D0017637

Creating the West

CREATING THE WEST
Historical Interpretations
1890–1990
GERALD D. NASH

The Calvin P. Horn Lectures in Western History and Culture, University of New Mexico, September 30–October 3, 1990

UNIVERSITY OF NEW MEXICO PRESS/ALBUQUERQUE

Library of Congress Cataloging-in-Publication Data

Nash, Gerald D.
  Creating the West: historical interpretations, 1890–1990 / Gerald D. Nash.—1st ed.
    p.   cm.—(The Calvin P. Horn lectures in western history and culture)
  Includes bibliographical references and index.
  ISBN 0-8263-1266-7 (cl.)—ISBN 0-8263-1267-5 (pa)
  1. West (U.S.)—Historiography.   I. Title.   II. Series.
F591.N37   1991
978'.0072—dc20   91-8584
                                                                   CIP

Map for the jacket and cover: Courtesy, Cartographic History Library, The University of Texas at Arlington Libraries. Photography of Frederick Jackson Turner: Courtesy, The Huntington, San Marino.

© 1991 by the University of New Mexico Press.
All rights reserved.
First edition.

Contents

Introduction

THE ONE HUNDREDTH ANNIVERSARY of the supposed closing
of the Western frontier in 1890 provides a good opportunity to review
the course of historical writings about the West during the past century.
In addition, an invitation to deliver the sixth annual Calvin P. Horn
Lectures in Western History and Culture at the University of New
Mexico prompted me to prepare the lectures that comprise the substance of this book. These dealt with four major perceptions of the
West which historians have reflected in their studies. As I reviewed
the literature I found that over the years historians have considered
the West as a frontier, as a region, as an urban civilization, and as a
mythical utopia. My primary aim in this volume is to provide a succinct
interpretive synthesis of these efforts since 1890. It is not to propound
a new hypothesis about the course of Western history. But my hope
is that such an analysis will provide context and perspective on the
subject which will be helpful in its future development.

In undertaking this survey of historical writing about the West, I
have chosen to focus on the ecology of historians who have been
associated with the field. I have borrowed this usage of the term *ecology*
from my mentor, John D. Hicks, to characterize the relationship between changes in the contemporary environment and the shifting
views of historians. I do not wish to imply that contemporary events
are the sole determinant of historical interpretations. That could be
misleading. As Robert Wohl noted in *The Generation of* 1914, the
generational approach to self-understanding may be confining and

misleading if it is used as the only norm for historical understanding.[1] On the other hand, the major events of any age do exert a very strong influence on those who experience them, and scholars are no exception. Obviously, historians have examined many aspects of this relationship so that to mention it again is hardly news. Yet it has not been explored in detail with specific reference to the study of the American West, a field in which an exploration of its philosophical assumptions could be fruitful. Hopefully, this study will also make a modest contribution to further inquiry along such lines.

In the context of such ecology it is almost a truism to note that each age interprets the past from its own particular perspectives. As Carl Degler noted in 1976:

> All historical interpretations are shaped by values. No interpretation can transcend the values that a historian brings to his or her own investigation of the past any more than historical figures at the time could escape their values. . . . The difference between historical antiquarianism and history is that the latter has a vital connection with the present while the former does not. In short, if historians did not change their minds as values shifted, their history would cease to be a living part of their culture—and thus incapable of illuminating the present with the past.[2]

Even those who would not agree fully with such an unabashed relativism would still emphasize the importance of contemporary affairs in shaping the perspectives of historians. As John D. Hicks, a more moderate relativist than Degler, once wrote:

> Each age . . . must write its history anew. In a sense this is inevitable and right. New problems, new circumstances, new developments demand new explanations, explanations frequently omitted from the handed-down versions . . . Frederick Jackson Turner . . . was himself a product of the receding frontier. Born in Portage, Wisconsin, the son of a local newspaper editor and minor politician, he knew about the Indian trade, the melting pot, the need for self-reliance in a new community, and the dominance of equalitarianism in the West long before he wrote these ideas into

1. John D. Hicks, "The 'Ecology' of the Middle Western Historians," *Wisconsin Magazine of History* 24 (June 1941), 377–84. Robert Wohl, *The Generation of* 1914 (Cambridge, Mass., 1979), 1–4.

2. Carl Degler, "Why Historians Change Their Minds," *Pacific Historical Review* 45 (May 1976), 183.

the significance of the American frontier. Had his birthplace been Boston, or Cambridge, or Concord, would his contribution to American history have been the same?[3]

In this constant shift of historical interpretations the passage of generations has been a significant element. Every generation has a particular outlook on its own and on other cultures which is significantly shaped by contemporary events. These events usually have their greatest impact during the first twenty-five years of an individual's lifetime. This is not to suggest that people never change their minds over a span of years. Yet their worldview, their *Weltanschauung,* their perspective on life and on culture, is often stamped by the particular events or ideas of their youth, frequently the most impressionable years of their lives. The philosopher José Ortega y Gasset recognized this tendency when he defined culture as:

> only the interpretation which man gives to his life, the series of more or less satisfying solutions he finds in order to meet the problems and necessities of life, as well as those which belong to the material order as the so-called spiritual ones. . . . Culture is the conception of the world or the universe which serves as the plan . . . riskily elaborated by man, for orienting himself among things, for coping with his life, and finding a direction amid the chaos of his situation.[4]

The theologian Martin Marty developed this theme further. He warned that the concept of "generation" could be taken too literally in the biological sense. Still, in seeking to grasp something as elusive as culture, the generational handle can be quite valuable. Differing interpretations of historical data often appear along generational lines. Marty noted that "Ortega was almost certainly too mechanical in his idea that cultural generations occurred fifteen years apart; he was more subtle when he recognized that several generations of coevals are alive at the same time. Those who have undergone a similar set of experiences at decisive stages in their life-careers tend to develop common outlooks. This is as true of those within the culture who endow with meaning both their fortune and their suffering—the religious—as it

---

3. John D. Hicks, "Changing Concepts of History," *Western Historical Quarterly* 2 (January 1971), 33–34.

4. Quoted in Martin Marty, "Religion in America Since Mid-Century," *Daedalus* 111 (Winter 1982), 151.

is of those who recognize and label the cultural change they perceive."[5]
In short, changes in historical interpretations are closely bound up
with the passage of generations.

Although the history of the West has been as prone to changing
interpretations as other fields of history it has also been distinctive
because it has been inextricably intertwined with American dreams
and myths. During the past century the American West has embodied
much of the American Dream, and the disentanglement of myth from
reality has been difficult at best. As Carl Becker once put it so well:
"In the history of history a myth is a once valid but now discarded
version of the human story, as our now valid versions will in due course
be relegated to the category of discarded myths."[6] Since 1890 perceptions of the West—not only by historians, but by scholars in many
disciplines, by politicians, and by average Americans—have undergone many changes. Our perspectives in 1990 are very different than
they were a hundred years ago. My goal is to analyze and describe the
paths which these multifold efforts have taken.

In a sense, this book is a record of the proceedings compiled by a
great seminar on the history of the West. The participants include
some of the best minds who have thought, spoken, and written about
the subject in the last one hundred years. Many are no longer living,
of course, but I have tried to bring the living and the dead to life. If
we can imagine that all of them could be brought together in one
large room the discussion would be lively, indeed. If there would be
little agreement on the significance of Western history in the larger
context of the American experience, yet they would provide various
perspectives, and also a context that would be constructive for future
development of the field. This volume, therefore, is also a record of
this ongoing seminar about the meaning and the scope of Western
history. My hope is that its deliberations may contribute to a greater
awareness of the subject's past, its condition at the present, and possible directions for the future.

Preparation of this book led me to incur many debts. I have bene-
fited from the encouragement of Mr. Calvin Horn, prominent Albuquerque businessman, who sponsored the lectures which bear his
name. Mr. David Holtby of the University of New Mexico Press, ably

5. Ibid., 151, 152.
6. Carl Becker, *Everyman His Own Historian* (New York, 1935), 247.

assisted by Larry D. Ball, Jr., provided much practical advice and support. My colleagues in the History Department at the University of New Mexico provided invaluable criticism. Most generous with time and advice was Richard W. Etulain whose encyclopedic knowledge of Western history is unrivaled. Ferenc Szasz shared insights from his special field of expertise which I found invaluable. Helping with the final preparations of this book were my colleagues at the University of Gottingen, where I served as the George Bancroft Professor of American History during 1990–1991. Although I have been the beneficiary of much help, I alone am responsible for the contents of this volume.

Albuquerque, New Mexico

Creating the West

ONE

The West as Frontier, 1890–1945

IN THE MINDS of most twentieth-century Americans the most familiar role of the West was that of a moving frontier. The definition of that frontier was rarely precise, however. Most often the frontier was thought to be a moving line of settlement across the continent of North America. That line originated with the arrival of the first settlers to New England's shores, and in ensuing years moved inexorably westward as successive waves of settlers carried it to the Pacific. By 1890 settlement had become so dense that supposedly the frontier came to an end—or so Frederick Jackson Turner proclaimed in 1893, after reading the latest report of the U.S. Superintendent of the Census in 1890. And with that pronouncement, Turner declared with much nostalgia, a major era in America's growth faded into history.

But while this momentous process was unfolding, the frontiering experience constituted the dominant influence on the shaping of American civilization. It molded the distinctive character of Americans, shaping traits such as individualism, hard work, and self-reliance; it was the major determinant of the democratic character of their political institutions; and it provided American cultural life with unique characteristics. Such, in brief compass, was the message conveyed by Turner in his famous essay on "The Significance of the Frontier in American History," read at the World Columbian Exposition in Chicago. The young University of Wisconsin professor could not know

3

at the time that his short paper would launch thousands of articles and books on the theme in the course of the next century.[1]

Almost immediately the reverberations of his essay reached beyond the halls of academe. The ideas which Turner propounded had been "in the air" for some time. Not only had journalists dealt with the issue, but contemporary politicians, particularly Populists, had talked about it for years. Nevertheless, few had stated the theme in such a penetrating and succinct manner as Turner did on that fateful day. Soon political leaders such as Theodore Roosevelt and Woodrow Wilson espoused the frontier theme, and within a few years writers, artists, and musicians joined them until it quickly entered into national consciousness and myth.

Turner was obviously more than a historian. He was also a poet, a prophet, a philosopher, and a master teacher—one who dominated the training of a generation of American historians. He explained the totality of the national experience to Americans, not merely one or another aspect. If Turner at times was a little vague or imprecise, or somewhat blurred, why, that only added to the mystique of his interpretation.

In the one hundred years after Turner delivered his message it underwent many transmutations. Yet it remained one of the seminal ideas with which to explain the growth and development of American civilization, not only within the United States but around the world. Ironically, Turner himself eschewed single-causation theories, but firmly believed in multiple causation. But scores of his disciples were far narrower than he, and much more rigid. And disciples he had, for he trained an influential generation of historians between 1890 and 1924. In a day when professional historians in the United States numbered no more than a few hundred, these individuals were able to exercise a dominant influence on the teaching and writing of American history.

During the Great Depression the Turner thesis attracted considerable attention. On the one hand, it enjoyed enormous popularity with New Dealers, from President Franklin D. Roosevelt himself to

1. Frederick Jackson Turner, "The Significance of the Frontier in American History," American Historical Association, *Annual Report*, 1893 (Washington, D.C., 1893), pp. 199–227, reprinted in Frederick Jackson Turner, *The Frontier in American History* (New York, 1920), 1–38. For a partial listing of publications, see Vernon E. Mattson and William E. Marion (comps.), *Frederick Jackson Turner: A Reference Guide* (Boston, 1985).

many of his chief advisers. It seemed to provide such a convenient rationalization for so many of their programs. Since the frontier was gone and the nation's growth presumably static, government deficit spending and social programs were now needed to take up the slack. It seemed so simple and so logical! On the other hand, after Turner's death in 1932 the critics became more vocal and kept up a steady flow of criticism which persisted throughout the World War II years. Within the broader context of Western history, the Turner thesis was considered fruitful in stimulating thought about the role of the West in American life, and, indeed, the nature of the American experience.[2]

Various events of Turner's lifetime conditioned his views of Western history and those of many of his contemporaries. The depression of the 1890s and the anguished cries of the Populists bewailing the decline of farming in America were but one indication of the sweeping changes overtaking the United States. By contrast, the emergence of great industrial cities in the Northeast and Middle West with large immigrant populations indicated that the nature of American society was undergoing a rapid transformation. Whether or not the frontier disappeared in 1890 was really incidental. In a sense it was only a symbolic rite of passage, signaling the transition from an Anglo-Saxon agrarian society to a multicultural and multiethnic state. With that change came the new problems of an industrial nation. In the economic sphere the concentration of wealth, monopolies, booms and depressions, and equality of economic opportunity now became major issues; in the social realm poverty, urban slums, crime, public health, education, and the exploitation of women and children came to the fore; and desecration of the environment and of natural resources were all but too visible. To the generation of 1890—as Henry and Brooks Adams noted so eloquently—one world was disappearing, and another was rapidly taking its place.[3]

It was not surprising, therefore, that historians of the West in the three decades after 1890 reflected a profound sense of nostalgia, fueled by a feeling of loss. To many of them the Turner thesis appeared to explain a great deal about the events occurring in their lifetime. It celebrated the passing of a glorious age in the nation's past and reflected

2. For a brief guide to the literature, see Rodman W. Paul and Richard W. Etulain (comps.), *The Frontier and the American West* (Arlington Heights, 1977).

3. Henry Adams, *The Education of Henry Adams* (Boston, 1918); Brooks Adams, *The Law of Civilization and Decay* (New York, 1896).

a sense of foreboding and pessimism about the future. Such nostalgia implied that while Americans had for centuries lived in a society that was open—with a series of new frontiers—henceforth they would be confined to a closed environment. These assumptions affected not only historians, but social scientists and a wide range of literati. Their visions began to be disrupted by the First World War, which forced them to expand their intellectual horizons by including a greater awareness of global perspectives in their study of the West.

Clearly, then, Turner did not develop his frontier thesis in an abstract vacuum, but in the context of the environment in which he matured and of his personal experiences. Numerous scholars have described these circumstances, among them Ray Allen Billington, Richard Hofstadter, and Lee Benson. The frontier conditions of his youth in Wisconsin between 1870 and 1890 left lasting impressions. During those years Wisconsin was just emerging from its status as a wilderness. As a boy, Turner knew the hunters and trappers who came into the small town of Portage where he lived. He knew, as well, the Indians whose presence there was still felt keenly. His lifelong love of hunting and fishing was developed in this somewhat idyllic environment. At least he perceived it as such, although by 1890 he found his home town far less attractive than it had once seemed.[4]

In addition to his Wisconsin background, Turner was also influenced by the intellectual climate from which he emerged. Both under his major undergraduate teacher at the University of Wisconsin, William Allen, and in his graduate studies at the Johns Hopkins University in 1889, Turner imbibed much about theories of evolution as expounded by Charles Darwin and Herbert Spencer. At Hopkins he was also exposed to the germ theory of his mentor, Herbert B. Adams, who taught that American political institutions evolved primarily from Anglo-Saxon and Teutonic traditions that had originated in Europe centuries before. The emphasis on forests as breeding places seems to have made a deep impression on Turner since it meshed with his own

4. Ray Allen Billington, *The Genesis of the Frontier Thesis: A Study in Historical Creativity* (San Marino, 1971), 9–15, and Billington, *Frederick Jackson Turner, Historian, Scholar, Teacher* (New York, 1973), 3–57; Richard Hofstadter, "Turner and the Frontier Myth," *American Scholar* 18 (Autumn 1949), 433–43; Hofstadter, *The Progressive Historians: Turner, Beard, Parrington* (New York, 1968), 3–164; Hofstadter, in Introduction to *Turner and the Sociology of the Frontier*, edited by Richard Hofstadter and Seymour M. Lipset (New York, 1968); Lee Benson, *Turner and Beard: American Historical Writing Reconsidered* (New York, 1960).

experiences in his Wisconsin boyhood. But he rebelled against this thesis and, instead, sought to demonstrate that indigenous American conditions, and not European influences, determined the patterns of the evolving civilization in the United States.

Turner frequently commented on contemporary conditions which were affecting his own views. He was concerned about the decline of the agrarian character of the nation in the face of the new industrialism. He viewed the rise of cities with distrust and expressed his distaste for the ways of the new immigrants who poured into them, particularly those from southern and eastern Europe. The changing face of the United States also led him to express nostalgia for the old order, for rural small-town America, for agrarian values and life-styles. Such feelings found an outlet in a new fascination with frontier life and the Old West, and the back-to-nature movement led by naturalists such as John Muir and conservationists like Gifford Pinchot and Theodore Roosevelt. Turner shared such thoughts but expressed himself more in terms of a professional historian. Clearly, he was very much a child of his own age. Like a barometer, he reflected the passing of the old order and bemoaned the advent of the new. Like many Americans, he replaced the perennial optimism of nineteenth-century America with a somewhat apprehensive pessimism about the future.[5]

But Turner firmly believed that each age must reinterpret the past. It is doubtful that he expected the Turner Thesis to remain unchanged over time. In his presidential address to the American Historical Association in 1910, he noted bluntly that

It is a familiar doctrine that each age studies its history anew and with interests determined by the spirit of the time. Each age finds it necessary to reconsider at least some portions of the past, from points of view furnished by new conditions which reveal the influence and significance of forces not adequately known by the historians . . . while this fact exposes the historian to a bias, at the same time it affords him new instruments and new insight for dealing with his subject.

If recent history, then, gives new meaning to past events . . . the origins and growth of which may have been inadequately described or even overlooked by historians of the previous generation, it is important to study the present and recent past, not only for themselves but also as the source of new hypotheses, new lines

5. Billington, *Genesis*, 15–62, 85–118; Billington, *Turner*, 58–131.

of inquiry, new criteria of the perspective of the remoter past. A just public opinion and a statesmanlike treatment of present problems demand that they be seen in their historical relations in order that history may hold the lamp for conservative reform.

These themes were amplified further just a few years later by Carl Becker, one of Turner's ablest students, in an extensive analysis of the relations of social problems to the writing of history.[6]

Turner's nostalgia about the passing of the frontier was shared by many of his contemporaries, including his erstwhile fellow student at Johns Hopkins University, Woodrow Wilson. The two had sat in the graduate seminar of Herbert Baxter Adams and developed similar interests and outlooks. Wilson had visited Turner in Madison just a few months before Turner read his famous "Frontier" essay in Chicago in July 1893, and had, in fact, discussed its contents with him at that time. Wilson largely agreed with Turner's views and also believed that the nation was at a crossroads in the 1890s. Although Wilson's writings during these years ranged over a wide spectrum of subjects, he did not ignore the West, and reflected the influence Turner had on him. Writing in 1895, for example, Wilson declared that he had been completely convinced by Turner that the frontier was "the central and determining fact of our national history." If American historical writing of his own times had major weaknesses, these were largely due to its having been written by easterners residing in the East or looking primarily to Europe. "The West is the great word of our history," Wilson proclaimed. But, like Turner, he bemoaned the fact that now, in 1895, "we have lost our frontier." He amplified this theme further in an essay which he wrote two years later. "The making of our own nation seems to have taken place under our very eyes," Wilson noted. "So recent and familiar is the story. . . . Yet we should deceive ourselves were we to suppose the work done, the nation made." And he posed a provocative question. "Is the history of our making as a nation indeed over, or do we still wait upon the forces that shall at last unite us? . . . The 'West' is not . . . a region at all, but, in Professor Turner's admirable phrase, a stage of development. . . . Now it lies without

6. Frederick Jackson Turner, "Social Forces in American History," *American Historical Review* 16 (January 1911), 225–26; Carl Becker, "Some Aspects of the Influence of Social Problems and Ideas upon the Study and Writing of History," *American Journal of Sociology* 18 (March 1913), 641–75.

outlet. The free lands are gone. Now communities . . . were caught in a fixed order of life."[7]

This mood of sadness about the perceived disappearance of the frontier was shared by popular writers such as Frank Norris, the novelist. In a mournful dirge entitled "The Frontier Gone at Last," Norris lamented that "Suddenly we have found that there is no longer any frontier. . . . And the Frontier has become so much an integral part of our conception of things that it will be long before we shall all understand that it is gone. We liked the Frontier, it was romance, the place of the poetry of the Great March, the firing line where there was action and fighting." With his vivid imagination he could see the West "where men held each other's lives in the crook of the forefinger. Those who had gone out came back with tremendous tales, and those that stayed behind made up other and even more tremendous tales."[8]

This refrain was also woven into many of Theodore Roosevelt's writings about the West. Although Roosevelt did not fully share all of Turner's assumptions about the West he, too, reflected that certain sadness about the passing of the frontier. Turner reviewed the first two volumes of Roosevelt's *Winning of the West* in 1889 and found much to praise. "It is the merit of Mr. Roosevelt's book," Turner wrote, "that he has given us a vivid portraiture of the backwoodsmen's advance, that he treats impartially and sensibly the relations of the pioneer and the Indians whom they dispossessed, that he has applied a scientific method of criticism to the material already existing, and that he writes in the light of the widest significance of the events which he describes." Turner also admired what he viewed as impartiality, objectivity, and the placing of "local history in the light of world history," values which he was imbibing then in the graduate program at Hopkins. In later years Turner complained privately that Roosevelt's emphasis on personalities rather than on institutions, and also his stress on violence and fighting tended to distort his account for the sake of melodrama. But outwardly their relationship was friendly. In fact, when Roosevelt was preparing the third volume of his *Winning of the West* in 1895, he wrote to Turner, "I have been greatly interested

7. Woodrow Wilson, "The Proper Perspective of American History," *Forum* 19 (July 1895), 544–59, and Wilson, "The Making of the Nation," *Atlantic Monthly* 80 (July 1897), 1–2.

8. Frank Norris, "The Frontier Gone at Last," *World's Work* 3 (February 1902), 1728.

in your pamphlet ["The Significance of the Frontier in American History"]. It comes at *the* right time for me, for I intend to make use of it in writing the third volume of my 'Winning of the West.'"[9]

The completion of that work deepened Roosevelt's nostalgia for the Old West. As he noted a few years later, "it was a land about to vanish forever." As a historian he wanted to capture that past before it passed on. As a political figure he also tried to enshrine its memory. Toward that end, he urged Congress in 1908 to create a commission on Country Life "to secure the necessary knowledge of the actual conditions of life in the open country." In explaining his reasoning, he noted that "no nation has ever achieved permanent greatness unless this greatness was based on the well being of the great farmer class . . . for it is upon their welfare, material and moral, that the welfare of the nation ultimately rests." A special charge to the commission was to recommend ways and means to improve the conditions of farmers in a technological society. When the commission eventually made its report it recommended that farmers improve their organizational skills and make use of business methods. This was to be done to achieve "a new and permanent rural civilization," a society that would blend the best of rural and urban America.[10]

Roosevelt's nostalgia was reflected not only in his own interest in Western history, but in his promotion of Western art by painters such as Frederic Remington and Charles Russell. As one historian who analyzed this relationship noted:

> They sensed that to come to grips with the western experience
> was to encounter certain aspects of American culture which the

9. Frederick Jackson Turner, "The Winning of the West," *The Dial* (August 1889), 7; on his later views of Roosevelt, see Turner's letter to Constance Skinner, March 15, 1922, reproduced in Wilbur R. Jacobs, *The Historical World of Frederick Jackson Turner* (New Haven, 1968), 57, 60–61; Merrill E. Lewis, "The Art of Frederick Jackson Turner," *Huntington Library Quarterly* 35 (May 1972), 241–42; on Theodore Roosevelt's note to Turner, April 10, 1895, see Elting E. Morison (ed.), *The Letters of Theodore Roosevelt* (8 vols., Cambridge, 1951–54), I, 440; see also David H. Burton, "The Influence of the American West on the Imperialist Philosophy of Theodore Roosevelt," *Arizona and the West* 4 (Spring 1962), 10.

10. Quote from Roosevelt, in Theodore Roosevelt, *Works*, edited by Herman Hagedorn (24 vols., New York, 1923–1926), IV, 454, and from Roosevelt to Lyman H. Bailey, August 10, 1908, in *Report of the Country Life Commission* (New York, 1911), 41–46; G. Edward White, *The Eastern Establishment and the Western Experience: The West of Frederic Remington, Theodore Roosevelt, and Owen Wister* (New Haven, 1968), 73, 78, 93, 178–79.

rush of industrialization threatened to sweep away. They were motivated to "Westernize" themselves in a way that earlier writers and
tourists were not. . . . Each sought for something in the West with
which he could identify . . . they can be seen to have a common
cultural foundation in the state of economic and social flux that
marked the latter portions of the nineteenth century. The Roosevelt generation's sense of instability led to a general search for sta-
bilizing forces in a fluctuating age. . . . The "Wild" West came
. . . to represent the stage of civilization in America before the
advent of industrialism, and as such it was both romantic and po-
tentially tragic.[11]

The lament over the passing of the frontier also found its way into
the nation's political consciousness. Progressives who were among the
most ardent supporters of Theodore Roosevelt utilized the frontier
hypothesis to justify their reform efforts and to rationalize Roosevelt's ideas about the New Nationalism. Among the most notable were
Herbert Croly and Walter Weyl, two journalists who influenced Roosevelt's speeches. In 1914 they founded the *New Republic*, which provided for a wider dissemination of their views. Although the two
differed in their interpretation of the frontier thesis, they shared a
belief that the frontier had now disappeared and that a new age was
dawning.

As Croly attempted to develop an ideology for progressive reform
in 1910 he borrowed extensively from Turner. "All the conditions of
American life have tended to encourage an easy, generous, and irresponsible optimism," he wrote. "As compared to Europeans, Americans have been very much favored by circumstance. Had it not been
for the Atlantic Ocean and the virgin wilderness, the United States
would never have been the Land of Promise." But the promise of the
future was much dimmer, according to Croly. "For two generations
and more the American people were, from the economic point of
view, most happily situated. . . . But such is no longer the case.
Economic conditions have been profoundly modified. . . . The Promise of American life must depend less than it did upon the virgin
wilderness . . . for the virgin wilderness has disappeared. . . . Ugly
obstacles have jumped into view." Croly's prescription for this dilemma
was a vast increase in the powers of the federal government to develop

11. White, *Eastern Establishment*, 185–86.

economic and social policies which could take up the slack created by the disappearance of the frontier.[12]

Weyl shared the assumption that the disappearance of the frontier required radical changes in national policies, in particular an expansion of the federal government. More than Croly, however, Weyl lamented what he considered to have been the negative impact of the frontier on the values of Americans. "Our conquest of the Continent, though essential to national expansion," Weyl wrote,

> did not aid . . . democracy. . . . On the contrary, the economic, political, and psychological developments inseparably connected with the struggle with the wilderness worked against the immediate attainment of a socialized democracy, and led to wild excesses of individualism which in turn culminated in the growth of a powerful and entrenched plutocracy. The conquest of the wide-stretching continent lying to the west of the Appalachians, gave to American development a tendency adverse from the evolution of socialized democracy. It made America atomic. It led automatically to a loose political coherence and to a structureless economic system. The trust, the hundred-millionaire, and the slum were latent in the land which the American people in the first century of freedom were to subjugate.[13]

Weyl accepted Turner's depiction of the frontier. "Our frontier . . . had been attained [by 1890]. . . . For the man who had girdled the trees and built log cabins in Tennessee or Ohio there was no chance in newly acquired lands in the Pacific or Caribbean. The western wave of migration . . . turned back upon itself. As the supply of free Western farms ceased, as the settlers, with no further place to go . . . the alternative which the frontier once offered to the city disappeared. The western march of the pioneer gave to Americans a psychological twist which was to hinder the development of a socialized democracy. The open continent intoxicated the American. It gave him an enlarged view of self. It dwarfed the common spirit. . . . It created an individualism, self-confidence, shortsighted lawlessness doomed in the end to defeat itself, as the boundless opportunities

12. Herbert Croly, *The Promise of American Life* (New York, 1909), 7, 16, 18.
13. Quotes from Walter Weyl, *The New Democracy: An Essay on Certain Political and Economic Tendencies in the United States* (New York, 1913), 348, 22; see also 25, 34–36.

which gave it birth became at last circumscribed."[14] Weyl detailed this tragic sequence to emphasize his proposed remedy—the creation of a welfare state by the federal government. As other publicists before him, and many who were to follow, he was utilizing his generation's perception of the frontier as a rationalization and defense of a political program, in this case the New Nationalism.

Most professional historians in the Progressive era embraced the Turner Thesis and similarly used it to rationalize contemporary reform movements. One of the most effusive was Frederic Logan Paxson. Although he received his doctorate at the University of Pennsylvania in 1907, Paxson early made himself a champion of the frontier thesis. In one of his first publications, "The Pacific Railroads and the Disappearance of the Frontier in America" (1907), Paxson stated unequivocally that "within recent years it has become commonplace in American history that the influence of the frontier is the one constant to be reckoned with in accounting for the development of American life during its first century of independent existence." Although a professional historian who professed to write "scientific" history, Paxson reflected the presuppositions of his era, using the Turner Thesis to rationalize the policies of the New Nationalism (although Roosevelt did not use that term until after 1911). "After 1885 the historical problem is the significance of the disappearance of the frontier," Paxson wrote. "In the change of epochs problems change as well. National organization replaces sectional; state activities tend to give way to federal; corporate organization succeeds individualistic; public regulation supersedes private initiative; and the imperative need for the creation of material equipment is transmuted into an equal necessity for the control of the activities to which the former need gave birth." And during the next decade Paxson followed these themes in books and articles designed for popular audiences and students.[15]

During this period the critics of the Turner Thesis were few. One cogent demurrer came from Agnes Laut, a journalist. In 1909 she observed that, very obviously, the frontier had not closed in 1890 as Turner had declared. At that very moment more than 500,000 Americans were scrambling over the Canadian prairies where they were

14. Weyl, *New Democracy*, 31–32.

15. Frederic L. Paxson, "The Pacific Railroads and the Disappearance of the Frontier in America," American Historical Association, *Annual Report*, 1907 (Washington, 1908), vol. 1, 118.

participating in one of the great land rushes of the twentieth century. The numbers involved exceeded those of the Oklahoma land rush of 1907. The frontier process seemed to be alive and well, Laut emphasized. But her article made few ripples.[16] Similarly, Edmund S. Meany, a young historian who was studying new towns in the Pacific Northwest, declared in 1909 that while the Turner Thesis might be applicable to communities east of the Rocky Mountains, he could not sustain its validity on their western side. Patterns of settlement in the Pacific Northwest did not at all follow the patterns outlined by Turner, Meany concluded. Unlike communities in the east, those of the Pacific Northwest were not spawned by the fur trade.[17] But professional historians paid little attention to these dissenters during this period.

Scholars in the social sciences also embraced the frontier hypothesis. One of Turner's most enthusiastic disciples was Ellen Churchill Semple, a geographer known for her pronounced environmental determinism. In *American History and Its Geographic Conditions* (1903), she heaped high praise on Turner. "American soil and the barrier of the Atlantic . . . modified European institutions and character," she wrote. "Without social classes and wealth, democracy reigned supreme. The daily struggle for existence amid the dangers of the wilderness produced a race of men, sturdy in their self-reliance, self-respecting in their independence, quick to think, strong to act." And she concluded: "The presence of the new West reacted most wholesomely upon the East . . . the stimulating effect of inexhaustible opportunity never allowed American opportunity to abate, and the democratic spirit of the ever youthful frontier fostered the spirit of democracy and youth in the whole nation."[18]

Semple went much further in her determinism than Turner ever did. "The story of the United States," she declared, "is that of a series of frontiers which the hand of man has reclaimed from nature and the savage, and which courage and foresight have gradually transformed from desert waste to virile commonwealth. It is the story of

16. Agnes C. Laut, "The Last Trek to the Last Frontier: The American Settler in the Canadian Northwest," *Century Magazine* 56 (May 1909), 99–110.

17. Edmond S. Meany, "The Towns of the Pacific Northwest Were Not Founded on the Fur Trade," American Historical Association, *Annual Report*, 1910 (Washington, 1911), 165–72.

18. Ellen Churchill Semple, *American History and Its Geographic Conditions* (Boston, 1903), 59, 67, 77, 112.

one long struggle, fought over different lands and by different generations, yet ever repeating the conditions and episodes of the last
period in the West." And in placing the frontier within the mainstream
of American history, she declared: "The greatest of American problems
has been the problem of the West."[19] Not all geographers in these
years were as enamored of the Turner Thesis as Semple, but she did
much to propagate it in her special sphere of interest.

Well-known sociologists were also impressed by Turner. As E. A.
Ross noted in 1908, "In the course of a decade there has come a wide
acceptance of Professor Turner's generalization that in America the
democratic spirit grew up in and spread from that portion of society
in the immediate presence of free land, namely the frontier. The
previous generation had just as many significant facts under its eye,
but persisted in accounting for American democracy by Providence,
the Fathers, the Puritan tradition, ethnic mixture, or climate."[20] Even
more profuse in praise was Algie Simons, one of the most popular
sociological writers of this period. In his *Social Forces in American
History*, he stated unequivocally "that with Jefferson a new political
force made itself felt in national politics. This was the frontier . . .
the one distinctive feature of American society. A full understanding
of its influence unlocks many difficult problems in that history." From
the perspective of 1911 "the history of the United States is the de-
scription of a mighty army moving westward in conquest of forest and
prairie. . . . The frontier has been the great amalgamating force in
American life." In a personal letter to Turner, Simons paid him full
tribute. "Your teachings were at the bottom of this (little) book," he
noted. An unabashed socialist, Simons utilized the closing of the
frontier as an argument for his advocacy of a welfare state.[21]

But it was the popular writers who parlayed the mood of the
professional historians to a wider audience, literary stylists like Emerson Hough and Hamlin Garland. In what was one of the finest dis-
tillations of the Turner Thesis, Hough gave vent to deep-seated feelings

19. Ibid., 1.
20. Edward A. Ross, "The Study of the Present as an Aid to the Interpretation
of the Past," Mississippi Valley Historical Association, *Proceedings*, 11 (1908–1909),
129.
21. Algie M. Simons, *Social Forces in American History* (New York, 1911), 134,
140. It is notable that Turner chose the identical title for his presidential address to
the American Historical Association when the book appeared. See Turner, "Social
Forces," in *American Historical Review*, 16, 159–84.

of nostalgia. His dirge was contained in a slim volume, *The Passing of the Frontier*, published in 1919 as one of the *Chronicles of America* volumes edited by Allen Johnson for the Yale University Press. Using colorful imagery, Hough lamented:

> Always it has been the frontier which has allured many of our boldest souls. And always back of the frontier, advancing, receding, crossing it this way and that, succeeding and failing, hoping and despairing, but steadily advancing in the net result has come that portion of the population which builds homes and lives in them. . . . We had a frontier once. It was our most priceless possession. It has not been possible to eliminate from the American West. . . . The frontier has been a lasting and ineradicable influence for the good of the United States. It was there we showed our fighting edge, our unconquerable resolution, our undying faith. There, for a time at least, we were Americans. . . . We had our frontier. We shall do ill indeed if we forget and abandon its strong lessons, its great hopes, its splendid human dreams.[22]

Hamlin Garland caught the spirit. Commenting on Hough, he wrote, "One might almost say [it] is a threnody, so deeply colored is it by the somber meditation of the gray-haired man yielding himself to a resurgent love of the stirring days of old. The men were full-sized and red-blooded in those days, he says . . . and mourns for the oldtime West." To Hough's refrain Garland added his own. "Over against the bitterness which springs from the congestion of great cities," he wrote, "I like to place the faith in which my pioneer sire wrought for over eighty years—a faith in the open spaces which enabled him to think of reform without violence and of the prosperity of others without bitterness or hate. So long as we have faith in the future and in the transforming effect of our winds and skies the gate of the sunset is open to the intellectual pathfinder, the trailmaker, the gold-seeker."[23] That came from the heart of a whole generation that looked back with increasing nostalgia on the West of their youth.

Although it is debatable whether Americans lost their innocence during the First World War, they did gain a more pronounced sense of their global significance which was reflected in the writing of Western history. Increasingly in the World War I decade historians of the

22. Emerson Hough, *The Passing of the Frontier* (New Haven, 1919), 1–2.
23. Hamlin Garland, "The Passing of the Frontier," *Dial* 6 (October 4, 1919), 286.

West showed a greater awareness of the international context of frontier development than they had in earlier years. Turner himself, always
sensitive to contemporary events, was a prime example. But others
who reflected the impact of the First World War included Herbert
Bolton, Carl Russell Fish, Clarence Alvord, and Samuel Flagg Bemis.
As they wrote about various aspects of the frontier, the contemporary
international importance of the United States was reflected in their
analysis of the past.

Even before United States entry into World War I Turner became
increasingly concerned about the international situation. He feared
German efforts which threatened American interests and was strong
for greater preparedness. Writing to Carl Becker on March 10, 1916
he said: "I am rather pained at the explanations I am forced to make
for . . . [the] failure [of the] Middle West to back up the President
when Germany cracked the whip." In the following year he joined
the National Board for Historical Service, a group of historians headed
by James T. Shotwell of Columbia University and Waldo Leland of
the Carnegie Institution who hoped to win support for the Allied
cause. When his friend Max Farrand questioned the role of historians
in engaging in efforts to shape public sentiments, or propaganda,
Turner vigorously defended his activities which he deemed eminently
proper.[24]

Once the United States had entered the war Turner's desire to
help his country's cause increased. In addition to his work on the
National Board for Historical Service he approached President Wilson
directly in November 1918 when the chief executive was gathering a
wide range of historical studies to take with him to the forthcoming
peace conference. As Carl Becker once noted of Turner: "If mankind
could once really understand what it has done and thought in the
past, is it not possible that it would stumble along now, and in the
future, with more intelligence and a more conscious purpose?" And,
Becker added, he was "always occupied primarily with the present,
and with the past as illuminating the present." Thus it was not surprising that Turner sat down to pen a comprehensive plan for a world
organization based on the experience of the American West. Entitled
"International Political Parties in a Durable League of Nations," the

---

24. Turner's letter to Becker is reproduced in Jacobs, *Historical World*, 143, and
his letter to Max Farrand, May 5, 1917, in ibid., 144–46. For communication to
Herbert Bolton, May 11, 1917, see ibid., 147–49; Billington, *Turner*, 345–48.

proposal sought to apply his frontier and sectional hypotheses to the problems of world organization. He noted that the American union was a result of the frontier experience and the consequent formation of sections. Americans had developed concepts of a League of Sections to govern themselves—an example which the Europeans could now adapt for the postwar world. What better opportunity to reemphasize America's sense of mission than to provide a model for the various nations of the world? It is not clear whether Wilson actually read Turner's proposal. Turner himself was somewhat hurt when he received an acknowledgment of his manuscript, not from the president himself but from his secretary.[25]

But if the example of the Western experience did not directly influence world organization, then the emphasis on international perspectives did affect historians of the West such as Herbert Bolton. Born in Wisconsin, and an undergraduate in Turner's classes at the state university, Bolton reflected multicultural and multinational perspectives in his writings. His relationship with Turner continued to be close. In fact, in 1916 Bolton invited his former teacher to offer summer-session courses at the University of California in Berkeley, an offer Turner accepted. At the same time, Bolton was publishing his influential essays on the Spanish borderlands and developing his views on the common elements of the nations in the Western hemisphere. In a certain sense, he was extending the Turner Thesis from a nationalist to an international dimension. As Bolton wrote:

> Professor Turner has devoted his life to a study of the Anglo-American frontier, and rich has been his reward. Scarcely less conspicuous in the history of the western world than the advance of the Anglo-American frontier has been the spread of Spanish culture, and for him who interprets, with Turner's insight, the methods and the significance of the Spanish-American frontier, there awaits a recognition not less marked or less deserved.[26]

25. Billington, *Turner*, 354–56; Carl Becker, "Frederick Jackson Turner," in *American Masters of Social Science*, edited by Howard W. Odum (New York, 1927), 273–318; Frederick Jackson Turner, "The Significance of History," *Wisconsin Journal of Education* 21 (October–November 1891), 230–34, 253–56. Turner noted that "each age writes the history of the past anew with reference to the conditions uppermost in its own time." Jacobs, *Historical World*, 124–25; Becker, in *American Journal of Sociology* 18, 666–67; quote from Carl Becker, *Everyman His Own Historian* (New York, 1935), 207–8, 224.

26. Herbert E. Bolton, "The Mission as a Frontier Institution in the Spanish-American Colonies," *American Historical Review* 23 (October 1917), 42–43; Jacobs, *Historical World*, 106–9.

Turner's close associate at the University of Wisconsin, Carl Russell Fish, was similarly affected by United States participation in the war to embrace global perspectives. In an essay published in December 1917, Fish argued that the frontier which Turner had identified in North America could now be considered in a worldwide context. "When we see in the United States people of all nations laboring for the conquest of the Mississippi Valley," Fish wrote,

> and employing money saved by New England and the Middle States or borrowed by them from Europe, when we see Russia borrowing French money to make Siberia habitable for Russian peasants, when Japan borrows in England, and Russia in France . . . we get glimpses of a new world. . . . These experiences on the frontiers . . . are unparalleled . . . but bring into clearer view general tendencies of the time. . . . The war itself has hastened the movement. . . . A study of the world frontier brings out the fact that no localities are independent in fact. The intergrowth of the world . . . frontier has . . . weakened the bulwarks of local independence; let us hope that with its international character the frontier may facilitate the integration of a world organization . . . adapted to the conditions of today.[27]

Other historians of the West reflected a similar global orientation. Although Clarence A. Alvord was not one of Turner's students, but received his doctorate from the University of Illinois, he provided the international context for his study of *The Mississippi Valley in British Politics*, published in 1917. In what was to become a classic work, Alvord traced the role of the frontier and the West in the international context of British imperial politics in the eighteenth century.[28]

The World War I era thus had a significant effect on historians of the American frontier. Instead of viewing westering in a narrow, nationalistic context or as a unique American phenomenon, as a previous generation had done, they now perceived it much more on a global

27. Carl Russell Fish, "The Frontier, a World Problem," *Wisconsin Magazine of History* 1 (December 1917), 140–41.
28. Clarence A. Alvord, *The Mississippi Valley in British Politics* (2 vols., Urbana, 1917). Samuel Flagg Bemis completed his doctoral studies at Harvard in 1916, with Turner's advice. Later a distinguished diplomatic historian who focused on the role of the West in American diplomacy during the early National period, his major works did not appear for another decade. They included *Jay's Treaty*, in 1923, and *Pinckney's Treaty*, in 1926.

scale. In one sense, they were reflecting a loosening of nineteenth-century isolationist feelings. What was surprising was the rapidity of this change in less than a decade. Historians who had been trained in the "scientific" school of history, as this generation had been, were apparently no less prone to contemporary trends than the unabashed romantic writers outside the historical profession. The World War I experience revealed that they were weather vanes who were acutely sensitive to the major currents of their times.

Between 1890 and 1920 Turner's frontier hypothesis enjoyed wide acceptance. In part, this was because it was so very much a product of his own times. His generation was keenly aware of the momentous changes engendered by the transition from an agrarian to an industrial society which took place in their own lifetimes. It was only natural that they felt a keen sense of loss about a familiar past, and feelings of apprehension about an unfamiliar future. The strong sense of nostalgia reflected both by historians and nonhistorians alike was the result. World War I provided still newer perspectives as it further jolted the United States out of its isolationist cocoon. The emergence of the United States as a world power had a deep impact on historians of the West who now sought out the international dimensions of their subject, which they had overlooked before.

More changes were to come in the 1920s. The decade witnessed a waning of much of the optimism that had characterized earlier years, particularly with the disillusionment that followed in the wake of United States participation in World War I. An increased pace of industrial and technological advance further diminished the importance of agriculture in American life, in an economic as well as in a cultural sense. The closing of the doors to large numbers of immigrants by the National Origins Act of 1924 also made contemporaries more aware that they were witnessing the end of an era—an era when immigration had been a major force in the shaping of American society. And with the burgeoning growth of cities, for the first time in the nation's history a majority of Americans came to live in urban areas. A recognition of this trend brought a new awareness of the urban dimension in American life, and in the West. Despite the resurgence of some isolationism in the 1920s, nevertheless Americans continued to have broader perspectives on their role in international relations than in earlier years.

Many of these trends were reflected in the writings of historians about the American frontier. One of these was a strong sense of pessimism, emanating from the nostalgic mood of the previous generation. Students of American culture now ascribed a wide range of negative influences to the frontier. As Turner and his generation had attributed the best uniquely American traits to the frontier, so now the critics of the 1920s blamed it for the worst. But an increasing number of historians discounted the significant impact of the frontier on American life altogether. Instead, they offered alternative explanations about the growth of American civilization. In deemphasizing the role of the frontier, they sought to alter the perception that it had played a central role in the shaping of the United States. By the end of the decade the consensus on the validity of the Turner Thesis began to show serious fissures.[29]

A more critical tone in the assessment of the frontier thesis became apparent immediately after the war. In 1920 Turner gathered a number of his best essays over the past few decades in a collection published as *The Frontier in American History*. As his biographer, Ray Allen Billington, has noted, Turner experienced great problems in writing full-length books. His only previous volume, *The Rise of the New West*, had been a painful experience. Now that Turner was approaching his sixtieth birthday, it was not at all clear to him or to his colleagues whether he would ever finish the "big book" of which he had often spoken, a culmination of his major researches. In lieu of such a magnum opus, he published the book of essays. But the reception historians accorded them, while respectful, was hardly enthusiastic. Allen Johnson of Yale University reflected some of the contemporary mood when he wrote that, in comparison to 1893, "what was then a fresh and exceedingly suggestive interpretation of our history has come to be almost a commonplace in American historiography, so completely have the younger historians made this point of view their own." Above all, Johnson criticized Turner for his vagueness. "It is somewhat unfortunate," he declared,

29. Turner himself commented on the changed mood. Writing to Arthur M. Schlesinger, Sr., on May 5, 1925, he noted that "I imagine that some of the attempts to minimize the frontier theme . . . are part of the pessimistic reaction against the old America that have followed the World War—the reaction against pioneer ideals, against distinctively American things historically in favor of Old World solutions . . . to write in terms of European experience, and of the class struggle incident to industrialism." Jacobs, *Historical World*, 164.

that Professor Turner nowhere defines in set terms what he means
by democracy, a word that appears on almost every page. There is,
indeed, no term which is used more carelessly in everyday speech
and in contemporary literature. . . . He often uses the word
loosely . . . and . . . has followed the careless usage of western
Americans. . . . The concept of democracy in the age of colonization was much narrower than at the present time. Measured by
contemporary events, the western American whom Professor
Turner describes was not a fullfledged democrat, nor even a be-
liever in equality.[30]

Among those who accentuated the negative impact of the frontier
on American culture—in contrast to Turner's positive evaluation—
was the philospher John Dewey. Writing about the American intellectual frontier in 1922, Dewey ascribed most of what he considered
the negative characteristics of American society to the frontier. He
particularly disliked the alleged frontier hostility to science and intellectual pursuits, and accused frontiersmen of being extreme evan-
gelicals who were irrational and given to hysteria. "The depressing
effect upon the free life of inquiry and criticism," Dewey wrote, "is
the greater because of the element of soundness in frontier fear. Impulses of good will and social aspiration . . . have become entangled
with its creed." To disillusioned intellectuals of the 1920s this influence
loomed large.[31]

Even some of Turner's closest associates, such as Joseph Schafer
of the Wisconsin Historical Society, dampened their enthusiasm about
the central role of the frontier. In a series of articles for the *Wisconsin
Magazine of History* during 1922 and 1923, Schafer suggested that
Turner's views about the frontier as a main source of American nationalism required modification. He doubted whether the frontier generated a spirit of nationalism which brought about an almost automatic
integration of newcomers and immigrants. Instead, in analyzing the
immigrant experience in Wisconsin, Schafer questioned whether the
frontier produced a melting pot. German ethnic groups in Wisconsin

30. Billington, *Turner*, 375–85; Billington, "Why Some Historians Rarely Write
History: A Case Study of Frederick Jackson Turner," *Mississippi Valley Historical Review*
50 (June 1963), 3–27; Allen Johnson, in *American Historical Review* 26 (April 1921),
542–43.

31. John Dewey, "The American Intellectual Frontier," *New Republic* 30 (May
10, 1922), 303–4.

tenaciously clung to their cultural practices and a strong sense of identity, not only for one, but several generations.[32] In short, Schafer was far less sanguine about the positive effects of the frontier than Turner.

If not all of the writers on the Western frontier in the 1920s evaluated its influence in negative terms, nevertheless they played down its supposed central impact and suggested alternative explanations to explain the America of their own time. During the decade, historians offered at least five competing hypotheses reflecting the major trends of the period. One was the economic interpretation of history, most brilliantly propounded by Charles A. Beard. Another was the thesis emphasizing the role of immigrants in national development, formulated with skill by Arthur M. Schlesinger, Sr. A third approach reflected the influence of Sigmund Freud as Henry Steele Commager emphasized the importance of psychological motivation on the frontier. Meanwhile, a bevy of cultural critics and writers like Lewis Mumford, Howard Mumford Jones, and historian Dixon Ryan Fox emphasized the primacy of cultural values as a determinant of American culture, rather than the frontier. And for a region like the South, Ulrich B. Phillips found that it was race, not the frontier, that determined that area's development.

As industries boomed and farmers failed in the 1920s, Charles A. Beard further developed his theory of clashing economic interests as a determinant of American civilization. While praising Turner for originally providing "a breath of fresh air," Beard found the thesis "too broad and sweeping. It is certainly questionable whether even up to that time [1890] the frontier or the whole agricultural West had exercised a more profound influence on American development than either the industrialism of the East or the semi-feudal plantation system of the South." Certainly free land and westward advance by themselves could not explain the course of American development. Beard also felt that ethnic divisions were greater than Turner held and that the impact of the West on national legislation and constitutional interpretations was far less than Turner claimed—without much evidence.

32. Joseph Schafer, "The Yankee and the Teuton in Wisconsin," *Wisconsin Magazine of History* 6 (December 1922), 125–45; ibid., 6 (March 1923), 261–79; ibid., 6 (June 1923), 286–302; ibid., 7 (September 1923), 3–19; ibid., 7 (December 1923), 148–71.

Nor was the West a primary stimulant of democracy. With his customary acerbity, Beard noted wryly that, rather, "it came in England which has not had any frontier recently." And in promoting his own thesis of economic determinism, Beard wrote of Turner that "strange to say he says very little indeed about the conflict between the capitalist and organized labor which has given us so many important chapters in our legislative and economic history. On this point our orthodox historians are silent. The tabu is almost perfect. The American Historical Association officially is as regular as Louis XVI's court scribes."[33]

By the end of the decade Beard had developed his theories of economic determinism further. Writing in 1928, he paid tribute to Turner as "the outstanding scholar of his generation, almost the only one who did not devote himself to rehashing hash. His frontier essay," Beard declared, "has exerted a greater influence on historical research and exposition than any other scholarly document composed since the landing of the first immigrants at Jamestown." But Beard attributed Turner's emphasis on agrarianism to the Populist turmoil of the 1890s. By the 1920s, Beard believed,

> the agrarian thesis is inadequate when applied to American politics and utterly untenable as the clue to American civilization in the large. The reason is simple. Besides agriculture, three other powerful economic forces have operated in the course of our affairs: *capitalism* in its manifold aspects such as manufacturing, commerce, banking, credit, and transportation, the *slave-planting system*, and *industrial labor*. Where the influence of one starts and another ends, no human eye can discern.[34]

While Beard was advocating economic determinism, the increasing role of immigrant Americans prompted historians like Arthur M. Schlesinger, Sr., to advocate immigration as a main theme in American development. Schlesinger had taken his doctorate at Columbia in 1916, where he studied with Herbert Osgood. Impressed by the sizable migrations to the United States between 1900 and 1914, he noted in 1921 that "the great Voelkerwanderungen, set in motion by the opening up of the Western hemisphere have been essentially unlike any earlier migrations in history. . . . In a large sense, all American

33. Charles A. Beard, "The Frontier in American History," *New Republic* 25 (February 16, 1921), 349–50.

34. Charles A. Beard, "Culture and Agriculture," *Saturday Review of Literature* 5 (October 20, 1928), 272–73.

history has been the product of these migratory movements from the Old World . . . The whole history of the United States . . . is . . . at bottom the story of the successive waves of immigration and the adaptation of the newcomers and their descendants to the new surroundings offered by the Western hemisphere." Although not making a complete break with the Turner Thesis, Schlesinger concluded that "the two grand themes of American history are, properly, the influence of immigration upon American life and institutions, and the influence of the American environment, especially the frontier in the early days, and the industrial integration of more recent times."[35]

The vogue of psychology in the 1920s also affected historical analysis of the Western frontier. One of these innovators was William A. McDougall, a leading behaviorist who was a professor of psychology at Harvard University. In his view, a nation passed through stages similar to those of individuals. These included youth, adolescence, and maturiy. The United States in 1925 was just entering a period of maturity. That phase was reflected in a marked decline of individualism in American life. Although McDougall believed that the frontier had some part in strengthening individualism, he placed a much greater emphasis on the psychological makeup of the colonists who came. "Only persons of independent disposition, of great initiative, and impatient of government control were likely in those early days to emigrate to the colonies," he wrote. But the end of the frontier led to the atrophy of individualism. The new immigration, the greater economic complexity of industrialism and the rise of corporations "have been the chief influencès in substituting, within some forty years, for the strongly marked and prevalent individualism of the earlier period an excessive and regrettable tendency to seek a remedy for all ills in action by the Federal Government."[36]

New psychological insights also affected interpretations of the frontier hypothesis in other ways. In 1927 Ole E. Rölvaag published his epic novel of frontier life, *Giants in the Earth*. A fictional account of the westward movement, Rölvaag challenged the importance of the physical impact of the frontier on individuals, but emphasized instead the psychological and spiritual influence. It was not man who subdued

35. Arthur M. Schlesinger, Sr., "The Influence of Immigration on American History," *American Journal of Sociology* 27 (July 1921), 72.

36. William McDougall, *The Indestructible Union: Rudiments of Political Science for the American Citizen* (Boston, 1925), viii, 99, 114, 171, 172.

the wilderness environment, Rölvaag declared. Rather, the environment crushed the human spirit, and robbed individuals of what civilization they had brought with them. The frontier was not a hopeful
place, but one of suffering and death, generating pessimism rather
than optimism. It was a very different place from that described by
Turner.[37]

The new generation of historians, as represented by Henry Steele
Commager, was quick to take up Rölvaag's theme. Commager was
himself a first-generation Danish-American who was particularly impressed by the saga of Scandinavian immigrants in the West. Writing
in 1927, Commager declared that Rölvaag's novel was

> the most penetrating and mature depictment of the westward
> movement in our literature. . . . It inspires this encomium because
> it chronicles as no other volume has the combination of physical
> and spiritual experience which is the very warp and woof of Amer-
> ican history. It indicates in the realm of fiction . . . that the story
> of America is not the story of physical and material development
> and expansion to the utter exclusion of the spiritual and psycho-
> logical. The westward movement ceases to be the victim of rom-
> ance and becomes a great . . . spiritual adventure. It ceases to be
> the proud epic of man's conquest of earth and becomes the tragedy
> of earth's humbling of man.

Commager then added an interpretive edge.

> For a generation American history has been concerned with the
> significance of the frontier. [This] approach [has] led us in history
> to a wholesome . . . economic realism . . . but we have not yet
> come out on the high road of understanding. . . . The develop-
> ment of American character and the American mind is to be dis-
> covered neither in statistics of population growth nor in the
> campfire songs of the western trails, but rather in the psychological
> experiences of the individuals and communities that participated
> in the great enterprise. It appears, indeed, that we are entering
> upon [the] era of psychological interpretation.

From that perspective, Commager noted, the frontier movement "was
a tragedy. . . . For the first time a novelist has measured the westward
movement with a psychological yardstick and found it wanting."[38]

37. Ole E. Rölvaag, *Giants in the Earth* (New York, 1928).
38. Henry Steele Commager, "The Literature of the Pioneer West," *Minnesota
History* 8 (December 1927), 319, 320, 324.

The new emphasis on psychological motivation also led students of American culture to give much greater emphasis to the role of cultural values as a determinant of major characteristics of life in the United States. Among these doubters of the Turner Thesis was Lewis Mumford, who expressed considerable skepticism about Turner's claim that the pioneer was conditioned largely by the frontier environment. "The truth is," wrote Mumford, "that he existed in the European mind before he made his appearance here." It was the European cultural and literary influences which shaped America's frontier.[39] This theme was reinforced in greater detail by the literary critic, Howard Mumford Jones, in his study of French influences on American culture. Although frontier conditions may have interacted with French culture, Jones declared, the psychological heritage of Frenchmen was far more important than the frontier in shaping American civilization.[40] These themes were placed in still broader context by a young social historian, Dixon Ryan Fox. Like Mumford and Jones, he was concerned with the transit of civilization from Europe to America, and in that transit he assigned only a minor role to the frontier. Instead, he placed prime emphasis on the movement of cultural values and institutions as a principal determinant of civilization in the United States.[41]

Many of the criticisms of Turner's frontier hypothesis were summarized in an effort to debunk it by John C. Almack, an education professor at Stanford University. "For thirty years American historical thought has been dominated by the frontier shibboleth," Almack complained shrilly.

It has come to be accepted . . . as the chief guide to historical interpretation. . . . It seems not unfair to say that both Professor Turner and his pupils have devoted more time to substantiating the theory by repetition than to testing its truth. . . . The frontier theory appears to be nothing more than a diluted type of Marxian determinism; its foundation an unmistakable materialism, conceiving of men as the slaves of forces over which they have little influence and no control. It assumes that hardships promote individual and social well being. It is not surprisng that our historians have been unable to escape this hangover from Puritanism.

39. Lewis Mumford, *The Golden Day* (New York, 1926), 47, and 48–81.
40. Howard Mumford Jones, *America and French Culture,* 1750–1848 (Chapel Hill, 1927).
41. Dixon Ryan Fox, "The Transit of Civilization," *American Historical Review* 32 (July 1927), 768.

Nor did Almack find the American frontier unique. "All people have had frontiers," he exclaimed. "While the frontier has been an important factor in American life," he concluded, "it has not been an important agency of progress. Side by side with elements of strength have been elements of weakness. The advances which have been made were made in spite of, not because of, the environment."[42]

During the 1920s, then, reactions to the Turner Thesis reflected many of the changing conditions of the decade. These included a more pronounced negativism toward American culture, and outright debunking. But most pronounced was the questioning of the context within which the frontier hypothesis had placed American history. During this decade scholars significantly broadened the framework of American history by focusing on economic determinism, immigration and ethnic influences, psychological factors, cultural values, and race as major determinants of the American experience. They replaced the somewhat simplistic theories of earlier decades with their uncovering of complexity. Most of their efforts were directed not so much at proving Turner wrong as to explore the great diversity inherent in the American experience. Of course, Turner himself always disclaimed the one-dimensional character of his frontier theory and emphasized the complexity and interaction of a wide range of influences. But it was his fate that most historians continued to identify him with the frontier hypothesis only—and it was against such a narrow context that the critics directed many of their complaints.

The Great Depression only stimulated these demurrers as historians undertook more searching analyses of the foundations of American society. The economic crisis raised serious questions about the very survival of American democratic institutions and about the proper role of government. And the New Deal coalition which Franklin D. Roosevelt fashioned focused much greater attention on immigrant Americans and minority groups than earlier movements. Thus, economic crisis, increased government involvement, cultural pluralism, and an awareness of totalitarian regimes in Europe were among some of the conditioning factors for the writing of Western history in the decade following the Great Crash.

Historians during this period could not help but reflect some of

42. John C. Almack, "The Shibboleth of the Frontier," *Historical Outlook* 16 (May 1925), 197, 198, 202.

these trends, although they continued to develop the themes of the 1920s. The depression deepened the pessimism already apparent in the previous decade. In a manner reminiscent of the Progressive era, politicians as well as historians now utilized the frontier thesis to justify increased government intervention. The concept of a closed society also received renewed emphasis. At the same time, scholars provided still more alternatives to the frontier theory, although it was widely accepted within the historical profession. Altogether, the depression seemed to quicken the pace of frontier studies, but from a decidedly contemporary perspective.

Turner's supporters took on a much more defensive tone than they had in previous years. Some merely reiterated or repeated the master rather than attempting to substantiate the thesis with empirical evidence. That was the case of Robert E. Riegel, a Dartmouth College professor who in 1930 published the first general textbook on Western history since Frederic L. Paxson had published his own two decades earlier. Riegel had studied at the University of Wisconsin and uncritically followed the Turnerian perspective. "The American frontier has been the most characteristic and vital of the forces which have distinguished the development of the United States from that of the Old World," he wrote. "For the greater part of three centuries dimly known mountain ranges, illimitable forests, unexplored streams and vast prairies lay to the west of more settled portions of the country. . . . A knowledge of the influence of the unsettled West is necessary to make [more] understandable the whole course of the development of the United States." A similar theme was reiterated by E. Douglas Branch, a journalist who wrote popular surveys of Western history during the decade.[43]

But most Turnerians had become rather cautious. Frederic L. Paxson, perhaps the leading defender of Turner until 1935 when he abruptly changed his views, sought to fend off the critics. In a series of lectures at Brown University, which were published in 1930, he defended the thesis without substantiation, but made concessions. "It has not been proved," Paxson said of the thesis, "and cannot be." Three years later he declared that a thorough examination of the Turner Thesis and its major points had not yet been made. This was

---

43. Robert E. Riegel, *America Moves West* (New York, 1930), 3; E. Douglas Branch, *Westward: The Romance of the American Frontier* (New York, 1930), vii, 592.

just a year after Turner's death, when his disciples rallied round the fallen leader. Still, Paxson now himself doubted that the frontier had had the nationalizing impact that Turner had claimed for it. "Even when Turner wrote there were forces in operation that were inconsistent with the idea of any complete amalgamation." In Turner's home state of Wisconsin, ethnic minorities rebelled against what they perceived as pressures for conformity. "It may be doubted," Paxson wrote, "whether Americans were ever as fully American as they appeared to be." And while the frontier might have encouraged democracy, "it is less clear that this is the sole or perhaps the principal cause of the democracy of the present. There have been other forces at work in the same direction." Still, Paxson had an emotional commitment to the thesis. "After a generation of general currency, the Turner hypothesis stands today as easily to be accepted as when it was launched. It was modest and reasonable when it gave new meaning to American History. When it is used as its framer framed it, it is as useful a guide as it ever was."[44]

In the wake of Turner's death other supporters tried to uphold the theory. Joseph Schafer of the University of Wisconsin, in particular, tried to ward off the strictures of Charles Beard. "The machine . . . is also, as Beard and others have pointed out, a force in historical development," he wrote. "It is much more probable today than it seemed in 1893, that industrialism is destined to triumph over frontier . . . democracy in the United States. Therefore, the technique of industrial advance, which involves the organization of capital . . . of labor, banking, transportation, trusts . . . is an essential study to one who would understand American history." Schafer also sought to reclaim the Turner Thesis from its overenthusiastic advocates.

> Turner, let us again remind ourselves, applied the frontier theory especially to the period which closed with the frontier's disappearance. He never claimed to have discovered in the frontier philosophy a universal solvent for American historical problems. His mind was almost uniquely free from dogmatism. In his teaching he missed none of the keys which interpret American development, whether economic, social, religious, psychological or what not.

44. Frederic L. Paxson, *When the West Is Gone* (New York, 1930), 91, 93; Paxson, "A Generation of the Frontier Hypothesis: 1893–1932," *Pacific Historical Review* 2, no. 2 (1933), 37–38, 45, 46, 51.

True, he did not place all before the public . . . but having be-
stowed . . . the frontier hypothesis . . . upon the world . . . he
could well afford to leave something for others to emphasize.

And in relating Turner to the rise of Mussolini and Hitler, Schafer
concluded: The "love of freedom . . . resultant of generations of pioneering, would rouse the entire West against any attempted *putsch*
on the Italian or the German model."[45]

Within two years after Turner's death, a group of historians gathered at a session of the Mississippi Valley Historical Association in
1933 to assess both Turner and his critics. Avery Craven, one of
Turner's ablest students, emphasized that his master's greatest contribution was the insight that "the occupation of new areas by the American pioneer was but the first step in an extended process" that transformed
a wilderness into a civilization. At the same time he admitted that
perhaps Turner had overemphasized the uniqueness of the American
experience. John D. Hicks, who had taken a doctorate under Paxson
at the University of Wisconsin, hoped to stake out a middle position
between Turner's critics and defenders. He argued that Turner's emphasis on the West as the most American part of America was his
greatest contribution. But he admitted that Turner had overemphasized the distinctiveness of the American experience and had under-
rated European influences. Moreover, he had neglected the
interdependence of East and West in the formation of a national
culture.[46]

But after 1934 the criticisms mounted. Even more than in the
1920s, scholars offered alternative explanations for American development other than the frontier. They emphasized the role of technology, economic interests, cultural values and institutions, ethnic
and immigrant influences, and, increasingly, the urban impact. The
West no longer played the central role in American life which an
earlier generation had assumed.

Several scholars stressed the important role of technology in Western development, an aspect largely untouched by the Turner Thesis.
Among them was Isaiah Bowman, an eminent geographer at Johns

45. Joseph Schafer, "Turner's Frontier Philosophy," *Wisconsin Magazine of History*
16 (June 1933), 468–69; Schafer, "Editorial Comment," ibid., 17 (June 1934), 465.
46. Dixon Ryan Fox (ed.), *Sources of Culture in the Middle West: Backgrounds
versus Frontiers* (New York, 1934), contains relevant essays by Avery Craven, 39–71,
and John D. Hicks, 73–101.

Hopkins University who had been a good friend of Turner's. Already
in the 1920s Turner had expressed slight irritation (privately) about
Bowman's questioning of the Turner Thesis. Just a year before Turner's
death, Bowman published a book that directly challenged Turner's
hypothesis and stressed the importance of technology in Western settlement. "Pioneering today does not conform to the American frontier
conditions of the nineteenth century," Bowman wrote. "Most of the
land in the United States was occupied before modern machine agriculture was developed. . . . The tools of conquest no less than new
fields of conquest are now in the mind of the enterprising settler. Mere
land is no longer a boon." And Bowman went on to attack another
aspect of the thesis concerning the 1890 closing of the frontier.

> It is frequently said that there is no longer an American "frontier."
> . . . Central and eastern Oregon belies the assertion. Central
> Montana has a like story to tell. The erroneous idea of a vanished
> frontier is due to a misconstruction of a statement in the report of
> the U.S. Bureau of the Census for 1890. . . . As a matter of fact,
> the frontier type of living is still the rule, not in one community,
> but in scores of communities . . . along the borders of the Great
> Basin . . . [and] on the plains and uplands east of the Rock-
> ies. . . . The West is still new.[47]

The importance of technology in Western settlement was also
underscored by a young Walter Prescott Webb, who in 1931 published
The Great Plains. Webb argued that the patterns of settlement in that
semiarid area differed appreciably from those in the humid frontiers
of the Middle West. The plains could not be settled until pioneers
developed or adapted special technologies to tame the wilderness and
the natives, technologies that included barbed wire, windmills, irrigation and the Colt revolver.[48]

An increasing awareness of technology also inspired another young
historian, James C. Malin of the University of Kansas, to question
Turner's emphasis on the closing of the frontier in 1890 and the
consequent emergence of a closed society. Such a conception Malin
found to be particularly wanting in the new air age upon which the

47. Isaiah Bowman, *The Pioneer Fringe* (New York, 1931), iii, 139; Jacobs, *Historical World*, 169–73, reprints correspondence between Turner and Bowman regarding
the book; Turner was also annoyed by Bowman's essay in the *Geographic Review* 21
(January 1931), 25–55. See Jacobs, *Historical World*, 168.
48. Walter P. Webb, *The Great Plains* (Boston, 1931), Preface, 8–9.

nation was entering. That clearly placed Turner's closed-space doctrines in doubt. In a period "of air communication, radio, television, and aircraft," Malin declared, the concept of the closing of the frontier seemed anachronistic. "The air age opens again a new world of possibilities," Malin proclaimed, "and some revival of hope after . . . a half century under the shadow of [Turner's] closed space."[49]

Understandably, the depression years also stimulated Marxian analyses of the frontier. Among the most cogent Marxian critics was Louis Hacker, a young historian at Columbia University. "Turner and his followers were the fabricators of a tradition which is not only fictitious but also to a very large extent positively harmful," Hacker declared in 1932.

> The Turner thesis is not proved so much as it is continually reiterated in [his] two volumes. . . . The historical growth of the United States was not unique; merely in certain particulars, and for a brief time, it was different from the European pattern largely because of the processes of settlement. With settlement achieved . . . class [not sectional] lines solidified, competitive capitalism converted into monopolistic capitalism under the guise of the money power, and imperialism—the ultimate destiny of the nation. The United States once again was returning to the main stream of European institutional development. Only by a study of the origins and growth of American capitalism and imperialism can we obtain insight into the nature and complexity of the problems confronting us today. . . . Perhaps the chief reason for the absence of this proper understanding was the futile hunt for a "unique American spirit" which Frederick Jackson Turner began forty years ago and in which he involved most of America's historical scholars from that time until now.[50]

Other Marxists similarly blamed the Turner Thesis for the confusion which was so prevalent during the early years of the Great Depression. Matthew Josephson, a prolific journalist and historian, argued that the "environment of the Frontier . . . created no social philosophy other than the anarchic individualism of the jungle." The combination of frontier values and industrial capitalism created an

49. James C. Malin, "Space and History: Reflections on the Closed-Space Doctrines of Turner and Mackinder and the Challenge of Those Ideas by the Air Age, Part II," *Agricultural History* 18 (July 1944), 107.

50. Louis M. Hacker, "Sections—or Classes," *Nation* 137 (July 26, 1933), 108–10.

exploitative society and a climate of opinion that deterred cultural endeavors. No recovery from the depression or the nation's cultural torpor could occur until Turner's hypothesis was purged from national awareness.[51]

This theme was further developed by Charles Beard, who was not a doctrinaire Marxist but espoused the idea of economic interests as major determinants of American life. During the depression Beard charged that the frontier thesis had foisted the myth of Rugged American Individualism on Americans. That created controversy over the need for governmental interference in the contemporary economic crisis. "The cold truth is," Beard wrote,

> that the individualistic creed of everybody for himself and the devil take the hindmost is principally responsible for the distress in which Western civilization finds itself. . . . Turner overemphasized, in my opinion, the influence of frontier economy on the growth of the democratic idea, on the formation of national policies and on constitutional interpretation. . . . Another problem that puzzled me in relation to the development of Turner's thesis . . . was the long neglect of the democratic impulses in Eastern idealism, of the labor movement. . . . [He] did not give due space to other features of American civilization, especially the planting and capitalistic aspects. Likewise overworked, in my opinion, was the "individualism" of the frontier. . . . Finally, did the closing of the agricultural frontier really make so much difference as Turner and his disciples imagined? The freehold frontier did have a lot of influence on American development, but how much and what kind is still an open question for me. That it does not "explain" American development I am firmly convinced. What does explain this development I leave to those who can write history as it actually has been. Yet I have no doubt that the elbowroom we have enjoyed here, the rich treasures we have fallen upon, used and misused, the freehold tenure in agriculture now declining, and absence of great landlordism from huge sections of the country have given the expressions of human nature in the United States some of the distinctive features we call American.[52]

It must be said that while Beard was critical of the Turner Thesis

51. Matthew Josephson, "The Frontier and Literature," *New Republic* 68 (September 2, 1931), 78.

52. Charles A. Beard, "The Myth of Rugged American Individualism," *Harper's* 164 (December 1931), 13–14, 14–22.

he had warm feelings toward Turner as an individual. As he noted in 1939,

> Personally Turner was one of the most modest and diffident schol-
> ars ever produced in America. He had none of Macauley's "orac-
> ular arrogance" and he had the "presentiment of Eve." The renown
> that came to him never turned his head. If anything it made him
> more cautious, and more critical in examining his own work. To
> students he was generous with his time and strength. With friends
> he was always genial and eager to share his discoveries. Until the
> curtain of night fell, he was . . . engaged in the quest of learning.
> His rounded life was an ornament to American scholarship and to
> the republic from which it sprang.

Thus, although Beard questioned many of Turner's theories, yet he admired the man. In fact, when the editors of the *New Republic* asked him to name books that had changed his mind, Beard chose Turner's *The Frontier in American History*.[53]

Somewhat surprisingly, Turner's foremost champion, Frederic L. Paxson, was moved by the depression to espouse the theory of class conflict. In 1935 Paxson declared that he would use the frontier mainly as a metaphor. "The frontier of 1935," he declared,

> is the social boundary where meet two great classes of Ameri-
> cans—those who have and those who want. It is a frontier which,
> like every other frontier, separates *this* from *that*. The this and the
> that of 1935 make a line of cleavage upon which the American
> future rests. The this and that of yesterday were geographic zones;
> for the old historic frontier separated the occupied areas of the
> United States from the region next beyond; the new frontier dif-
> fers from the old in that on either side lie the horizontal strata of
> social class, instead of regional sections meeting upon a single so-
> cial plane. But whether the metaphor be good or bad, it remains
> true that American policy has ever generated most rapidly along
> some line of friction.

In assessing the twentieth century, he concluded that "frontiers persisted in a different sense. The lines could no longer be traced across
the map, but through the heart of American civilization they thrust

53. Charles A. Beard, "The Frontier in American History," *New Republic* 97 (February 1, 1939), 359; also in Malcolm Cowley (ed.), *Books That Changed Our Minds* (New York, 1939), 61–71.

cleavages between class and class. Social strata, more sharply defined with each new decade, broke down the importance of geographic section, while the frontiers that separated class from class became the battleground of new ideas. The old frontiers separated communities . . . ; the new . . . were boundaries between classes."[54]

The global nature of the depression only reinforced the views of some historians that cultural influences rather than the frontier were a prime force in the United States, and that the nation was not as unique as Americans had believed in an earlier age. Benjamin F. Wright, in an analysis of American culture, accused Turner of Middle Western isolationism, a kind of provincialism against which Sinclair Lewis had railed in *Main Street*. He especially emphasized Turner's preoccupation with the Middle West. "Turner was emphatically a native of that important section," he wrote.

> His theory of the frontier was, among other things, a middle western view of pioneer civilization. It was the people and the institutions of that and of similar areas that he always had in mind when he wrote of the frontier. Those frontiers that were materially different in culture, or lack of it, he almost invariably left out of that account. . . . The seeming scarcity of distinction among the descendants of pioneering stock in other regions seems not to have interested him.[55]

Wright also placed much emphasis on the view that cultural influences were more significant than the frontier. In examining various Western political institutions, Wright attacked Turner for his failure to recognize that American democratic institutions derived from European cultures, not from the frontier. Many frontier political practices such as universal suffrage were not indigenous, but were imported by the pioneers from England or the older Eastern states. Although Wright did not reject all of Turner's insights, he concluded that the "conception of the frontier as it appears in Turner's essays, is largely a myth."[56] A similar point was made by Fletcher Green, a southern scholar. After close analysis of state constitutions in the South, Green

54. Frederic L. Paxson, "The New Frontier and the Old American Habit," *Pacific Historical Review* 4, no. 4 (1935), 309, 322.

55. Benjamin F. Wright, review of Turner's *The Section in American History*, in *New England Quarterly* 6 (September 1933), 633.

56. Benjamin F. Wright, "American Democracy and the Frontier," *Yale Review* 22 (December 1930), 349–50; Jacobs, *Historical World*, 167–69.

concluded in 1932 that democratic features were usually included not by representatives from the frontier sections, but by those from older tidewater areas who were usually steeped in English law.[57]

Even one of Turner's own students, Thomas P. Abernethy, reinforced this theme. In a close study of political institutions in Tennessee he contradicted Turner's assumptions although, in 1932 when Turner was still alive, he dedicated his book to the master. Abernethy found that on the Tennessee frontier the settlers and speculators who were most prominent were ruthless and exploitative, and often antidemocratic. Their experience in no way reinforced the Turner assumption that the frontier was responsible for political democracy. Abernethy further expanded on his views as president of the Southern Historical Association in 1938. "In the development of our ideas and habits of popular government," he said,

> at least three forces have combined to produce the present-day result. The philosophical doctrines of seventeenth and eighteenth century Europe, as expounded by Locke, Rousseau, and others played a leading role . . . the frontier was a mighty force during a succession of generations, and lastly, the Industrial Revolution which so powerfully affected the development of democracy in nineteenth century England. . . . The Jeffersonian regime developed under the influence of the first of these; the Jacksonian under the second; and the New Deal under the third. It is true that Europe had the leading part in shaping the first and last of these forces, but is there any reason why we should make such disproportionate ado about the . . . frontier . . . just because it was peculiarly American?[58]

The continuing movement of Americans to cities during the 1930s was clearly reflected in the development of an urban interpretation of the national experience. Arthur Schlesinger, Sr., had first presented this view in 1922, but in a very muted and low-key fashion which paid homage to Turner. More than a decade later Turner was dead, and Schlesinger published the first book to offer an urban interpretation of American history, complementing and perhaps displacing

---

57. Fletcher M. Green, *Constitutional Development in the South Atlantic States, 1776–1860* (Chapel Hill, 1930), 297–304.

58. Thomas P. Abernethy, *From Frontier to Plantation in Tennessee* (Chapel Hill, 1932); Abernethy, "Democracy and the Southern Frontier," *Journal of Southern History* 4 (February 1938), 12–13.

the frontier thesis. In the introduction to the volume, Dixon Ryan Fox, the editor of the series in which the work appeared, obliquely criticized the previous isolation of American historians who had emphasized the uniqueness of the American experience. Schlesinger, he noted, "recognizes that Americans formed a part of the larger human family and had behind them the general history of mankind; their achievements, therefore, are measured by world standards—a procedure rare among American historians." In a veiled reference to Turner, Fox noted that "such writers, too . . . have been accustomed to emphasize the longtime influence of the frontier upon American civilization and the disastrous effects of the passing of free fertile lands. The present volume is devoted, rather, to describing and appraising the new social force which waxed and throve while driving the pioneer culture before it: the city." In this book, and in his consequent presidential address to the Mississippi Valley Historical Association in 1940, Schlesinger was more explicit in offering an urban interpretation of American history which, he argued, largely ignored the importance of towns and cities in the settlement of the West.[59]

As the first generation of American-born children of the immigrants who came to the United States at the beginning of the century matured, they developed the theme of immigration as an alternative to the frontier hypothesis. One of the ablest descendants was Marcus Hansen, who charged that the Turner thesis directly stymied efforts of American historians to study the European origins of American culture. He himself was a second-generation Danish-American. Commenting on the Turner Thesis, Hansen felt that most historians were simply parroting Turner's ideas without advancing fresh concepts themselves. "Turner simplified what he knew," Hansen wrote. "His disciples further simplified the idea in order that their undergraduate listeners might understand. . . . Consequently, there has come to maturity a generation of Americans who . . . know that once the frontier meant opportunity; and a surprisingly large number of them believe that all opportunity in the United States ended with the census of 1890." The immigrant, however, Hansen declared, played a far more important role in shaping American civilization than the frontier. "Without the influx of millions of Europeans, the clocklike progression

59. Dixon Ryan Fox, in Arthur M. Schlesinger, Sr., *Rise of the City, 1878–1898* (New York, 1933), xiv; Arthur M. Schlesinger, Sr., "The City in American History," *Mississippi Valley Historical Review* 27 (June 1940), 43–66.

across the continent could not have occurred. The population would not have been so mobile. There would have been a frontier, to be sure, but not the kind of frontier that produced the now accepted historical consequences."[60] During the same period, another young historian, Carl Wittke, came to almost identical conclusions. Wittke, a first-generation German-American, noted that it was not the frontier that shaped America, but the immigrants who transmitted European culture to the New World.[61] Hansen's premature death in 1938 precluded further development of the theme by him, for he had planned a three-volume work on the subject.

Since the Great Depression focused, above all, on problems of unemployment, it was not surprising that Turner's suggestion that the West served as a safety valve for eastern discontent came in for closer scrutiny. Criticism arose early in the decade when Anne Bezanson, an economic historian, noted in 1932 that statistics on labor turnover did not substantiate the hypothesis that eastern working men who were unemployed could find solace in free lands of the West. A detailed study of Iowa by William J. Petersen in 1934 also questioned the safety-valve thesis.[62] A full-fledged assault on it was taken up in the following year by Carter C. Goodrich, an economic historian at Columbia University, who noted the "sheer absence of direct evidence in its support." At the same time, James C. Malin undertook a painstaking analysis of population movements in Kansas and concluded that "economic depression was usually associated with declining numbers of farm operators during the frontier stage. It has been generally assumed by followers of Frederick Jackson Turner that unfavorable conditions in the East . . . resulted in the flow of population westwards to free and cheap land. . . . The data in the study does not seem to bear out such a theory."[63] That point was reiterated by Fred Shannon in 1935 as he demonstrated that the number of people migrating from

60. Marcus L. Hansen, *The Immigrant in American History* (Cambridge, Mass., 1940), 64–65.

61. Carl Wittke, *We Who Built America* (New York, 1939).

62. Anne Bezanson, "Some Historical Aspects of Labor Turnover," in *Facts and Factors in Economic History*, edited by Arthur H. Cole et al. (Cambridge, Mass., 1932), 692–708; William J. Petersen, "Population Advance to the Upper Mississippi Valley, 1830–1860," *Iowa Journal of History and Politics* 32 (October 1934), 312–53.

63. Carter C. Goodrich and Sol Davidson, "The Wage-Earner in the Westward Movement," *Political Science Quarterly* 50 (June 1935), 161–85; James C. Malin, "The Turnover of Farm Population in Kansas," *Kansas Historical Quarterly* 4 (November 1935), 339–72.

farms to cities in depression times was far greater than the number of those moving from cities to farms. These critics did much to undermine the safety-valve theory, and indirectly supported the notion that in its absence, government compensatory programs were necessary.[64]

Turner's suggestion that free lands acted as a safety valve was further questioned by the exhaustive studies of public lands in the skilled hands of Paul W. Gates. During the heyday of the New Deal, when Americans were conscious of much overlapping and confusing legislation, Gates demonstrated that a similar situation had pervaded federal land policies in the nineteenth century. As a result, public land laws rarely accomplished their objectives. Instead of promoting settlement by yeoman farmers, the land laws were often manipulated by speculators and corrupt public officials who promoted the concentration of landownership in the hands of a few large corporations or landowners. Nor was it possible for a person of moderate means to secure the capital necessary to till a small homestead. Turner's idea of "free lands" thus was a myth, for the actual administration of federal and state land laws did not allow large numbers of poor men to take advantage of new Western lands. Even the Homestead Act of 1862, which Turner cited as a prime example of "free land" legislation, rarely operated as its framers had hoped.[65]

Americans slowly shed some of their isolationist sentiments as the decade of the 1930s progressed, and historians of the West were quick to pick up the cues. By 1933, when President Roosevelt was publicizing his Good Neighbor policy toward Latin America, historian Herbert Bolton took the opportunity to reemphasize his belief in the historical unity of the nations in the Western Hemisphere. In a burst of enthusiasm, Bolton urged extension of the Turner Thesis to the entire Western Hemisphere, although his effort required considerable imagination and glossing over discordant facts.[66] By 1942 a young historian, William Diamond, published the previously unpublished manuscript that Turner had submitted to President Wilson in 1919 on "International Political Parties in a Durable League of Nations," to underscore

64. Fred A. Shannon, "The Homestead Act and Labor Surplus," *American Historical Review* 41 (July 1936), 637–51.

65. Paul W. Gates, "The Homestead Law in an Incongruous Land System," *American Historical Review* 41 (July 1936), 652–81.

66. Herbert Bolton, "Epic of Greater America," *American Historical Review* 38 (April 1933), 448–74.

the relevance of the frontier experience to a new international organization. Global awareness was also reflected in Arthur Schlesinger, Sr.'s presidential address to the American Historical Association in 1943, when he discussed "What, Then, Is the American, This New Man?" His themes were quite un-Turnerian, for he now criticized Turner's thesis as too narrow and nationalistic. Openly calling for modification of Turner's hypothesis, Schlesinger declared: "The American . . . is the product of the interplay of his Old World heritage and New World conditions."[67] Times had changed!

But while scholars were actively debating diverse approaches to the study of the West, the Turner Thesis had entered popular consciousness. Politicians, in particular, had used the frontier thesis to rationalize their public programs in the Progressive era, and they were to do the same during the New Deal. The perception that the closing of the frontier had transformed the United States into a closed society with limited potentials for further growth appealed to New Dealers because it rationalized their advocacy of government compensatory programs in the absence of the frontier. It was a most convenient myth, although many, of course, believed that it was an accurate perception of reality.

President Franklin D. Roosevelt himself espoused this view, and provided a cue for many members of his administration. In his famous 1932 campaign address to the Commonwealth Club of California at San Francisco, Roosevelt said, alluding to the nation's rapid growth in the nineteenth century:

> The happiest of economic conditions made that day long and splendid. On the western frontier, land was substantially free. No one . . . was entirely without opportunity. . . . At the very worst there was always the possibility of climbing into a covered wagon and moving west where the untilled prairies afforded a haven for men for whom the East did not provide a place. . . . The turn of the tide came with the turn of the century. We were reaching our last frontier; there was no more free land.

67. William Diamond, "American Sectionalism and World Organization, by Frederick Jackson Turner," *American Historical Review* 47 (April 1942), 545–51; Diamond, "Introduction to a Manuscript by Turner Entitled 'International Political Parties in a Durable League of Nations,'" ibid., 47 (April 1942), 545–47; Arthur M. Schlesinger, Sr., "What Then Is the American, This New Man?" ibid., 48 (January 1943), 225–44.

But in 1932 he saw very different conditions.

> A glance at the situation today only too clearly indicates that
> equality of opportunity as we have known it no longer exists. . . .
> Our last frontier has long been reached. . . . There is no safety
> valve. . . . All this calls for a re-appraisal of values. . . . Our task
> now . . . is . . . the soberer less dramatic business of administering
> resources, . . . of distributing wealth and products more equitably.
> The day of enlightened administration has come.[68]

Historians who approved of the New Deal enthusiastically embraced this doctrine. Writing in 1933, Henry Steele Commager applauded Roosevelt's abandonment of laissez-faire, realizing "it had been
born in the American wilderness and of the boundless resources of
the American continent." Now that the frontier was closed, "old
theories of individualism and laissez-faire were no longer applicable."[69]
Curtis Nettels noted that while "there was not an historian in the
Roosevelt Brains Trust [yet] a strong current running through the
philosophy of the New Deal may be traced directly to the interpretation
of American society developed" by Turner. The engineers of the New
Deal viewed the passing of the frontier as the passing of an automatic
adjuster of the nation's economic ills, and therefore "something must
be put in its place." That something was the New Deal.[70]

Some of the New Dealers were not always consistent in their use
of the frontier hypothesis. Secretary of Agriculture Henry Wallace
accepted the concept of the closed frontier in 1890, and in his book,
New Frontiers, published in 1934, wrote that "we are no longer a
pioneer nation with free lands." On the other hand, he argued that
Turner's view of the United States in the twentieth century was not
relevant. New frontiers were needed, frontiers characterized by cooperative achievements (such as the New Deal) rather than by individualism and free enterprise.[71]

Historians who were not sympathetic to the New Deal remarked

68. Text of Franklin D. Roosevelt's speech, in New York Times, September 24,
1932, p. 6, also reprinted in The Public Papers and Addresses of Franklin D. Roosevelt
(13 vols., New York, 1938–50), I, 746–47, 750, 751–52.

69. Henry Steele Commager, "Farewell to Laissez-Faire," Current History 38 (August 1933), 513–20.

70. Curtis P. Nettels, "Frederick Jackson Turner and the New Deal," Wisconsin
Magazine of History 17 (March 1934), 257–58.

71. Henry A. Wallace, New Frontiers (New York, 1934), 249–62, 274–75, 276–
87.

on the questionable use of the frontier thesis to justify contemporary social programs. Without Turner's frontier hypothesis, Marcus Hansen lamented, "the New Deal would have been politically much more difficult to achieve." Charles A. Barker of the University of Texas and James C. Malin of the University of Kansas concurred in this appraisal. They rejected the notion that Americans in the 1930s were caught in a closed society, in an era of closed opportunity, from which there was no escape except through New Deal programs.[72]

Yet the belief that the American system was encapsuled in closed space also profoundly affected the thinking of economists during the Great Depression. Even the most eminent practitioners, such as Professor Alvin Hansen of Harvard University, the leading Keynesian in the United States, accepted the assumption uncritically, without giving it much further thought. It fit so nicely with their preconceptions. If the United States was a nation with limited or no opportunity to grow, that required deficit spending by the federal government to compensate for the economic stimulus once provided by the frontier. "It is not possible, I think," Hansen wrote, "to make even an approximate estimate of the proportion of the new capital created in the nineteenth century which was a direct consequence of the opening of new territory. . . . What proportion of new capital formation in the United States went each year into the Western frontier we do not know, but it must have been very considerable. . . . The opening of new territory and the growth of population were together responsible for a very large fraction—possibly somewhere near one-half of new capital formation in the nineteenth century." And in reflecting the pessimism of the 1930s, he added: "These outlets for new investments are rapidly being closed. . . . This movement ended in the Great Depression."[73]

Hansen represented the mainstream of economic thought in the 1930s and 1940s and so dominated the field that dissident voices were rarely heard. One of those dissidents was George W. Terborgh, an economist who had worked at the Brookings Institution and was the economist of a trade association, the Machinery and Allied Products Institute. In his book, *The Bogey of Economic Maturity*, offered as a

72. Hansen, *Immigrant*, 53–76; Charles A. Barker, "Three Types of Historical Interpretation," *Southwestern Historical Quarterly* 45 (April 1942), 323–34; Malin, "Space and History, Part II," *Agricultural History* 18 (July 1944), 107–26.

73. Alvin Hansen, *Fiscal Policy and Business Cycles* (New York, 1941), 43, 360.

pamphlet in 1939 and published in 1945, he directly attacked the concept of the closed society espoused by Hansen and his followers. If the frontier did end in 1890, he inquired, what significance could it have for the 1930s? Certainly, the passing of the frontier in 1890 did not inaugurate an era reflecting a dearth of investment opportunities in the half-century that followed. "There is no historical evidence," he declared, "that the completion of the first wave of western settlement impaired the functioning of the American economy. There has been no significant 'afterglow' effect since the frontier disappeared. Indeed, investment opportunity per capita appears to have been on the whole greater in the older states during the past fifty years than in the younger. This leaves the spectre of the vanishing frontier a bedraggled and disreputable scarecrow." But Terborgh was a voice crying in the wilderness, although the nation's economic experiences after 1940 fully substantiated many of his arguments. [74]

Despite critics, between 1930 and 1945 the frontier hypothesis enjoyed widespread acceptance among historians and the public. A Canadian historian, George W. Brown, summed it up well in 1938 when he wrote: "One cannot but be struck with the emphasis given to Turner's influence in contemporary discussions of American historical writing. Although there was a reappraisal of the Turner thesis . . . the importance of Turner remains, and historians are still frequently judged by the degree in which they appear to have been affected by Turner's influence." The critics had not so much demolished the thesis as they had modified it. [75]

That point was conceded by even the most devoted Turnerians, such as Avery Craven. Assessing his mentor's role in 1939, Craven noted that "Frederick Jackson Turner wrote less and influenced his own generation more than any other important historian." He quoted Louis Hacker to the effect that for forty years Turner "so completely dominated American historical writing that hardly a single production of that time has failed to show the marks of his influence." To this, Craven added: "The explanation is simple. It is found in a wealth of suggestive ideas packed into short essays which interpret rather than narrate, and in a stimulating personality which stirred students to

74. George W. Terborgh, *The Bogey of Economic Maturity* (New York, 1945), 65, 76.

75. George W. Brown, "Some Recent Books on the History of the United States," *Canadian Historical Review* 19 (December 1938), 412.

curiosity and inspired them to independent research. Turner was both
a 'first-class mind' and a great teacher." Craven was careful to place
Turner within the context of his own times.

> The historian is the child of his age. New shifts in interests alter
> values and outlooks. History must be rewritten by each generation
> for itself. It would be asking too much that Turner be to another
> generation what he was to his own. It is probably fair to say he
> generalized too much for the whole West from the Old Northwest
> which he knew so well. He may have insisted a bit more on the
> uniqueness of the American experience than the facts warranted,
> and he may not have stressed the industrial-agricultural conflicts
> enough. . . . His faith in America's future may have been too
> great, his hope for democracy too high. These were common faults
> of his day. But the questions he asked are more or less permanent
> ones for those who would know how America came to be what it
> is. His answers may not exactly fit when the pattern is entirely
> unfolded. He would be among those greatly surprised if they did. I
> at one time asked him why he did not answer a critic who had
> distorted in order to criticize. He only chuckled and said: "I've al-
> ways been surprised that there has not been more of criticism." He
> was too eager for truth to care for praise or blame.[76]

In one of the first histories of American thought, Ralph Gabriel
of Yale University in 1940 appraised Turner's contribution as he perceived it at the time. "Whitman transformed the democratic faith
into magnificent verse," he wrote,

> Turner into immortal history. When Turner's writings are used as
> source material, they suggest the importance of the democratic
> faith for American thought as the twentieth century opened. . . .
> He overemphasized, to be sure, the importance of the frontier; a
> study of Emerson would have given him new insights. But his over-
> emphasis was his strength. His thesis stirred not only national but
> sectional pride. It was, in fact, an expression of that loyalty to
> one's province which Josiah Royce urged as the only sound foun-
> dation of nationalism. Before his death Turner had become a
> prophet among historians. Since his passing his fame has mounted.
> Detractors have appeared, but they have found the students of the
> master fierce contenders. The emotionalism of the battle suggests

76. Avery Craven, "Frederick Jackson Turner," in *Marcus W. Jernegan Essays in
American Historiography*, edited by William T. Hutchinson (Chicago, 1937), 252,
269.

that more than a scientific hypothesis is at stake. The controversy over the Turner thesis affects tenaciously held social beliefs. One suspects that the fame of Turner will not decline until the American democratic faith has waned.[77]

In 1942 another Yale historian, George W. Pierson, undertook a survey of the attitudes which American historians held about the Turner theory. He prepared a questionnaire which he sent to 220 historians in the field, of whom 106 replied. Major criticisms included the charge that it was too vague and general, too simplistic and all-inclusive. Most respondents felt that Turner and his supporters were too greatly influenced by the cultural, regional, and patriotic preferences of their own times. Both critics and defenders agreed that Turner's influence in the classroom was greater than in print. Walter P. Webb noted that "the hypothesis is generally sound, but its implications—for today and for the future—have never been grasped." Henry Steele Commager commented: "I have the feeling that the 'frontier' has been chewed too much. I wish historians would stop arguing about it and develop some new interpretations. Also, I wish they would copyright the idea so as to prevent every literary critic, sociologist, criminologist etc. from using it and abusing it."[78]

A somewhat surprising response came from a man who in the next generation was to become Turner's champion, Ray Allen Billington. In 1942, he declared:

> Most glaring of the Turner errors is probably his stress on the lone frontiersman and the effect of the frontier on rugged American individualism. Certainly the few careful studies of frontier communities . . . show that the *group* was more important in the west than in the east. American individualism developed from opportunity, not from isolated living. . . . Even the casual reading I have done convinces me that the frontier community was far from a complete plateau—that democracy was not automatically bred by wilderness conditions. Each frontier had its aristocracy and its lower classes.[79]

On the basis of his survey, Pierson concluded that the defenders

77. Ralph H. Gabriel, *The Course of American Democratic Thought* (New York, 1940), 258–59.

78. George W. Pierson, "American Historians and the Frontier Hypothesis in 1941," *Wisconsin Magazine of History* 26 (September 1942), 36–60, and ibid., 26 (December 1942), 170–85.

79. Ibid. (December 1942), 152.

of the thesis still far outnumbered the detractors. "A pronounced majority seems a long way from abandoning certain central propositions. . . . The hold of the grand Turnerian hypothesis . . . may . . . be less firm than the overall totals would indicate," Pierson declared. "Hardly a proposition in the theory but numbers today a substantial group of opponents or doubters."[80] Several decades of criticism and changing times had certainly taken their toll.

Later observers of the historical controversies over the Turner Thesis between 1893 and 1945 might wonder what the fuss was all about. Turner himself had made it quite clear, not only in his teaching but also in his published writings, that he was certainly not advocating a singular interpretation of American development. He held decidedly pluralistic views. As he stated quite clearly in 1910:

> Is it not well before attempting to decide whether history requires an economic interpretation, or a psychological, or any other ultimate interpretation, to recognize that the factors in human society are varied and complex; that the political historian handling his subject in isolation is certain to miss fundamental facts and relationships in his handling of a given age or nation, that the economic historian is exposed to the same danger; and so of all the other special historians. . . . But the point on which I would lay stress is this: The economist, the political scientist, the psychologist, the geographer, the student of literature, of art, of religion— all the allied laborers in the study of society—have contributions to make to the equipment of the historian.[81]

If, despite Turner's disclaimers, his thesis aroused so much controversy, this was due perhaps to the deeply felt emotions and attitudes which many Americans—historians included—held about their vision of American society, in their own times as well as in the past. The Turner Thesis quite simply stirred passions about the nature of society in the United States. As in the 1980s, historians read their own ideological assumptions into their analysis of what had happened in the West. Some like Charles Beard viewed the American epic as a clash of economic interests. Marxists were sure they could discern class struggle. Nationalists perceived a triumphant march to a national

80. Ibid., 154.
81. Turner, "Social Forces," in *American Historical Review* 16 (January 1911), 231, 232.

identity. Liberals viewed the disappearance of the West as a justification for their own programs advocating more government intervention. Conservatives could rationalize the decline of individualism as
a consequence of the closing of the frontier. The search for meaning
in Western history was as much a search for meaning in contemporary
times as it was an investigation of the past.

TWO

The West as Frontier, 1945–1990

THE END of the Second World War brought a new generation into the historical profession, and with them came changing perspectives on the frontier. The men and women who had been born in the nineteenth century and who had lived through the momentous changes in American life at the turn of the century had either retired or passed away. Historians who succeeded them were born in the twentieth century, usually of urban backgrounds, with very different perspectives on the frontier. Their own particular background and the contemporary events of their lifetimes did much to shape their distinctive interpretations of the frontier experience in the second half of the twentieth century.[1]

That period had a profound impact. The experiences of war—World War II, the Korean conflict, and Vietnam—contributed to the waning of the optimism which had once so characteristically been associated with the frontier. Instead, a growing pessimism and negativism became a hallmark of this generation. Moreover, the emergence of the United States as a world power after 1945 led these historians to have a very different image of themselves and the nation. In contrast

1. Peter Novick, *That Noble Dream* (Cambridge, 1988), 138–68, 282–92, 320–415.

to the somewhat narrow nationalism common in Turner's youth, they were imbued with global perspectives—a comparative view of the American frontier—measuring it against frontiers around the globe. Nor was this generation one of generalists like many of their predecessors. Proliferation of knowledge in all fields and the rapid growth of the historical profession after 1945 led to increasing specialization of frontier studies. And given the large number of new historians with increasingly varied racial, ethnic, religious, and social backgrounds, it was not surprising to witness the breakdown of consensus on any single theory such as the Turner Thesis. That consensus was destroyed further by the social fragmentation occurring in American society. By the 1950s the civil rights movement underscored the neglected role of blacks, and soon thereafter, Hispanics and Indians in American life, and that emphasis extended to the frontier. A decade later, the women's rights movement gathered force. Meanwhile, the Vietnam war encouraged the rise of the New Left, which stressed class conflict in American life. And major environmental problems by the 1970s quickly forced themselves on the consciousness of most historians. By 1990, race, class, gender, and environment had become major concerns of this generation of frontier historians.

Nor could the scholars of this era espouse the simplicity of an earlier generation. The compartmentalization of knowledge revealed levels of complexity which tended to inhibit broad generalizations or hypotheses such as the Turner Thesis. By 1990 historians knew much more about the frontier than Turner had divined a hundred years earlier. But paradoxically, they were far less sure than he had been about its impact, and its significance, in American development.

During the fifteen years immediately after the conclusion of the war, at least four major trends in the writing of frontier history emerged. First, historians reflected a new awareness of America's role as a global power. No longer did historians view the frontier as a unique American historical phenomenon. Instead, they placed its development in a broad international context and eagerly sought comparative experiences in other nations. A second trend was similarly affected by the World War II experience, namely a view of the West as an open, growing society, not a closed one as had been fashionable in the 1930s. The wartime experiences dispelled this assumption and exposed it for the myth it was. Historians no longer considered the United States as a closed civilization because of the supposed closing of the frontier in 1890. Rather, in an age of affluence they now regarded the nation—and the West—as capable of unlimited and extensive growth, constituting an open system, geographically as well as intellectually. It fit the mood of a nation that saw itself as the world's leading power. A third major trend was the emphasis on the dominance of cultural influences in shaping the frontier, and far less emphasis on environmental conditions stressed by earlier generations. Such a perspective was in part due to a related trend, a renewed emphasis on the use of social science theories and methods in the study of the frontier. These unraveled complexities that brought a deeper understanding of the manifold influences of the frontier.

Sometime about 1960 the positive self-image of Americans began to disintegrate, resulting in significant changes in the perception of the role of the frontier. The major new emphases of frontier historians now mirrored the nation's preoccupations, a new self-consciousness about race, class, poverty, gender, and the natural environment. That led to a significant shift in *Weltanschauung*. Historians no longer espoused the hope and optimism of the postwar decade. Reflecting a loss of self-confidence, and increasing pessimism, they now busied themselves with condemning much in America's past, including the frontier. While this mood was as much an emotional as well as an intellectual response, it also reflected the knowledge that the frontier process had been far more complex than previous generations had perceived. An accumulation of hundreds of detailed, specialized studies replaced a naive innocence and simplicity of earlier years. One result of this experience was a disinclination to embrace single-causation theories such as Turner's. Multicausation processes seemed more plausible. But whatever their particular orientation, the scholars who wrote about the frontier between 1945 and 1990 closely reflected far-reaching changes in national life, and in the process changed the nature of frontier studies. Their search for the West did not succeed in changing popular images of the frontier in their day, however. But a cultural lag between history written by professionals and by popular writers had existed in earlier years and was hardly new. After all, it was a reaction to romantic narratives about the frontier that had prompted Frederick Jackson Turner in his own day to attempt a more analytical and interpretive account.[2]

2. Turner, "The Significance of History," *Wisconsin Journal of Education* 21, 230–34, 253–56; Burton, "Influence of American West . . . on Theodore Roosevelt," *Arizona and the West* 4, 5–26; Lewis, "Art of Frederick Jackson Turner," *Huntington Library Quarterly* 35, 241–55.

A realization that World War II inaugurated a new era sparked a series of surveys of the field of Western history in the ensuing decade. One of the first was by Earle D. Ross, a historian at Iowa State College, who belonged to Turner's generation. In reviewing an era of prairie historiography, Ross reiterated traditional incantations by noting that Turner had done more than any other single individual to stimulate interest in regional history. Ross did not provide explicit evidence for his conclusion, but struck a defensive note by admitting that the Turner Thesis was in fact predicated "largely upon the unique conditions of the Prairie West." Similarly, James Frost, in reviewing the literature concerning the Turner Thesis in the preceding twenty years for the benefit of social studies teachers, concluded that in his estimation the Turner Thesis was still valid, although he adduced no evidence to document his conclusion. But John Caughey came to a similar determination after examining articles dealing with the Turner hypothesis in a wide range of professional journals between 1930 and 1947.[3]

In the post–World War II era the impact of the Turner Thesis was as important in Canada as in the United States. In 1948 Morris Zaslow evaluated the Turner Thesis, which he viewed as a direct outgrowth of Turner's middle western environment. In summarizing the views of Canadian historians writing about the West, he noted that "Canadian history of today is . . . to a considerable degree [influenced] by the frontier hypothesis." And a few years later, J. M. Careless, a noted Canadian scholar, demonstrated effectively that Turner had had a very decisive impact on the interpretations of Canada's most distinguished historians of the past generation.[4]

Perhaps the most persuasive demonstration of the widespread acceptance of the Turner Thesis in post–World War II America was by John Caughey, who in 1952 took a poll of historians concerning their favorite books in American history. For the period of works published between 1920 and 1935, Turner's *The Frontier in American History*

3. Earle D. Ross, "A Generation of Prairie Historiography," *Mississippi Valley Historical Review* 33 (December 1946), 391–410; James Frost, "The Frontier Influence— A Perspective," *Social Education* 11 (December 1947), 361–63; John W. Caughey, "The Mosaic of Western History," *Mississippi Valley Historical Review* 33 (March 1947), 595–606.

4. Morris Zaslow, "The Frontier Hypothesis in Recent Historiography," *Canadian Historical Review* 29 (June 1948), 153–67; J. M. S. Careless, "Frontierism, Metropolitanism, and Canadian History," ibid. 35 (March 1954), 1–21.

placed second, just behind Vernon Parrington's *Main Currents in American History. The Rise of American Civilization,* by Charles and Mary Beard, ranked third; followed, in order, by *The Colonial Period of American History,* by Charles M. Andrews; Carl Becker's *The Declaration of Independence;* Ulrich Phillips, *Life and Labor in the Old South;* Edward Channing's *History of the United States;* Samuel Eliot Morison's *Maritime History of Massachusetts;* A. M. Schlesinger's *New Viewpoints in American History;* and *The Populist Revolt,* by John D. Hicks.[5]

The decline of isolation in American life and the adoption of global perspectives by a majority of Americans in the post–World War II era was early reflected in writings about the frontier. One of the first to jump into the fray was Carlton J. Hayes. In his presidential address to the American Historical Association in 1945, he noted that

> it is now over half a century since Frederick Jackson Turner assisted in Chicago at the international celebration of America. Almost without critical test . . . the frontier hypothesis in that paper met with prompt and well-nigh unanimous acceptance by historians of the United States. . . . I wonder, however, if the time has not come when our historians might profitably broaden their conception of the frontier . . . a frontier of what? The advancing frontier of North America, like similar frontiers in South America, Australasia, and South Africa [was] a frontier of Europe.

Hayes then alluded to the changed international position of the United States—as compared to 1893.

> It is no longer a question of creating a great American nation. It is now a question of preserving and securing this nation in a world of nations. Nor is it now a question of isolationism versus internationalism. This has finally been determined by the Senate's almost unanimous ratification of the Charter of the United Nations. The question now is whether as a nation we are going to be sufficiently informed and intelligent about foreign conditions, sufficiently free from provincialism, to ensure the effective operation of the United Nations. . . . Towards satisfactory solution of this question American historians . . . can make major contributions. One . . . would be to put much greater emphasis than in the past on cultural history. . . . The American frontier is a frontier of European or

5. John W. Caughey, "Historians' Choice: Results of a Poll on Recently Published American History and Biography," *Mississippi Valley Historical Review* 39 (September 1952), 299.

"Western" culture. This culture, however modified by or adapted
to peculiar geographic and social conditions in America or elsewhere, is still, in essential respect, the culture . . . of the regional
community of nations on both sides of the Atlantic. . . . The Atlantic community has lost none of its potential importance for us
and for the world. We must look anew to it and strengthen our
ties with it if we are to escape the tragedy of another world war.
To this end the historical guild in America can immeasurably contribute.[6]

On the other side of the Atlantic, the famous British historian,
Arnold Toynbee, took up a similar refrain in 1947. American culture
was not, he wrote, a unique result of the frontier experience as Turner
had argued. Rather, it was a direct consequence of the expansion of
European culture.

The frontier which the American people had carried into the
Great Plains, and across them, [came] out of the eastern forests of
northern Europe . . . a phase of global movement westward. In
the United States, the descendants of West European colonists had
occupied effectively vast habitable spaces which previously had
been virtually empty or else had been occupied ineffectively and
utilised inefficiently by their former inhabitants. But this had been
happening not only in the United States; it had been happening
also in Canada, in southern South America, in Australia, in New
Zealand. Moreover, this effective occupation of more or less empty
spaces had not been the only form that the West European peoples' expansion had taken. While they had been supplanting the
world's surviving food-gathering, hunting, and pastoral nomadic
peoples, they had also been subjugating the civilized, but technologically backward agricultural peoples of Mexico and Peru and
Asia and Africa. In one or the other of these two ways the West
European peoples and their overseas daughter-nations had been expanding literally all over the planet in the course of the four hundred years that came to a climax in the nineteenth century.[7]

Other historians embellished the theme, if from varying perspectives. Herbert Heaton, an economic historian at the University of

6. Carlton J. H. Hayes, "The American Frontier—Frontier of What?" *American
Historical Review* 51 (January 1946), 199, 200, 214, 216.
7. Arnold S. Toynbee, introduction to Walter P. Webb, *The Great Frontier* (Austin, 1964), vii–x; see also Arnold S. Toynbee, "Encounters Between Civilizations,"
Harper's 194 (April 1948), 289–94.

Minnesota, in 1946 urged American historians to abandon their academic isolation in the same manner in which the United States as a nation was just then abandoning isolation as a national policy. Such a perspective applied to the study of the frontier, he declared, should lead them to a comparative approach whereby they would compare the American frontier to those of other Wests around the world. Heaton stressed that the American frontier, rather than being a unique phenomenon, shared many similar characteristics of frontiers elsewhere.[8] That point was reiterated further by Max Lerner, a distinguished writer on the nature of American civilization. In the past, wrote Lerner, it was Turner whose frontier theory stressed, above all, the uniqueness of the American experience. The frontier hypothesis was "a crucial link between the theories that explain American greatness in terms of individualism and those that explain it in terms of . . . the nation's separation from world forces." Lerner attributed Turner's popularity to his glorification of American uniqueness, yet in the context of the world in 1947 such uniqueness no longer seemed believable.[9]

Perhaps the global outlook of frontier historians in the 1950s was most emphatically reflected in the writings of Walter P. Webb, one of the West's most notable historians. In 1951 he published *The Great Frontier*, in which he criticized Turner for "having treated the frontier as if it were something exclusively American, as if the United States were the only nation that had felt the powerful influence of access to vacant land." Instead, Webb argued, "the American frontier concept . . . needs to be lifted out of its present national setting and applied on a much larger scale to all western civilization in modern times." Webb then proceeded to try to accomplish that task, to "globalize" the frontier thesis. "What happened in America was but a detail in a much greater phenomenon, the interaction between European civilization and the vast raw lands into which it moved. Europe's frontier predated that in America and was much greater than that of the United States. The frontier of Europe was almost . . . as important in determining the life and institutions of modern Europe as the frontier of America was in shaping the course of American history." Ironically,

8. Herbert Heaton, "Other Wests than Ours," *Journal of Economic History* 6, Supplement (1946), 50–62.

9. Max Lerner, "History and American Greatness," *American Quarterly* 1 (Fall 1949), 214.

like Turner, Webb concluded that this frontier was now gone and that Americans had to confront "the problems now facing a frontierless society." Apparently, Webb had not shed his depression era outlook completely. With lingering vestiges of that perception, he concluded that a four-hundred-year boom, which had first begun with the sixteenth-century explorations of the Western hemisphere, had now run its course with the completed settlement of the United States.[10]

The global outlook of frontier historians in the 1950s had various themes, of course, one of which was to relate the frontier to the Cold War of the decade. As early as 1952, Lawrence S. Kaplan, a diplomatic historian, declared that Turner, whom he considered the most important writer of American history in the twentieth century, was also intensely nationalistic and expansionist. "He may have been seized by the expansionist fever of his day," Kaplan wrote, "fever that can be diagnosed as imperialism." In analyzing the imperialists of Turner's generation, Kaplan suggested that in Turner they found "what they still lacked, namely the historical justification of imperialism."[11]

This theme was still more fully developed just a few years later by William Appleman Williams, a young diplomatic historian with some affinity for Karl Marx. Williams declared that "a set of ideas, first promulgated in the 1890s, became the world [view] of subsequent generations of Americans and is an important clue to understanding America's imperial expansion in the twentieth century." Williams did not provide conclusive evidence for his assertion, but wove it into a complex and challenging fabric to explain American foreign policy. One of these crucial ideas, he felt, was the Turner Thesis. Turner's concept that America's unique and true democracy was the product of an expanding frontier. Williams placed great weight on Turner's hypothesis as a major determinant of United States diplomacy for more than half a century. Indeed, he wrote, Turner "was the apostle of the revival movement that restored the faith of the conquerors of North America and made them international crusaders." A few years later, in 1961, Williams embellished his theme further by arguing that Americans had used expansion on the frontier as an escape from

10. Webb, The Great Frontier; quotation from Webb, "Ended: Four Hundred Year Boom: Reflections on the Age of the Frontier," Harper's 203 (October 1951), 26, 27, 33.
11. Lawrence S. Kaplan, "Frederick Jackson Turner and Imperialism," Social Science 27 (January 1952), 13, 14.

dealing with their internal problems. Williams was obviously profoundly influenced by the contemporary currents of the Cold War.[12]

The global perceptions of this period were also reflected in the work of many historians who were advocating more intensive study of comparative frontiers. Norman Harper applied the Turner Thesis to Australia, asserting that "the process . . . could be a universal one, certainly applicable to Australia." Silvio Zavala and Robert E. Riegel experimented with applying the Turner Thesis to Latin America, while W. R. Mead tried it out on Finland. Dietrich Gerhard advocated further investigation of the frontier experience in Canada, Australia, South Africa, Germany, and Russia. Perhaps Walker Wyman summarized well the mood of this decade's historians at a conference to honor Lyman Draper—a great collector of manuscripts—at the University of Wisconsin. "The significance of Turner's propositions is that they have been so widely held as assumptions about the American past. It is now time to reconsider the frontier in the perspective of world history,"[13] Wyman wrote in 1957. But alas, much of the research on comparative frontiers was undermining the Turner Thesis because historians increasingly concluded that cultural influences were far more important than environmental factors in explaining the distinctive features of various national frontiers.

Nevertheless, by 1960 a new subfield of comparative frontier history had come into being. In reviewing this literature, M. W. Mikesell, a geographer, concluded that

> the growing body of comparative research . . . deserves serious attention. . . . Recent attempts to compare the westward movement in American history with the advance of settlement in other parts of the world . . . [are significant]. The principal failing of Turner and his followers, and most of his critics, has been a neglect of

12. William Appleman Williams, "The Frontier Thesis: An American Foreign Policy," *Pacific Historical Review* 24 (November 1956), 379–95; Williams, *The Contours of American History* (Cleveland, 1961), 376–77.

13. Norman D. Harper, "Turner the Historian: 'Hypothesis' or 'Process'? With Special Reference to Frontier Society in Australia," *University of Kansas City Review* 18 (Autumn 1951), 76–86; Silvio Zavala, "The Frontiers of Hispanic America," in Walker D. Wyman and Clifton B. Kroeber (eds.), *The Frontier in Perspective* (Madison, 1957), 35–58; Robert E. Riegel, "Current Ideas of the Significance of the United States Frontier," *Revista de Historia de America* 33 (June 1952), 25–43; W. R. Mead, "Frontier Themes in Finland," *Geography* 44 (July 1959), 145–56; Dietrich Gerhard, "The Frontier in Comparative View," *Comparative Studies in Society and History* 1 (March 1959), 205–29; Wyman and Kroeber (eds.), *Frontier in Perspective*, xix–xx.

comparative research. Without the perspective afforded by knowledge of developments in foreign areas, it is not possible to interpret the significance of the American frontier.

After reviewing some of the most important writings in the field
Mikesell noted that

> the most challenging feature of Turner's thesis was his assertion
> that the frontier was a major influence in the formation of na-
> tional institutions. The evidence drawn from other parts of the
> world neither confirms nor denies this claim. Comparative study
> has made no major contribution to this aspect of the Turner con-
> troversy because the concept of national character is vague at best
> and has multiple causes. . . . Little can be expected from compar-
> ative study unless research proceeds in a more systematic manner.[14]

This latter point was also made by Richard Hofstadter as he pondered the meaning of the Turner Thesis for the postwar generation.
"American historical writing in the past century has produced two
major theories or models of understanding," Hofstadter declared, "the
economic interpretation of politics associated with Charles A. Beard,
and the frontier interpretation . . . identified with Frederick Jackson
Turner . . . but . . . it is the frontier thesis that has embodied the
predominant view of the American past." Looking back, Hofstadter
felt that Turnerians treated it "not as a theory to be tested, but as an
all-sufficient assumption which could be used to explain what they
had found. With repetition, the frontier thesis . . . became less a
working hypothesis than an incantation. But the strength of Turner's
thesis, which had influence far beyond the historical profession, rested
upon the appeal of the frontier to the American imagination." Hofstadter believed that it appealed "to the common desire to root native
history in native soil." Reflecting the emphasis of his own generation
in rejecting isolationism in American diplomacy, Hofstadter noted
that

> the central weakness of Turner's thesis was in its intellectual isola-
> tionism. Having committed himself to an initial overemphasis on
> the uniqueness of the historical development of the United States,
> Turner compounded the error by overemphasizing the frontier as a

14. Marvin W. Mikesell, "Comparative Studies in Frontier History," *Annals of
the Association of American Geographers* 50 (March 1960), 69.

factor in this development. The obsession with uniqueness . . . diverted the attention of historical scholarship from the possibilities of comparative social history . . . factors outside the frontier process . . . social classes . . . [and] European immigration. . . . The mingling of peoples that took place in the United States must be placed alongside the presence of "free lands" in explaining American development.

Perhaps reflecting some present-mindedness of his own, Hofstadter surmised that "the closure of the American gates after the First World War becomes an event of broader significance than the disappearance of the frontier line in 1890." Yet Hofstadter found much to admire in Turner. His openness was appealing, although "he propagated less inquiry among his disciples than among his critics."[15]

The global persuasion among frontier historians reached its apogee about 1960 and was well reflected by a young cultural historian, William Goetzmann. "It has always been permissible, of course, for the Western historian to say with Turner, that 'to the frontier the American intellect owes its striking characteristics,'" Goetzmann wrote.

But perhaps in celebrating and studying the great story of the westward movement the Western historian has taken too narrow a view. Perhaps he has really been guilty of underestimating the extent of this impulse to move into the unknown and uncharted wildernesses of the world. Might it not be possible that this experience in the American West was an experience that was characteristic of the whole of America rather than just a part of it? Indeed, there is reason to suspect that the impulse for expansion over the globe might even be as characteristic of European civilization as a whole as it was for those hardy pioneers way out West. It might even be that one of the reasons for the enthusiastic acceptance of the myth of the American West was its very centrality to the whole of American experience at that particular time and place in the nineteenth century, and perhaps even today.

Goetzmann reflected on recent influences by noting that "the recent interest in cultural history, and the corresponding use of new source materials has begun to afford the historian new points of view toward all aspects of American history. . . . The historian has become more conscious of American behavioral patterns as they exist within the

15. Richard Hofstadter, "Turner and the Frontier Myth," *American Scholar* 18 (Autumn 1949), 433, 435, 437–38, 442–43.

whole context of modern European experience." And in reiterating the global context of frontier history, Goetzmann concluded that

> the experience in the American West seems somewhat less than unique. Rather it appears as a part of a much larger whole—a great synthesis which extends all the way from the picturesque trappers' rendezvous in Cache Valley to the dimly lit study of Humboldt in Potsdam. When we have worked long enough and hard enough at studying this whole complex of ideas and emotions, we may perhaps arrive at a different view of our national and international history. . . . With particular regard to our own American West, we will have broken away from the old Turnerian tyranny which has failed to satisfy us for a number of years but which is still too valuable emotionally to part with completely.[16]

While a large number of frontier historians were influenced by the global awareness of the post–World War II era, others were impressed by the affluence and rapid economic expansion of the nation between 1945 and 1960. Clearly, the Second World War had demolished the assumption of most Western historians, politicians, and a wide range of scholars that the closing of the frontier had made the United States into a closed society with severe limitations on future growth. One of the first to question that theme—so dominant in the 1930s—was Wendell Berge, in 1945 the Assistant U.S. Attorney General for antitrust policies. Reflecting on the enormous economic expansion of the West in wartime, he asserted that the Turnerians had been wrong when they "assumed that the passing of the geographic frontier also meant the disappearance of broad opportunities for economic development." Including his own recent experiences, he noted that "the stark adversities of war compelled us to re-examine our economic potential and to recast our thinking. It soon became apparent that far from being mature or senile our economy had been asleep to its own powers, both in terms of technical progress and in terms of the fields awaiting exploration and enterprise." Berge foresaw a bright future for the West in 1945. "The West is once more the frontier on which the question of America's economic expansion will be decided," he declared. "All its trails have not been blazed. Even though its mountains have been mapped, its rivers charted and its elements classified, the

16. William Goetzmann, "The West and the American Age of Exploration," *Arizona and the West* 2 (Autumn 1960), 266–67, 278.

full economic greatness of the West is undiscovered. It need not remain so. If the West recognizes its own right to grow and acts upon that recognition, and if the rest of the country understands how deeply the common interest will be affected by what happens in the West, discovery will soon follow."[17]

Not all of the writers on the frontier during these years charged Turner with being an apostle of closed space. Max Lerner, as he reviewed the debate between pro- and anti-Turnerians in the preceding decade, looked for a middle ground. He believed that much of the discussion had centered "too much on the validity of the Turner thesis and too little on the implications to be drawn from it." In his reading of Turner, the hypothesis also included the "industrial and capitalist revolution taking place at the same time as the frontier settlement," thus demonstrating that the American frontier experience was not "a genesis which began and closed . . . but a continual genesis."[18]

Even historians who accepted many aspects of the Turner Thesis found the closed-space doctrines troubling. Writing in 1947, Paul F. Sharp pointed out that the Canadian experience was directly relevant to that of the United States. "The passing of the frontier," Sharp declared, is "seen in a somewhat different perspective when a continental viewpoint is adopted." The Turnerians were wrong when they proclaimed the end of the frontier in 1890. "The first two decades of the twentieth century were marked by one of the greatest land rushes in North American history," when more than one million Americans swarmed over the Canadian prairies in an effort—not always successful—to engage in homesteading and agricultural settlement. Sharp concluded that "the theory of the passing of the Frontier in 1890, like other broad generalizations, does not stand the test of close examination." The last frontier, truly, "was the Canadian West" which remained open for "nearly three decades after 1890. Frederick Jackson Turner interpreted the frontier as a past phenomenon, but even as he wrote, thousands of his fellow countrymen were seeking in Canada the economic and social opportunities he described as characteristic of a frontier society."[19]

17. Wendell Berge, *Economic Freedom for the West* (Lincoln, 1946), 1–2.

18. Max Lerner, "America—A Young Civilization?" *Antioch Review* 6 (Fall 1946), 369, 371.

19. Paul F. Sharp, "The American Farmer and the 'Last Best West,'" *Agricultural History* 21 (April 1947), 65–75.

The most direct attack on the closed-space concept of the Turner Thesis came from James C. Malin of the University of Kansas, who disagreed profoundly with every aspect of Turner's thought. In arguing that the sense of space was central to Turner's hypothesis, Malin also questioned the validity of his use of the concept. "The historian must free himself not only from the space theory," Malin wrote in 1946, "but from all forms of single factor interpretations." He urged, instead, greater emphasis on themes such as science and technology, communications, and urbanization. And as he himself began to develop an ecological interpretation of history of the Great Plains, he kept up his barrage in the 1950s with a variety of articles and books.[20]

Again, it was the British historian Arnold Toynbee who placed the doctrine of the closed frontier in a broad global context. Reflecting the impact of economic affluence in the 1950s, Toynbee stated that an

> unexpected feature of the chapter of history through which we are now living is that the Western peoples are not going to be ruined by the halting of their geographic expansion. . . . Ruin might have seemed to be staring them in the face, since for five hundred years their expansion at other peoples' expense was apparently the basis of their prosperity. Yet the United States was never before so prosperous as she has been since the closing of her frontier, which happened about seventy years ago; and the West European countries have never been so prosperous as they have been since they gave up, or lost, their former colonial empires during and after World War II.[21]

The two strands so effectively combined by Toynbee—an awareness of global trends and a rejection of the concept of a closed frontier—led directly to a third major trend in the writing of frontier history, one which stressed the impact of cultural rather than environmental influences. A concern with the primacy of cultural factors was certainly not new during this period. It had been manifest in earlier years, but an increasingly larger number of historians between 1945 and 1960 came to embrace such an interpretation. Contemporary events did

20. James C. Malin, "The Turner–Mackinder Space Concept of History," *Essays in Historiography* (Lawrence, 1946), 1–44; see Robert P. Swierenga (ed.), *James C. Malin: History and Ecology* (Lincoln, 1984), for selections from Malin's writings and a bibliography of his works.

21. Toynbee, in Introduction to Webb, *The Great Frontier*, x.

much to strengthen their awareness. Cold War tensions with the Soviet Union, the rise of the Third World, and the civil rights move-ment at home made frontier scholars much more sensitive to the role of cultural influences than in previous decades.

The focus on the cultural determinants of frontier life took various forms. One of the pioneers of American social history, Dixon Wecter, analyzed the cultural advance of the frontier West as reflected in schools, colleges, and libraries. That led him to conclude that Turner's claim about the frontier as an instrument transforming American cul-ture was inaccurate. In fact, Wecter argued, just the opposite was true. Eastern culture imported into the West transformed the frontier, and had at least as great an impact on shaping the emerging West as frontier conditions. The same theme was developed even more forcefully and broadly in 1955 by Earl S. Pomeroy. "The Westerner has been fun-damentally imitator rather than innovator," he declared in a seminal article. "His culture was Western European rather than aboriginal. He was often the most ardent of conformists." Pomeroy questioned the extent of frontier influence on the East. "The effects that he [Turner] thought he saw seem to have other causes, if they exist at all."[22]

Other historians pursued this theme along different paths. Thomas J. Wertenbaker, one of the most distinguished historians of the colonial South, directly challenged the Turner Thesis on cultural grounds. It was simply untrue, he declared, "that American democracy was born on the frontier. American democracy was born in Westminster Hall."[23] Following a similar line of argument, Louis B. Wright, a well-known student of American culture, argued forcefully that eastern civilization was brought by pioneers to the West without being dramatically trans-formed by the frontier environment. Turner and his cohorts, Wright declared, "have been inclined to romanticize the rebelliousness of the West against the 'effete East' [and] to magnify the political liberalism, the independence, the originality, and the 'progressivism' of the settlers in the . . . frontier." Expanding his views a few years later, Wright criticized Turner for completely overlooking the eastern minority of

22. Dixon Wecter, "Instruments of Culture on the Frontier," *Yale Review* 36 (Winter 1947), 242–56; Earl S. Pomeroy, "Toward a Reorientation of Western History: Continuity and Environment," *Mississippi Valley Historical Review* 41 (March 1955), 579–600.

23. Thomas J. Wertenbaker, "The Molding of the Middle West," *American His-torical Review* 53 (January 1948), 223–34.

culture bearers who transplanted "elements of traditional civilization on each successive frontier." American culture was formed by European and East Coast sources, not by the frontier.[24]

Other scholars of this period also accentuated the importance of cultural rather than environmental influences. Walter Agard stressed the importance of Greek and Roman classics in shaping the outlook of the founders of cultural institutions in the old Northwest. Although Turner claimed that people on the frontier shed their European past, Agard concluded that "as we examine the evidence furnished by architecture, education, and the churches, libraries, and press, we find that they [the classics] provided intellectual and artistic nourishment." This view was propounded even more vigorously by a specialist in American literature, Arthur K. Moore, in his book about culture on the Kentucky frontier. "Turner's widely applauded interpretation," Moore declared, "is selective, uncritical, and lacking in rear vision." Turner was quite wrong when he assumed that "men in a state of nature could . . . create an adequate culture virtually from nothing," or when he "tended to slight the continuing influence on the emigrants of some of the noblest concepts of the enlightenment." Instead of producing a superior American culture, the frontier produced one that was clearly inferior to its European counterpart. If there were constructive influences on the Kentucky frontier, these were primarily of European or eastern origins, and rarely indigenous.[25]

Some historians of this era also emphasized that the cultural contributions of European immigrants deserved much greater emphasis. In comparing the frontier and urban melting pots, Edward Saveth declared, Turner was aware of the impact of various ethnic groups but chose not to assign them a prominent place in his theory. Moreover, Turner's main sympathies were with English and German immigrants who were important on the nineteenth-century frontier of the Middle West. He ignored or disliked immigrants from southern and eastern Europe because they were oriented toward cities, and, in his view, were "a loss to the social organism of the United States." Yet, in all

24. Louis B. Wright, "The Westward Advance of the Atlantic Frontier," *Huntington Library Quarterly* 11 (May 1948), 261–75, and Wright, *Culture on the Moving Frontier* (Bloomington, 1955), 11–45.

25. Walter Agard, "Classics on the Midwest Frontier," in Wyman and Kroeber (eds.), *Frontier in Perspective*, 165–83; Arthur K. Moore, *The Frontier Mind* (Lexington, 1957).

fairness, Saveth wrote, "Turner was cognizant of a number of valid approaches to the immigration problem . . . as he suggested to Marcus L. Hansen [a young historian of immigration], European peoples not only exerted an important influence upon America but that, conversely, what the peoples accomplished in America was not without effect in Europe. This, he told Hansen, one learns 'by studying the reactions in Europe itself.'"[26]

Another aspect of a focus on cultural factors came in 1950 when Henry Nash Smith raised study of the West as myth to new levels of sophistication. That the West had a function as a major strand of American myth was not a novel idea, of course, but Smith's analysis of popular literature broke new ground in Western cultural history. "The influence of the West on American thought at the level of unsystematic popular ideology [is a] parody of the Frontier Hypothesis: a statement in vulgarized terms of ideas which Turner advanced as a general interpretation of American history," Smith wrote. He wondered aloud as to why Turner had had such an enormous impact and concluded that his "influence on historical scholarship has been unfortunate."[27]

A number of other historians pointed out cultural influences on the West which Turner had virtually ignored. Arthur Bestor noted that communal utopian societies on the outer margins of settled areas had very few of the frontier characteristics sketched out by Turner. And Perry Miller, the foremost student of Puritanism in the 1950s, emphasized the profound cultural impact of seventeenth-century Puritanism on the wilderness environment. Turner had done more to confuse than to clarify the relation of the Puritans to the frontier, Miller charged in his Errand into the Wilderness. "He was the foremost victim of his fallacy," Miller argued, "rather than the master of it." Instead, Miller emphasized the European determinants of American culture. One of Miller's students, Alan Heimert, carried on the attack further by challenging Turner's interpretation of Cotton Mather's view of the frontier. Heimert charged openly that Turner's treatment of the

26. Edward N. Saveth, American Historians and European Immigrants, 1875–1925 (New York, 1948), 136.

27. Henry Nash Smith, "The West as an Image of the American Past," University of Kansas City Review 18 (Autumn 1951), 29–40. A fuller discussion is in Smith, Virgin Land: The American West as Symbol and Myth (Cambridge, Mass., 1950).

Puritan response to the wilderness appeared overly simplistic in the light of research of the 1950s.[28]

Historians also uncovered a major gap in the frontier theory, namely Turner's neglect of the vital role of law. That omission was emphasized especially by Clarence E. Carter, who in the 1950s was editing the *Territorial Papers of the United States*. Law, Carter declared, was clearly one of the most fundamental institutions to shape American society, a vital ingredient of an incipient culture. Yet Turner completely ignored the enormous influence of the law which was shaped not by the wilderness but by Anglo-American legal principles brought by the settlers.[29]

During a period of economic affluence such as the 1950s, it was not surprising that some historians sought to use the concept of affluence in explaining the growth of the West and American society. The most brilliant such effort was that of David Potter, a distinguished American Studies scholar, who utilized abundance as a means to explain the essential character of Americans. To do that, he had to cope with the Turner Thesis, which had sought to provide a similar explanation by focusing on the frontier. Potter maintained that by confining his explanation of American development to the tracing of various stages of the frontier, Turner implied that "nothing distinctly American would be left, except as a residue, after the pioneer stage had been passed." Because of such an assumption, Potter noted, Turner cut himself off from other influences such as technology, urban growth, and human aspirations to a higher standard of living, "all of which have contributed quite as much as the frontier to the fluidity and facility for change in American life."[30]

The cultural historians who were writing about the frontier between 1945 and 1960 did much to expand the context of the subject. By underscoring the significance of cultural conditions—whether in the realm of ideas, art, music, education, or the law—they were subtly

28. Arthur Bestor, "Patent Office Models of the Good Society: Some Relationships Between Social Reform and Westward Expansion," *American Historical Review* 58 (April 1953), 505–26; Perry Miller, *Errand into the Wilderness* (Cambridge, Mass., 1956), 1–2; Alan Heimert, "Puritanism, the Wilderness, and the Frontier," *New England Quarterly* 26 (September 1953), 361–82.

29. Clarence E. Carter, "The Transit of Law to the Frontier: A Review Article," *Journal of Mississippi History* 16 (July 1954), 183–92.

30. David Potter, *People of Plenty* (Chicago, 1954), quotes on 155–56.

changing an understanding of the foundations of Western development. Environmental conditions which had loomed so large to earlier generations seemed far less important to historians who lived in an age when technological developments altered climates, reduced distances, facilitated communication, and seemingly decreased the dominance of environmental influences. And the affluence of the period further induced widespread feelings that Americans had mastered most challenges posed by the forces of nature that might have seemed intimidating to their ancestors.

Such confidence was strengthened further by a fourth major trend of frontier historians in these years, namely the impact of social science research on their work. In view of their contemporary interest in economic development, particularly in underdeveloped nations, economists in these years evinced a greater interest in the history of the West than at any other time. Sociologists also found the West a fertile ground for testing of their theories, while political scientists utilized it for similar purposes. The perspectives they provided furnished still new dimensions for historians of the frontier.

Economists and economic historians were especially prone to attack the methodologies of Western historians. In the words of Richard Hofstadter in 1950, Western historians should rejoice with the recognition "how far . . . scholarship has advanced from the simple formulas of Turner's generation." Greater methodological sophistication, Hofstadter believed, would go "far to reassert the importance of the West in more moderate, acceptable and intellectually sophisticated terms." Vernon Fowke, an economic historian, questioned Turner's methodology. The Turner Thesis, he wrote, lent "credence to a hypothesis . . . that history is comprised of the examination of a succession of conceptual anachronisms devised in each case by the historian's generation for the solution of contemporary problems and applied as an afterthought to the reconstruction of the past. . . . Turner advanced the frontier thesis as a tool of analysis of the past at a time when major concern was arising over the frontier's disappearance." Economist Douglas Dowd, urging study of the comparative economic growth of the West and South, criticized Turner's narrowness. "Western development was *ancillary* to that taking place to the east of it," he wrote.[31] And Lee Benson, a young economic historian, argued that

31. Richard Hofstadter, review of Henry Nash Smith, *Virgin Land,* in *American*

Turner derived much of his frontier hypothesis from Achille Loria, an Italian economist who was his contemporary. Turner merely adapted Loria's theories slightly and then pronounced them as his own handiwork. Benson especially singled out Turner's notion of an "ever retreating frontier of free land" and the idea of a continual "rebirth of American life" as concepts directly derived from Loria's writings, duly cited by Turner.[32]

In hoping to introduce historians to greater methodological sophistication, the Economic History Association in 1956 devoted an entire special program to the history of the economic development of the West, viewed as an underdeveloped region. Such a perspective was derived from dominant economic thought of the 1950s, when economic development was *the* dominant issue for most economists, especially with reference to Third World nations for whom the United States at the time was establishing special aid programs. More than a dozen scholars explored the theme in various dimensions. Perhaps the most notable contribution was that of economist Douglass North, who utilized development theory and statistical analysis to criticize Turner's frontier hypothesis. His focus was on "the pace of westward development and the influence of the international economy." He concluded that it was not the frontier but international capital flows that shaped American economic growth between 1815 and 1860. To him, "the demand for certain staple commodities in the European . . . market" were the primary influence on westward expansion, rather than the existence of free lands in the West.[33]

Contemporary sociological analysis also inspired a number of historians writing about the frontier in the 1950s. Thus, Stanley Elkins and Eric McKittrick attempted to utilize recent sociological theories to provide a factual data base for Turner's frontier hypothesis. They were particularly impressed by the experiences of community building

---

Quarterly 2 (Fall 1950), 279; Vernon C. Fowke, "National Policy and Westward Development in North America," *Journal of Economic History* 16 (December 1956), 461; Douglas F. Dowd, "A Comparative Analysis of Economic Development in the American West and South," in ibid. 16, 558–74.

32. Lee Benson, "Achille Loria's Influence on American Economic Thought: Including His Contributions to the Frontier Hypothesis," *Agricultural History* 24 (October 1950), 182–99.

33. Douglass C. North, "International Capital Flows and the Development of the American West," *Journal of Economic History* 16 (December 1956), 493–505.

in suburban housing projects of the 1950s and considered that experience to be analogous to the establishment of frontier communities a century earlier. Borrowing their conceptual framework from recent sociological theory dealing with community analysis, Elkins and McKittrick sought to demonstrate an organic relationship between the frontier and the creation of democratic institutions. While Turner's insights might have been "crude in form," they declared, they "remained the closest thing we have had to a seminal contribution to the theory of American history." With considerable enthusiasm, and reflecting the faith of many behavioral scientists that they had truly made social analysis into a science, they concluded that it was exciting to contemplate that "a host of [contemporary] problems may be examined with fresh interest if we put in testable terms facts which he [Turner] knew by instinct."[34]

Some historians applied sociological theories in other ways. In studying frontier claim clubs in nineteenth-century Iowa, Allan Bogue utilized sociological and social psychology concepts to analyze community formation. Like Elkins and McKittrick, Bogue concluded that the application of social science theories and methodologies corroborated Turner's insights in regard to the stimulation which the frontier experience provided for pioneers engaged in social innovation.[35]

Political scientists applauded such efforts by historians to borrow social science approaches. One of the influential members of that specialty, Pendleton Herring—who also headed the influential Social Science Research Council in the 1950s—wrote approvingly about what he considered Turner's present-mindedness. He argued that "the most penetrating thinkers are partly the exponents of their own times and . . . the sensitive reactors to their environment." Turner intended his thesis to be a hypothesis, not an iron law that was applicable to all periods in the American experience. If Turner had such a great impact, that was because he "hit upon a hypothesis which gave fresh

34. Stanley M. Elkins and Eric L. McKittrick, "A Meaning for Turner's Frontier, Part I: Democracy in the Old Northwest," *Political Science Quarterly* 69 (September 1954), 321–53, and Elkins and McKittrick, "A Meaning for Turner's Frontier, Part II: The Southwest Frontier and New England," ibid. 69 (December 1954), 565–602.

35. Allan G. Bogue, "Pioneer Farming and Innovation," *Iowa Journal of History* 56 (January 1958), 1–36, and Bogue, "The Iowa Claim Clubs: Symbol and Substance," *Mississippi Valley Historical Review* 45 (September 1958), 231–53.

relevance in the 1890s for all that had transpired in the preceding century."[36]

Perhaps the most comprehensive attempt to document the frontier thesis by use of newly developed social science theories and methods in the 1950s was made by Merle Curti and his assistants at the University of Wisconsin. They undertook to examine community development in Trempeleau County, Wisconsin, in great depth to test Turner's assumption that "the ready accessibility of free or almost free land promoted economic equality and that this was followed by political equality." Their method was "combining long-accepted methods of historical investigation with certain quantitative methods used in the social sciences." This exhaustive inquiry led Curti "to support . . . the main implications of Turner's theory about the frontier and democracy." Moreover, he urged others to embark on similar detailed studies for other areas rather than to indulge in reincantations of the Turner Thesis, a practice in which some of Turner's defenders had indulged. Curti did not touch on the question as to whether he himself had perhaps built certain assumptions favorable to the Turner Thesis into his own elaborate study.[37]

Between 1945 and 1960 frontier historians accomplished a great deal in broadening the context of the study of the West. Possibly no other comparable period of just fifteen years was as fruitful. They had placed American frontier expansion in a global context; they had come to view it as a dynamic, ongoing process which had not necessarily run its course by 1890; they had found a new appreciation of the significant role of cultural influences in the shaping of the West; and they had introduced new theories and methods from the social sciences which—although these varied in their usefulness—brought additional perspectives to an understanding of the West. In their efforts, they reflected some of the self-confidence which was a reflection of the affluent society in the United States during this period. Few could have predicted in 1960 that this mood—and with it, the suppositions of historians—would change quickly and radically within the space of a few years.

Sometime about 1960, the ebullient optimism that had been visible

36. Pendleton Herring, "A Political Scientist Considers the Question," *Pennsylvania Magazine of History and Biography* 72 (April 1948), 118–36.

37. Merle Curti et al., *The Making of an American Frontier Community* (Stanford, 1959).

in the post–World War II era was transformed into an increasingly negative and self-critical outlook by large numbers of Americans. Many in the United States grew more apprehensive about the future and became less self-confident. Some of the smug optimism of the 1950s turned into a pervasive pessimism, and at times even into nihilism. Now racism, sexism, poverty, urban social problems, militarism, and American intervention in Vietnam became common elements of criticism and self-doubt. A whole generation of younger historians, especially those born in the Great Depression, reflected these changing preconceptions, some identifying with New Left persuasions.

The years between 1960 and 1990 also witnessed a further expansion of the historical profession. College and university enrollments increased from 1960 to 1975. By 1970 the American Historical Association reported 20,000 members. A reflection of this growth was the decision of several Western historians such as Ray Allen Billington to organize a new professional organization devoted to their specialty, namely the Western History Association, founded in Santa Fe in 1961. The volume of writings by Western historians grew enormously in this era. More articles and books touching on the frontier appeared from 1960 to 1990 than in the entire half-century before.[38]

Historians of the frontier, no less than others, were significantly affected by the changes swirling about them and reflected them clearly in their writings. Among the general trends in this period was a penchant for specialization. As scholars found ever-increasing complexity in their detailed studies of limited subjects, they came to eschew broad generalizations or hypotheses such as the Turner Thesis. It seemed as if for every single broad theory there were dozens of exceptions, and generalizations were not appropriate.

Certainly, a number of specific trends were discernible. In the first place, historians reflected a decided negativism, or pessimism. They concentrated mainly on what they felt was wrong with the frontier— and America—and largely ignored what was right. The concentration

38. Membership fluctuates yearly and statistics are approximate. See Joan Hoff Wilson, "The Plight of a Mom and Pop Operation," *OAH Newsletter* 13 (May 1985), 2; on the Western History Association see *Western Historical Quarterly* 15 (January 1984), 111; Howard R. Lamar, "Persistent Frontier: The West in the Twentieth Century," *Western Historical Quarterly* 4 (January 1973), 5; for references see Mattson and Marion, *Turner: A Reference Guide.*

on the global context of the frontier—born in the idealism of inter-
nationalism after World War II—now largely waned. Instead, scholars
now became preoccupied with domestic issues. They focused on race,
gender, and class, reflecting the civil rights movements of their day.
Unlike their predecessors, they viewed the frontier not as a positive
force in American civilization, but as a destructive element that brought
a variety of problems and undesirable characteristics into American
life. Although many frontier historians continued to stress the primacy
of cultural influences on Western development, after 1970 the growing
consciousness of environmentalism in the nation was soon reflected
in a renewed emphasis on the importance of environmental conditions
in the West. The impact of social science research continued to be a
notable factor in the field. As a result of these trends, it was not
surprising that most frontier historians abandoned the idea that a single
theory could explain what had been revealed as the complexity of the
frontier experience, and instead looked for multicausation or pluralistic
explanations.

Contemporary historians were well aware of many of the changes
sweeping the field. As Charles Crowe noted in 1966:

> We are still very much in the midst of a continuing anti-Progres-
> sive reaction. . . . The violent and tragic events of this generation
> cast at least some doubt on the simplistic explanations and on the
> personal devotion to the gospel of progress of many older histori-
> ans. The Progressive rationale seems increasingly superficial and
> inadequate. . . . Many scholars are increasingly put off by the tale
> of American history as an orderly march of events towards a "solu-
> tion" or near solution of one problem after another.

In addition, the passage of time had altered perspectives. "The profession itself has changed in many ways." Not only did research grants
lead to the challenging of old cliches, but "the social sciences have
intruded with methodological and conceptual tools." More and more
monographs were being written by individuals of urban backgrounds
and diverse ancestry. American history had ceased to be a near monopoly of scholars with WASPish backgrounds.[39]

39. Charles Crowe, "The Emergence of Progressive History," *Journal of the History
of Ideas* 27 (January–March 1966), 123, 124.

Western history was in no way insulated from these changes. Writing in 1970, Burton Bledstein, a young Wisconsin historian, remarked that

> the liberal critics of Turner have often spoken from the perspective of an urban, collectivist, corporate, and technological society—"the new industrial state." They defined themselves best against nonprofessional types: the Puritan and the Philistine in the twenties, the Pioneer in the thirties, the Fascist and Communist in the forties, the Populist in the fifties. The types easily blended, allowing fascism, for example, to enter Populism. Moreover, taken together, the attacks on the Philistine, the Pioneer, and the Populist reflected the critical liberals' attitudes toward an entire century—the nineteenth. Twentieth century corporate America had found a "usable past" in the previous century—a past that helped explain the violence that persisted in modern life, despite institutions, education, government, and affluence.[40]

Contemporaries in the 1960s read their own concerns into the Turner Thesis. It

> touched upon the politics of polarization in America, where the middle vanished when issues were raised. The thesis described the lack of communication between Americans who related to each other on the basis of their human prospect. It embraced violence as an irreducible quality in democratic life. It recorded the toil of society in a nation of aggressive, irritable, and frightened men who desperately needed to believe both in their decency and in their good will. It suggested that American institutions were required to legitimize their existence by a democratic creed as well as by an environmental function. . . .

But the thesis might have new meanings in the 1970s.

> The frontier thesis emerged from an historical moment of emotional insight . . . as stated in the social turmoil of the tortured 1890s . . . in its fullness [it] may have interpretive value to the generation of historians maturing in the 1970s—a generation lacking faith in the liberal social vision built upon ethnicity, pluralism, and consensus; a generation disillusioned with the pragmatic claims for the ameliorative and the accommodating influence of

40. Burton J. Bledstein, "Frederick Jackson Turner: A Note on the Intellectual and the Professional," *Wisconsin Magazine of History* 54 (Autumn 1970), 51.

twentieth century social institutions; a generation that appears to be concerned with the implications of democracy as equality of person beyond democracy as equality of opportunity; a generation again concerned with the content in addition to the conditions of a democratic ideal; a generation nourishing a more desperate instinct for intellectual survival than the critical liberals.[41]

Amid all of the wide-ranging debate swirling about the nature of Western history between 1960 and 1990, one island of stability remained in the person of Ray Allen Billington. Almost single-handedly, he engaged in a crusade to defend and propogate the Turner Thesis, quite independent of the strictures pointed out by hundreds of its critics. In elegant and eloquent prose, Billington took it upon himself to elaborate upon the thesis in a steady stream of articles and books. Concerned about what he perceived as the decline of Western history, he argued vigorously for the validity and relevance of the Turner Thesis in the years before 1890 as well as thereafter. From his positions at Northwestern University and at the Huntington Library, he emerged as Turner's major champion who hoped to attract a younger generation to the fold. Although he was not unmindful of the critics, he tended to bypass them rather than engage in confrontations.[42] But when William N. Davis conducted a survey of the field of Western history in 1964, he reported that while only 19 of 285 respondents openly advocated a departure from Turnerian views, the times, they were a-changing. "The ideas of Turner . . . are still dominant," Davis reported, "but such is the force . . . of the anti-, un- and non-Turnerian groups that it would appear only a matter of time until they attain majority status."[43]

Some of these forces were reflected in the growing mood of pessimism that began to affect historians about 1960. In discussing freedom and the frontier, for example, Richard A. Bartlett in 1959 felt

41. Ibid., 55.
42. For a listing of Billington's writings, see Mattson and Marion, *Turner: A Reference Guide,* 254; Martin L. Ridge, "Ray Allen Billington (1903–1980)," *Western Historical Quarterly* 12 (July 1981), 245–50, and Ridge, "Ray Allen Billington, Western History, and American Exceptionalism," *Pacific Historical Review* 56 (November 1987), 495–511.
43. William N. Davis, "Will the West Survive as a Field in American History? A Survey Report," *Mississippi Valley Historical Review* 50 (March 1964), 680.

that the Turner hypothesis still had relevance because it helped Americans to understand themselves, especially in regard to their freedoms.
But in his day he felt that

> frontier freedoms are being crushed by the insecurity of modern so-
> ciety, and especially when we think of the Cold War. A man can-
> not swagger when he must glance over his shoulder in fear of
> attack by an adversary. A man who has begun to doubt his own
> ability . . . is no longer a free man. . . . Today's American is los-
> ing more than the sense of confidence . . . he is losing that spirit
> of freedom which every frontiersman felt. . . . This spirit . . . is
> the golden heritage of our frontier youth . . . this heritage can be
> and must be coaxed and nurtured back to blazing life.[44]

The nagging sense of insecurity was reflected in eloquent language
during the following year by C. Vann Woodward, in his presidential
address to the American Historical Association. Woodward proclaimed
that the age of security for the United States was past. Events since
1945, he noted, have an "effect upon our view of the past. Throughout
. . . its history the United States has enjoyed a remarkable degree of
military security, physical security from hostile attack and invasion."
That security was now gone. Development of aircraft and missiles had
brought a new vulnerability to the nation. Referring to Turner, Woodward declared that "in 1893 the first period of American history . . .
was brought to an end by the disappearance of free land. Perhaps it
was not premature to suggest that another epoch of American history
was closed even more suddenly sixty years later by the disappearance
of free security." And he added that "if the influence of free land may
be considered significant in the shaping of American character and
national history, it is possible that the effect of free security might
profitably be studied for contributions to the same end."[45]

A negative view of the frontier was also provided by Warren Sussman in his analysis of the attitudes which American intellectuals
expressed about the frontier hypothesis between 1910 and 1930. As
Sussman interpreted them, leading American thinkers during these
years rejected the Turner Thesis because they saw the frontier experience as useless in explaining the nation's past,

44. Richard A. Bartlett, "Freedom and the Frontier: A Pertinent Re-examination," Mid-America 40 (July 1958), 138.
45. C. Vann Woodward, "The Age of Reinterpretation," American Historical Review 66 (October 1960), 2, 3, 5.

and the uses to which that past had been put. The frontier became the scapegoat for all that was wrong with contemporary
America. It had created a dangerously incomplete psychological
type which reigned as national character; it was responsible for
American lawlessness and for political corruption . . . it made the
achievement of a high culture . . . difficult . . . it created an environment which was simply hostile to the life of the mind. The
revolt against this particular "useless past" was part of a larger revolt against what was considered to be the Midwestern domination
of American life and values. It was made by intellectuals who were
born or educated in the East, the urban United States. But significantly it accepted in general outline the same essential thesis
about the nature of American history that had been advanced . . .
by Frederick Jackson Turner . . . it admitted that American development had been the creation of the frontier process. Yet it in-
sisted that the consequences of that process had been detrimental.
. . . The debate . . . was over values. . . . Yet . . . the stress on
the problem of values and ideologies related to the study of the
past itself may not have been without important consequences. It
[was] . . . responsible for a search among professional students of
history . . . for . . . a more usable past, a new way of viewing the
history of America.[46]

Sussman reflected his generation's search for new ideologies,
prompted in part by President John F. Kennedy's call for new frontiers.
"I am suggesting," he wrote,

that what followed from this kind of history was . . . an ideology
and moreover one which was in striking ways to become in part
the official American ideology since at least 1893. If from 1893 to
1963 Americans find themselves committed to a search for new
frontiers to replace the one that Turner announced was no more,
they do so in large part because the study of history pointed the
way ideologically. It is precisely because this did become a major
ideological force, adapted to many ends in the America of the
twentieth century, that there has been such a wide-scale public debate on the validity of the so-called Turner thesis and that important groups of American intellectuals found it necessary to discuss
the values which followed from a frontier America, values which

46. Warren I. Sussman, "The Useless Past: American Intellectuals and the Frontier Thesis, 1910–1930," *Bucknell Review* 11 (March 1963), 17.

some were trying to preserve in our century while others equally vigorously were trying to disavow them.[47]

Among historians who tended to such disavowal were several who stressed the negative impact of the frontier. Writing in 1964, Curtis Martin challenged what he termed "the myth of Turner's self-sufficient and self-reliant West." Reflecting contemporary concerns with the Great Society, he argued that the West had always been heavily dependent on government, and Eastern financial support for its development. "Government had a greater impact upon the West than the West had upon government," he wrote. "The myth of the individualistic, isolated, self-sufficient Westerner is largely that—a myth."[48] In a different context, T. Scott Miyakawa similarly questioned the frontier's role in promoting individualism. In studying Protestant denominations on the frontier, he found that they were not "lone individuals in an atomistic society [but] members of disciplined groups and an increasingly organized society." Mirroring the organizational society of the 1960s, Miyakawa challenged the validity of Turner's view on the relationship between the frontier and individualism, nationalism, supposed reversion to primitivism, and the alleged rejection of seaboard and Old World culture by pioneers.[49]

Increasing pessimism about social disorder in the 1960s was also expressed by Louis B. Wright who had written extensively about culture in the West. By 1964 he was greatly concerned about the seeming increase of chaos in American society, and read his concern into the frontier thesis. In his analysis of culture and anarchy on the frontier, he criticized the disorderly elements in frontier society and praised those pioneers who brought traditional cultural values with them. "These were the people who struggled to reproduce the best of the older civilizations they had left," he declared approvingly. That experience, he emphasized, had direct relevance to the social problems of the 1960s. Reading his contemporary concerns into the frontier past, he concluded that "upon intelligent and cultivated citizens rests

47. Warren I. Sussman, "History and the American Intellectual: Uses of a Usable Past," *American Quarterly* 16, part 2, Supplement (Summer 1964), 254–55.

48. Curtis Martin, "Impact of the West on American Government and Politics," *Colorado Quarterly* 13 (Summer 1964), 51.

49. T. Scott Miyakawa, *Protestants and Pioneers: Individualism and Conformity on the American Frontier* (Chicago, 1964), 7–8, 21, 130, 202, 224–40.

the heavy responsibility of saving society from the chaos of the cheap and tawdry."[50]

No longer did historians view the frontier as having promoted mobility and success in the United States. Reflecting contemporary pessimism, Gilbert C. Fite in 1966 emphasized the large number of individuals who experienced failure on the frontier. "Thousands of people helped conquer the frontier," Fite observed, "but thousands more were conquered by it." In articulating a realistic view, quite in contrast to Turner's self-congratulatory pronouncements, Fite concluded that "pioneers [found] grim realities turned their daydreams into nightmares."[51]

Perhaps the most trenchant analysis of the increasing negativism of frontier historians was made in 1968 by Harold Simonson, a literary scholar. "Today's students of American history study Frederick Jackson Turner's frontier hypothesis far more critically than they did in the 1890s," he wrote. "We now think, for example, that in explaining American development primarily in terms of Western expansion Turner overlooked such influential groups as Southern agrarians, Eastern capitalists, and Middle West progressives; and that in homogenizing a complex American society into what he called a 'composite nationality' he stereotyped Americans and gave far too important a role to the geographic and climatic factors." But above all, Simonson focused on the impact of the idea of an open frontier on American attitudes that emphasized optimism. "Jumping off [to reach the frontier] meant keeping ahead of oppressive complexities. It meant new adventure, new history, new being. It meant the American dream of virgin land, a golden gate, an open road. In short, it meant Eden." Simonson felt that Turner had caught this vision in his "Frontier" essay. "Using the poet's language, and sharing his vision, Turner described what he thought the significance of the frontier to be. He saw it as a boundless Eden wherein America's fulfillment would take place." But in the 1960s Simonson detected a more tragic vision. "As we see more clearly today . . . the West was no longer another Eden . . . the Westerner was no longer another Adam. The immense implications of an open frontier were now to be eclipsed by those of a closed one. The informing

50. Louis B. Wright, "Culture and Anarchy on the Frontier," in Carroll Camden (ed.), *Literary Views: Critical and Historical Essays* (Chicago, 1964), 131–43.

51. Gilbert C. Fite, "Daydreams and Nightmares: The Late Nineteenth-Century Agricultural Frontiers," *Agricultural History* 40 (October 1966), 285.

metaphor changed from endless space to the solid wall." Nevertheless, he believed that in the 1960s Americans were desperately seeking to hold on to optimism by refusing to confront stark realities of their day. "The dream," he noted, "is re-enacted every day as we sit before our television sets or turn the slick pages of our magazines. Answers to problems require only that we tune in again tomorrow or buy the economy-sized package. . . . No wonder that in avoiding tragedy Americans still look back to a time when the myth assured us no walls existed, to a time of perpetual youth and innocence." And, approvingly citing Daniel Boorstin, he concluded that "coming of age requires the courage to disillusion ourselves."[52]

The pessimism that historians began to reflect after 1960 was in part fueled by a profound guilt complex that stemmed from America's alleged mistreatment of minorities, women, and the poor, a feeling that was also prompted by the civil rights movement of these years. This increased concern contrasted sharply with the self-confidence and even smugness that had characterized earlier generations of frontier historians. That group had praised the egalitarian influence of the frontier; historians between 1960 and 1990 turned the tables and chronicled what they perceived as inequalities and injustices suffered by the hitherto "forgotten people" on the frontier—Indians, blacks, Hispanics, and women. In a similar negative vein—and reflecting contemporary environmental concerns—a growing number of scholars severely criticized the ravishing of the natural environment by successive generations of Westerners. To a considerable extent, then, historians were finding the frontier responsible for what they considered to be major ills of their own times (1960–1990): racism, sexism, inequality, and the wanton destruction of nature.

Some of the first criticisms of Turner for ignoring minorities came in the later 1950s. In 1957 Irving Hallowell, a historian of Indian affairs, took Turner to task for slighting the influence of Native Americans on the westward movement. "It is . . . the Indian's continuing presence throughout our whole colonial and national history that has given many aspects of our culture a special coloring," wrote Hallowell.[53] A year later, Gilman Ostrander, who had just received his doctorate at Berkeley in 1956, was more explicit. He charged that the

52. Harold P. Simonson, "The Closed Frontier and American Tragedy," *Texas Quarterly* 11 (Spring 1968), 56, 57, 58, 59, 60, 61.

53. A. Irving Hallowell, "The Backwash of the Frontier: The Impact of the Indian on American Culture," in Wyman and Kroeber (eds.), *Frontier in Perspective*, 230.

frontier hypothesis was based on the assumptions of Turner's generation "that political habits are determined by innate racial attributes." But by 1958 such perspectives had changed. "The Turnerian hypothesis concerning the frontier origins of American democracy has remained possible only by the implicit retention of . . . old and no longer reputable racial assumptions," Ostrander charged.[54] A year later, Jack Forbes, with a new Ph.D. from the University of Southern California, wrote in a similar vein. "Unfortunately for the Indian," Forbes declared, "Turner . . . did not duly consider the role of the native. His own studies were concerned exclusively with the white intruder. . . . The Indian is clearly not a part of this frontier. He is, rather, a part of the environment on which the frontier acts." Yet Forbes believed that the Indian also had a frontier, and "this [Indian] frontier surely is a part of the American frontier."[55]

Within a few years, other historians broadened the attack. Burton Williams, a student of James C. Malin who had already criticized Turner earlier, charged Western historians with racial myopia. "Students of the West are, by and large, trapped in a morass of historical tradition," Williams wrote. This was

> largely the result of a near-religious devotion to the late Frederick Jackson Turner and his Frontier Hypothesis. Indeed, the Turner disciples have exceeded their master in their dedication to his cause. . . . One needs only to examine the more popular texts dealing with the West. . . . Ray Allen Billington's *Westward Expansion* . . . devotes eleven pages to the Turner thesis and a scant forty some odd pages to the age of exploration . . . by the Spanish, Portuguese, and French. The remaining some 700 pages read somewhat like a history of the English people—continued in America. . . . The book concludes with the emergence of Populism in the 1890s with the suggestion that the Populists laid the foundations for "the new world of cooperative democracy that is America's future." As for Riegel, and Athearn, they very nearly omit all New World colonists, including the native Indian population, save for the British colonists. The westward trek of these "Americanized" Anglo-Saxons begins virtually on line one, page one. No doubt such approaches to . . . the frontier can be justified

54. Gilman Ostrander, "Turner and the Germ Theory," *Agricultural History* 32 (October 1958), 258–61.
55. Jack D. Forbes, "The Indian in the West: A Challenge for Historians," *Arizona and the West* 1 (Autumn 1959), 206–15.

if the goal is to chronologically trace the westerly migratory habits of our British forebears. And this, indeed, is what Athearn, Billington, and Riegel and many others have done. Adherence or objection to the Turner thesis has long been a test of historical fellowship. There is, however, far more to the history of the American West than the narrow spectrum exposed by a religious application of the Turner thesis.[56]

A former disciple of Turner, Wilbur Jacobs, echoed this view. "Over the years we have created and accepted as true our own version of early American Indian history," he wrote in 1969.

> We have been all too inclined to glorify our ancestors, to portray them as heroic frontiersmen who conquered the wilderness and subdued the wild natives, thus setting the foundations of the new republic. This tendency in American history owes much to the frontier thesis of Frederick Jackson Turner who tended to ignore minority groups, especially the Indians. But we can no longer afford to be satisfied with a version of our history designed primarily to obscure the more dubious actions of our ancestors. There is a need to reexamine the Indian side of our colonial history. The need is pressing and the reassessment of the evidence has already begun. . . . In this new history a central theme will undoubtedly be the persistent struggle of the Indian to preserve his lands and way of life.[57]

Younger scholars suggested specific guidelines for the writing of this new history. Jack Forbes declared that "to the Turnerians . . . the Frontier consisted solely in Anglo-Americans" and to the exclusion of "the Indians who opposed [their] expansion." Forbes criticized such an ethnocentric approach. Instead, he proposed a framework in which "the frontier is an instance of dynamic interaction between human beings and involves such processes as acculturation, assimilation, miscegenation, race prejudice, conquest, imperialism, and colonization." Such a perspective obviously reflected a somewhat negative view of

56. Burton J. Williams, "The Twentieth Century American West: The Old Versus the New," *Rocky Mountain Social Science Journal* 6 (October 1969), 163, 164.
57. Wilbur R. Jacobs, "British Colonial Attitudes and Policies towards Indians in the American Colonies," in Howard Peckham and Charles Gibson (eds.), *Attitudes of Colonial Powers toward the American Indian* (Salt Lake City, 1969), 100.

America's past, in stark contrast to the upbeat, optimistic version of the frontier sketched by Turner.[58]

This being an age of specialization, younger scholars busied themselves with attacking special aspects of the Turner Thesis as it related to Indians. David Nichols argued that Turner largely ignored Indian influence on American civilization. To him, natives were merely part of the landscape. Christine Bolt charged that white historians simply failed to give adequate treatment to Indians, people of another race. Lawrence Hauptman analyzed the image of Indians on the frontier as reflected in school textbooks before 1890. In this literature, he argued, various historians developed negative stereotypes of Indians and mythologized the frontier. That imposed a highly negative and inaccurate image of Native Americans in the minds of most people in the United States. And Turner's theory accepted rather than dispelled the myth. The mythical aspect of the Turner Theory was also criticized by William Robbins, a New Left historian who declared that the conquest of the American West was an important aspect of American expansion and imperialism—and the conquest of native peoples. Historians who eulogized this brutal process were merely accepting "the dominant values of the American imperial system."[59] America's past was dark, indeed.

But the most comprehensive plea for the reconsideration of the Indian on the frontier came from Wilbur Jacobs, in various books and articles published during the decade after 1969. Jacobs decried the glorification of frontiersmen, which he ascribed "to the frontier thesis of Frederick Jackson Turner who tended to ignore minority groups, especially the Indians." Jacobs urged a complete reevaluation of American history. "I am suggesting that we revise certain of our traditional ideas about the frontier in American history with a hope of seeking a balance. . . . If we are going to tell the whole story of Indian–white

58. Jack D. Forbes, "Frontiers in American History," *Journal of the West* 1 (July 1962), 63, 64, 65.

59. David Nichols, "Civilization Over Savage: Frederick Jackson Turner and the Indian," *South Dakota History* 2 (Fall 1972), 383–405; Christine Bold, "Return of the Native: Some Reflections on the History of American Indians," *Journal of American Studies* 8 (August 1974), 247–59; Lawrence M. Hauptman, "Mythologizing Westward Expansion: Schoolbooks and the Image of the American Frontier before Turner," *Western Historical Quarterly* 8 (July 1977), 269–82; William G. Robbins, "The Conquest of the American West: History as Eulogy," *Indian Historian* 10 (Winter 1977), 7–13.

relations, we must make an all-out attempt to picture the clash of cultures so that there will be an understanding of both cultures, not just one. Thus, to give more attention to the Indian side is not necessarily to plead for the Indian point of view. . . . We need to ask ourselves if the history of the United States is only the history of white people, or if it also includes the American Indian, as well as other ethnic minorities." Indeed, Jacobs noted, "The Turnerian theme of progress and development as an explanation of frontier advance is largely an interpretation of Euro-American white history. . . . It has little to do with Indians, blacks, orientals, Mexican-Americans, or other minorities that make up the bulk of population in large American cities."[60]

Jacobs believed that the unfair treatment Americans accorded Indians was also reflected in the nation's foreign policies. "Nations today that are led by a powerful white citizenry are still often unsympathetic to the aspirations of native peoples," he wrote in the midst of the Vietnam imbroglio. "The popularity of Frederick Jackson Turner's theory in North America and in Australia is evidence of the historians' concern for the development of white civilization and the exploitation of the land. Native peoples play only a minor role in this widely accepted interpretation. . . . Turner . . . treated Indians . . . as if they were some kind of geographical obstacle to the westward movement of whites." On the basis of such reconsideration of the baneful impact of the frontier, Jacobs concluded that "the frontier theory . . . represents not only an interpretation of history but also an attitude that historians have taken toward the land, native people, and the expansion of white civilization."[61]

Such changing attitudes toward Indians also affected historical interpretations about the role of blacks on the frontier. Until 1960 historians had largely neglected the subject. Thereafter, a series of increasingly critical studies appeared. New Left writers such as Staughton Lynd charged that Turner, along with Beard, was responsible for obscuring the significance of slavery by shifting attention from slavery

60. Wilbur R. Jacobs, "The Indian and the Frontier in American History—A Need for Revision," *Western Historical Quarterly* 4 (January 1973), 43, 44.

61. Wilbur R. Jacobs, "The Fatal Confrontation: Early Native–White Relations on the Frontiers of Australia, New Guinea, and America—A Comparative Study," *Pacific Historical Review* 40 (August 1971), 307, 308.

to the frontier. In the condemnatory tone characteristic of many scholars of this period, Lynd wrote that Turner ignored the Southwestern
frontier because its influence was "to coarsen and brutalize the peculiar
institution, not to humanize it."[62] Eugene Berwanger, in a sober and
detached analysis, documented many of the racist attitudes which
blacks experienced on the nineteenth-century frontier. James Fisher,
in analyzing the black community in California from 1850 to 1950,
declared that the Turner hypothesis simply ignored blacks because
they did not experience "individualism, economic equality, freedom,
. . . and democracy."[63] In surveying available works on blacks in 1975,
Lawrence De Graaf noted that "the greatest limitation of those works
that employ the racism and collective minority themes is that their
perspective was often influenced too heavily by the climate of opinion
in the 1960s, just as the blindness of many earlier scholars to ethnic
history was due to their infatuation with the ideas of Frederick Jackson
Turner." He hoped that scholars in the future would produce works
"that will give western black history a significance that transcends
contemporary modishness."[64]

Historians who were concerned with other minorities such as Hispanics or particular ethnic groups tended to study these peoples within
the context of the West as region, rather than considering their presence on the frontier. That was particularly true of the work of Fred
Luebke, who suggested that settlers on the Great Plains frontier were
hardly a homogeneous group as Turner and popular myth would have
it. Rather, they represented a multitude of different nationalities who,
over the years, retained many aspects of their culture. Joseph Schafer
had made the same point about Germans in Wisconsin a half-century
before, but at that time was one voice crying in a wilderness.

The increased consciousness of minority groups also brought a
greater sensitivity to the role of women on the frontier. One of the
first to raise the issue was David Potter, in a 1964 essay discussing
women and the American character. Potter urged modification of the

62. Staughton Lynd, "On Turner, Beard, and Slavery," *Journal of Negro History*
48 (October 1963), 235–50.

63. Eugene H. Berwanger, *The Frontier against Slavery: Western Anti-Negro Prejudice
and the Slavery Extension Controversy* (Urbana, 1967); James A. Fisher, "The Political
Development of the Black Community in California, 1850–1950," *California Historical
Quarterly* 50 (September 1971), 256–66.

64. Lawrence B. DeGraaf, "Recognition, Racism, and Reflections on the Writing
of Western Black History," *Pacific Historical Review* 44 (February 1975), 49.

Turner Thesis as it pertained to women. "If we accept Turner's own assumption that economic opportunity is what matters," Potter wrote, "and that the frontier was significant as the context in which economic opportunity occurred, then we must observe that for American women . . . opportunity began . . . where the frontier left off." Such a perspective reversed many prevailing views about the frontier as a door to opportunity, and emphasized its negative impact.[65] Even so, studies of women in the West were slow in coming. It was only a decade later that T. A. Larson wrote a suggestive piece on women on the frontier, in which he blamed Turner for setting the pattern of belittling their importance. Many of those who followed Turner unthinkingly did the same, resulting in great neglect of the subject.

> In his famous essay Turner includes the sentence, "Kit Carson's mother was a Boone." It is the only mention of the female sex in the entire essay. Other historians likewise give the impression that women played insignificant roles in Western history . . . Ray A. Billington, Thomas D. Clark, Robert Athearn and Robert Riegel. . . . In short, standard textbooks used in college and university courses in Western history come closer to ignoring women entirely. Were women really that insignificant in the American West? The census returns . . . show that . . . there were large numbers of women in many parts of the West. The 1870 census enumerated 172,145 women over 21 years of age . . . pioneer women contributed importantly to society's good.[66]

By the middle of the 1970s the increasing momentum of the women's movement stimulated a bevy of new studies about women's role on the frontier. Pioneers in the field such as Glenda Riley, Sandra Myres, Judith Austin, and Joan Jensen uncovered a dimension in Western history that most previous historians had simply neglected. As Riley aptly noted:

> That women have been relatively invisible in western history is now widely understood, but why they have been invisible is not.

65. David M. Potter, "American Women and the American Character," in John A. Hague (ed.), *American Character and Culture: Some Twentieth Century Perspectives* (Deland, Fla., 1964), 65–84; and Frederick C. Luebke, "Ethnic Group Settlement on the Great Plains," *Western Historical Quarterly* 8 (October 1977), 405–30.

66. T. A. Larson, "Women's Role in the American West," *Montana: The Magazine of Western History* 24 (Summer 1974), 4, 5.

. . . These women were virtually ignored because, until the emergence of the feminist movement in the 1960s, women's lives were
usually regarded as unworthy of study. This attitude was complicated by the fact that the fourteen-to-sixteen hour day demanded
of pioneer women did not leave them much leisure time to record
their thoughts and activities in the diaries and journals which
serve as source materials for later historians.

As a consequence of this condition, Riley believed that male historians
created stereotypes to fill the vacuum. "The historian of the frontier
has faced essentially two alternatives in studying frontier women: to
cast them in masculine terms (tough, sexual, political) or to cast them
in 'feminine' terms (domestic, submissive, yet sturdy, moral). . . . A
third and more significant result has been the proliferation of accounts
regarding female suffrage on the frontier." A rewriting of Western
history was necessary, Riley declared, because to Turner "women were
an invisible or perhaps non-existent force."[67]

By 1990 the volume of articles and books on the role of women
on the frontier had increased significantly. Along with most other
studies of the West during these years, they stressed the primacy of
cultural rather than environmental influences on frontier women.
Thus, in a comprehensive volume on *The Female Frontier*, Riley argued
that neither plains nor prairies structured the life of women. Rather,
traditional cultural patterns such as female patterns of domesticity and
motherhood were the dominant formative elements that determined
female life-styles on the frontier.[68]

Indeed, the emphasis of ethnic and women's historians on the
importance of cultural determinants in shaping Western life was only
one—albeit important—aspect of the broader aspect of the major
emphasis on the impact of culture, and not of environment, a new
focus so characteristic of the years from 1960 to 1990. Since the post–
World War I era, frontier historians had increasingly placed much
greater weight on cultural factors than on natural phenomena. Perhaps
this reflected an assumption that Americans had mastered nature and
had subordinated it to serve their own desires. That assumption was
to be rudely disrupted by environmental challenges that surfaced by

67. Glenda Riley, "Images of the Frontierswoman: Iowa as a Case Study," *Western
Historical Quarterly* 8 (April 1977), 190, 191.

68. Glenda Riley, *The Female Frontier: A Comparative View of Women on the Prairie
and the Plains* (Lawrence, 1988).

1990, but until then it permeated most writings on the American frontier.

Ethnic and gender historians contributed greatly to a growing awareness of cultural difference in American society which shaped the outlook of frontier historians. By 1960 they were devoting more attention to cultural differences rather than to viewing the frontier as a great equalizer which produced a homogeneous American identity. William Goetzmann noted, in 1963, that he considered Turner's emphasis on environment as a shaping force on the frontier to be overblown. Even the mountain men, Goetzmann wrote, were not influenced primarily by their raw-wilderness surroundings. Intensive research on such individuals revealed that they were influenced far more by Eastern civilization than by the frontier.[69] Douglas Leach pursued the same theme in a book on the Northern colonial frontier between 1607 and 1763. He concluded that "much of the evidence that Turner gathered on the colonial frontier was exceptional rather than typical, selected for the very reason that it did seem to sustain his hypothesis." Writing in 1966, Leach believed that transplanted European culture had a much greater effect on colonial life-styles than the frontier.[70]

As other historians studied various institutions on the frontier during these years, they came to similar conclusions. When Miyakawa examined the role of churches on the frontier, he found that their cultural inheritance was the most significant factor in their development. "Social background, and traditions of the settlers . . . were among the major forces shaping western society," he wrote. "The frontier provided the physical setting and the limits, but did not determine the pioneer social organization and culture." That position was defended also by Ben Vorpahl, who analyzed Presbyterian denominations on the frontier. That church, Vorpahl noted, constituted "a kind of exception to the frontier hypothesis." Presbyterians did not stand in awe of the vast spaces before them, and were affected only minimally by environmental considerations. The ideas of the Presbyterians did more to mold life on the frontier than did their

69. William H. Goetzmann, "The Mountain Man as Jacksonian Man," *American Quarterly* 15 (Spring 1963), 402–15.

70. Douglas E. Leach, *The Northern Colonial Frontier, 1607–1763* (New York, 1966).

surroundings.[71] Even a confirmed environmentalist like Walter P. Webb said, in 1960, that he now felt the value system of the pioneers had been shaped more by the Old Testament and the Bible than by the environment of the frontier.[72]

Historians continued to stress the enormous importance of law and legal institutions in the shaping of the West. In discussing the transmission of English law to the frontier, William B. Hamilton concluded that Turner's hypothesis about political institutions evolving in response to frontier conditions was simply unwarranted in the light of evidence. American law was neither unique, nor original, and largely dependent on English precedents. "English law was transported to America where it was received and took root," he wrote. And the rapid growth of legal history as a specialized field during these years contributed greatly to a deeper appreciation of the role of law as a major force in the formation and development of frontier communities.[73]

The extraordinarily one-sided emphasis which frontier historians gave to the influence of cultural factors was bound to stimulate an eventual reaction to their neglect of environmental forces. Moreover, the growth of environmental consciousness in the United States throughout this period undoubtedly called attention to the significance of ecology. If some historians at the beginning of the century had erred in being environmentalists, so this later generation was one of culturalists, intent on stressing cultural influences. Yet even the environmental historians reflected a preoccupation with the importance of culture. Whereas the environmentalists at the turn of the century had stressed the primacy of natural phenomena, the historians in the three decades after 1960 emphasized the role of cultural values which Americans held as they confronted the wilderness environment. Thus, they considered issues of class, race, and gender to be as crucial in the realm of nature on the frontier as in society.

Erstwhile Turnerians became some of the earliest converts to the

71. Miyakawa, Protestants and Pioneers, 239–40. Ben M. Vorpahl, "Presbyterianism and the Frontier Hypothesis: Tradition and Modification in the American Garden," Presbyterian Historical Society Journal 45 (September 1967), 180–92.

72. Walter P. Webb, "Geographical–Historical Concepts in American History," Annals of the Association of American Geographers 50 (June 1960), 86.

73. William B. Hamilton, "The Transmission of English Law to the Frontier of America," South Atlantic Quarterly 67 (Spring 1968), 243–64, and Hamilton (ed.), The Transfer of Institutions (Durham, 1964), v, vi.

cause of environmental frontier history. Among these, Wilbur Jacobs was vocal. "Although in his later years Turner had serious reservations about unlimited population growth and a never-ending exploitation of non-renewable resources," Jacobs wrote in 1978,

> this line of thought did not reach his published writings. Far ahead of Turner in understanding environmental social costs was a contemporary of his, Thorstein Veblen. . . . We look to the past, not to discern what must be, but to understand environmental themes which help to explain origins of ecological transformation taking place in our lifetime. We may then catch a glimpse of our newly forming frontiers which forecast the environmental future of America.[74]

Another former Turnerian who was profoundly impressed by the newly emerging environmental consciousness of the period was Thomas D. Clark. A well-known student of the Southwestern frontier, Clark lamented, in 1972, that the real significance of the frontier experience was in the enormous wastefulness it had fostered and the despoliation of America's resources that had resulted. "At this point in the twentieth century," he wrote,

> the opening of the American frontier seems like a saga of an ancient time. In this age of sprawling urban communities and threats of a population explosion the whole attitude of Americans has had to accept changes. . . . Large masses of late twentieth-century Americans seem almost separated completely from the past of their country. Every issue of a newspaper or half-way serious magazine, newscast, or commentary on the quality of current American life reigns us up for our past shortcomings. . . . streams of most rivers are polluted. . . . the air itself carries various charges of poisions. . . . This is certainly not a reiteration of the promise of a continent which piqued the imagination of man. . . . it is not a realization of the great dream that a free people would reap the bountiful rewards of nature, and enjoy them in an idyllic condition where there was space to expand the soul and freedom to erase the problems of the crowded and impoverished Old World. At the outset the American pioneers believed they would never nurture a society in which cities became blighted, large areas of

74. Wilbur R. Jacobs, "The Great Despoliation: Environmental Themes in American Frontier History," *Pacific Historical Review* 47 (February 1978), 16, 17, 26.

land would become impoverished, and people would find themselves as completely dissociated from the soil as those displaced
English peasants. . . . The great promise of the frontier was that
biting poverty would never rob our people of hope. . . . Yet these
are problems of modern America.

The pessimism reflected by a mature scholar like Clark was as deeply
seated as that of the younger writers of this period.[75]

Other historians now blamed the frontier for encouraging environmental desecration. Writing in 1977, Harlan Hague criticized Turner
for not detecting the notion of most Westerners in the nineteenth
century that land and natural resources were inexhaustible. "Farmers,
miners, and cattlemen all believed that the West was a great cornu-
copia which could not be used up, and the country's resources were
vastly exploited." Such wanton exploitation led to enormous waste.
Now viewing the Turner Thesis in a negative light, Hague suggested
that it illustrated that "the belief in the inexhaustibility of resources
in the West generated the unique American acceptance of waste as
the fundamental tenet of a life-style." Hopefully, Americans would
learn from that experience to be more prudent in the future.[76]

While many historians during this period concentrated on tracing
cultural influences on the frontier, a significant number continued to
utilize social science theories and methods in their research. Economists seem to have lost interest in the frontier after 1960. On the
other hand, that of sociologists, psychologists, and geographers increased. The reciprocal relationships between them and historians
flourished.

Once American economic aid to underdeveloped countries ceased
to be a major issue in public policies—as in the 1950s—many economists found their interest in the frontier waning. Yet some retained
a confidence that the behavioral science methods of the 1950s would
produce a truly scientific discipline. One of these was Elias Tuma, who
in 1972 reflected a present-mindedness not untypical of his generation
of social scientists. Tuma was particularly critical of Turner's methodology. He decried the lack of evidence for his generalizations, the
absence of precise data, the breadth of Turner's generalizations, and

75. Thomas D. Clark, "The Heritage of the Frontier," West Virginia History 34
(October 1972), 1–2, 15–17.

76. Harlan Hague, "Eden Ravished: Land, Pioneer Attitudes, and Conservation,"
American West 14 (May-June 1977), 30, 66.

his tendency to express opinions. "In general," wrote Tuma, "Turner is satisfied with qualitative measurements such as 'important,' 'significant,' or 'influential' with no documentation." Imbued with the importance of statistics, scholars like Tuma ascribed their own fascination with quantitative data to an earlier age, and found Turner wanting.[77]

On the other hand, various frontier historians successfully applied sociological concepts to their studies. One was Robert Berkhofer, who emphasized Turner's dependence on the contemporary social thought of his own day. That thought, Berkhofer maintained, was outdated by the 1960s. Frontier historians should therefore utilize the sociological concepts of their own times. Utilizing such theories, Berkhofer reversed some of Turner's major assumptions. The frontier was not an area demanding innovation, as Turner claimed, but instead provided the opportunity for the firmer establishment of old and transplanted institutions. Allan Bogue's studies of pioneer adjustments similarly applied recent sociological theories to individualism, social cooperation, and political participation, although he found affirmation rather than rejection of the Turner Thesis more relevant in his writings.[78]

At the same time, some sociologists found the Turner Thesis still suggestive for the development of their own field. Everett S. Lee, in 1961, considered its usefulness as a special case of more general theories of migration with which sociologists of the decade were then much concerned. "Most of us are now several generations removed from our pioneer forebears," he wrote.

> Most of us have been rendered cautious by the reception accorded more monistic explanations of national character. It now seems obvious that the Turner thesis is too simple an explanation for such complexities as American democracy and American character, so after forty years of general and enthusiastic acceptance it is now the fashion to attack Turner's propositions. It can fairly be said that the supporting evidence was meager and that the thesis was not so much proved as reiterated. Nevertheless, there is great intuitive appeal in this theory, and few are willing to abandon it entirely. In part, the Turner thesis still commands credence because . . . Turner . . . was developing a special case of a more

77. Elias H. Tuma, *Economic History and the Social Sciences* (Berkeley, 1971), 82, 93–217.

78. Robert F. Berkhofer, Jr., "Space, Time, Culture and the New Frontier," *Agricultural History* 38 (January 1964), 21–30; Allan Bogue, "Pioneer Farming," in *Iowa Journal of History* 56, 1–36.

general theory of migration. . . . Migration is one of the most important factors in American civilization.[79]

The frontier hypothesis thus could be used as a stepping stone to broader sociological theories.

If Turner could not have foretold some of the uses to which sociologists would put his theory, he might have been even more surprised by the psychologists. By 1966, Allan Beckman was discovering hidden psychological themes in the frontier hypothesis. Using psychoanalytic concepts, Beckman focused on the mythic and anthropomorphic content of the frontier hypothesis. Its popularity, he argued, was "due to the fact that it symbolically depicted a universal wish-drama of childhood." To a psychoanalyst, it all seemed clear. As Beckman noted:

> In spite of a wealth of criticism adverse to the Turner thesis it is still a popular theme. The initial, as well as continuing appeal must be explained. Here, individual depth psychology can add light where other explanations fail. . . . The great appeal of the Turner thesis . . . comes from the fact that it depicts a universal problem that each person in his individual development attempts to solve. Since man gets some relief from his inner tensions by seeing on the outside similar problems which others, more or less, seemed to have solved, it may be anticipated that prose, poetry, and even historical writings that contain symbolically depicted psychic themes of a universal nature will be popular.

Psychoanalytic theory provides an understanding of Turner's relationship with the father figures in his life. "It also makes understandable Turner's rebellion against some, like [Herbert B.] Adams, and his need to feel that he was a disappointment to others such as Edward Channing and Max Farrand. It explains why Turner was never able to achieve additional historical insights and why he tended to repeat his original statement again and again." Beckman concluded that "the great popularity of the Turner thesis has been . . . discerned and understood by the reader who, after all, had experienced and played out in his own imagination this very same drama; so he had *a priori* knowledge of the theme. And it was because of this experience that

79. Everett S. Lee, "The Turner Thesis Reexamined," *American Quarterly* 13 (Spring 1961), 78, 83.

the reader tended to suspend judgment and accept the hypothesis as an a priori truth."[80]

Other psychoanalysts found different meanings. Fred Schroeder announced that the frontier was notable for developing the superego of Americans. In comparing Turner to Freud, he declared that the frontier was a movement from selfish individualism to the superego or group conscience. From this stage emerged "a new and historically unique super-ego which has developed out of the shared guilt and primal sin (egotism and selfishness) of the frontier." Schroeder's reasoning was suggestive, for as he wrote:

> Like some of the critics of Freudian psychology, I occasionally object to having my inner life analyzed from the point of view of men whose circle of acquaintances consists of a majority of mental cases. . . . But both Freud and Turner were intensely interested in the processes of acculturation and civilization. For Freud a major question was how cultures developed; for Turner . . . how the specific American culture had developed. To the psychoanalyst Freud, many of the neurotic aberations of disturbed men and women might be understood and subsequently remedied if one could determine the social forces which repress and transform the wild instincts to which the human animal is heir. For the historian Turner, the national characteristics which paradoxically seem to unify a people whose varied cultural ancestries should properly produce disparateness might be explained if one could find a common process of acculturation. . . . Both men were concerned with questions of liberty in civilized societies.

Such insights contributed to an understanding of the persistence of the Turner Thesis, a formulation that had roots not only in historical analysis but in national myth.[81]

Some psychologists developed the technique of content analysis during these years. Ronald Carpenter, in examining the rhetoric of the Turner Thesis, found a stylistic identification with the rhetorical style of Turner's contemporary, Governor Robert LaFollette. Since Turner had presented his ideas as a rhetorically oriented discourse, it

80. Allan Beckman, "Hidden Themes in the Frontier Thesis: An Application of Psychoanalysis to Historiography," *Comparative Studies in Society and History* 8 (April 1966), 361–62, 382.

81. Fred E. H. Schroeder, "The Development of the Super-Ego on the American Frontier," *Soundings* 57 (Summer 1974), 189, 190.

could be understood best in that context rather than as historical theory.[82]

Somewhat less speculative than the psychologists were geographers who—while mainly concerned with the West as a region—also offered their insights to frontier historians. One of these was Merlin P. Lawson, who emphasized that the environment of the frontier was rarely a stationary one as most historians simply assumed. As he noted,

> the myth of the Great American Desert was derived from the no-
> tions of a few men rather than from the probable reality of the
> experienced environmental conditions. The "illusion" of the Great
> American Desert has not been considered from a climatological
> perspective; no serious attempts have been made using historical
> methods and techniques to establish the actual climate of the re-
> gion during the period of the desert image. Explanations con-
> cerned with the derivation of the notion of a trans-Missouri desert
> as perceived by early American explorers neglect the possibility of
> climactic variability sufficient enough to justify the disparaging ac-
> counts of the territory. By establishing the statistical relationship
> between tree growth and climatic characteristics, spatial recon-
> structions of moisture conditions in the western United States per-
> mit analysis of exploratory experience in perspective with climatic
> stress. One must conclude that Stephen Long, the explorer re-
> sponsible for naming the Great American Desert in 1820, wit-
> nessed serious drought conditions on the High Plains exceeding
> that experienced by previous expeditions, thus suggesting that the
> desert notion had substantial merit. . . . The "real" past environ-
> ment is [not] changing.[83]

Not only the geographers, but the psychologists and the sociologists, among social scientists, contributed much to weaving a tapestry
of much greater complexity for the Turner Thesis than had existed
before 1960. The simplicity that had accompanied the Turner hypothesis in its earlier years was gone. In its place had sprung up a wide

82. Ronald H. Carpenter, "The Rhetorical Genius of Style in the 'Frontier Hy-
pothesis' of Frederick Jackson Turner," Southern Speech Communication Journal 37
(Spring 1972), 233–48, and Carpenter, "The Stylistic Identification of Frederick
Jackson Turner with Robert M. LaFollette: A Psychologically Oriented Analysis of
Language Behavior," Wisconsin Academy of Sciences, Arts, and Letters, Transactions 63
(Madison, 1975), 102–15.

83. Merlin P. Lawson and Charles W. Stockton, "Desert Myth and Climatic
Reality," Annals of the Association of American Geographers 71 (December 1981), 527,
535.

range of explanations concerning the development of the frontier West and its impact upon the course of American civilization. It was not surprising, therefore, that after 1960 many historians questioned single-causation explanations such as the Turner Thesis and instead offered hypotheses based on a multiplicity of influences. Even those who did not reject Turner's hypothesis outright often urged that it be supplemented by the consideration of other variables.

That was certainly true of Rowland Berthoff, who in 1961 offered a new conceptual framework for analyzing American social history. "The westward movement which since Frederick Jackson Turner's time has figured as a special field claiming fundamental importance," Berthoff wrote, "had better be considered as only one of a number of kinds of physical and social movements." Berthoff was part of a new generation of historians who had not known the great figures in the profession before World War II personally and were often likely to be more critical as a result.[84] That was also true of Lee Benson who, reflecting the negativism of his age group, went out of his way to write a book attacking Turner and Charles A. Beard. As Benson noted:

> In recent decades a tendency has developed to view Frederick Jackson Turner and Charles A. Beard as though their seminal ideas derived from, and represented, radically different theories of history. This book challenges that view and argues that their surface differences should not obscure their fundamental similarities. Searching for an overarching theme that would help them comprehend and summarize American experience, Turner and Beard both drew upon European models. Both adopted eclectic approaches that inconsistently combined concepts taken from the "economic interpretation of history" and from economic determinism. Consequently, they both presented theses that are ambiguous and self-contradictory.[85]

A similar theme was followed by Peter Coleman, a young historian from New Zealand. "The Turners and the Beards began with an idea which allowed them to impose an imaginative synthesis upon American History before a problem had been adequately investigated," he declared. "Turner and his followers are especially criticized because they too readily accepted a thesis that resulted from a 'premature and

84. Roland W. Berthoff, "The American Social Order: A Conservative Hypothesis," *American Historical Review* 65 (April 1961), 499.

85. Benson, *Turner and Beard*, vii.

irresponsible synthesis.' The Turners have done a disservice to the historical profession by 'enticing scholars into fruitless or meaningless investigations' while leaving more important questions untouched."[86]

It was in the 1960s, also, that James C. Malin brought his lifelong crusade against the Turner Thesis to its culmination. In crystallizing his attacks on the thesis, Malin wrote in 1961 that Turner had been too simplistic. A full study of the frontier would take into consideration "its geological history, its ecological history, and the history of human culture since the beginning of occupancy by primitive men. In terms of time, such a study should not cease in 1890 but extend to the present. New issues and new cultural values would then be considered." Unlike some of Turner's critics, who were mainly negative, Malin also developed a positive alternative to Turner's formulation.[87]

Although comparative frontier history was far less popular between 1960 and 1990 than it had been between 1945 and 1960, several of its proponents continued to attack Turner for his nationalistic orientation. Reflecting the impact of globalism and cultural pluralism, Louis Hartz criticized the nationalistic, single-causation orientation of the earlier historians such as Turner, Parrington, and Beard. In charging that their views reflected the suppositions of their own age, Hartz was apparently unaware that he himself was following in a very similar pattern. A comparative approach, he declared, would eliminate American provincialism, and place the American experience in an international context. It would "link us to humanity, not through the discovery of superior virtue, but through the discovery of a common dilemma: the conservation of the cultural fragment and the challenges it encounters." Hartz's Harvard colleague, philosopher Morton White, took similar aim at Turner, whom he apparently had not read with care. He castigated him as one who was "influenced by a single-minded regularism."[88]

Multiple causation in Western history was by now a theme of an

86. Peter J. Coleman, "Beard, McDonald, and Economic Determinism in American Historiography," Business History Review 34 (Spring 1960), 113–21.

87. James C. Malin, "On the Nature of the History of Geographical Area, with Special Reference to the Western United States," in The Grassland of North America: Prologomena to Its History (Lawrence, 1961), 471–86; see also Swierenga (ed.), History and Ecology, 129–30 for quote.

88. Louis Hartz, "American Historiography and Comparative Analysis: Further Reflections," Comparative Studies in Society and History 5 (July 1963), 365–77; Morton White, Foundations of Historical Knowledge (New York, 1965), 61–66, 84.

increasing number of historians. John Caughey, the dean of California historians, declared in 1974:

> We western historians, I submit, must break out of our self-imposed imprisonment in the early and antique West. We must change the parameters and deal with the whole West. When we succeed in projecting western history in its full dimensions, the several state and local histories will gain a much needed coherence. . . . And the stage will be set to establish awareness of the significance of the West in American history, a significance too long clouded by our obsession with the frontier.

Coincidentally, at about the same time, the first general history of the West in the twentieth century appeared, as if to underscore Caughey's complaint. Such an extension of the chronology of Western history reflected, in part, the enormous population growth of the West since 1945 and its increasing economic and political importance in national life.[89] Paul W. Gates, in analyzing agricultural development in the years from 1815 to 1860, concluded that "pioneering in the new cotton areas of the West was something very different from the process described by Turner . . . and others of the 'frontier' school of historians."[90] And Earl Pomeroy, in discussing scholarship concerning the Pacific Coast, argued that it was "out of touch with the contemporary world" because historians stressed the differences between the past and present rather than dwelling on continuities. "Their writings tended to offer escape into a romantic past rather than [offering] solutions to the present," and made it "hard to believe the announcement that the frontier was gone."[91]

Some scholars hoped a new hypothesis would replace Turner's. In offering such a hope, Harry Scheiber in 1969 declared that

> the history of the West is clearly in trouble today, so far as its future as a distinct and unified field of research and teaching in American history is concerned. It is an open secret in the profession that many of the scholars responsible for training students in

89. John W. Caughey, "The Insignificance of the Frontier in American History, or 'Once Upon a Time There Was an American West,'" *Western Historical Quarterly* 5 (January 1974), 16; Gerald D. Nash, *The American West in the Twentieth Century* (Albuquerque, 1977).

90. Paul W. Gates, *The Farmer's Age: Agriculture, 1815–1860* (New York, 1960), 138–44.

91. Earl Pomeroy, "Old Lamps for New: The Cultural Lag in Pacific Coast Historiography," *Arizona and the West* 2 (Summer 1960), 107–26.

this field question how long it can survive without a fundamental reorientation of its subject matter and its relevance to basic social research. . . . The plight of Western history, I think, lies principally in the continuing failure of scholars to produce an acceptable unifying framework—some principle of selection, some lodestone. . . . Lacking such an accepted framework, western history has become an obliging receptacle for trivia and a convenient label for studies whose significance might otherwise be readily challenged. Of course . . . Turner did attempt to provide a unifying framework. . . . But by claiming everything, he risked admitting *anything* to the province of American history . . . and thereby imperiled its integrity. Until such basic conceptual issues are settled . . . the failure of the Turner legacy leaves History of the West in quest of a purpose.[92]

In many respects, John W. Ward, an American Studies scholar, summed up well the view of his generation on the frontier experience. Writing in 1966, Ward declared that

if the movement out of society, away from the East when it becomes more and more like Europe, the movement toward nature and the frontier is, as Turner insists it is, the really American part of our experience, then consider what his reading of the American tradition leaves out. The world of Western frontier farmers leaves out . . . Boston and New York and Philadelphia and Charleston. It leaves out, even gladly rejects, the contribution Europe has made to the development of our national experience. It leaves out a number of Americans: Hawthorne and Melville, Henry James, Willard Gibbs and Henry Adams. It leaves out, in other words, a range of experience and attitudes that are indispensable to the realization of our stature as fully developed human beings. It leaves out the consideration of sophisticated ideas and all art. It leaves out no less than the sense of the past itself and its embodiment of tradition. . . . It leaves out the city and the technology that was implicit in the urban, industrial Chicago where Turner stood when he spoke. All these are somehow not really American.[93]

By 1990, then, historians had arrived at a very different perception

92. Harry N. Scheiber, "Turner's Legacy and the Search for a Reorientation of Western History: A Review Essay," *New Mexico Historical Review* 44 (July 1969), 231, 232, 245.

93. John W. Ward, "Cleric or Critic? The Intellectual in the University," *American Scholar* 35 (Winter 1965), 108.

of the frontier than they had held four and a half decades earlier. The larger number of historians writing about the frontier were critical of Turner. Most did not reject the thesis outright so much as they proposed substantial revisions or additions. What was most striking was their pessimistic outlook. The frontier they viewed no longer had a positive impact on American society but was responsible for many of the ills, many of the problems which they perceived in their contemporary era. They saw it as the instigator of violence, anti-intellectualism, racism, sexism, and environmental desecration. Instead of being a spawning ground for desirable American character traits such as individualism and self-reliance, through their negative lens it was an area that bred crudity and was devoid of culture. Instead of symbolizing freedom, historians like Hofstadter accused it of promoting paranoia and totalitarian tendencies. The image of the frontier drawn by this generation was a dark one. Perhaps it reflected their own pessimism about the future, their disillusionment with their own present, and a decreasing confidence in the attainment of the American Dream.

Nor did the historians of this era reflect the nationalistic pride of earlier generations. No longer did they find the American frontier unique. It was merely a part of worldwide patterns of settlement in which the American experience was not exceptional, as Americans had once believed. And amidst the many influences that had formed American society—almost all of them cultural—the frontier was only one of many. Certainly it was not the dominant factor in the American experience, as earlier scholars had proclaimed. Detailed monographic research and more sophisticated social science theories and methods seemed to indicate that the processes of nation-building were far more complex than earlier historians had imagined. Instead of the nation's distinctive pride, the frontier had become its shame, its albatross. Fortunately, this vision did not necessarily constitute famous last words about the frontier. It did reflect the worldview of many historians during the second half of the twentieth century who read their own preconceptions into a significant part of Western history.

THREE

The West as Region, 1890–1990

IN THE CENTURY after 1890 historians viewed the West as a region from a variety of perspectives, conditioned by the contemporary conditions of their own day. Between 1890 and 1920, when the trans-Mississippi area was the nation's youngest and most recently settled, they perceived it mainly as a geographical entity, distinguished by climate, topography, and environmental factors. Sometime about 1920 such perceptions changed with increasing awareness of diverse cultures in the Southwest, Pacific Northwest, and the Plains, whether Indian or Hispanic. Literary critics and writers came to emphasize the cultural distinctiveness of the West, and from 1920 to 1945 many historians followed their lead. World War II altered these perspectives. The enormous growth of population and consequent increase of economic and political power between 1940 and 1945 led historians in the postwar era to view the West as an economic and political region. By the 1960s a new generation adopted different perspectives, however. Profoundly influenced by the social issues of their lifetime—ethnic, racial, gender, and ideological disputes—they came to emphasize the primacy of cultural and social determinants of regionalism. Moreover, the development of psychology led an increasing number to view regionalism as being the product mainly of perceptions—of rational

or irrational attitudes in people's minds. By 1990, therefore, the characteristics of Western regionalism had gone through an extensive transformation.

Such a transformation was of course conditioned by major changes
in American life during this period. Turner and his generation were
conditioned by the hardships of the agricultural depression of the
1890s, as is well known. That experience underscored the important
differences between the industrialized East and the underdeveloped
West. It also induced a strong sense of nostalgia. But by the time of
World War I a new generation who had not personally lived through
the industrialization process became imbued with a new global consciousness stimulated by the war. Woodrow Wilson's idealism and his
advocacy of a League of Nations inspired many, including Turner, to
dream of Western regionalism as providing a model for the reorgani-
zation of the world. The American West, and the other major sections
of the United States, would serve as a prototype for a new world
organization that would bring peace and democracy to the world as it
had to the American nation. These noble goals were not attained in
the 1920s, and the disillusionment led to a new-found appreciation
of the nonindustrialized areas of the West and of cultural nationalism
in the 1920s and 1930s. World War II provided still other perspectives,
as between 1945 and 1960 regional historians regarded the West as
America's Third World, much like other underdeveloped regions abroad.
With the questioning of many traditional beliefs in three decades after
1960, historians came to regard Western regionalism as determined
by major issues of the period: racial, ethnic, or gender discrimination,
or alleged corporate abuses. In their search for the West as a region
scholars had moved far from the geographical determinism of the
1890s, and had increasingly stressed the primacy of the cultural determinants of regionalism. Moreover, while historians during the first
half of the century had largely viewed Western regionalism as a positive
force in American life, those who wrote after 1945 tended to lament
many of its supposed destructive influences.

If Turner and his contemporaries tended to view the West as a
region defined by geographic boundaries between 1890 and 1914, that
was in part due to some of the events of their own lifetime. After all,
the United States did not fill out its continental boundaries until late
in the nineteenth century. It was only in 1869 that the intrepid Major
John Wesley Powell became the first to explore the mighty Colorado

River and to map out and describe much of the semiarid West which many Americans still regarded as the Great American Desert. This was also the period of the last Indian wars, symbolized perhaps by the tragic Battle of Wounded Knee in 1890. Moreover, in 1889 and 1890 Congress finally admitted some of the more sparsely populated territories to statehood in the Union: North Dakota, South Dakota, Washington, and Montana in 1889, and Wyoming and Idaho in 1890.[1] It was hardly surprising, therefore, that the generation of the 1890s tended to view the West as a new region defined largely by distinctive geographical and environmental features.

Such a perception was reinforced by contemporary geographers and their theories, mostly imported from Germany where many American scholars during these years received their training. One of the dominant figures in the field was Friedrich Ratzel, who was an avowed advocate of geographic determinism. A prolific writer, his *Political Geography*, published in 1897, had a widespread impact in the United States (and on Turner). In France, Vidal de la Blanche worked out similar themes. Several notable scholars in England also traced the influence of physiographic features on the political development of regions around the world, A. J. Herbertson among them. The views of these European academicians were well known in the United States, where William Morris Davis of Harvard University pioneered with new methods of regional analysis. In the West, Eugene W. Hilgard of the University of California became a distinguished innovator, developing imaginative methods of soil analysis, and relating differences in soil to geographical variables. At the same time, a number of distinguished statistical cartographers emerged in the United States, men like Fletcher M. Hewes and Henry Gannett. In 1883, these two men compiled *Scribner's Statistical Atlas of the United States*. This volume brought a great amount of statistical data together, which they correlated effectively with social, economic, and political trends. Gannett also proposed various theories in this study concerning the grouping of states in sectional alignments.[2]

1. On Powell, see Wallace Stegner, *Beyond the Hundredth Meridian: John Wesley Powell and the Second Opening of the West* (Boston, 1954). A brief overview of Indian wars is in William T. Hagan, *American Indians* (Chicago, 1961). On statehood, see John D. Hicks, *The Constitutions of the Northwest States*, University Studies Series, University of Nebraska, vol. 23 (Lincoln, 1924), and Earl Pomeroy, *The Territories and the United States, 1861–1900: Studies in Colonial Administration* (Philadelphia, 1947).

2. Griffith Taylor (ed.), *Geography in the Twentieth Century* (London, 1951), 64–

These varied influences had an impact on historians as well as others who were grappling with the rapidly changing identity of the West as a region. As they pondered the newly emerging distinctions between the East and the West, their emphasis focused on geographical characteristics. That was understandable since a sparsely settled area as yet had little population, an underdeveloped economy, and few cultural institutions. The geographical features loomed much larger than the cultural attributes of the inhabitants. Thus, although scholars such as Josiah Royce, John Wesley Powell, Ellsworth Huntington, Ellen Semple, Alfred P. Brigham, and Frederick Jackson Turner differed in their approaches to defining the West as a region, they all emphasized environmental conditions as a major determinant.

One of the earliest and most imaginative attempts to delineate Western regionalism was made by the philosopher and historian Josiah Royce. A native Californian who had been born in the first decade after the Gold Rush (in 1855), Royce reflected some nostalgia for the California of his youth when he wrote his analysis of *California* three decades later (in 1886). Keenly aware of German and English trends in contemporary philosophy, he was particularly impressed by the emphasis on community and its relation to nationalism in the works of Otto von Giercke in Germany, and Francis W. Maitland and James Pollock in England. Royce emphasized the need for "vigorous development of a highly organized provincial life to offset dead national conformity that tends to crush the individual." Unless such regional entities emerged, he feared that the nation "was in danger of becoming an incomprehensible monster, in whose presence the individual loses his right, his self-consciousness, and his dignity." Thus, he believed that the development of a sense of place, in geographical environs, was necessary to develop a sense of community. Royce concluded that California and the Far West in the 1880s had developed such a regional character. He analyzed this adaptation by the response of Californians to the geographical features of the state, to their social diversity, and to the economic realities with which they dealt. Royce feared that

76, on nineteenth-century and French geography; Billington, *Turner*, 209–12; Preston E. James, *A History of Geographical Ideas* (New York, 1972) provides an excellent general survey. Michael C. Steiner, "The Significance of Turner's Sectional Thesis," *Western Historical Quarterly* 10 (October 1979), 437–66; Fulmer Mood, "The Origin, Evolution, and Application of the Sectional Concept," in Merrill Jensen (ed.), *Regionalism in America* (Madison, 1951), 5–98.

the rapid growth of California might lead to the loss of this special sense and warned that "the time has come to emphasize with a new meaning and intensity the positive value, the absolute necessity . . . of a whole provincialism as a saving power" against the forces of constant mobility and alienation.[3]

Although he was a geologist, John Wesley Powell, director of the U.S. Geological Survey in the years from 1881 to 1894, had a keen sense about the history and ethnology of the West as a region. In a suggestive essay which he published in 1896, Powell identified the physiographic regions of the United States. While he did not draw precise boundaries for the West, he suggested various delineations. He believed that these were in constant flux, shifting in response to changing environmental as well as cultural conditions. But his depiction of the Columbia Plateau, the Basin Ranges, and the Pacific Mountains was one of the first serious attempts to suggest guidelines for a regional approach to the West. In fact, his study influenced many of his contemporaries. Among them was Frederick Jackson Turner, who accepted his classification as uncritically as he had the interpretations of the frontier by the superintendent of the census in 1890, Patrick Porter. As Turner wrote: "My work in American History is based on natural physiographic divisions outlined by Powell in his *Physiographic Regions of the United States*. I find it revolutionizes the study, and I hope sometime to work out a work along those lines." In the following year, Turner gave a lecture in which he said: "Let us imagine . . . that the United States were one great plain without varied geographical features. At once the fact would impress itself upon us that there was nevertheless a geographical element of profound importance. This society would be affected by the vast space open to

3. Josiah Royce, *Basic Writings*, edited by John J. McDermott (2 vols., Chicago, 1969), vol. 2, 1070, 1074, 1083–84; Richard W. Etulain, "Frontier, Region, and Myth: Changing Interpretations of Western American Culture," *Journal of American Culture* 3 (Summer 1980), 268–84. Royce noted in his *Provincialism* that he hoped for "the vigorous development of a highly organized provincial life to offset dead national conformity that tends to crush the individual." He feared the nation was "in danger of becoming an incomprehensible monster, in whose presence the individual loses his right, his self-consciousness, and his dignity." See Earl Pomeroy, "Josiah Royce: Historian in Quest of Community," *Pacific Historical Review* 40 (February 1971), 14.

its occupation."[4] Powell's influence was obviously pervasive and, through Turner, influenced the views of Western historians on regionalism to a considerable extent.

Neither Turner nor Powell was a geographical determinist, but there were others in their day who fell into that category, including Ellsworth Huntington, Alfred P. Brigham, and Ellen Churchill Semple. Huntington, a geographer at Yale from 1907 to 1915, gave pointed expression to his views in *Civilization and Climate* (1915). Turner was well aware of his position.[5] Brigham was a geography professor at Colgate University for thirty years after 1891. As one of the founders of the field of human geography in the United States, he did much to shape geographic thought in his lifetime, stressing the influence of the earth on man. His influence on historians was considerable because Albert Bushnell Hart, the editor of the American Nation Series, asked him to contribute the first volume in this widely respected publication to which Turner also gave his first book. Published in 1903 as *Geographic Influences in American History*, the study had great impact in its day, and delineated the West exclusively in geographic terms.[6] Even more explicit were the works of Ellen Churchill Semple. She had studied at the University of Leipzig and was one of Ratzel's leading disciples in the United States. Between 1906 and 1923, she lectured at the University of Chicago and wrote several influential books, including *American History and Its Geographic Conditions* (1903) and *Influences of Geographic Environment* (1911), in which she viewed the West as a product of its natural environment. And if she was not quite as strident, Katherine Coman of Wellesley College, in her book *Economic Beginnings of the Far West* (1911), directly linked economic development to geographic conditions.[7]

But it was Turner, of course, who focused more directly on the West as a distinct region. He was deeply influenced by Royce and

4. Frederick Jackson Turner, in Robert B. Block, "Frederick Jackson Turner and American Geography," *Annals of the Association of American Geographers* 70 (March 1980), 32; Billington, *Genesis of the Frontier Thesis*, 209; Steiner, "Turner's Sectional Thesis," *Western Historical Quarterly* 10, 454.

5. Ellsworth Huntington, *The Climatic Factor* (New York, 1914), and *Civilization and Climate* (New York, 1924).

6. Alfred P. Brigham, *Geographic Influences in American History* (Boston, 1903).

7. Ellen Churchill Semple, *American History and Its Geographic Conditions* (Boston, 1903), and *Influences of Geographic Environment* (New York, 1911); and Katherine Coman, *Economic Beginnings of the Far West* (2 vols., New York, 1911).

Powell, and by the work of the geographic determinists. He himself never took an extreme position because, as he admitted in 1908, "I haven't quite gotten sure of what I think myself on the degree of control of geographical factors." However, he read deeply in the works of Europeans like Ratzel and de la Blanche and was greatly impressed by the work of the eminent American geologist George Perkins Marsh, whose book *Man and Nature* he assigned in his American History courses. Turner utilized the emphasis on the geographical determinants on history to fashion his own ideas about the West as a region. In his desire to show the predominance of American conditions—rather than European influences stressed by many of his contemporaries—on the shaping of American civilization, the geographic factors obviously loomed large.[8]

Turner's interest in the West as a region (he used "section" and "region" interchangeably) developed gradually over a period of years. It is likely that his initial interest was stimulated by his influential college teacher William F. Allen, who alerted him to the importance of sections. In his courses, Allen used an outline he had prepared in 1876 entitled *History Topics for the Use of High Schools and Colleges,* which gave much attention to regional differences between New England and the Middle West. In addition to his reading, Turner in 1898 also enrolled in a seminar given by his famous University of Wisconsin colleague in geology, Charles Van Hise, on the physiography of the United States. In later years, Turner declared that "my interest in the section in American History was contemporaneous with my interest in the frontier." His own background in Portage, first a frontier and then part of a region, reinforced his academic interests, which only crystallized in his later years.[9] As he pondered the problem he hoped to facilitate closer relationships between historians and geographers. In 1907, he organized a session on geographical influences at the American Historical Association meeting in Madison, to which he invited Miss Semple. That intrepid geographer roundly scolded historians for ignoring geographical influences, which led to a biting

8. Frederick Jackson Turner to Claude Van Tyne, April 25, 1908, Turner Papers, Henry L. Huntington Library, San Marino, California, quoted in Block, "Turner and American Geography," *Annals of the Association of American Geographers* 70, 39; Steiner, "Turner's Sectional Thesis," *Western Historical Quarterly* 10, 452, 455.

9. On Allen, see Billington, *Turner,* 25–26, 49–50, 213, 215, 225; Billington, *Genesis of the Frontier Thesis,* 15–26, 213; quote in Steiner, "Turner's Sectional Thesis," *Western Historical Quarterly* 10, 440.

rebuttal by George Lincoln Burr of Cornell University, who dismissed her determinism. Miss Semple was quite blunt. "My experience is that historians as a rule do not know geography," she said. "They may know the natural features . . . in their field, but they are unable to interpret these in effect, because they are ignorant of the rest of the world." The session proved to be disillusioning for all concerned, including Turner, who was chair. Miss Semple had the final word when she wrote her friend, Alfred Brigham: "My experience at Madison . . . leads me to think that the historians represent a big field for propaganda. They are not an open-minded set of men. . . . Merely mention geographic factors in the Historical Association, and the fur flies." Henceforth, Turner would study geographic influences on his own, and he spent the next fifteen years accumulating more data on the subject.[10]

By the time of the First World War, contemporary international events were prodding Turner to develop his ideas on sectionalism further. As his biographer, Ray Allen Billington noted, at the turn of the century Turner believed that sectional forces such as rural discontent, urban unrest, and free silver were shaping national policy. By the time of World War I, Turner extended his vision to include the entire world and to view sectionalism as a guide for a new international order. Already in 1915, he began to speculate about a world organization that could transcend the nationalist loyalties of Europeans. He crystallized his thoughts in two essays which he penned in 1918. One was a twenty-three page manuscript entitled "Syllabus of Considerations on the Proposed League of Nations." The other was a seven-page memorandum, "International Political Parties in a Durable League of Nations," which he sent to President Wilson for possible use at the Versailles Peace Conference. He felt hurt when he did not receive a direct acknowledgment from the president, whom he had known for thirty years, but from his secretary. In both of these essays, Turner stressed the parallels between geographic sections in the United States

10. Quote in Block, "Turner and American Geography," Annals of the Association of American Geographers 70, 40–41; Frederick Jackson Turner, "Report on Conference on the Relation of Geography and History," Annual Report of the American Historical Association for 1907 (Washington, 1908), vol. 1, 46–47; for Semple's paper, see Ellen Churchill Semple, "Geographical Location as a Factor in History," Bulletin of the American Geographical Society 40 (1908), 65–81; on Burr see George Lincoln Burr, "The Place of Geography in the Teaching of History," New England History Teachers Association, Annual Report for 1907 (Boston, 1908), 1–13.

and the nations of Europe. He placed great emphasis on the influences that had held the sections together in the United States and presented them as a model for the world.[11]

At the same time, he developed his ideas on regionalism further in a series of lectures which he gave at the Lowell Institute in 1918. There, he outlined the concepts of sectionalism which he later presented in his book *The United States, 1830–1850.* "The frontier and section," he said, "lie at the foundation of what is distinctive in American history." The American experience could be understood only by studying sectional conflicts and their resolution through compromise, and war. Reflecting on his current thinking, he noted that "these relationships between sections are to the United States what international relations are to Europe; a section is in fact a denatured nation."[12]

Apart from the discussion about the League, other influences were leading Turner to refine his regional concepts between 1918 and 1920. The slow pace at which he was writing his Big Book was a constant embarrassment which he felt even more keenly as his retirement was approaching. Promulgation of his sectional thesis, on which he had been mulling for three decades, would lead him to retirement in a blaze of glory. Moreover, the visible decline of a sense of community in the United States as it was becoming an urban nation provided a further impetus for developing a theory of regionalism. Perhaps, as Royce had suggested, regionalism could cement the disruptive forces in American society.[13]

Ironically, however, most historians at the time were stressing nationalizing rather than provincial tendencies in American life. In contrast to the 1890s, Turner was now not as closely attuned to his contemporaries. Even the professional geographers—men like Isaiah

11. Billington, *Turner*, 209, 345–56; William Diamond, "American Sectionalism," *American Historical Review* 47, 545–51. See George T. Blakey, *Historians on the Home Front: American Propagandists for the Great War* (Lexington, 1970), for a detailed account.

12. James R. Mock and Cedric Larson, *Words that Won the War: The Story of the Committee on Public Information, 1917–1919* (Princeton, 1939), 158–86. Two of Turner's essays which reflected his global perspectives during these years include "Sections and Nation," *Yale Review* 12 (October 1922), 1–21, and "Geographical Sectionalism in American History," *Annals of the Association of American Geographers* 16 (June 1926), 85–93. See Billington, *Turner*, 374 for quote.

13. Billington, *Turner*, 379–85; Steiner, "Turner's Sectional Thesis," *Western Historical Quarterly* 10, 459–60.

Bowman and Carl O. Sauer—were rejecting regionalism as a geographic concept, and were instead emphasizing the impact of cultural rather than environmental influences in shaping regions.[14] The changed mood did not presage a favorable reception for Turner's sectional thesis.

That formulation he made in two stages. The first effort came in an article he wrote in 1922 for the *Yale Review*. Again, he referred to the contemporary international situation which he believed placed American sectionalism in a worldwide context. Although he felt that the differences between sections in the United States were not as great as between European countries, the comparisons were valid. "Like an elastic band the common national feeling and party ties draw sections together, but at the same time yield in some measure to sectional interests when these are gravely threatened." And he emphasized that "Congress was like a diplomatic assemblage, preserving the balance of power. . . . We in America are in reality a federation of sections rather than of states."[15]

The culmination of what he hoped was a lifetime of thought on the subject came in 1925 when Turner published "The Significance of the Section in American History" in the *Wisconsin Magazine of*

14. Block, "Turner and American Geography," *Annals of the Association of American Geographers* 70, 40–41; Turner's major critics included Isaiah Bowman, Andrew Clark, and Carl Sauer among geographers. After Turner's death, Bowman wrote to the editor of the *Geographical Review:* "Turner's ideas were curiously wanting in evidence from field studies that could easily have been made even in Wisconsin as well as in Montana, Texas, and Utah. He represents a type of historian who rests his case on documents and general impressions rather than a scientist who goes out for to see. If I had been asked to say whether my views were contrary to Turner's I should have said that they were not so contrary as *variant*." Bowman to Gladys M. Wrigley, March 6, 1944, quoted in chapter 7, "The Pioneer Fringe," in Geoffrey J. Martin, *The Life and Thought of Isaiah Bowman* (Hamden, Conn., 1980). Sauer declared that "Turner's . . . concept . . . is easy and wrong. If Turner had ever read Eduard Hahn or any account of culture history, he would hardly have fallen into this evolutionary error of a standard series of cultural stages." Sauer to Richard Shryock, November 27, 1940, Sauer Papers, quoted in Block, op. cit., 41; Clark stated that "the obvious implications of strong degrees of environmental influence, if not control, led the thesis to be embraced warmly by the geographers contemporary with its early twentieth-century heyday, and then, often almost as uncritically, rejected by latter-day geographers in a methodological revulsion against the naivete of a single factor causation." Andrew Hill Clark, *Acadia: The Geography of Early Nova Scotia to 1760* (Madison, 1968), 383. Billington ignored the negative reaction of the geographers but rather emphasized approval from Turner's students. Billington, *Turner*, 398. Such an emphasis can be deceptive.

15. Turner, "Sections and Nation," *Yale Review* 12, 380.

History. As the essay on the frontier had announced his entry into the historical profession, so this piece would frame his formal retirement. As in 1893, Turner delivered his remarks to a live audience, this one at the Wisconsin Historical Society. In accepting the invitation to deliver the principal address there in January 1925, Turner noted that "I have always tried to have what an astronomical friend of mine calls a 'bright idea' when I have addressed that organization. I should like to do something worthwhile." As his biographer, Billington, noted: "He did his best, but the result was a sad anti-climax." He presented "the usual history of the sectional conflicts of the nineteenth century, the usual predictions that sectional antagonisms would deepen as mobility lessened, the usual plea for government policies that would keep friction to a minimum. . . . Yet he had little to add to a story that was already well known. . . . The address . . . stirred none of the excitement of his frontier thesis. . . . Turner had little to add." Turner was deeply disappointed, but believed his critics to be wrong. "I am possessed with the idea that twenty years from now my Sections paper will travel along with my frontier as interpretations," he wrote to his friend A. M. Schlesinger, Sr., in May 1925. At the time, he was giving a course of seven lectures on the subject at the University of Wisconsin. "He was sure he would find eager students and faculty . . . but somehow his listeners failed to catch fire as they did when he talked of the frontier." As Augustus C. Krey, one of his former students, commented sadly: "His audience dwindled day by day; the spark was gone."[16]

Soon after the end of the First World War, the generation of Western historians who had emphasized the geographical determinants of regionalism saw a waning of their influence. The gradual disappearance of frontier conditions in the West was one factor in that trend. And while for a few years the controversy over the League of Nations had focused renewed attention on regions, the failure of the Senate to ratify the Treaty of Versailles led to waning interest in that issue. But the remarkable technological changes between 1890 and 1920 also changed the perspectives of a new generation of historians. Unlike their predecessors, they had not themselves experienced the

16. Frederick Jackson Turner, "The Significance of the Section in American History," *Wisconsin Magazine of History* 8 (March 1925), 255–80; Augustus C. Krey, "My Reminiscences of Frederick Jackson Turner," *Arizona and the West* 3 (Winter 1961), 381; Billington, *Turner,* 396–98.

transformation of frontier areas in their lifetime. Gone were the days when Ratzel and Huntington spoke with authority. Historical fashions had changed. Scholars now deemphasized the impact of physiographic factors and instead stressed the cultural determinants of regionalism.

Such an emphasis was partly moored in a recognition that American society in the 1920s was undergoing a period of especially rapid changes. The growth of population in urban areas was still accelerating; ethnic diversity was becoming increasingly visible in the West and East; life-styles were noticeably changing, underlining differences between country and city, and as a result many came to challenge the traditional values of the Protestant Ethic. World War I deepened disillusionment and doubts. The conflict also intensified feelings of nationalism and the resultant nativism of the 1920s. Such shocks led some Americans to feel a loss of community, alienation, or anomie.

These major currents in American life also provided the context for a strong regional movement in the United States during the 1920s, a movement paralleled in many European nations during the period. Regionalism and nationalism were, to a considerable extent, a reaction to the fading—or collapse—of traditional societies. In Europe this was dramatized by the collapse of empires; in the United States, by the gradual dominance of an urban civilization and the decline of the agrarian society fashioned in the nineteenth century. In literature, folklore, and art, regionalists were seeking new symbols of community to counter the waning influence of the old.

And in seeking to define the distinguishing features of the West as a region, most historians, social scientists, writers, and artists now came to emphasize cultural rather than geographical determinants. Many Western universities now became centers for regional cultural activities. At the University of Texas, folklorist J. Frank Dobie developed the folklore of the Southwest. At the University of Oklahoma, folklorist B. A. Botkin made that subject academically respectable. Mari Sandoz at the University of Nebraska uncovered the native lore of the Great Plains. In New Mexico, Santa Fe and Taos became major art and literary centers which celebrated the three major cultures of the Southwest—Indian, Hispanic, and Anglo. Important writers took the West as their theme—Wallace Stegner, Paul Horgan, Erna Fergusson, Oliver La Farge, John Steinbeck, William Saroyan, Dashiell Hammett, and Carey McWilliams. In the Pacific Northwest, Robert Cantwell, Richard Neuberger, and Stuart Holbrook began to write about the distinctive features of that area. Although the scope of these activities varied greatly, the common thread was a quest for regional and subregional identity in the midst of a rapidly industrializing society in which centralizing and nationalizing influences were prominent.[17]

Since a substantial segment of the movement for Western regionalism sprang from literary and artistic efforts, it was not surprising that historians of the period gave greater importance to cultural determinants of American life than their predecessors had done a decade earlier. Herbert Bolton, for example, wrote extensively about Spanish influences on the Borderlands. "The old Spanish Borderlands," he declared, "were the meeting place and fusing place of two streams of European civilization, one coming from the south, the other from the north. . . . Throughout these Hispanic regions now in Anglo-American hands . . . there are . . . marks of Spanish days on the southern border. We see them in social, religious, economic, and even in legal practices." Some of his students, such as Gilbert Garraghan and Colin B. Goodykoontz, followed his orientation by amplifying educational and religious determinants of Western history. One of the most prolific Western historians, LeRoy Hafen, stressed the role of technological developments in transportation in modifying the Western environment. "During the past century Western America has witnessed an interesting evolution in transportation methods," he declared. "The long reach from the ox-team to the motor car and airplane has not been made in a single bound. . . . Each adopted mode of travel brought man nearer his goal of speed and economy." Cultural historians were more openly critical of Turner's emphasis on wilderness environment. Percy Boynton of the University of Chicago acidly quoted Turner's statement that "the wilderness masters the colonist." He retorted that "to focus attention on this aspect of American life as recorded in literature, is to eliminate a major proportion of the literature."[18]

Historical geographers were also attacking the suppositions of geographical determinists. At the same time that Turner was putting the

17. A recent brief survey of the movement in the 1920s is in Richard M. Brown, "The New Regionalism in America, 1970–1981," in William G. Robbins, Robert Frank, and Richard E. Ross (eds.), *Regionalism and the Pacific Northwest* (Corvallis, 1983), 37–42. See also Carey McWilliams, *The New Regionalism in American Literature* (Seattle, 1930), 7–20, and Nash, *American West in Twentieth Century*, 116–34.

18. James F. Willard and Colin B. Goodykoontz (eds.), *The Trans-Mississippi West* (Boulder, 1930), 36; for Bolton, 43–63; for Garraghan, 65–86; for Goodykoontz, 103–21; for Hafen, 163–74; for Boynton, quote on 165.

finishing touches on his sectional hypothesis, rooted to some extent in geographical characteristics, Carl O. Sauer was beginning his life-long effort to emphasize the primacy of cultural variables in explaining American—and Western—landscapes. After his pathbreaking essay on "The Morphology of Landscape," in 1925, Sauer amplified his views on the West before the end of the decade. "The first hopes of a science of society have been abandoned," he wrote. "The great mechanistic concept of man, measurable, responsive, predictable, now impresses us as a deceptive analogy borrowed in vain from the physical sciences. . . . Even in the West we are dealing today largely with cultural landscapes, for the transforming hand of man is seen conspicuously in unsettled and uncultivated tracts as well as in those taken over by agriculture and town sites."[19]

A contemporary writer and historian, Carey McWilliams, aptly characterized the mood.

> The manner and the extent to which regionalism has coped . . . are obvious. By developing regional centers it encourages native expression; by recounting local legends it develops a useable past: it gives the artist a feeling of familiarity with his environment. It marks out the region as unique and invites rhapsody. . . . The art-ist comes to view his environment not as an indifferent and apa-thetic locality against which he must revolt and ultimately escape from, but as "the common mother, this beautiful and mystic earth."

McWilliams then tied the movement to what he perceived as con-temporary trends. "Regionalism rationalizes this desire for a sense of community," he wrote, "just as it does the desire to break with irrec-oncilable and conflicting traditions and the desire to live in a region where familiarity has allayed the fear of a stalking hostility in na-ture. . . . The new regionalists reveal a typical modern tendency in their attempt to escape from the tumultuous present into the glamorous past."[20]

One striking exception to the emphasis on the cultural dimensions of regionalism during this period came in the writings of Walter P. Webb, who espoused an unabashed environmentalism. But, then,

19. Sauer, in ibid., 267, 277; Sauer, *The Morphology of Landscape,* University of California Publications in Geography 2 (Berkeley, 1925), 19–53.
20. McWilliams, *The New Regionalism,* 35, 36.

Webb enjoyed his role as outsider and rebel. In *The Great Plains,* published in 1931, Webb clearly reiterated his theme. "The Great Plains environment . . . constituted a geographic unity whose influences have been so powerful as to put a characteristic mark on everything that survives within its borders. Particularly did it alter the American institutions and cultural complexes that came from a humid and timbered region." But, as Professor Richard Etulain has noted cogently, when Webb returned dejectedly from the University of Chicago without the desired doctorate, "a spirit of revenge seems to have motivated him to write a book that would defend his region . . . and prove his abilities as a scholar. *The Great Plains* was Webb's answer." Webb also shared the feelings of some Americans in the 1920s that the literary giants of the decade—Hemingway, Faulkner, Fitzgerald, and Sinclair Lewis—were too negative and despairing of their native land. "These Americans searched for a voice that would . . . reveal . . . and praise the struggles for existence in a pressure ridden environment. . . . He wished his book to be not only a satisfactory scholarly work but also a defense against those who . . . belittled his region."[21]

If the search for community was a common motivation of regionalists in the 1920s, it became an even more pronounced preoccupation in the succeeding decade. Not only historians, but folklorists, social scientists, social planners, and a wide range of federal, state, and local government officials became increasingly concerned with the formulation of theoretical concepts of regionalism and their application. In fact, some universities specialized in regional studies, including Vanderbilt, the Universities of North Carolina, Oklahoma, Nebraska, and New Mexico, where many academic disciplines were affected by the movement.[22]

Among the influences making for this increased interest, the Depression must rank high. As few other experiences, the Depression created a terrifying sense of insecurity in most Americans and prompted an intensified search for community, for roots, for an indigenous primal

21. Webb, in Willard and Goodykoontz (eds.), *Trans-Mississippi West,* 339; Webb, *The Great Plains,* preface; Etulain, "Frontier, Region, and Myth," *Journal of American Culture* 3, 275; Gregory M. Tobin, *The Making of a History: Walter Prescott Webb and "The Great Plains,"* (Austin, 1976). Walter Rundell, Jr., "Walter Prescott Webb: Product of Environment," *Arizona and the West* 5 (Spring 1963), 4–28.

22. Brown, "New Regionalism," in Robbins (ed.), *Regionalism,* 42–45; Michael C. Steiner, "Regionalism in the Great Depression," *Geographical Review* 73 (October 1983), 430–46.

America that seemed to have disappeared. The economic crisis also prompted increased popular interest in the past, in the hope that historical awareness might bring greater order and structure to the tumultuous and seemingly chaotic present. As John Dos Passos noted at the time: "A sense of continuity with generations gone before can stretch like a lifeline across the scary present."[23] Amid such turmoil, Americans yearned for a sense of place.

As students of American culture sharpened regional distinctions during this period, historians focused more narrowly on one aspect of this regionalism in the West—on its colonial status, due to its exploitation by the East. One of the most popular writers on this theme was the well-known journalist Bernard De Voto. In 1934, he charged that the West was nothing less than a plundered province. Such exploitation, he charged, had done much to define a Western identity. "Looted, betrayed, sold out, the West is a man whose history has been just a series of large-scale jokes," he wrote. The East had bled the natural resources of the West, making it "the one section of the country in which bankruptcy . . . has been the determining condition from the start." Yet De Voto retained a sense of optimism. "History has precedents," he declared. "The long pull may show . . . that the dispossessed have the laugh on their conquerors."[24]

De Voto's shrill cries were reinforced in 1937 by Walter P. Webb, in his *Divided We Stand*, an angry indictment of alleged Eastern exploitation of the West. Taking an extreme stand on regional differences, Webb declared that "I believe that there have developed in this country three fairly distinct cultures . . . each with its own mores, ways of life, culture complexes." Referring to North, South, and West, Webb charged that "back of the North's present might and behind its increasing control of . . . the West is its undisputed command of the mighty forces of the industrial production of America. . . . At the present time the North owns 80 or 90 per cent of the wealth of the United States. . . . The economic imperial control by the North over the . . . West . . . grew stronger as the political imperialism grew weaker." And one of his admirers, regionalist John Crowe Ransom,

---

23. Dos Passos quote in Steiner, "Depression," 434.
24. Bernard De Voto, "The West: A Plundered Province," *Harper's* 169 (August 1934), 355–64.

added that "we all know about the inequalities of the economic structure. . . . The North owns and operates the national economy; the
South and West work under its direction."[25]

Within a decade of W. P. Webb's complaint, other historians took
up the theme, sharpening the image of the West as a distinct region
shaped by political and economic rather than environmental forces.
That historians would become more conscious of colonialism was not
surprising since the United States after 1937 was becoming more
involved in foreign crises that were to lead to World War II. In that
conflict, the self-determination of nations and the dissolution of colonial empires was one major issue. One of the young historians who
explored the subject with reference to the West was Earl S. Pomeroy,
who undertook the first serious analysis of the territorial system and
its administration in the American empire. In that study, Pomeroy
emphasized a multiplicity of cultural influences, but he focused on the
importance of political institutions in giving form to the West as a
region. True, Pomeroy admitted, "the natural environment was more
proximate than the institutional." As for the territorial system, "it
may be that its chief significance is negative: being weak, it allowed
a freer play of other influences, personal, economic, physiographical,
spiritual."[26]

The colonial theme was also utilized by Wendell Berge, Assistant
U.S. Attorney General, in his *Economic Freedom for the West*. Writing
in 1945, he noted that "to the West, intelligent regionalism . . . means
not only a far greater degree of local economic autonomy; it means
the reconstitution of a point of view, the recapture of the spirit of
adventure in economic affairs. . . . A vital Western regionalism will
have as its premise the understanding that it is part of a joint enterprise
in which the country as a whole will lose if the West is held down."
Berge believed that wartime experiences had done much to stimulate
regional feelings. "A new kind of regionalism . . . has stirred nearly
every corner of the country. Regional abilities not previously recognized . . . were released during the years of the war. . . . This regionalism is no longer the result of accentuated differences but rather
a progressive desire . . . to develop the best possible qualities . . . of

25. Walter Prescott Webb, *Divided We Stand: The Crisis of a Frontierless Democracy*
(New York, 1937), 3, 4, 26, 30; John Crowe Ransom in *Saturday Review of Literature*
17 (December 18, 1937), 6–7.
26. Pomeroy, *Territories*, 94, 99, 107.

their environment in order to participate more effectively in the larger life of the nation."[27]

During the war, John Kinsey Howard wrote his Pulitzer Prize–winning book *Montana: High, Wide, and Handsome,* to protest the colonial exploitation of the West. He hoped that the West as a whole would have a brighter future than Montana had in the past. His prime goal for writing about Eastern exploitation of Montana was to demonstrate that its "unbalance in population will affect all America; and that is the reason for singling out a state whose economy seems most precarious in the hope that discussion of its experience may encourage sympathetic understanding of steps already taken to aid . . . balanced development. . . . The social problem . . . is to prevent the urban east from exploiting . . . the . . . west."[28]

A more aggressive stance was taken by A. G. Mezerick, a prolific journalist of the era. "Why, at this time, a book which stresses the divisions within our country?" he asked. "The internal stresses which were with us before the war are still with us, and more significantly, the war . . . was the instrument with which the corporate clique in the East strengthened its grip on the economic life of the South and West. There can be no internal harmony as long as Eastern corporate power enforces . . . centralized control of major industry, banking and distribution." But 1945 was a year of decision.

> Western America has a post-war plan. Simply stated, it is to wage war against the financial monopoly now held by the East. The goal is industrial self-determination. . . . The West is playing for a new empire . . . by utilizing Alaska and its alliance with the undeveloped Canadian Northwest, to become self-sufficient. . . . Then boldly it expects to ship finished products through the Panama Canal to undersell the East in the South and Southwest, and finally to hit the jackpot—the domination of the world's greatest market—Asia. It will be a breathtaking fight that may change the pattern of our economy.[29]

Many of these arguments against colonialism were crystallized further by De Voto at the end of the war. "New Deal measures, war

27. Berge, *Economic Freedom,* 16.

28. Joseph Kinsey Howard, *Montana: High, Wide, and Handsome* (New Haven, 1943), 6, 7.

29. A. G. Mezerick, *The Revolt of the South and West* (New York, 1946), ix, xiv, 290.

installations, and war industries have given the West a far greater and more widely distributed prosperity than it has ever had before," he wrote in 1946. "Moreover, during the war a fundamental revolution took place; power and industrial developments in the West have made a structural change in the national economy." De Voto felt that the freeing of the West from colonial status was a moment awaited by many Westerners. "The West sees all this in terms of its historical handicaps; colonial economic status and absentee control. The ancient Western dream of an advanced industrial economy . . . is brighter than it has ever been before. For the first time there are actual rather than phantasmal reasons for believing that the dream can be realized."[30]

Between 1920 and 1945 historians and other students of the West tended to eschew geographical determinism and instead emphasized the importance of cultural determinants in shaping regional characteristics of the West. The Great Depression, and also the Second World War, encouraged historians and other writers to view the West from a regional perspective. In a sense, they were reflecting the feelings of millions of Americans who, when beset by the tribulations of depression and war, sought solace from the turbulent and rapidly changing present in a clearer appreciation of a supposedly more stable past. And as the disruptions of this period induced much greater mobility among Americans, their search for stability, community, and a sense of identity increased in intensity. The concept of region helped to provide for these psychic needs. And as skilled writers for large popular audiences, De Voto and Webb helped to satisfy such yearnings. As in the case of Turner, they were not strictly original, but reflected widely held beliefs of their contemporaries. The sharpened consciousness of the West as a region also led scholars to develop the subtheme of colonialism, of viewing the region as an exploited possession of the older East. The time was ripe for the resurgence of such a perspective, since Americans after 1937 gave their support to the dissolution of colonial empires around the world. The theme of Western colonialism thus seemed particularly relevant. With the end of World War II and the emergence of Third World nations, contemporary events overtook this outlook, however, as historians soon reflected the newer trends of the 1950s.

30. Bernard De Voto, "The Anxious West," *Harper's* 193 (December 1946), 489, 490.

Certainly, the years between 1945 and 1960 ushered in a new era as Depression America became a memory and Americans entered upon a period of unprecedented affluence. If anomie continued to be a problem for many people in the United States, as David Riesman reminded them in 1950, nevertheless the search for a sense of community as embodied in Western regionalism was not as intense during these years of prosperity as it had been in times of economic crisis. The emergence of the United States as a superpower also brought more intensified global perspectives to most Americans, and certainly affected those who viewed the West as an underdeveloped or colonial region. The Second World War had also inaugurated the G.I. Revolution, the enormous expansion of enrollments in higher education which led to an unprecedented expansion of all professions, including history. Now joining the historical guild were younger scholars who brought new perspectives, not only from their own experiences in the war but from a much wider range of ethnic and cultural backgrounds than any previous generation. As a consequence, interpretations in Western history were bound to be affected by this as well as by other contemporary trends.[31]

That was also to be true of the analysis of the West as a region. Yet it must be said that interest in the West as a region flagged, when compared to earlier periods. Most students of the West during these years centered their attention on the frontier, or on the West as myth. Perhaps this was because the concept of the West as a region had never really caught fire or captured the imagination of scholars and nonscholars the way the frontier did in the 1890s. Turner himself had been deeply disappointed by the reception he received in 1925 in regard to his sectional thesis, although he did not lose faith in it. But his prognosis at that time—that it would take at least twenty years for it to be appreciated—was not fulfilled. The concept of the regional West remained vague and difficult to define. Whatever the reasons for its lack of popularity, historians remained much less impressed by it than social scientists. Sociologists, anthropologists, and geographers were among the most active between 1945 and 1960, along with some

31. Gerald D. Nash, *The American West Transformed: The Impact of the Second World War* (Bloomington, 1985), 212–16; David Riesman, *The Lonely Crowd* (New York, 1950). On changes in the historical profession, see Novick, *That Noble Dream*, 281–360.

economists, in seeking a more precise delineation of Western regionalism. Those historians who did write about the West as region continued the earlier trend in deemphasizing environmental influences.
Instead, they focused increasingly on cultural factors, political, economic, or ecological forces.

Perhaps the most ambitious effort to analyze the West as a region
which stressed cultural perspectives came out of a conference on American regionalism sponsored by the University of Wisconsin in 1949.
The participants included scholars from a wide range of disciplines
who sought to crystallize much of the work in the field over the past
two decades. Fulmer Mood contributed a brilliant essay on the evolution of the sectional concept from 1750 to 1900, while Vernon
Carstensen briefly traced its development to 1950. Merrill Jensen, the
editor of the book that emerged from this symposium, was quite candid
about his objectives. "The vast number of books and articles dealing
with regional questions have often lacked a depth of perspective," he
declared, "and hence a significance they might otherwise have had."
In analyzing the reasons for this trend, Jensen noted that "it was plain
that the concept of 'region' meant different things to different academic
disciplines, to administrators of state and federal governments. . . .
The nature of a 'region' varies with the needs, purposes, and standards
of those using the concept." The eminent regional sociologist Rupert
Vance perhaps provided the most concise definition of a region when
he said that a "region [is] a unit of areal and cultural differentiation.
Many definitions of the region reinforce each other."[32]

Vance's focus on regions as a product of cultural development was
reflected by various Western historians of the period. Among these
was Howard Lamar, who utilized the theme of the West as a colonial
region shaped by the political institutions of the United States Territorial system. In a study of Dakota Territory, Lamar worked out the
implications of his analysis. "It is one of the themes of this study," he
wrote, "that government, both federal and local, was a highly important factor in making the settlement of Dakota possible; therefore
. . . the settler's concept and use of government must be closely examined."[33]

32. Jensen (ed.), *Regionalism in America*, vii, 3, 5–118, 119–42.
33. Howard Lamar, *Dakota Territory, 1861–1889: A Study of Frontier Politics* (New
Haven, 1956), ix.

Leonard J. Arrington, on the other hand, focused on the importance of economic and religious influences in the shaping of the Utah region. Like Lamar, he was deeply impressed by the contemporary importance of government in shaping newly developed areas.

> At a time when government is exercising a potent influence in molding the economy of all of us, and when "advanced" countries are sending billions of dollars, and some of their finest experts, to underdeveloped areas to stimulate economic growth and expansion, it does not seem out of place to discuss the role of the Church of Jesus Christ of Latter-Day Saints in developing the economy of the Mountain West. While the general recipe for development has long been recognized to include systematic planning, organized cooperation, patient sacrifice of consumption in favor of investment . . . the economic institutions and policies of the Church . . . have never been described in detail. The economic development of Mormon Country is of particular significance for four reasons. 1) It illustrates the problems associated with the settlement and growth of an isolated, mountainous, and semi-arid region. 2) It dramatizes the strengths and weaknesses of attempting a comprehensive development program without outside capital. 3) It represents one of the few regional economies in modern history founded for a religious purpose. 4) It offers an interesting case study of American pioneering experience, generally.

Reflecting on contemporary public policies, Arrington sought to "suggest the positive role which a government, whether secular or theocratic . . . can play in the building of a commonwealth."

Arrington also believed that the Mormon experience was relevant to the underdeveloped regions of the world in the 1950s. "The Mormons demonstrated the effectiveness of central planning and voluntary cooperation," he wrote,

> in developing a semi-arid region. As the waste involved in the short-sighted, unplanned and ruthless exploitation of other Western frontiers became more apparent, the Mormon pattern became increasingly appreciated, became recognized as prophetic of the pattern which the entire West would ultimately have to adopt. By government decree and otherwise, this pattern is being followed in many parts of the world, at times with conscious knowledge of the Mormon antecedent. The design of the Kingdom, once despised as

backward, is now part of the heritage which Americans are passing on to governments and peoples around the world.[34]

A still broader approach was developed by James C. Malin, who emphasized broad ecological factors which he believed were essential to the growth of the West as a region. Borrowing heavily from studies by contemporary natural and social scientists, he drew upon a wide range of disciplines. In addition, Malin was reacting strongly to the New Deal programs of the 1933 to 1945 period, for he vigorously opposed central planning by the federal government and the general expansion of all kinds of governmental programs. Throughout his life, he was consistent in opposing New Deal liberals who claimed that such programs were necessary because of previous unwise policies by private enterprise. To him, such rationalizations were based on assumptions about the dominance of environmental influences which he rejected because they were unproven.[35]

In a series of books and essays between 1945 and 1960, Malin outlined his case for an ecological interpretation of the West as a region. Malin argued that historians needed to consider not only the relation of the Western economic system to the environment, but to the total ecosystem of the region—including the complex cycles relating human beings to climates, soils, and wildlife. Immersed in natural and physical sciences as well as ecological history of the Kansas grasslands, Malin included "all the elements that enter into a situation as historical activity, especially facts and thoughts formulated by the sciences in areas not traditionally recognized by historians. . . . Ecology deals with groups or assemblages of living organisms in all their relations, living together, the differences between plant, animal, and human ecology or history being primarily a matter of emphasis." Malin thus developed a broad and unified conception of the West as a region in which humans—and their cultural attributes—were the central factor. As he viewed the regional history of the Great Plains and the adaptation of agriculture there by individuals with a European-forest culture background, he found an explanation for their very slow adjustment to the treeless region. Where they succeeded, he concluded, it was only because of individual ingenuity. The human mind was the

34. Leonard J. Arrington, *Great Basin Kingdom: An Economic History of the Latter-day Saints, 1830–1900* (Cambridge, Mass., 1958), vii, 411, 412.

35. See introduction by Swierenga (ed.), *Malin*, xiii–xxix, 87–90, 111, and quotation on 106.

cardinal factor in the process. While the environment set certain limits, people could adapt to it in a myriad of ways. With a critical jab at Turner, Malin wrote that "historians and geographers placed too much emphasis . . . upon space and not enough on people in time, and in the capacity of man to unfold the potentialities of the mind in the discovery of new properties of the earth."[36] The process of adaptation was not finite, but infinite.

If historians like Malin stressed the importance of cultural determinants in shaping the West as a region during these years, social scientists pursued that theme even more rigorously. This was a time when many Americans believed that they had the restructuring of their own nation—and the world—securely in their grasp. Economists, anthropologists, and geographers in the 1950s, often stimulated by American regional development programs overseas, developed new theories and techniques which they applied fruitfully to the American West. Their work was to have an increasing impact on historians.

Economists, in particular, developed a special interest in the West as a region because between 1945 and 1960 economic growth and development became the major focus of their discipline. That emphasis was stimulated not only by the enormous expansion of the American economy during these years, but also by American-aid programs overseas. The Marshall Plan and the Point Four efforts by the Truman administration were only among the most prominent. The Committee for Economic Development—a private research and public policy organization—created a Special Area Development Committee to pursue such specialized studies. A new research institution, Resources for the Future, sponsored a massive study of regionalism, with obvious implications for the West. And the growing number of economists with special interests in regions organized the Regional Science Association. Its journal, *Regional Science,* provided an important forum for economists, demographers, and sociological theorists whose interests focused on regional growth and development throughout the world, but also with some reference to the West.[37]

36. James C. Malin, "Geographical–Space Concept: Anglo-American New-Land Version," in *The Contriving Brain and the Skillful Hand* (Lawrence, 1955), 338–436. See also Malin, "The Grassland of North America: Its Occupance and the Challenge of Continuous Reappraisals," in Swierenga (ed.), *Malin*, 3–20.

37. Harvey Perloff et al., *Regions, Resources, and Economic Growth* (Baltimore, 1960), and Perloff, *How a Region Grows* (New York, 1963), a shorter, popular version.

Not surprisingly, in 1956 the Economic History Association devoted its annual program to the American West as an underdeveloped
region, America's own Third World. The scholars who presented papers there concerned themselves with aspects of Western regionalism
which previous Western historians had hardly touched. Vernon Fowke,
a Canadian historian, compared United States and Canadian economic growth in their respective Wests. While he found many similarities, he concluded that different cultural values as well as the
absence of sectionalism in Canada differentiated their respective patterns of development.[38]

The most comprehensive interpretation of Western regionalism
came from Douglass North, an economist who reflected many of the
international perspectives of Americans during this period, when the
United States was at its height as a world power. Rather than finding
the dynamics for Western expansion in domestic influences, he found
the most vital causes to exist overseas. Using abstract economic theories, he argued that the wealth of resources in the West did attract
capital and labor, but that these could not have developed the region
without foreign capital. It was such investments that made transportation possible to provide crucial access to markets and a concentration
on export staples. It was this combination that provided the spark for
economic growth of the West from the colonial era to 1860. Thus, it
was cultural determinants such as international mobility of capital, a
growing European demand for American products, and the transfer of
European technology to the New World which boosted Western economic growth. Such an analysis did not explicitly reject the Turner
Thesis, but nevertheless focused on international economic conditions
and European cultural values, rather than conditions in North America, as the dominant themes in Western regional development.[39]

Not all economic historians fully agreed with North. Among them,
Douglas Dowd argued that comparison of the West with Third World
nations was somewhat strained. Reflecting the value that Americans

38. Fowke, "National Policy," *Journal of Economic History* 16, 461.

39. North, "International Capital Flows," in ibid. 16, 493–505; North, "Location
Theory and Regional Economic Growth," *Journal of Political Economy* 63 (June 1955),
243–58; and James N. Tattersall, "The Turner Thesis in the Light of Recent Research
in Economic History," Western Economic History Association, *Proceedings*, 1958 (Pullman, 1959), 46–51.

placed on change, the West underwent a constant stream of trans-
formations in its development, including a series of booms, in contrast
to Third World nations, which often languished with static economies
over the course of centuries.[40]

Think-tanks like Resources for the Future made their own efforts
to identify regional characteristics of the West. From the perspective
of its theoreticians, the West was comprised of four subregions, including the Mountain states, the Plains, the Southwest, and the Pacific
Coast. Within those divisions, economists like Harvey Perloff identified indicators of growth, and then applied statistical analysis to
variables such as population, personal income, location of industries,
exports, and other internal determinants. In many ways, the Resources
group was continuing the regional studies that had captured the imagination of economists and planners during the New Deal, when the
National Resources Planning Board had hired a staff of Keynesian
economists and specialists in location theory to chart plans for the
West's (and other regions') future. In the 1950s the Resources economists were developing that tradition further, with the aid of computers and a new breed of theories. Their studies concluded that
investment in human resources, natural resources, and in capital fa-
cilities were the keys to active growth. These factors were obviously
determined by cultural values. Although the studies by Resources for
the Future were aimed largely at policymakers inside and outside government, they contributed new perspectives to an understanding of
Western economic growth.[41]

Meanwhile, anthropologists were also developing a sharper regional image of the West, one emphasizing cultural determinants.
Their approach was circuitous rather than direct. Some were engaged
in the study of Indian cultures in the West, and were increasingly
conscious of cultural pluralism west of the Mississippi River. Others
were involved in community analysis. Thus, building on the work of
the Lynds in the 1930s and Stouffer in the 1940s, Conrad Arensberg
focused intensively in the 1950s on identifying regional characteristics
of American communities. Similarly, Evon Vogt extended his studies
of Zuni culture to non-Indian communities by analyzing a Mormon
community in New Mexico through intense cultural analysis. Both

40. Dowd, "Comparative Analysis," *Journal of Economic History* 16, 558–74.
41. Perloff, *Regions, Resources, and Economic Growth,* passim.

Arensberg and Vogt concluded that cultural traditions and values were the most important variable in the shaping of distinctive regional communities in the West. Their studies also convinced them that cultural traits were often heavily influenced by historical circumstances in formulating distinctive regional patterns. Cultural inheritance and value systems, these anthropologists concluded, were the key factors in shaping the West as a region.[42]

Anthropologists like Arensberg and Vogt—and others such as Alfred L. Kroeber, Clyde Kluckhohn, and Robin Williams—had a direct influence on various historians of the West who attempted to integrate their findings into historical accounts. Thus, Allan Bogue's analysis of the social theories of Western pioneers and their views toward community drew heavily on the contemporary literature in anthropology and social psychology. Similarly, Robert Berkhofer revealed his absorption in cultural anthropology in his study of Indian–white relations. In attacking environmentalism, Berkhofer charged that Turner had been too heavily influenced by Spencerian doctrines, and that he had accepted uncritically Darwin's emphasis on society as an organism. That led Turner to relate American space—the physiographic regions—to what he perceived as social organisms. But by the 1960s, Berkhofer believed, social scientists had demonstrated clearly that cultural factors were far more important than environmental conditions in shaping societies, their social values, and their institutions. Resources, Berkhofer explained, are what a society wishes to exploit. Their value is not fixed, but culturally determined. The dominant factors shaping the West as a region were cultural, and included nationality, class, and historical heritage.[43] Geographical conditions might have been a limiting factor, but certainly they were not determining.

Professional geographers joined the chorus of social scientists who were emphasizing the significance of cultural as compared to environmental influences. The intellectual godfather of the cultural approach to Western regionalism was Carl O. Sauer, for many years a professor

42. Conrad M. Arensberg, "American Communities," *American Anthropologist* 57 (December 1955), 1143–62. Evon Vogt in ibid., 1163–73, and *Modern Homesteaders: The Life of a Twentieth Century Frontier Community* (Cambridge, Mass., 1955).

43. Alan G. Bogue, "Social Theory and the Pioneer," *Agricultural History* 34 (January 1960), 21–34; Robert F. Berkhofer, Jr., *Salvation and the Savage: An Analysis of Protestant Missions and American Indian Response, 1787–1862* (Lexington, 1965), and "Space, Time, Culture, and the New Frontier," *Agricultural History* 38 (January 1964), 21–30.

at the University of California in Berkeley who became a dominant figure in the field between 1945 and 1960. At Berkeley, he also worked closely with his colleagues, particularly Kroeber in anthropology, Herbert Bolton in history, and also Robert Lowie in anthropology. "One has not fully understood the nature of an area," he wrote, "until one has learned to see it as an organic unit, to comprehend land and life in terms of each other."[44] That was why he felt that regional geography was not fully developed in the United States during much of his lifetime (1889–1975).

Like many geographers, Sauer's views were also shaped by his perceptions of contemporary trends. He became increasingly pessimistic about the future by 1960 as he witnessed the growth of bureaucratic, centralized states, whether capitalist or noncapitalist, which he viewed as major threats to human, pluralistic societies. State power combined with technological skills and materialistic values of twentieth-century industrial states resulted in the reduction of both cultural and natural diversity. As he wrote to a friend in 1948:

> The economists and the geographers ought to be doing some long, long thinking about changes that are under way in the draught on resources and their distribution and *control.* And about the growth of populations. There's going to be a bitter harvest of dead sea fruit coming out of the sowing of our whole modern philosophy of materialism and its god, the all-powerful State. It's interesting to live in an apocalyptic time, but discouraging when the signs are wanting that register the approach of the redemption.

He feared the decline of an agriculturally diverse rural society and the rise of a culturally more homogeneous industrial urban civilization that destroyed cultural diversity through the destruction of local communities. Given his orientation, he feared social activists of the liberal stripe who advocated planned communities and regional development. Cohesion in communities, he believed, would come about best through the diversity of their members brought together by local customs and tradition.[45]

The postwar era thus witnessed efforts by social scientists and historians to develop more precise criteria for the understanding of

44. Sauer, following Bluntschli in *Morphology,* 26.

45. Sauer, "Morphology," 45; J. Nicholas Entriken, "Carl O. Sauer, Philosopher in Spite of Himself," *Geographical Review* 66 (October 1984), 387–408, quotation on 393; James J. Parsons, "Carl Ortwin Sauer," ibid. 58 (January 1976), 83–89.

the West as a region. The years between 1945 and 1960 reflected a declining interest in the West as region when compared to the previous period (1920–1945). To a considerable extent, students of the West transformed their emphasis—from concentrating on environmental forces to a focus on the cultural determinants of Western history in a national as well as an international context. Social scientists were more active in these endeavors than historians. In fact, the economists, anthropologists, and geographers provided the conceptual tools and methodologies which historians of the next generation would readily adopt and integrate into their own studies. If the period was not notable for a large volume of books and articles on Western regionalism, it was distinctive in serving as an era of gestation. It was germinating a flood of new studies based on the social sciences, which were to pour from the pens, typewriters, and computers of students of the West from 1960 to 1990.

If not all historians would agree with the contemporary critic, William O'Neill, that in the 1960s the United States fell apart, yet few could deny that the decade saw the emergence of new perspectives that would affect that generation for the next three decades. To some degree, the changing views were a result of well-known demographic trends which saw the coming of age of the post–World War II baby-boom generation. This group had been too young to experience the Great Depression. Rather, they were the children of the affluent society, confident of their own abilities, of their righteousness. They were ready to undo many of the world's wrongs, whether poverty, war, sexism, or social and racial discrimination. Moreover, having been born into an age stressing instant gratification, they were impatient and sought perfection here and now. Such tendencies affected many aspects of American life, and also left a deep impact on the nation's professions.[46]

Historians of the West as a region were also influenced by these profound cultural and psychological changes and reflected them in the new approaches they developed. Their major emphasis in the next thirty years came to be on cultural rather than environmental determinants of the West. Moreover, not unlike previous historians, they tended to be present-minded. In reading their contemporary problems

46. William O'Neill, *Coming Apart: The United States in the* 1960s (Chicago, 1971).

into past Western history, they displayed a profound negativism and, at times, pessimism about the region's (and America's) past. Their analysis was highly critical. While students of the West between 1890 and 1960 had largely stressed the positive role of the West in the development of the nation, this generation focused mainly on what they perceived as the negative or destructive impact of the West on the nation's heritage. Although nurtured by unprecedented financial support in their educational development and research grants not available to previous generations of academics, they found little in the West's past that was right, but saw a great deal of what they considered wrong. With their questioning of the values and the assumptions of the past generation of historians, they raised new issues and interpretations. In addition, they tended to eschew broad theories or interpretations, and instead focused more narrowly on highly specialized topics analyzed in depth. They distrusted the sweeping generalizations of historians like Turner, Webb, and the regionalists of the 1930s and 1940s, and were drawn to write about the popular issues of their own day, such as ethnic minorities, women, blacks, Native Americans, Hispanics, and cultural pluralism. The impact of environmental influences on the West received minimal attention until in the 1980s a new wave of environmental historians renewed emphasis on this theme, although in a cultural or ideological context.

But historians were not alone in developing the regional history of the West during these years, for social scientists now devoted considerable attention to the subject. Geographers, political scientists, anthropologists, and sociologists made significant contributions to the development of concepts which viewed the West as a region. Not only did they sharpen concepts that defined regionalism, but they revealed complexities that had escaped earlier generations. That stimulated historians to write about the region, using social science concepts and methods. Both social scientists and historians stressed the primacy of cultural factors in the shaping of the West, particularly those that reflected the great public issues of their day. These included ethnic diversity, the role of women, and the place of Indians, blacks, and Hispanics in the West. The overwhelming number of these studies tended to be highly specialized rather than broad and often emphasized in-depth analyses. Thus, while the literature concerning Western regionalism was large, it tended to be scattered in a great many different directions, rather than focusing on a few major themes.

Geographers were among the most active in seeking to define Western regionalism in a cultural context. Among those who took the cultural emphasis of Sauer to its extreme was Raymond Gastil, who developed what amounted to cultural determinism—not unlike the geographical determinism of Ellsworth Huntington several generations before in its stridency. Gastil was very much a child of the 1960s, both in his outlook and in his negativism concerning American society. In explaining his motivation he noted, "This is an age of reevaluation, of testing, of trying to get a feel for the balance of good and evil in our society. . . ." Writing in 1975, he declared that "although there always have been problems, we wonder why the wealthiest and most powerful nation in the world still has the injustice, poverty, violence, and ugliness that it does." Like many of his generation, his prime purpose was "to change the course of American society."[47]

In pursuit of that aim, Gastil declared flatly that physical features of a landscape had virtually no influence at all in shaping human communities. In his view, it was mainly the cultural environment that determined the nature of regions and their unique characteristics. A region, Gastil proclaimed, is a place that exhibited cultural homogeneity. Historical experience revealed that different people living in the same environment usually made very different uses of it, thus proving that the cultural dimension was the dominant factor in the development of landscapes. He claimed, moreover, that the culture of first, initial settlers left a particularly deep imprint on a region. Reflecting the antiestablishment attitude of his generation, he charged that in the United States this gave elite groups in business, education, religion, and politics a special advantage in determining the cultural characteristics of the American West while the masses of people in that area were powerless. The other regions in the nation were similarly shaped by the cultural values of the first settlers. "The cultural traits developed by these people in the formative period," Gastil declared, "and secondarily by variations in the cultures of peoples that dominated later settlements," set regional patterns. "Regions will be formed where there are large areas of relative homogeneity in these factors and regional borders will be placed, when possible, where there are important discontinuities."[48]

47. Raymond Gastil, *Cultural Regions of the United States* (Seattle, 1975), 3, 5.
48. Ibid., 27.

Considerably less extreme than Gastil in developing concepts to identify the West as a cultural region was Wilbur Zelinsky, a prominent cultural geographer. In a book about the cultural geography of the United States, published in 1972, he delineated five regions, based on cultural traits such as religion, ethnicity, foods, housing, and language. Like Gastil, he concluded that the first group of settlers in an area had the greatest impact in grafting a regional culture. But, less doctrinaire, he concluded that the interactions between settlers and their physical habitat created the dynamics of cultural change.[49]

As Zelinsky developed his ideas further in succeeding years, he came to stress not only cultural but also psychological determinants of a regional identity. These he characterized as vernacular regions. To Zelinsky, a region was what masses of people perceived it to be. In that emphasis, Zelinsky was reflecting a tendency of social scientists of his generation to focus not so much on elites but on large groups, or masses, of the population. In a stimulating essay published in 1980, he noted that a region is "the product of the spatial perception of average people." Interest in regional, ethnic, and historical questions had been increasing throughout the world since 1960, he declared. That was because a region represented a shared, spontaneous image of territorial reality, local or not local, hovering in the minds of the untutored. Although he continued to emphasize the importance of cultural influences on regions such as the West, increasingly his emphasis shifted to include the importance of perceptions by common people which were rooted in the realm of folk culture.

The vernacular region which Zelinsky described had deep roots in the past, and in the years from 1960 to 1980. He noted that popular regions were recognized in eighteenth- and nineteenth-century Europe, where folk culture was a potent social and psychological phenomenon. It was reflected not only in territorial boundaries but in administrative areas—in Russia, Germany, France, Spain, and England. The United States had a different experience, however. It developed a much more volatile and unstable society, characterized by migration and movement. But as the United States became of age in the twentieth century, Americans became more conscious of their rootlessness and deliberately set out to find roots. As they became

49. Wilbur Zelinsky, *The Cultural Geography of the United States* (Englewood Cliffs, 1973).

aware of the pressures for nationalization and standardization of culture—particularly with the rise of the mass media—after 1950 a grassroots regionalism began to assert itself. Such a search for social and territorial identity was often connected to a resurrected ethnic or racial heritage. The movement was prominent in the American West, but also manifested itself in Canada, Great Britain, France, Yugoslavia, Belgium, Spain, and the Soviet Union. In the American West it was reflected in the emergence of black, Chicano, Hawaiian, and Native American nationalism. These led to the emergence of distinctive regions after 1950, reflecting popular perceptions of ethnicity. Zelinsky suggested that they were a result of spatial sorting of special interests. Such a quest resulted in new regional journals, regional museums, festivals, and a growing interest in folklore and nostalgia, not to speak of historic-preservation movements. Zelinsky believed that the perceptual and psychological studies of geographers in the 1970s were a direct response to this newly emerging need.[50]

The cultural dimension of Western regionalism was popularized for a wide audience in 1981 by Joel Garreau, a journalist who published his widely acclaimed *Nine Nations of North America* at that time. Traveling widely throughout the United States, Garreau found his sources not so much in manuscript collections or archives, but in scores of interviews with people in all walks of life and in contemporary newspapers and magazines. From this evidence he concluded, in somewhat bombastic style, that cultural traits—far more than physical features or economic realities and historical experiences—defined regions in the United States such as the West. Much like the professional cultural geographers of his day, Garreau concluded that the attitudes of residents in particular areas determined definitions of a region. No wonder that professional geographers accorded his book a cordial reception since his views coincided so closely with their own. The nine nations that Garreau perceived were Mexamerica, embracing the Southwest and Baja California; Ecotopia, the Pacific Coast, stretching

50. Wilbur Zelinsky, "North America's Vernacular Regions," *Annals of the Association of American Geographers* 70 (March 1980), 1, 2; Zelinsky, "Personality and Self-Discovery: The Future of Social Geography of the United States," in Ronald Abler et al. (eds.), *Human Geography in a Shrinking World* (North Scituate, Mass., 1975), 108–21. See also Harold R. Isaacs, *Idols of the Tribe: Group Identity and Political Change* (New York, 1975).

from Alaska south to San Francisco; the Empty Quarter, which included much of western Canada, Idaho, Nevada, Utah, and northern Colorado; and the Breadbasket, stretching from the Great Lakes westward across Canada and much of the Great Plains. The other areas he discerned were outside traditional Western areas, and included Dixie—the South—New England; Quebec; the Foundry—the Middle Atlantic and Middle West east of Chicago—and the Caribbean Islands. "Whatever our political maps may say," Garreau wrote, "our continent is not divided into fifty states and three countries. What we really are is The Nine Nations of North America."[51]

Although more traditional geographers were not quite prepared to place such great weight on the psychological and cultural manifestations of regionalism, yet they too emphasized the important role of cultural influences in shaping environmental adaptation. The most distinguished representative of this group was Donald Meinig, who elaborated a comprehensive interpretation of the whole sweep of Western history. The author of outstanding studies of the Great Plains in the 1950s and of the Columbia River Basin a decade later, he integrated these specialized studies into his broader theory.[52]

In dealing with the whole region of the West, Meinig argued in 1970 that, indeed, there was not one West, but many Wests. From his perspective, the West had been fashioned by four major influences. These included the size and the quality of the population, its mobility—or circulation—political areas, and cultural influences. The distinctive features of the West could be recognized according to these variables, although Meinig also underscored a fifth characteristic—already stressed by Zelinsky—namely popular conceptions of what constitutes a region. A region was what masses of people perceive it to be. It was a mental image, a perception in the minds of millions of individuals inside or outside a particular area.

According to Meinig, four stages characterized Western regional development. The first was a nuclear one and came with the initial settlement by Europeans from the sixteenth to the nineteenth centuries. That was followed by a second stage which saw the formation of the West as a true region. As cultural clusters of various settlers

51. Joel Garreau, *The Nine Nations of North America* (Boston, 1981).
52. Donald W. Meinig, *The Great Columbia Plain: A Historical Geography, 1805–1910* (Seattle, 1968), and *Southwest: Three Peoples in Geographical Change, 1600–1970* (New York, 1971).

evolved in this same period, they formed subregions such as Mormon Utah, Hispano New Mexico, the Oregon country, northern California, southern California, and others throughout the trans-Mississippi West. Political boundaries and institutions further helped to define regional character during these years. The third stage was the regional–national stage from 1890 to 1960. During these years, agricultural settlement slowed, except where it was stimulated by irrigation development and large federal water-diversion projects. But the most important development in the West during this phase was the concentration of population in towns and cities. Urbanization was the major force, leading, in turn, to much greater ethnic, racial, and cultural diversity.

The fourth stage was a metropolitan–national stage, extending from 1960 to 1990 and beyond. This was characterized by the growth of huge metropolitan clusters and megalopolises such as Los Angeles, the San Francisco Bay area, and the Seattle–Puget Sound region. New metropolitan areas also arose, such as Phoenix, Tucson, San Diego, Albuquerque, and Las Vegas. These centers had direct jet connections with each other and also with major national cities such as Washington, New York, and Chicago.

If the West continued to display regional characteristics, Meinig argued, that was not due mainly to locational or environmental factors. Rather, it was a cultural phenomenon, a matter of attitudes and behavior, of life-styles which were perceived by people throughout the United States and the world. Very likely, therefore, the West would continue to be seen as a distinctive region. Its urban population was particularly fluid and mobile, impermanent in residence, dispersing widely for recreational activities, and knit together by television, jet travel, electronic communications, computers, and national corporations.

Meinig concluded that westering as a national phenomenon "has continued to be a major feature of American life. In depressions as well as booms, the image of the West as new country where one might embark upon a new life in more congenial circumstances has persisted as a powerful attraction. To a very considerable degree, industry has followed the population as well as lured it." Moreover, despite a rapid increase of population in the West from 1945 to 1990, Western regionalism was very much alive. The eleven Western states contained only 16 percent of the total United States population, but 38 percent of the nation's land area. Many parts of the West were not caught up in rapid growth, including Montana, Wyoming, and Idaho. But during this period attitudes toward growth also began to change as the negative impact of population increase on the natural environment became clearer, whether in air and water pollution or the exhaustion of mineral or land resources. This growing awareness of the environment by the 1970s brought an increased appreciation of the physical and cultural distinctiveness of the West, and reinforced its regional character.[53]

Thus, although varying in emphasis, this generation of geographers emphasized the dominance of cultural and psychological determinants of Western regionalism. Their interpretations were a far cry from the environmental determinism of Huntington and Semple at the beginning of the century. They reflected a deeper understanding of the role of psychological perceptions and complex variants of cultures than the earlier generation. And as technological changes had wrought major modifications of geographical environments—jet travel, air conditioning, computers, communications, irrigation—they focused on manmade changes rather than on nature. In their view, a region was first and foremost a cultural phenomenon, or the result of psychological perceptions, and only secondarily an entity grounded in geography.

Like the geographers, political scientists between 1960 and 1990 were also drawn to the study of the West as a region, stressing its distinctive political behavior. Some, like Ira Sharkansky, criticized historians for their lack of rigorous analytical frameworks in the study of Western regionalism. What historians needed, he declared, was far greater precision in the delineation of regional characteristics, more emphasis on empirical analysis, especially statistical examination of variables such as population diffusion, economic distinctions, and natural resources.[54]

Others, like Daniel Elazar, placed greater emphasis on cultural influences in the development of Western regionalism. In Elazar's view, the West and its subsections were distinguished mainly by differing cultural attitudes—such as views toward government, or the qualities which the inhabitants ascribed to their leaders, or assumptions they

53. Donald W. Meinig, "American Wests: Preface to a Geographical Interpretation," Annals of the Association of American Geographers 62 (June 1972), 159–84, quotes on 174, 181, 182.

54. Ira Sharkansky, Regionalism in American Politics (New York, 1970), 4, 18, 174.

made about the proper role of government. Such attitudes, he believed, had their roots in the older regions of the United States because
Elazar, like Max Weber, Carl O. Sauer, or Seymour Lipset, and other
social scientists held that the values of the original settlers in a region
like the West determined much of the cultural matrix within which
succeeding generations developed the area. As a result of his studies,
Elazar concluded that the federal system embodied many of these values
and set the tone for both national as well as regional political and
social organization.[55]

An even broader model for the West as a region was proposed by
Richard Jensen, a historian who was representative of political sociologists and quantitative political analysts of this era. Like them, he
was less interested in individuals than in economic, social, or political
group behavior. Jensen stressed cultural rather than environmental
determinants, factors such as value systems, life-styles, class, race, and
religion. These variables he subsumed within the broad concept of
modernization which, Jensen concluded, revealed a great deal about
various stages of regional development.[56]

Using different perspectives and methods, political scientists concerned with Western regionalism came to conclusions that were similar
to those of scholars in other disciplines. Man-made or cultural influences, they argued, were of prime significance in explaining the regional distinctiveness of the West. It must be said, however, that
because of the nature of their craft, political scientists were less concerned about changes over time than about the West of their own
contemporary generation.

At the same time, anthropologists continued to provide Western
historians with concepts and methods emphasizing the cultural dimension of Western regionalism. Beginning in the postwar era, anthropologists utilized either Clyde Kluckhohn's or Alfred Kroeber's
approach in formulating historical studies, with an emphasis on distinctive subregions of the West defined by cultural groupings. Thus,
Harold E. Driver, one of Kroeber's disciples, spent a lifetime inves-
tigating Indian cultures of both North and South America, but with
notable studies of tribes in the West. Edward Spicer specialized in

55. Daniel Elazar, *American Federalism: A View from the States* (New York, 1966),
112, 130, and his *Cities of the Prairie* (New York, 1970), 3.

56. Richard Jensen, "On Modernizing Frederick Jackson Turner: The Historiography of Regionalism," *Western Historical Quarterly* 11 (July 1980), 311, 316, 322.

Indian tribes of the Southwest and their variant cultures. John C. Ewers focused mainly on the unique cultural traits of the Plains Indians, and pioneered with descriptions of their arts and crafts. Evon Vogt, one of Kluckhohn's students, wrote about changing cultures of Indian veterans of World War II, and produced notable studies of culture changes among the Navajos. Anthony F. C. Wallace, one of the most historically minded anthropologists of this period, was notable for tracing the impact of cultural and psychological influences on the Eastern Indian tribes. Meanwhile, Robert C. Oswalt followed culture changes among the Eskimos in Alaska.[57] Whatever their specialization, however, the conceptual and methodological approaches of the cultural anthropologists emphasized the primacy of cultural variables in the diverse civilizations which they studied. Historians of the period were duly impressed by their conclusions.

Similarly, sociologists between 1960 and 1990 were underscoring the importance of culture in shaping the regional character of the West. In addition to influencing the work of Western historians such as Allan Bogue, they themselves became involved in dealing with aspects of the region's history. Preeminent was Seymour Lipset, who

57. Harold E. Driver, *Hoof Rattles and Girls' Puberty Rites in North and South America* (Baltimore, 1950); Driver, *Comparative Studies of North American Indians* (Philadelphia, 1957); Driver, *The Contributions of A. L. Kroeber to Culture Area Theory and Practice* (Baltimore, 1962); *Ethnology and Acculturation of the Chichineca-Jonaz of Northeast Mexico* (Bloomington, 1963); Driver and James L. Coffin, *Classification and Development of North American Indian Cultures* (Philadelphia, 1975). Edward A. Spicer, *Pascua: A Yaqui Village in Arizona* (Chicago, 1940); Spicer (ed.), *Perspectives in American Indian Cultural Change* (Chicago, 1956); Spicer, *Cycles of Conquest: Impact of Spain, Mexico and the United States on the Indians of the Southwest, 1533–1960* (Tucson, 1962); Spicer, *The American Indians* (Cambridge, Mass., 1980). John C. Ewers, *The Horse in Blackfoot Indian Culture* (Washington, 1955); Ewers, *The Blackfeet: Raiders on the Northwest Plains* (Norman, 1958); Ewers, *Crow Indian Beadwork* (New York, 1959); Ewers, *Artists of the Old West* (New York, 1965); Evon Z. Vogt, *Navajo Veterans: A Study of Changing Values* (Cambridge, Mass., 1951); Vogt, *Navajo Means People* (Cambridge, Mass., 1951); Vogt (ed.), *People of Rimrock: A Study of Values in Five Cultures* (Cambridge, Mass., 1966); Vogt (ed.), *Culture and Life: Essays in Memory of Clyde Kluckhohn* (Carbondale, 1973); Anthony F. C. Wallace, *The Modal Personality Structure of the Tuscarora Indians* (Washington, 1952); Wallace (ed.), *Men and Cultures* (Philadelphia, 1960); Wallace, *Culture and Personality* (New York, 1970); Wendell H. Oswalt, *Napaskiak: An Alaskan Eskimo Community* (Tucson, 1963); Oswalt, *Alaskan Eskimos* (San Francisco, 1967); Oswalt, *Eskimos and Explorers* (Novato, Cal., 1979); and Robert L. Oswalt, *Kashaya Texts* (Berkeley, 1964). See also one of the most influential anthropologists, Clifford Geertz, *Interpretation of Cultures* (New York, 1973).

approached the West with perspectives that were broader than those used by most historians.

A primary emphasis of sociologists like Lipset was to focus on the importance of the unique cultural characteristics of the West as a region when compared to similar physiographic areas elsewhere. Lipset borrowed some of his theoretical framework from the great German sociologist Max Weber. The latter had postulated that differences in social structure of different regions or nations could often be linked to specific historical events which set one process—or value system— into motion in a particular society, and a very different system in some other area. Historical events, Weber held, established distinctive values and predispositions, and these, in turn, affect the progression of succeeding events. Thus, Turner declared that the frontier promoted values such as individualism and egalitarianism—which later shaped the West as region. But such was not the influence of the frontier in other societies, and was not a necessary consequence. In Australia the agricultural frontier had an inhospitable climate, and was not very conducive to settlement by families. The harsh environment also required considerable sums of investment capital. The impact of the frontier on Australian regional development, therefore, was much less marked than in the United States because the population was so much smaller, and was from the beginning concentrated in urban areas.[58]

Lipset also found that the Canadian settlement experience contrasted with that in the United States. In its formative years Canada was on constant guard against the expansionist tendencies of Americans, and could not leave its newly settled Western regions unprotected or autonomous. Moreover, by 1850 it had become an established British tradition that the power of civil authority should first be established in a new area before settlers would be allowed to populate it. The Northwest Mounted Police usually moved in before any settlers. Canada had no vigilantes and relatively little Indian warfare. Pervasive government controls tended to weaken expressions of individualism among settlers.[59]

58. Seymour M. Lipset, "History and Sociology: Some Methodological Considerations," in Seymour Lipset and Richard Hofstadter (eds.), *Sociology and History* (New York, 1968), 37–38. Seymour M. Lipset, *Agrarian Socialism: The Cooperative Commonwealth Federation in Saskatchewan* (Berkeley, 1950).

59. Lipset, "History and Sociology," 39; Lipset, *The First New Nation* (New York, 1963), 160, 250–52, 255–59; Lipset, *Revolution and Counter-Revolution: The United States and Canada* (New York, 1968), 35, 57–59.

Lipset also synthesized the work of other sociologists to corroborate his theme that cultural influences were more significant than environmental conditions in shaping the West as a region. For example, the experience of the western regions of Brazil was relevant. Although Brazil was the largest nation in Latin America and the best endowed with natural resources, it did not enjoy the prosperity of the United States. One sociologist tried to explain the differences by noting:

> The bandeirantes [flag bearers] were the explorers and settlers of the interior of Brazil, as pioneers were the conquerors and colonizers of the great unoccupied heartland of the United States. The difference lies in their motives and ideals. The Brazilian bandeirantes were perhaps the last wave of colonial conquistadores. The American pioneers, though of all kinds, were predominantly Reformation settlers. The resulting civilizations set up by the two groups of wilderness conquerors were therefore quite different, despite many elements common to both.

Bandeirantes wanted to get rich quickly, and then leave, while Englishmen and Americans wanted to establish new homes. The experience of the West in Argentina provided similar evidence. There, the frontier did not influence social organization nor a democratic outlook in emerging regions. Argentinian agriculture developed as in Australia—with huge ranches employing hired labor. Large landowners opposed homesteading by small farmers. Other evidence could be gathered to support Weber's thesis—Lipset argued—that the core values of the generation of initial settlers exert a profound influence on the consequent settlement of a region. American democracy, therefore, came from the inheritance of English values and institutions and the Calvinist work ethic rather than from environmental conditions.[60] The findings of sociologists dealing with Western regionalism thus dovetailed with those of contemporary anthropologists, political scientists, and geographers.

In fact, their emphasis encouraged a number of historians to utilize a comparative approach in their study of the West. Among them was Howard Lamar who by 1980 was urging this approach on his colleagues. "The dominant tradition in historical scholarship," Lamar wrote,

60. Lipset, "History and Sociology," 39–42, quote on 39; Adolph A. Berle in Vianna Moog, *Bandeirantes and Pioneers* (New York, 1964), 9, 119–21, 171; Charles Wagley, *An Introduction to Brazil* (New York, 1963), 74–75.

is one that deals in single cases. The time, energy, and talents of the typical historian are fully engaged in the discovery, organization, and interpretation of data on the history of his own society or his own culture. This focus has created a tendency for mainstream historians to refrain from questioning some of the most fundamental assumptions that are current in their own environments. . . . The cultural chauvinism that is a regular concomitant of human conflict is, wittingly or unwittingly, propagated by many historians.

Lamar then turned his critique on Frederick Jackson Turner. "The irony of Frederick Jackson Turner's lasting eminence," he wrote, "is that he thought he was describing a zone, a process, a period, and an outcome that were unique to the American experience. What he was actually describing . . . was one example of the . . . capitalist system and European settlers, which in turn constitute a particular species of a process that takes place whenever one people intrudes into terrain occupied by another. . . . That [is] a universal and still ongoing process."[61]

Comparative historians such as Robin Winks also reflected the emphasis of the social scientists on the importance of cultural factors in the shaping of the West as region. Reflecting a global outlook, Winks criticized American historians for defining regions through geography, although very few had done so since the 1920s. Instead, Winks argued that the West had been shaped mainly by cultural influences. "But the main indicators of regional identity must at root be emotional," Winks proclaimed, much like contemporary geographers. "The region . . . like the nation . . . draws upon the oldest and most primitive feelings of mankind—the need for security achieved through social groups."[62] Similar words had been written almost a hundred years before by Josiah Royce.

Indeed, the effort to reemphasize the important psychological impact of Western regionalism as a source of identity was intensified by a number of historians after 1979. In that year, Michael Steiner undertook a searching reappraisal of Turner's sectional thesis as it seemed

61. Leonard Thompson and Howard Lamar (eds.), *The Frontier in History: North America and Southern Africa Compared* (New Haven, 1981), 3–5, 314; see also Lamar, *The Far Southwest, 1846–1912: A Territorial History* (New Haven, 1966), 5–6.

62. Robin Winks, "Regionalism in Comparative Perspective," in Robbins (ed.), *Regionalism*, 13–18.

resuscitated by the social-science research of the previous three decades. As Steiner noted: "Despite the fact that more has been written
about Frederick Jackson Turner than any American historian, relatively little attention has been given to his sectional thesis. . . . Historians have tended either to slight the sectional concept or to reject
it as a piece of misguided thinking. They have dismissed it as a sub-
terfuge hiding the unpleasant fact of class conflict, as a simplistic
exercise in environmental determinism, or as a case of 'arrested development' and an escape from challenging social concerns." Steiner
believed that in a time of alienation, historians would do well to take
another, and closer look, at the sectional hypothesis. "More than any
other historian," he declared,

> Turner draws attention to the vital fact that our culture varies
> over space—a fact that receives increased consideration as scholars
> become more aware of the segmentation and diversity that under-
> lie our culture. And beyond providing an essential interpretation
> of the past, Turner's conviction that the growth of sectional or re-
> gional identity would offer a counterforce to many of the destruc-
> tive cultural traits engendered by the frontier and an antidote for
> the homelessness of mass society has profound implications for the
> present.

Steiner was convinced that in 1979 Turner's sectional thesis was
more relevant than ever.

> Turner realized that frontier characteristics of rootless individual-
> ism and restless mobility isolated Americans from themselves as
> well as from their environment. Sectionalism, he argued with rea-
> soning that seems even more convincing today, could not only fos-
> ter a sense of community amid the incorporation of life into larger
> more impersonal units but also insure a healthier relationship to
> the land. Implicit in the sectional thesis is the desire to instill rev-
> erence and affection for the portion of the earth that has nurtured
> us, to learn to meet the promise of the land rather than mine it
> and move on in the traditional American manner. . . . Our
> heightened awareness in recent years of dwindling global resources
> and the inefficiency of large-scale organization and massive central-
> ization should open our eyes to the value of Turner's sectional
> concept.[63]

63. Steiner, "Turner's Sectional Thesis," *Western Historical Quarterly* 10, 437–38,
439, 465–66.

Adding to the growing volume of studies emphasizing cultural influences in the shaping of the West as region was a volume on the New Deal in the West by Richard Lowitt. Emphasizing the importance of the federal government in the shaping of the region, Lowitt analyzed the work of the Department of the Interior and the Bureau of Reclamation, in particular. The development of new power projects, Lowitt argued, and the opening of new lands by irrigation as well as tree planting on the Plains significantly affected the Western environment and how Westerners perceived it. Land that had been considered the heart of the Great American Desert now became fruitful. Like many historians of his generation, Lowitt stressed the primacy of man-made changes in the Western environment, with special emphasis on government. And in a volume concerning the impact of the Second World War on the West, Gerald Nash followed similar themes.[64]

In fact, the growing number of works on Western regionalism in this period prompted Richard M. Brown to proclaim in 1983 that he discerned an important revival of the regional approach to the study of the West in the quarter-century after 1960. Brown reviewed previous cycles of regional interest in the 1920s and 1930s, and chronicled the declining interest in the subject during the 1950s. That, he surmised, was due to nationalizing influences such as television, jet travel, and interstate highways. He saw the revival of interest in regional identity as a product of persistent regional identities and a search by Americans for roots, as reflected also in a rising interest in local history. Brown credited much of the revival to government programs such as those of the National Endowment for the Humanities, the National Endowment for the Arts, legal requirements for environmental impact statements, widespread historic preservation activities, and the Bicentennial programs of the 1970s. The result of these varied efforts resulted in what he perceived as a new regionalism in the West which, not surprisingly in view of its origins, stressed the importance of cultural determinants.[65]

The importance of cultural variables in the West as region was also an assumption in a widely ranging survey of the West by Patricia Limerick. Like many historians of the 1960s generation, she reflected

64. Richard Lowitt, *The New Deal and the West* (Bloomington, 1984); Nash, *American West Transformed.*
65. Brown, "New Regionalism in America," in Robbins (ed.), *Regionalism*, 45–95.

the negativism and disdain for previous interpretations. In contrast to scholars of the first half of the twentieth century who had celebrated the conquest of the West as one of America's great achievements— even as a heroic saga—she chronicled what she perceived as a shameful legacy of conquest. In her account of the forming of the West, the record was one of unmitigated suppression, of women, of Native Americans, of blacks, and of Hispanics, not to speak of wanton despoliation and destruction of the natural environment. Clearly, the value system of a civilization which engaged in such widespread and consistent pillage was open to serious question.[66] This perception reflected the *Weltanschauung* of many of the social critics of the 1960s.

Of course, Limerick was not unusual in transmitting the major concerns of her own generation, as most historians between 1960 and 1990 closely reflected an intense interest in race and gender in the West. The strong emphasis on cultural influences led to the creation of a number of subdisciplines in Western regionalism. These included ethnic history, the history of women, of blacks, of Hispanics, and of Asian-Americans. Historians expanded the study of Native Americans in the West, compared to earlier periods. A survey of the writings on the American West as region reveals that between 1960 and 1990 the study of minority groups and women attracted more attention than any other major topic in the field.

This groundswell was clearly visible in studies of ethnicity in the trans-Mississippi West. Theodore Saloutos wrote of Greeks in the region, Andrew Rolle studied the Italians, and Fred Luebke focused on Germans. Luebke, in particular, was concerned with the broader role of immigrants in the West, tying it also to the mainstream of immigration history in the United States. The study of ethnicity, Luebke argued, introduced a new dimension into the regional analysis of the West. It allowed for a more precise examination of the interaction of culture and environment over time, and provided comparison in time, space, and culture so as to determine regional characteristics more precisely. He criticized Turner for largely ignoring non-English immigrants, and took even sharper aim at the environmental determinism of Walter P. Webb. Instead, he emphasized the central role of cultural influences such as language, religion, historic ethnic awareness, folklore, and tradition in shaping the civilization of the West.

66. Patricia Nelson Limerick, *The Legacy of Conquest: The Unbroken Past of the American West* (New York, 1987).

Its physical contours, Luebke argued, were not a major factor in forging civilization, even if they set certain broad limitations. Obviously, Luebke was drawing some of his concepts from the cultural anthropologists of his era. Moreover, his emphasis fit into the mainstream of contemporary research in American history, preoccupied with the importance of culture, and the central role of cultural pluralism in American life. "Environmental factors have influenced spatial distribution," he wrote, "but social and cultural variables—especially kinship and religion—seem generally to have been more important."[67] In many ways, Luebke was advocating the study of immigration history which Marcus Hansen had inaugurated for the East a generation earlier, but which Western historians had ignored for many years, perhaps because of their undue concern with the environmental uniqueness of the West.

Between 1960 and 1990 Western historians also did much to clarify the history of women in the region. Although scholars had not totally ignored women in their writings before 1960, they had underemphasized their importance or treated them in stereotypical terms. Usually, they sketched them as "gentle tamers," as the demure civilizers who brought social and cultural graces to the West, either as wives of pioneers or as schoolteachers. Other types that appeared in the saga of the West included "wild women," the occasional women outlaws or hell-raisers such as Calamity Jane, or the ubiquitous prostitutes and dance-hall women who frequented frontier communities.[68]

But with the rise of the women's rights movement after 1960, and particularly after Betty Friedan published *The Feminine Mystique* in

67. Theodore C. Saloutos, "Cultural Persistence and Change: Greeks in the Great Plains and Rocky Mountain West, 1890–1970," *Pacific Historical Review* 49 (February 1980), 77–103; Andrew F. Rolle, *The Immigrant Upraised: Italian Adventurers and Colonists in an Expanding America* (Norman, 1968), 4, 6, 28–30, 100; Frederick C. Luebke, *Immigrants and Politics: The Germans of Nebraska, 1800–1900* (Lincoln, 1969), xii, xxix; see also Luebke's articles, including "Ethnic Group Settlement on the Great Plains," *Western Historical Quarterly* 8 (October 1977), 405–30, "Ethnic Minority Groups in the American West," in Michael Malone (ed.), *Historians and the American West* (Lincoln, 1983), 387–413, and "Regionalism and the Great Plains: Problems of Concept and Method," *Western Historical Quarterly* 15 (January 1984), 19–38.

68. Joan Jensen and Darlis A. Miller, "The Gentle Tamers Revisited: New Approaches to the History of Women in the American West," *Pacific Historical Review* 49 (May 1980), 173–213. By 1990 the history of children and families in the West was just beginning to be developed. See Elliott West, *Growing Up with the Country: Childhood on the Far Western Frontier* (Albuquerque, 1989).

1963, the advocates of women's importance demanded that their perceptions find a place in Western history. Already in 1958, Dee Brown, a journalist, had published a general work on Western women, *The Gentle Tamers*, which challenged at least some of the prevailing images of women in the West. Brown wondered whether women's roles had not been much more varied than the stereotyped versions projected, as carriers of cultural gentility. By the 1970s Friedan and her followers had stirred up enough ferment to lead to hundreds of new articles on women in the West and the publication of bibliographies on the subject. In its totality, this new body of literature presented very different perspectives of women in the West. Most authors rejected the stereotypes in most of the existing writings about the West as region. Instead, they presented women as individuals, not as types. This meant also that they emphasized differences among women as a group, whether by personality, class, ethnic origins, or race. Women's historians now wrote of women in a great variety of roles, outside the stereotyped categories sketched by earlier writers. Some women had been independent homesteaders; others were heads of households, or managed cattle ranches. Moreover, women of different cultural backgrounds had very different experiences in the West, whether in their choice of occupations, in their political roles, or in their relations with other women of different ethnic or cultural backgrounds. These studies uncovered an entirely new—and large—dimension in the study of Western regionalism.[69]

Within two decades the field of Western women's history had made a significant impact on historians of the region. In surveying the literature in 1980, Joan Jensen and Darlis Miller noted that "a newer, ethnically broader and more varied image of women in the West is today challenging the older view. This view rests on a multicultural approach which calls for an evaluation of the experiences of all ethnic

69. Dee Brown, *The Gentle Tamers: Women of the Old Wild West* (New York, 1958); Julie Roy Jeffrey, *Frontier Women: The Trans-Mississippi West, 1840–1880* (New York, 1979); Sandra Myres, *Westering Women and the Frontier Experience, 1800–1915* (Albuquerque, 1982); Glenda Riley, "Women of the Great Plains: Recent Developments in Research," *Great Plains Quarterly* 5 (Spring 1985), 81–92, and *Women and Indians on the Frontier, 1825–1915* (Albuquerque, 1984); Susan Armitage and Elizabeth Jameson (eds.), *The Women's West* (Norman, 1987), and Armitage, "Women and Men in Western History: A Stereoptical Vision," *Western Historical Quarterly* 16 (October 1985), 381–95; Sarah Deutsch, *No Separate Refuge: Culture, Class, and Gender on an Anglo-Hispanic Frontier in the American Southwest, 1880–1940* (New York, 1987).

groups of women within a historical framework incorporating women's history into western history. This process will necessitate the rewriting of western history."[70]

The increased awareness of minority groups which gripped Americans during these years was also reflected by historians who now devoted greater attention to the role of blacks in Western regions. Before 1960 blacks were rarely mentioned by writers of textbooks about the West. True, before 1940 less than 2 percent of the population west of the Mississippi River was composed of blacks. Yet they had played various roles in the region since its first settlement. That black regiments had been important components in the United States Army's Indian campaigns in the West from 1865 to 1890 was common knowledge, yet the historical literature rarely examined their activities in detail. That might have been, Kenneth Wiggins Porter suggested in 1971, because white Americans did not associate blacks with heroic images of cowboys, gunslingers, trappers and explorers, so that in the realm of historical writing they became invisible. Until the civil rights movement of the 1950s focused attention on black contributions to the building of America, black historians themselves, including Carter G. Woodson, Charles H. Wesley, Benjamin Quarles, and John Hope Franklin also ignored the presence of blacks in the West, preoccupied as they were with the South and migrations northward. It took the Black Power movement of the 1960s, and an increasing concern of blacks for their racial identity and their past history, to jolt historians into looking more deeply into the black experience in the West.[71]

The first fruits of this aroused awareness did not appear until the 1970s. Then, a spate of books and articles began to appear, some by journalists such as William Katz who wrote *The Black West*, a survey that covered the period from 1850 to 1910. Although the presence of black cowboys in the nineteenth-century West was sometimes mentioned in the accounts of contemporary diarists, it took two English professors to underscore that fact in *The Negro Cowboys*. Even if their estimate that as many as 20 percent of working cowboys were black was very likely erroneous, still a more realistic figure of 5 percent would have made the complete neglect of blacks in Hollywood western

70. Jensen and Miller, "Gentle Tamers Revisited," *Pacific Historical Review* 49, 174.

71. Kenneth Wiggins Porter, *The Negro on the American Frontier* (New York, 1971); De Graaf, "Western Black History," *Pacific Historical Review* 44, 23, 24, 25.

films inexcusable. Since real cowhands—as opposed to the mythical variety—were often marginal men, hardworking, poorly paid, and living under primitive conditions, it was hardly surprising that they counted blacks among them.[72]

Other books detailed the military accomplishments of black soldiers in the West, and examined black colonization efforts in Kansas and Oklahoma in the half-century after the Civil War. The emphasis of much of this literature was on the positive contributions of blacks to the West, and a pluralistic, multicultural society. As the writers of textbooks on Western or state history revised their volumes—Billington and Caughey served as fine examples—they now revised their works to include more materials on blacks. Yet in the 1970s historians writing about blacks did not place them in the broader context of Western history, but tended to emphasize their contributions—perhaps reflecting the guilt feelings common of their own times.[73] Nevertheless, by the 1980s the total impact of this literature was to emphasize cultural pluralism as a force in Western regionalism.

The emphasis on ethnic pluralism could not fail but to focus attention on Hispanics in the West, given their large numbers in California, Texas, New Mexico, and other areas of the Southwest. Study of Spanish-speaking peoples had not been fully ignored before 1960, but had developed in a very different context. When Herbert Bolton first developed the history of the Borderlands at the University of California between 1911 and 1940, he had brought an awareness of the Spanish influence in the New World directly into the mainstream of American history. But his emphasis, and that of this disciples, was more on the initial exploration and settlement, on leaders rather than followers, leaving much of the social, economic, and cultural life of Spanish-speaking peoples in subsequent years untouched in the histories of the borderlands.[74]

The regional movement of the 1920s, however, began to create a

72. William Loren Katz, *The Black West* (Garden City, New York, 1971); Philip Durham and Everett L. Jones, *The Negro Cowboys* (New York, 1965).

73. William H. Leckie, *The Buffalo Soldiers: A Narrative of the Negro Cavalry in the West* (Norman, 1967): Arlan F. Fowler, *The Black Infantry in the West, 1869–1891* (Westport, 1971). See also Robert G. Athearn, *In Search of Canaan: Black Migration to Kansas, 1879–1880* (Lawrence, 1978), and DeGraaf, "Western Black History," *Pacific Historical Review* 44, 33–39.

74. Herbert Bolton (ed.), *Spanish Exploration in the Southwest, 1542–1706* (New York, 1925).

greater awareness of the social and cultural distinctiveness of Spanish-speaking peoples in communities scattered throughout the Southwest. Their language, customs, folklore, and religion now came to be romanticized by literary figures seeking an escape from urban, industrial America. Mary Austin, Mabel Dodge Luhan, and Alice Corbin Henderson, among others, brought an awareness of the distinctive cultures of the Spanish-speaking people of the Southwest to the consciousness of Americans outside the region. The Great Depression and the New Deal strengthened the cultural identity of these "forgotten people," to use the phraseology of George Sánchez, one of their spokesmen. New Dealers, especially in the arts, music, theater, and writing programs of the Works Projects Administration (WPA) strengthened the consciousness of a unique cultural identity. And a new generation of Hispanic scholars, such as Carlos Castañeda and George I. Sánchez at the University of Texas, wrote about their people. The first comprehensive volume about this subculture appeared in 1948 when Carey McWilliams published his *North from Mexico*. If the seeds of ethnic consciousness had been laid in the 1920s and 1930s, World War II fertilized these seeds and laid the foundations for much greater cultural awareness in the 1950s.[75]

The political activism of Hispanics in the 1960s found direct reflection in the increasing interest of historians and political activists in the history of Hispanics, Mexican-Americans, and Chicanos, a term applied to peoples of the Southwest who were of mixed Spanish, Mexican, and Indian heritage. The first Chicano historians of the 1960s included Raymond Paredes, Ernesto Galarza, and Leonard Pitt, who admitted freely that the social and political impact of contemporary Chicano protest movements provided them with the inspiration to delve into Chicano history.[76]

In the two decades after 1970 the literature of Chicano history in the Southwest proliferated. New journals appeared as outlets for an increasing flow of articles on various levels of quality. Some of the writers were preoccupied with what they perceived as the racism of

75. George I. Sánchez, *Forgotten People: A Study of New Mexicans* (Albuquerque, 1940); Carey McWilliams, *North from Mexico: The Spanish-Speaking People of the United States* (Philadelphia, 1949).

76. Leonard Pitt, *The Decline of the Californios: A Social History of Spanish-Speaking Californians, 1846–1890* (Berkeley, 1966); Ernesto Galarza, *Merchants of Labor: The Mexican Bracero Story* (Santa Barbara, 1964); Raymund Paredes, *The Evolution of Chicano Literature* (New York, 1989).

whites, or colonialism. A whole spate of works belabored this theme, from Rudolfo Acuna's *Occupied America* to Matt S. Meier and Feliciano Rivera's *The Chicanos*. These advocates ignored ethnic and racial as well as class differences within the Hispanic community, or variant religious and social groupings.[77] By the 1980s less strident scholars began to investigate the complexity of the Spanish-speaking communities in greater depth and from more scholarly perspectives.

But the writings on Chicano history reflected the broader trends of historians writing about the West as region by emphasizing the importance of cultural influences. Those historians who were writing about Hispanics in the Bolton era were concerned with an ethnic group within a reasonably well-defined geographical area. But the Chicano historians of the 1960–1990 period were mainly preoccupied with a cultural group, and its communities which were not necessarily confined to a particular region like the Southwest. Thus, they reflected the strong emphasis on cultural rather than environmental influences that were so pervasive in much of the writing about the West as a region in the 1960–1990 era.

Although Indians had not been neglected in Western history before 1960, historians had often presented them from a somewhat stereotyped perspective. Some scholars tended to view them as an impediment to the western advance of white men. They analyzed their civilizations through white men's eyes, particularly because most written records of Indian–white relations were based on historical sources produced by whites rather than Indians. Even in the historical record—just as on the battlefield—Indians were vastly outnumbered and at a disadvantage. Moreover, their cultures often did not provide for written records but were based on oral traditions, not all of which were preserved. The work of anthropologists like Clark Wissler, Alfred Kroeber, and Clyde Kluckhohn after World War I began to detail various aspects of Indian culture, and to reveal the diversities and complexities of their civilizations. But the gist of these detailed studies

77. Rodolfo Acuña, *Occupied America: A History of Chicanos* (3d ed., New York, 1987), and also Matt S. Meier and Feliciano Rivera, *The Chicanos: A History of Mexican Americans* (New York, 1972); Juan Gómez-Quiñones and Luis Leobardo Arroyo, "On the State of Chicano History: Observations on Its Development, Interpretations, and Theory, 1970–1974," *Western Historical Quarterly* 7 (April 1976), 155–85.

did not have a substantial impact on historians until after the Second World War.

Like other minorities, Indians were caught up in the civil rights movements of the 1960s. While no one organization could claim to be spokesperson for all of the Indian tribes in the West, the majority of Indian activists believed in the need for greater cultural awareness of their racial heritage, and intensified action to preserve their culture in the face of powerful leveling influences in American society. It was this activism that led Wilcomb Washburn to note in 1971 that "the impetus for the . . . support of Indian studies comes not from historical, but from racial reasons."[78]

Consequently, the two decades after 1970 saw the appearance of what one historian dubbed as the "New Indian History." This reflected current Native American concerns about losing their cultural distinctiveness and their identity, unless they took a more strident role in preserving their traditions. In such an effort, historical studies obviously had an important place. The New Indian History thus placed primary emphasis on Indians themselves, on Indian viewpoints affecting society and culture, and on the essential elements of Indian personality and culture. Such a focus was less concerned with Indian–white relations, which had been of prime interest to historians before 1960. Now the emphasis shifted to aspects of ethnic survival, and cultural continuity amid a larger society in the constant turmoil of change. Indians were no longer passive, faceless, inscrutable figures, but individual personalities in their own right who looked at the world through their own special cultural prisms which were as valid as those of white society. Invariably, such an emphasis prompted greater attention to diversities within Indian societies—including the multiplicity of cultures and languages, customs, migrations, and contacts with other peoples. Such an approach disrupted existing stereotypes of Indians as a faceless group. Nor was the tribe a dominant concern in the institutional study of Indian civilizations since tribal governments had often been imposed by the white man's laws. More indigenous were factions within Indian societies which historians now began to study with greater intensity. And in reflecting a trend in the writing of contemporary American social history to detail the experiences of

78. Wilcomb E. Washburn, "The Writing of American Indian History," *Pacific Historical Review* 40 (August 1971), 261.

ordinary individuals, historians of Indians now began to study the lives of average Indians in their communities rather than to concentrate on the deeds of leaders.[79]

The architects of the New Indian History within a regional context were many. Some concentrated on sketching the broad outlines of the New Indian History, such as Wilcomb Washburn, Reginald Horsman, and Robert F. Berkhofer. Others dealt with the social organization and institutions of Indian tribes, such as the studies of Indian education by Margaret Szasz, of Indian police by William T. Hagan, and of Indian women by Gretchen Bataille and Kathleen M. Sands. Various writers, such as Brian W. Dippie and Alvin Josephy, suggested new perceptions of Indians. But the majority of Indian historians still focused on government policies toward Native Americans. What was distinctive during this period was a new emphasis on the twentieth century, as compared to the almost total concentration on the years before 1890 by previous generations. The magisterial studies of Francis P. Prucha provided the most comprehensive overview of American Indian relations yet written and did much to stake out new dimensions in the field, for the years after 1890 especially. A general work of smaller compass was Peter Iverson's survey of the experience of Plains Indians in the twentieth century. Other scholars focused on particular eras, particularly the New Deal period, which was examined in depth by Lawrence C. Kelly, Donald Parman, Kenneth Philp, and Graham Taylor. A few, like Donald Fixico, ventured into the years between 1945 and 1960 to analyze the controversial policy of termination. And some historians eschewed more traditional modes of analysis by subjecting the perceptions which whites had of Indians to closer analysis. These diverse approaches unearthed dimensions in Native American history which placed Western regionalism in a new context, particularly in emphasizing its multicultural characteristics.[80]

79. Robert F. Berkhofer, Jr., "The Political Context of a New Indian History," *Pacific Historical Review* 40 (August 1971), 357–82.

80. Wilcomb E. Washburn (ed.), *The American Indian and the United States: A Documentary History* (4 vols., New York, 1973); Hagan, *American Indians*; Alvin Josephy, *The Indian Heritage of America* (New York, 1968); Donald L. Parman, *The Navajos and the New Deal* (New Haven, 1976); Kenneth R. Philp, *John Collier's Crusade for Indian Reform, 1920–1954* (Tucson, 1977); Brian W. Dippie, *The Vanishing American: White Attitudes and United States Indian Policy* (Middletown, 1982); Lawrence C. Kelly, *The Assault on Assimilation: John Collier and the Origins of Indian Policy Reform* (Albuquerque, 1983). The most prolific scholar has been Francis Paul Prucha; see

It was during these years, also, that historians concerned with the West as a region first gave greater attention to the role of Orientals. Their main focus was on the evacuation of Japanese-Americans from the West Coast in World War II, an experience that attracted a large number of historians, including Roger Daniels and John Modell. But slowly the awareness of other East Asians in the history of the West alerted an as yet small number of scholars. H. Brett Melendy chronicled the experience of Koreans, East Indians, and Filipinos who had been left largely invisible by most regional accounts. Works by Roger Daniels and Harry Kitano also touched on these groups, yet the history of Orientals in the West by 1990 was still the least developed field of ethnic studies.[81]

By 1990 the ethnic histories of various groups and of women had broadened perceptibly and revised their place in the development of the West as a region. They were no longer represented as simple or standardized stereotypes, but as highly diverse groups and individuals with well-developed cultural identities. If they had often been the losers in the battle for the continent, this was not necessarily due to the inferiority of their cultures, but to their status as minorities. In the larger context of the West, minorities underscored the cultural pluralism of the region and the dominant role of cultural influences, rather than environmental conditions, in the shaping of the emerging civilization. If the regional distinctiveness of the West was due to cultural rather than geographical factors, then the contributions of the various ethnic, racial, and gender groups to that distinctiveness was an important component of the greater whole.

But the heavy emphasis on the cultural determinants of Western regionalism by historians in the years from 1960 to 1990 virtually ignored the influence of the natural environment. The concentration of some scholars on the preeminence of cultural variables was as one-sided as the environmentalism of their predecessors had been a century before. Such a perspective reflected a present-mindedness that was

The Great Father: The United States Government and the American Indians (2 vols., Lincoln, 1984); Donald L. Fixico, Termination and Relocation: Federal Indian Policy, 1945–1960 (Albuquerque, 1986).

81. Roger Daniels, Concentration Camps, U.S.A. (New York, 1971); Harry L. Kitano, The Japanese-Americans: The Evolution of a Subculture (Englewood Cliffs, 1969); H. Brett Melendy, The Oriental Americans (New York, 1972); Melendy, Asians in America: Filipinos, Koreans, and East Indians (Boston, 1977); John Modell, The Economics and Politics of Racial Accommodation (Urbana, 1977).

beginning to be challenged by the emergence of new environmental problems after 1960. During these years issues such as air and water pollution, strip-mining, and the disposal of nuclear wastes helped to spawn increasingly popular environmental protection movements which, in turn, provided an impetus for historians. Yet unlike environmental concerns of former years, the historians of this era placed them in a cultural context. Their focus was not so much on the physiographic features of the Western environment, but on the cultural adaptations to this environment by the various peoples on the North American continent. Thus, they concentrated on cultural values and attitudes about the natural habitat which emanated from different social groups in the United States. Although they reasserted the importance of the West's natural endowment in defining it as a region, they emphasized the cultural impact which Americans had left on it over centuries of settlement.

One of the most forceful advocates of the new environmental history was Donald Worster, who placed the subject in a global context. In a volume about the Dust Bowl of the 1930s, Worster traced the destructive impact of policies which he attributed to the cultural assumptions of an exploitative capitalist system. What he did not mention—but was obvious to many readers—was that any economic system, whether socialist, communist, or merely subsistence, is bound to have some impact on the environment. Capitalism was no exception, and perhaps not quite as villainous as he painted it. In a later work, *Rivers of Empire*, Worster developed this argument even more powerfully. He charged that the policies of the United States Bureau of Reclamation between 1902 and 1980 had resulted in the damming of the West—with dire consequences for the salting of the region in the future. The diversion of rivers, the mindless use of technology to change the natural ecology of the West, whether by water diversion or destruction of wildlife and their habitats, boded ill for the West. It would result in eventual exhaustion of scarce waters, the silting and salting of its soils, the destruction of valuable species of animals, and such a serious disruption of ecological balance that it might take centuries to repair, if ever. Worster's call was "leave the land alone." His hope was to arouse greater ecological awareness in his readers.[82]

82. Donald Worster, *Dust Bowl: The Southern Plains in the 1930s* (New York, 1979); Worster, *Rivers of Empire: Water, Aridity, and the Growth of the American West* (New York, 1986).

The book made a significant contribution in raising questions about the future development of the West as a region, questions which others in the era had not posed as powerfully or effectively as Worster.

From the viewpoint of Western historiography, what was significant about the views of Worster and the environmental historians of this period was their effort to redress the balance between environmental and cultural influences shaping the West as region. A generation of historians and cultural geographers between 1960 and 1980 had all but discounted environmental factors as major shaping forces of the West. The environmental historians in the decade of the 1980s were providing a much needed balance by underscoring the continued importance of physiographic conditions, even while they placed considerable emphasis on the cultural choices made by various interest groups on how the environment was to be used or exploited. Their view was succinctly expressed by Richard White, when he noted:

> If, after all, the environment did not shape human institutions, if instead, it was [the] human culture and institutions which increasingly shaped the environment, then concern should center on human thought and human policies. The problem was that in such a formulation, nature sometimes became little more than an intellectual construct. Nature does not dictate, but physical nature does, at any given time, set limits on what is humanly possible. Humans may think what they want, they cannot always do what they want, and not all they do turns out as planned.[83]

Other environmental historians echoed these themes, even while placing considerable emphasis on cultural determinants. Environmentalist Marc Reisner echoed Worster's complaint about Western water policies, while Stephen J. Pyne stressed the impact of European migrations on natural ecosystems of North America and the close connections between cultural and environmental changes. Martin Melosi focused on the interrelation of population congestion and pollution. Even critics of environmentalism, such as Aaron Wildavsky and Mary Douglas, agreed on the primacy of cultural considerations in influencing environmental changes.[84]

83. Richard White, "American Environmental History: The Development of a New Historical Field," *Pacific Historical Review* 54 (August 1985), 335.

84. Marc Reisner, *Cadillac Desert* (New York, 1986); Stephen J. Pyne, *Fire in America: A Cultural History of Wildland and Rural Fire* (Princeton, 1982); William

Between 1960 and 1990 a new generation of scholars—historians and social scientists—reflected changing conceptions about regions by introducing contemporary issues. One major trend of this period was the extraordinary expansion of the field of Western regionalism. It could be argued that more changes transformed the subject in these thirty years than in the preceding seven decades. Topics that had barely been perceived, and even less likely investigated, were now subjected to closer inquiry. The very concept of a region was significantly modified by cultural geographers who developed new perspectives. Anthropologists left a deep imprint on Western historians by emphasizing the cultural influences which they considered preeminent in Western regional development. To a considerable extent, they stimulated historians who now delved into ethnic and immigration history. That, in turn, led to intensive specialization, and a response to contemporary civil rights issues. The result was the proliferation of subfields embracing the history of women, Hispanics, blacks, and Indians.

Another trend was fragmentation of the field. Whereas the generation before 1960 had sought to cope broadly with the entire West as region, and its subregions, the generation in the three decades after 1960 tended to deal with small topics. True, they probed in much greater depth than their predecessors, and with sharper analytical tools. In the process, they achieved greater sophistication. But specialization also had a price, for it was achieved in part at the expense of breadth. By 1990 much more was known about the complexities of regionalism than in prior years. At the same time, the concept of region was more diverse than ever and a unified perspective still lay in the future.

Between 1890 and 1990 scholars studying the West as region responded closely to the major contemporary issues of their day. Those who were writing about the West between 1890 and 1920 were influenced by a strong feeling of nostalgia brought on by the supposed closing of the frontier and the exhaustion of free land. Such a perception led them to emphasize the importance of geographical and environmental determinants in Western regionalism. By the 1920s

Cronon, *Changes in the Land: Indians, Colonists, and the Ecology of New England* (New York, 1983); Martin Melosi, *Coping with Abundance: Energy and Environment in Industrial America* (Philadelphia, 1985); Aaron Wildavsky and Mary Douglas, *Risk and Culture: An Essay on the Selection of Technical and Environmental Dangers* (Berkeley, 1982).

that perception was waning as the United States became a predominantly urban society with a maturing culture. Western historians reflected these currents by deemphasizing the role of geographical determinants of Western regionalism and focusing instead on the importance of cultural influences. No wonder that Turner did not receive a favorable response to his sectional hypothesis in 1925. The times—and the mood—had changed markedly since his early success in 1893. The Great Depression strengthened the tendency to emphasize the cultural characteristics of the West as region, as Americans searched eagerly for a more clearly defined sense of community in a time of crisis. That was also true of the World War II era when Western regionalism contributed to a strong sense of national identity. But as the crises of Depression and war waned, Americans lost much of their interest in regarding the West as region. In the affluent society between 1945 and 1960, sociologist David Riesman argued, Americans lost their sense of identity and community under the nationalizing pressures of the mass media and jet travel. The West as a region still served contemporary issues, however. As the United States became a global power with a variety of overseas aid programs, Western historians viewed the region as the nation's own underdeveloped region which could serve as an example, as a laboratory, for the United States development programs around the world.

That perception was rudely disrupted by the social turmoil of the 1960s and the Vietnam War. As in other crises, Americans again eagerly sought a sense of identity which they had seemingly lost in their vast bureaucratic, technological, postindustrial society. The search for roots led again to renewed appreciation of the West as region. At the same time, Western regionalism could be wedded to cultural identity, which provided another route to a newly defined sense of community. Contemporary civil rights and gender rights movements directly influenced a large number of historians who now combined these two strands with a major emphasis on the primacy of ethnic, racial, and gender characteristics in the development of the West as a region. In the process, they emphasized the importance of the cultural determinants of Western regionalism so strongly that they all but ignored the environmental context. This one-sided tilt produced a reaction from environmental historians after 1980—themselves reflecting a growing environmental consciousness in the nation—who reemphasized the ecological and geographical limitations within which the cultural growth of the West as region had taken place.

In considering the writings of scholars about the West as region between 1890 and 1990, one trend stood out predominantly—a drastic change of mood. Whereas historians between 1890 and 1960 had viewed the region as a positive and constructive force in American civilization, the generation after 1960 reflected a profound negativism and disenchantment. Before 1960 historians largely viewed the West as providing for diversity, dynamism, and creative change. After 1960, scholars nurtured by affluence, federal grants, loans, and affirmative action programs had a far more pessimistic perspective. In their view, the cultural values which Americans had used to develop the West as a region had a mostly destructive impact. Their task—as they saw it— was to chronicle this destruction. And so they wrote at length about the destruction of earlier native cultures; of ethnic and racial conflicts; of white Anglo exploitation of blacks, Indians, and Hispanics; of the suppression of Orientals; and the subordination of women at the hands of men. Nor did they ignore the wanton destruction of the West's natural environment. It was a bleak indictment, indeed. Perhaps it reflected a pervasive sense of pessimism and self-doubt about the future, or guilt feelings about the past. But as Earl Pomeroy had noted in 1970, historical interpretations about the West often revealed more about the values, attitudes, and assumptions of the scholars writing about the region than they did about the area itself.[85] The ecology of historians was as revealing as the ecology of the West.

85. Pomeroy, "Rediscovering the West," *American Quarterly* 12 (Spring 1960), 30.

FOUR

The West as Urban Civilization, 1890–1990

THROUGHOUT THE PAST one hundred years some historians of the West have sought to find a key to understanding it by studying its towns and cities rather than its more sparsely populated areas. Despite a variety of landscapes, they declared, the area could be comprehended best by considering it as an urban civilization. Although such a view first made its appearance in the 1890s, it became more widely held after 1960. This was in direct response to a rather obvious but dominant development in American, and Western, society, namely, rapid urbanization. Americans moved from the countryside to the cities in increasing numbers after 1890, a trend that was already noticeable when Turner announced the end of the frontier. In 1900 five of ten Americans lived in towns or cities; by 1920 seven of ten; and by 1980 nine of ten. The interests, and the emphases, of historians closely mirrored this radical change in American life-styles and the consequent shift of values, political power, economic activity, and social behavior, and the emergence of new social problems. But perspectives changed slowly, given the strong hold of the frontier thesis on the profession. Interest in the role of Western cities was somewhat muted between 1890 and 1960. But with the population explosion experienced by most Western cities and their suburbs, the concentration on urban studies by historians and sociologists mushroomed. In the course of the next thirty years, the urban interpretation emerged as a major approach to the study of the West.

At the same time that Turner was propounding his frontier hypothesis, one of his contemporaries was developing an urban interpretation of the American experience. That individual was Adna Weber, at the time the deputy commissioner of labor statistics for the state of New York. Weber completed his doctoral dissertation on urban growth in 1899 at Columbia University. Like many of his fellow graduate students at the time, he was greatly influenced by the work of German scholars. During a stay in Germany, he studied with some of the great names of the era. These included men like E. Blenck, director of the Royal Prussian Statistical Bureau in Berlin; Johannes Conrad of the University of Halle; and Max Sering at the University of Berlin. At Columbia University, E. R. A. Seligman and John B. Clark directed his work, both of them distinguished economists. In a particular reference to cities of the American West, Weber wrote:

> In a new country the rapid growth of cities is both natural and necessary, for no efficient industrial organization of a new settlement is possible without industrial centres to carry on the necessary work of assembling and distributing goods. A Mississippi Valley empire rising suddenly into being without its Chicago and smaller centres of distribution is almost inconceivable to the nineteenth century economist. That America is therefore the "land of mushrooming cities" is therefore not at all surprising. But, on the other hand, it is astonishing that the development of the cities in a new country should outstrip that of rural districts which they serve. The natural presumption would be that so long as land remains open to settlement the superfluous population of the older States or of Europe would seek the fundamental or food producing industry of agriculture, and build up cities only in a corresponding degree. Yet in the great cereal regions of the West the cities have grown entirely out of proportion to the rural parts, resulting there, as in the East and in Europe, in an increasing concentration of the population.

Such cities, Weber declared, grew in direct response to the necessities of economic development. "In the latest decade, 1880–1890," he wrote, "the development of the United States was industrial rather than agricultural, and the migration was cityward, instead of westward. While the number of farms and the cereal production have increased but little, the manufacturing interests have prospered as never before. The decade 1880–1890 saw an exceptionally rapid development of the manufacturing industries."[1]

Weber accurately foresaw the growth of Western cities. "The large urban population of the Mississippi Valley is counterbalanced by a large rural population, while the Western States have a comparatively small rural population. The net result is that in the Western States a larger percentage of the people dwell in cities than do the people of the North Central States. 44.8% of Western population lives in towns of 1000 or more. That was more heavily urban than in any other part of the nation except the North Atlantic states." He noted that it was somewhat surprising to find so large a proportionate number of town dwellers in the Far West as compared to the Middle West. The probable explanation, he surmised, was the difference in the physical features of the two regions. While in the Central States agriculture was the staple industry, employing mostly small farmers, "in the Pacific states commerce brings men together in towns, and agriculture does not call for a dense population as it is carried on so largely on large estates, or ranches. The average size of a farm in the Western States, according to the census of 1890 being 324 acres as compared with 133 acres in the North Central States." Weber noted that California, Colorado, Utah, and Washington were more than one-fourth urban. California already outranked Pennsylvania in its urban aspect. In Wyoming, Montana, and Oregon more than one-tenth of the population lived in towns or cities. Weber predicted the West's future development with considerable accuracy. "The historical trend in the distribution of population in the United States is for an ever increasing proportion of the people to dwell in towns."[2]

Weber was not the only urbanist of the 1890s, however. At about the time Turner announced his frontier hypothesis, a respected economist and statistician, Carl Boyd, wrote that "the great cities of America are growing less rapidly than the smaller ones." That was particularly true of the West. "The only inference to be drawn . . . is that in an era of rapid colonization the growth of the new centres of distribution

1. Adna F. Weber, *The Growth of Cities in the Nineteenth Century*, Studies in History, Economics, and Public Law, Columbia University, vol. 11 (New York, 1899), passim, and especially 20, 27, 30, 33–34; see also Josiah Strong, *Our Country* (New York, 1891), 157.

2. Weber, *Growth of Cities*, 30, 33–34.

may overshadow the development of older commercial centres." Boyd also accurately perceived the spatial patterns of Western cities. "The movement towards the suburbs, which is stronger in America than elsewhere with the exception of Australia, not only necessitates frequent annexations of territories, but even then baffles the statistician."[3]

During this same decade, a well-known historian, Edmund James, then teaching at the University of Chicago, also developed an urban interpretation. Writing in 1899, he declared that

> the growth of urban population during the past century in Europe and the United States has been so marked as to excite the universal attention of students of our social, industrial, and political conditions. Not only has the population living in cities increased enormously in absolute numbers during the last one hundred years throughout the world affected by European civilization; but the proportion of the total population dwelling in cities has increased in almost as remarkable a manner. . . . The United States forms a striking example of this development. Owing to the enormous extent of its unoccupied and unsettled territory, and the rapid rate at which it has occupied the wilderness, we should have expected to find simply this tendency to diffusion, but parallel with it has gone a tendency to concentrate in cities.

James then focused more directly on cities of the West. "A remarkable phenomenon in this connection is the growth of cities in the more sparsely settled states," he wrote. "The appearance of such urban conglomerations . . . in what are chiefly agricultural states is one of the most striking facts of our social life. The three Pacific States, with a remarkable sparse population on the whole, showed in 1890 a population of 901,644 in cities of 8,000 or more inhabitants while the rest of the population, rural and village together, only amounted to 969,643."

James lamented that the implication of this urban development in the nation's history was not always fully appreciated. He warned against simplistic interpretations drawn from statistical tables. "In order to get a fairly adequate idea of the real facts concerning . . . urban life,

3. Carl Boyd, "Growth of the Cities in the United States during the Decade, 1880–1890," *Publications of the American Statistical Association* 3 (September 1893), 416; Weber, *Growth of Cities*, 36.

any particular fact should be studied from a number of different viewpoints. The population of a given city, for example, should be compared with the population of other cities, the density of population with the density of population of other cities . . . in order to avoid erroneous conclusions that might be deduced from a single table or a single set of tables."[4]

The emphasis on an urban dimension of American history was developed further during the first two decades of the twentieth century by historians who heeded James H. Robinson's call for a "New History." Robinson, a prominent historian at Columbia University, urged his colleagues to give greater emphasis to social and economic affairs. He first made his appeal in 1912, and soon counted a number of converts. These included young scholars just embarking on their careers, such as Arthur M. Schlesinger, Sr., as well as those who were well established, such as Turner himself. Throughout his life, Turner always remained sensitive to changes in American life which provided new perspectives for historians. In fact, Turner was profoundly impressed by the rapid rise of urbanization in the United States by the time of the First World War and its impact on the West. Turner joined the Harvard faculty in 1910, at just about the time that Schlesinger, Sr., was about to start his graduate studies at Columbia University. Within a few years, Turner openly acknowledged the importance of cities. Writing to Schlesinger on April 18, 1922, he said:

> I am not sure but more . . . attention should be given to the phenomena of great city development and the results and problems in many fields incident thereto. . . . What you say of my frontier studies being fundamentally an economic interpretation interests me. Personally, I don't know. There is in this country such an interrelation of ideals, economic interests, frontier advance (or recession, if you prefer) and regional geography, that it isn't easy to separate them. One whose activity has been more continuously in an urban environment would no doubt lay more stress than I have in my published essays on the importance of the economic revolution substantially, but I am aware of its importance.[5]

Clearly, Turner was conscious of his own youth in a frontier region

4. Edmund J. James, "The Growth of Great Cities," *Annals of the American Academy of Political and Social Science* 13 (January 1899), 1, 3, 10, 30.

5. Frederick Jackson Turner to Arthur M. Schlesinger, Sr., April 18, 1922, reproduced in Jacobs, *Historical World*, 155.

which predisposed him to a frontier interpretation. But he was just as aware of the possibility that a historian bred in an urban context would lean more heavily to an urban approach. Nevertheless, in 1922 he had moved beyond a singular stress on the frontier, and had finished his essay on "The Significance of the Section in American History." During the next three years, however, his thinking moved much closer to emphasizing the role of cities in Western development. As he wrote to Schlesinger, he was engaged in drafting an essay on "The Significance of the City in American History," an essay he never completed. But he noted that he expected American historians to fashion an urban interpretation of the nation's history within one or two decades, and expected it to have deep-seated influence.[6]

Schlesinger paid due homage to Turner and reflected the relativism that drove them both. When in 1922 he published his book of essays *New Viewpoints in American History,* he included a quotation from Turner's address to the American Historical Association in 1910. There, Turner had noted, "A comprehension of the United States of today, an understanding of the rise and progress of the forces which have made it what it is, demands that we should rework our history from the new points of view afforded by the present." When the book appeared, Schlesinger sent a copy to Turner, who was appreciative despite the fact that Schlesinger was beginning to question the importance of environmental influences. In pointing to an urban interpretation, Schlesinger noted that

> the geographic factor has played an important part in shaping the history of the American people no thoughtful person can deny. The conformation of the Atlantic Coast, the mountains and plains and virgin forests of the interior, the frequency of water courses and the variations of climate and soil have all left their impress upon the manner and quality of American development. Not only were the interrelations of Europe and the western hemisphere affected by geographic conditions but, from first to last, the internal development of America was strongly modified by the same influences.[7]

6. Billington, *Turner,* 492–93; Turner's letter is quoted in Arthur M. Schlesinger, Sr., "The City in American History," *Mississippi Valley Historical Review* 27 (June 1940), 43, and reproduced in Jacobs, *Historical World,* 163–65. The Turner Papers at the Henry Huntington Library contain extensive notes on the importance of cities, in file drawers 14 A and 15 C.

7. Schlesinger, Sr., *New Viewpoints,* 23, 29; Jacobs, *Historical World,* 153–55.

But after having paid due homage to such factors, Schlesinger accurately predicted the future directions of American historiography by noting that historians would increasingly stress the importance of cultural influences. "In all probability," he wrote in 1922,

> the influence of natural conditions on American national develop-
> ment will be less important in the future than it has been in the
> past. The age of steam and electricity has neutralized many of the
> effects which proved vital determinants of political and social
> progress in the past. Mountains have been conquered by the rail-
> road and the telegraph; unproductive soils have yielded to irriga-
> tion and fertilization; rivers have been rendered navigable and
> their courses changed. The long contest between Man and Nature
> in America has been decided in favor of Man; and for the future,
> Man seems determined to create the kind of physical environment
> which is best adapted to his fullest development.

And the cities provided that development in the context of the American experience.[8]

Schlesinger gave much fuller expression to his urban hypothesis in his volume about *The City in History*, 1878–1898, which appeared in 1933. In introducing the volume, Dixon Ryan Fox, one of the editors of the *History of American Life* series in which the volume appeared, was more explicit than Schlesinger himself. "The United States in the eighties and nineties was trembling between two worlds," Fox wrote,

> rural and agricultural . . . urban and industrial. In this span of
> years the fateful decision was made. Traditional America gave way
> to a new America, one more akin to Western Europe than to its
> own former self, yet retaining an authentic New World quality.
> The author recognizes that Americans formed a part of the larger
> human family and had behind them the general history of man-
> kind . . . a procedure rare among American historians. Such writ-
> ers, too . . . have been accustomed to emphasizing the long-time
> influence of the frontier upon American civilization and the disas-
> trous effects of the passing of free fertile lands. The present volume
> is devoted, rather, to describing and appraising the new social
> forces which waxed and throve while driving the pioneer culture
> before it: the city. In the ever widening reach of its influence the
> author finds the key to an understanding of the most multifarious

8. Schlesinger, Sr., *New Viewpoints*, 43.

developments. . . . Aside from the part played by urban leadership in building a new structure of industry and trade . . . the city is envisaged as the dominant force of all those impulses and movements which made for a finer, more human civilization. Education, literature, science, invention, the fine arts, social reform, public hygiene, the use of leisure, the "good life"—all these were given lift and direction by those who lived in urban centers. As rumour of the city's fascination and its opportunity reached the far flung countryside, a downward trek set in, which in magnitude recalls the hosts who once had sought a larger life in the unpeopled wilderness.[9]

Schlesinger himself was as yet more muted, perhaps in deference to Turner, a mentor and friend. "Underlying all the varied developments that made up American life," he declared,

was the momentous shift of the center of national equilibrium from the countryside to the city. Long foreshadowed, it had at last become an actuality. A civilization traditionally rural was obliged to learn how to come to terms with a civilization predominantly urban. The process was painful and confusing to those who clung to the older mores. . . . But to untold numbers of others it meant the attainment of a new Promised Land, the release of energies and ambitions which the constricted opportunities of the farm had always denied. The city had come, and it was clear to all, it had come to stay.[10]

After Turner's death, Schlesinger sharpened his urban interpretation. While paying homage to Turner in his presidential address to the Mississippi Valley Historical Association in 1940, Schlesinger noted that Turner had formulated his ideas in an atmosphere of profound agrarian unrest.

Today, however, it seems clear that, in the zeal to correct older notions he overlooked another order of society which, rivaling the frontier even in the earliest days, eventually became the major force. The city marched westward with the outposts of settlement, always injecting exotic elements into pioneer existence, while in the older sections it steadily extended its dominion over politics, economics, and all other interests of life. The time came in 1925

9. Arthur M. Schlesinger, Sr., *The Rise of the City*, 1878–1898 (New York, 1933), 423; Fox in ibid., xiv, xv.
10. Schlesinger, Sr., *Rise of the City*, 436.

when Turner himself confessed the need for an "urban reinterpretation of our history." A true understanding of America's past demands this balanced view—an appreciation of the significance of both frontier and city.[11]

And when he revised the essay nine years later, he further sharpened his interpretation. "A reconsideration of American history from the urban point of view need not lead to the distortion which Professor Turner feared," he declared. "It should direct attention to a much neglected influence and, by so doing, help to illuminate the historian's central problem: the persistent interplay of town and country in the evolution of American civilization."[12]

At the same time that he was promoting an urban interpretation in his own writings, during the 1930s Schlesinger was also encouraging some of his graduate students at Harvard University to follow his lead. One of the first to do so was Carl Bridenbaugh, a Philadelphian who wrote his dissertation on cities in the colonial period. It was eventually published in 1938 as *Cities in the Wilderness.* Bridenbaugh sought to explain that life in the colonial West developed mainly in an urban context rather than exclusively under frontier conditions. Echoing his mentor, Bridenbaugh wrote:

> Emerging from forty years' preoccupation with the frontier in early American history, historians are now beginning to realize that much that was characteristic of life in the colonies did not necessarily bear the stamp of frontier democracy and individualism. Commercial as well as agrarian interests dictated political if not also social revolution; most of the intellectual activity and much of the social and political advance of the eighteenth century depended on an urban rather than rural environment; certainly a large part of our radical thought came neither from farm nor forest but from seaboard towns. I believe the colonial city, though it never embraced more than ten per cent of the population of the colonies, exercised a far more important influence on the life of early America than historians have previously recognized. . . . One of the most important aspects of this study I believe to be the role played by the towns in the transit of civilization from Europe to America.[13]

11. Schlesinger, Sr., "The City," *Mississippi Valley Historical Review* 27, 43.
12. Arthur M. Schlesinger, Sr., *Paths to the Present* (New York, 1949), 210.
13. Carl Bridenbaugh, *Cities in the Wilderness* (New York, 1938), v–vi.

Bridenbaugh directly questioned the frontier hypothesis.

The developments of a hundred years of life under relatively urban conditions created a society at once distinct from that of rural regions, whether tidewater or back country, and even further removed from that of the westward reaching frontier. The communal attitude toward the solution of the physical and social problems of diversified populations dwelling together in close propinquity, and the constantly widening outlook which material progress, commercial expansion, and contact with the larger world of affairs made possible, were its distinguishing characteristics. In general, this society was more cooperative and social, less individualistic in its outlook toward problems of daily life, far more susceptible to outside influences and examples, less aggressively independent than the society of frontier America. At the same time it was more polished, urbane, and sophisticated, more aware of fashion and change, more sure of itself and proud of its achievements . . . than the rural society of the colonial back country. Because its outlook was eastward rather than westward, it was more nearly a European society in an American setting. It had appropriated various points on the American continent and transformed them as nearly as possible into likenesses of what it had known at home. It was itself less transformed in the process than might have been expected, because the contact with the homeland never ceased, but rather increased with the passage of years. Its importance to American life was therefore great. Here were centers of the transit of civilization from Old World to New. . . . It was well for the future of national America that its society should not remain completely rural and agricultural, isolated and self-sufficient, ignorant of outside developments and distrustful of new ideas from abroad, as it might well have done had there been no cities.[14]

Social historians quickly adopted some of Bridenbaugh's themes. In their volume on *The Completion of Independence,* John A. Krout and Dixon Ryan Fox in 1944 noted that "urban life, then, perhaps more largely than today, when rural isolation has been broken down by the modern miracles of transportation and communication, formed the substance of American civilization. It was in the cities that men

14. Ibid., 481.

by mutual imitation changed toward what they considered improvement."[15]

The ripples of the urban interpretation were also felt in the Middle West, where one of Frederic Paxson's students, Bayrd Still, turned his attention to urban influences in the West. As early as 1935 he published an article in which he emphasized the important cultural impact of Chicago in the middle of the nineteenth century, when the Middle West was still largely a frontier. By 1940 Still amplified his urban vision. Undue emphasis on agrarian influences by a whole generation of historians in the previous decades, he argued, had seriously obscured the westward movement of towns and cities which played a vital role in the taming of the wilderness. Town builders and promoters, Still declared, were at least as significant as farmers in extending the path of American civilization westward. In challenging the frontier thesis, Still maintained that the Western city facilitated agricultural development of the West, rather than vice-versa. If the nineteenth-century West enjoyed economic abundance, that was due largely to opportunities afforded by the growth of towns and cities. Such a perception was not entirely novel, Still noted, because contemporaries—unlike historians between 1890 and 1940—were well aware of the trend. The *Milwaukee Sentinel*, on May 26, 1845, for example, declared that "in no other country have towns and villages sprung up so suddenly as in this. . . . cities grow up here to more importance in ten years than they do in Europe in a century."[16]

At the same time, some historians were afraid that a full-blown urban interpretation of American history would impose the same kind of limitations—a straitjacket—which they felt the Turner Thesis had already imposed on the field. That point was made in 1941 by William Diamond, a young historian at Johns Hopkins University. Diamond felt that after 1940 Schlesinger was responding to social science critics of his 1933 book on *The Rise of the City*, who had charged that he was not sufficiently theoretical. One of these was Albert Lepawsky, a political scientist, who in 1933 urged historians to "do with the city

15. John A. Krout and Dixon Ryan Fox, *The Completion of Independence* (New York, 1944), 10.

16. Bayrd Still, "Evidences of the Higher Life on the Frontier," *Journal of the Illinois Historical Society* 28 (1935), 81; Still, "Patterns of Mid-Nineteenth Century Urbanization in the Middle West," *Mississippi Valley Historical Review* 28 (September 1941), 187–206, quote on 187–89.

what Turner and his students did with the frontier. . . . use it as a means of explaining the problems and the pace of American life in the post-frontier period of American history." Diamond was concerned about Schlesinger's use of the city as a causal factor in American life, and his assertion that "cities . . . exerted an important influence on the struggle for manhood suffrage, the effort to abolish war, and the anti-slavery cause, and . . . economic dependencies and spheres of influence." As a causal factor, Diamond felt, Schlesinger needed to provide clearer and more precise definitions of urbanization. In that connection, he cited the already extensive sociological literature on cities that had grown by 1941, which reflected considerable diversity among social scientists studying urban affairs. As Louis Wirth, an eminent urban sociologist at the University of Chicago, noted in 1938: "Despite the preponderant influence of the city in our civilization . . . our knowledge of the nature of urbanism and the process of urbanization is meager." "Which of the many meanings of 'city' and 'urban' Professor Schlesinger prefers is not certain," Diamond stated, "for nowhere in his essay [the presidential address to the Mississippi Valley Historical Association in 1940] is there an explicit definition of terms." Diamond wondered whether changes that were cultural in origin could be mistaken for being urban. Yet rural communities, no less than urban centers, could reflect such changes, even if perhaps more slowly. His point was that differences between rural and urban society might not have been as great as an undue emphasis on urban influences would imply. And some cultural traits might not be products of city life at all but results of environmental changes. Diamond concluded, "The danger of not distinguishing between the results of urban life and those of cultural change common to both city and country . . . was summed up by Professor Wirth when he warned against confusing urbanism with capitalism and industrialism." And Diamond further added:

> Unless the concept "city" is carefully analyzed, students in their enthusiasm for a fresh and attractive reinterpretation of American history may make of the "city" another "frontier" and fall into the difficulties inherent in Turner's "hazy and shifting" concept. Students of urbanization, reading phrases like the "contrast between urban and frontier conceptions of democracy" cannot but be disturbed at the way in which the "frontier" became a bottleneck of American historiography.[17]

17. William Diamond, "On the Dangers of an Urban Interpretation," in Eric F.

By 1945 the first foundations for an urban interpretation of the American experience had been laid by historians who questioned the dominant influence of the frontier. In the 1890s both historians and social scientists had quite properly stressed the importance of cities in American life. But while the social scientists had gone ahead and continued to develop urban studies in succeeding years, the historians restricted themselves increasingly to the Turner Thesis. Perhaps this was due in part to Turner's strong influence in the historical profession. In a larger sense, however, it may have been related to the emotional role of the Turner Thesis rather than to its scholarly dimension. It was, after all, part of the American Myth. The generation between 1890 and 1945 reflected a strong nostalgia for the lost civilization of the nineteenth-century West. That—as Turner had so eloquently proclaimed—defined the national identity of the American people and was a major component of the self-image of Americans. On the other hand, a self-image of America as an urban civilization, similar to that of Europe, was not as attractive or acceptable to Americans of Turner's generation. If, as Ortega y Gasset noted, a cultural lag of at least one generation is characteristic of historical perceptions and interpretations, then it is understandable why the urban dimension of Western history was slow in developing between 1890 and 1945 and why historians only developed it more fully in succeeding years.

Undoubtedly, other influences in historical writing on the West also conditioned the urban interpretation of Western history. The growing emphasis on the cultural influences on Western life by historians went hand in hand with a greater focus on towns and cities, since they served largely as the repositories of culture. Moreover, the lessening of nationalist perspectives and a greater awareness of global trends gradually reinforced urban perspectives. Nor could historians indefinitely ignore major developments in urban sociology during these years. Thus, while preoccupation with the frontier hypothesis might have suppressed an urban interpretation for about a generation, it was unlikely to delay it much beyond that time.

And between 1945 and 1990 the enormous growth of towns and cities increasingly forced itself on the consciousness of historians. In 1945 seven of ten Americans lived in urban areas; by 1990 more than

---

Goldman (ed.), *Historiography and Urbanization: Essays in Honor of W. Stull Holt* (Baltimore, 1941), 106, 110; see *American Journal of Sociology* 39 (September 1933), 253, for review by Albert Lepawsky.

nine out of ten did so. The movement of Americans from the country to the city, begun in the nineteenth century, had largely been completed. As a result, the life-styles of Americans changed accordingly, profoundly influenced by urban styles. The change was particularly noticeable in a young region like the West, where it appeared more dramatically than in older areas. Before 1945 the West contained few major cities with populations over 500,000 people. But between 1945 and 1990 the West came to contain the fastest-growing cities in the United States, with more than a half-dozen populated by more than a half-million individuals. The West had become primarily an urban civilization as four of five Westerners lived in its metropolitan areas.[18]

So drastic was this change that historians could not fail to take note of its importance. Beginning in the postwar era, therefore, a growing number of scholars began to explore the urban dimension of Western history. They did not confine themselves to the twentieth century, but applied the urban perspective to the whole range of Western history. Beginning with broad general studies and histories of individual cities, historians by the 1970s began to delve into increasingly specialized aspects of city growth. In the process, they developed a new perspective on the West by 1990, one that focused on an urban civilization.

The Second World War did much to stimulate further development of the urban interpretation of the West. In addition to the works of Schlesinger and Bridenbaugh, the extensive writings of sociologists and political scientists on urban affairs drew attention to the subject. Moreover, in 1938 Lewis Mumford published *The City in History*, a complex interdisciplinary work which placed further emphasis on the role of cities in developing civilizations around the world. In addition to these writers, the experience of the wartime years underscored the importance of cities in the West. The war stimulated the growth of Western cities as no other event before it. Cities like San Diego doubled their population in four short years. Los Angeles gained more than 400,000 new residents. Phoenix grew from 20,000 to 60,000; places like Las Vegas zoomed from 8,000 to 40,000. Population growth occurred in cities; sparsely populated areas in the West actually lost population. Thus, the war did much to change the image of the West.

18. Nash, *American West in the Twentieth Century*, 189–289; Michael P. Malone and Richard W. Etulain, *The American West: A Twentieth-Century History* (Lincoln, 1989), 120–294.

No longer was it an area characterized by wide, open spaces—although it still had these in abundance. It had become the depository of boom-ing cities—urban oases—which contained more than four-fifths of its population.[19]

The years from 1945 to 1960 also witnessed a striking reorientation in the field of American history. In the words of John D. Hicks, a well-known contemporary historian, the ecology of the profession changed drastically. Whereas the previous generation of historians had been born in rural areas of New England or the Middle West, the new emerging generation tended to be of urban background, with many sons and daughters from first- or second-generation immigrant stock.[20]

That trend was already evident in the early stages of the war. Ecology, as Hicks used the term, described the mutual relationship between organisms and their environments. His main point was that biologists as well as historians are, to a considerable extent, creatures of the conditions that surround them. For all their gallant efforts to achieve objectivity, they always betrayed a close connection with the environment about them. If the revelation was not new or highly original, it needed to be emphasized if historians were to retain some perspective. "American writers of American history are particularly prone to reflect their environment in their writings," Hicks wrote.

> New Englanders have generally shown a calm confidence in the superiority of the culture from which they have sprung, and have not failed to note the deep and abiding influence of New England ways upon the whole American nation. Writers from the Middle Atlantic states have often emphasized nationalism, less perhaps, because Middle Atlantic horizons were particularly wide than be-cause the Middle States could never have hoped to stand alone, and required the support of every other section to live at all. His-torians of the South have almost invariably stood out as convinced regional apologists, determined . . . to take their stand by Dixie Land. Historians of the Middle West and of the Far West are little different. Westerners no less than easterners survey the historical scene from the vantage point of their own locale.

19. Lewis Mumford, *The City in History* (New York, 1938); Nash, *American West Transformed,* 56–87.

20. John D. Hicks, "The 'Ecology' of Middle-Western Historians," *Wisconsin Mag-azine of History* 24 (June 1941), 376, 377; Novick, *Noble Dream,* 22–24, 169–75, 361–66.

Hicks placed Turner within this broader context. "It was a matter of great importance that Turner began to write at a time when the memory of the frontier was still fresh in his mind." As Turner himself confessed: "Is it strange that I saw the frontier as a real thing and experienced its changes? . . . Is it strange that I preached on the frontier?" To which Hicks added: "Is it strange that other historians of the Middle West, some of Turner's generation and some of the next, should have been stirred by the same motives that inspired Turner? . . . It is but natural that native historians of the Middle West . . . should have emphasized the West in their writings." On the other hand, it was harder for the succeeding generations of urbanites to understand frontier conditions. As Hicks noted:

> How could any city-bred easterners . . . ever hope to know Turner's Middle West? It is not surprising that during the last few years there has been a tendency . . . to break away from the Turnerian approach. Today the sound of industry has drowned out the sounds of the woodmen's axe. . . . the graduate students of the past two decades have been recruited from the cities. . . . Like Turner and his generation they see the field of history from the vantage point of their own environment. Speak of the rise of big business, the growth of cities, the problems of labor . . . and they stand on familiar ground. But to this generation, which has learned of the frontier only from books, the Turner hypothesis seems to be only a succession of overstatements. . . . Unfortunately, however, some of those who rail most bitterly against the way in which Turner wrote his environment into his history insist on doing precisely the same thing with theirs.[21]

This trend became even more evident in the succeeding decade when, in 1953, Hicks took another look at the American historical profession. "Again the scene is shifting," he declared,

> and again a new generation is taking over. The newcomers, like their predecessors, have been conditioned in part by cataclysmic events—in their case the Great Depression and World War II. The young men now arriving . . . at the age of forty have never known placid times as adults. They were just finishing high school when the Panic of 1929 broke; they were in college and graduate school,

21. Hicks, "'Ecology,'" *Wisconsin Magazine of History* 24 (June 1941), 378, 379, 380, 382, 384.

if they could manage it during the bleak years of the Depression. . . . Their lives were deeply affected by the raging conflict . . . [World War II]. Even the postwar years have been full of abnormalities. The new generation . . . has a right to feel . . . grim and suspicious. It finds difficulty in accepting readily all the old values. Its faith in the future is considerably short of buoyant. . . . It is . . . worried about . . . the world, the United States, themselves. . . . They are surcharged with disillusionment. They are products of the city rather than of the country; they are urban-minded, not rural-minded. . . . It is inevitable, therefore, that our new historians, brought up in the new environment, should take a diminishing interest in the old, rural America. . . . For these "asphalt flowers," as Charles A. Beard . . . once called them, the significance of the American frontier, which made good sense to rural-minded Americans, makes almost no sense at all. . . . They tend . . . to be not only present-minded, but also city-minded.[22]

One of the first to emphasize the importance of cities in the West, among the writers of this period, was Carey McWilliams in 1949. "Isn't it absurd to attempt a social and cultural analysis of the intermountain West, with its vast area and paucity of population, through a study of its 'cities,' scarcely one of which measures up . . . to the dimension of real urban status?" he asked.

Nevertheless, the cities of the West, paradoxical as the statement may sound, are socially more important than their counterparts in the other major regions. Where people are so thinly distributed over such vast areas the concentration of population, no matter how small they may be . . . come to possess a unique importance. . . . With a population of 23,000 Reno would ordinarily be placed in the category of small towns, but in Nevada, with a statewide population slightly in excess of 100,000, it looms large as a city. . . . While these Rocky Mountain cities may be the nation's small towns, they are by every standard the big cities of the West: big in relation to the territories they serve, big in relation to total state population, big in relation to the functions they discharge. . . . Cheyenne *is* Wyoming; Denver *is* Colorado; Reno *is* Nevada. In this sense, therefore, these cities are more truly capitals than cities many times their size.[23]

22. John D. Hicks, "American History," *Saturday Review of Literature* 36 (March 14, 1953), 14, 15.
23. Carey McWilliams, "Introduction," in Ray B. West (ed.), *Rocky Mountain Cities* (New York, 1949), 7, 8, 9.

Always imaginative and suggestive, McWilliams also advocated a broad urban approach to the study of the West. In 1949 he was also rethinking the larger dimensions of Western history as he put the finishing touches on another book, *California: The Great Exception.* An urban perspective, he declared, made it possible to view "the West . . . from a new point of view: from its centers, not its fringes; from the places where its interests are articulated, not where they are most dispersed. This reverses, of course, the usual procedure, for far more has been written about the fringes of Western life—out where the West begins—than about its centers. It differs also from the usual appraisal by having been written from the inside out, with the insight born of experience and the candor which affection permits." And with a finality that was surprising for the time, he declared: "An understanding of the capitals of the West provides the key to an understanding of the region."[24]

That theme was taken up by an increasing number of historians in the decade of the 1950s. In 1952, Blake McKelvey, one of Schlesinger's former students who was then writing a history of Rochester, New York, made a brief survey of the status of urban history. He found the field still undefined and rather small. To provide it with some sense of direction, he suggested that the task of urban historians was "to measure the extent to which the ideals and aspirations of . . . society found expression, growth, or rebirth in urban centers." Only a few scattered studies of individual cities were available. In regard to the West, Charles M. Gates had embarked on an exploratory essay entitled "The Role of Cities in the Westward Movement," which he read at the 1950 meeting of the Mississippi Valley Historical Association. Gates stressed the close relation between urban growth and agricultural development and urged historians to take note of changing urban–rural relations during successive stages of the westward movement.[25]

Within a year, Constance Green, a social historian, attempted to provide a more comprehensive urban interpretation of the westward migrations of the nineteenth century. Delivering four lectures at the University of London, her purpose was to emphasize the importance

24. Ibid., 10, 23.
25. Blake McKelvey, "American Urban History Today," *American Historical Review* 57 (July 1952), 919–29; paper by Gates summarized in *Mississippi Valley Historical Review* 37 (September 1950), 277–78.

of urban growth as contrasted to the frontier. In the book published in 1957 as *American Cities,* Green declared that

> cities have played an important part in the development of the United States since the founding of the nation. City enterprise . . . was a force as powerful in peopling the country as the restless urge that drove the trapper on into the wilderness and the homesteader in his wake. For hard on their heels came men intent upon exploiting the new country in other ways—by marketing furs and hides, by lending money and giving credit; in short, by building up the life of older cities and by founding new. The swift rise of cities is a feature of American history no less significant and dramatic than the swift march of the frontier.

Green eschewed the geographical determinism of an earlier generation and presaged the emphasis on cultural influences that was to be characteristic of most historians during the latter half of the twentieth century.

> Though geography determined the pattern of American expansion across the continent and the rise of cities at strategic points, the men and women who seized the opportunities thus prodigally offered left their own indelible marks upon the country and the nation. . . . With the maturing of the machine age in the United States . . . shifting economic opportunity partly explains the impulse of Americans to be constantly "on the move," just as the lure of free land accounted for much of it in the earlier years.

Green thus provided one of the first comprehensive efforts to develop an urban interpretation for the westward movement.[26]

In a less theoretical vein, Lewis Atherton in 1954 sought to underscore the importance of towns in the growth of the Middle West. "The history of the Middle Border," he proclaimed in that year, "has been largely the history of its towns. Even today, when automobiles have greatly reduced the necessity for decentralized trade centers, villages a few miles apart speckle the midwestern countryside." And in his detailed narrative, he provided evidence to indicate how the manifold aspects of an unfolding civilization were, in one way or another, closely related to stimulation provided by small urban communities.[27]

26. Constance M. Green, *American Cities* (London, 1957), 2, 3, 4.
27. Lewis Atherton, *Main Street on the Middle Border* (Bloomington, 1954), 3.

But perhaps the most notable addition to the emergence of Western urban history came in 1959, when Richard Wade published his book, *The Urban Frontier: The Rise of Western Cities, 1790–1830*. "The rural West has had many historians," Wade wrote. "Its growth, influence, and importance are well known. Yet it is not always well understood that from almost the very beginning there was also an urban West . . . before the surrounding area had fallen to the plow. From the earliest days [cities] became centers of economic activity for the whole region, the focuses of cultural life, and scenes of great social change. . . ." Wade crystallized some of the same themes that Carey McWilliams had outlined a decade earlier. "The towns were the spearheads of the frontier," he noted. "Planted far in advance of the line of settlement, they held the West for the approaching population." In developing his themes, Wade did not necessarily reject the Turner Thesis as much as he supplemented it. "By 1830, then, the West had produced two types of society," he wrote,

> one rural, and one urban. Each developed its own institutions, habits, and living patterns. . . . The West was large enough to contain both movements comfortably. Indeed, each supported the other. . . . Yet the cities represented the more aggressive and dynamic force. By spreading their economic power over the entire section, by bringing the fruits of civilization across the mountains, and by insinuating their ways into the countryside, they speeded up the transformation of the West from a gloomy wilderness to a richly diversified region. Any historical view which omits this dimension of Western life tells but part of the story.[28]

Clearly, the urban historians of the West during the 1950s were groping for a sharper analytical framework, perhaps one that would suggest structure for the broader process of urbanization. That was clear from some of the studies that appeared, which provided a spur for a new generation of historians who prided themselves on their familiarity with the social sciences and interdisciplinary research. One of these was Eric Lampard, a young British-born historian who was trained at the University of Wisconsin. In 1961, he published a suggestive essay on "The Study of Urbanization" in the *American Historical Review*. As a European, Lampard took a broader and perhaps more

28. Richard C. Wade, *The Urban Frontier: The Rise of Western Cities, 1790–1830* (Cambridge, Mass., 1959), 1, 341–42.

detached view of the American urbanization experience than scholars in the United States. "After all," he declared,

> Americans had been taught [in the nineteenth century] that the United States was born in the country, that its most cherished institutions and ways of life were uniquely shaped in the rustic mold. The yeoman, the pioneer, the frontiersman, the cultivator, and their near neighbors . . . were the idealized types, the original and noblest representatives of the nation's spirit and character. This agrarian view of society was supported by much literary and statistical evidence. During the nineteenth century it hardened into ideology.

Lampard sought to set forth the reasons that explained the neglect of cities by American historians. "What American historians brought back from their pilgrimage abroad [in the late nineteenth century]," he noted,

> was a methodological passion for particularism and formal documentation. Up to a point this was salutary, but when historians looked for conceptual frameworks to explain American development, they mistook the phenomena of variation and difference for "uniqueness." It was easy to believe, in Frederick Jackson Turner's words, that the "true point of view" could be found in "The Great West." For all but political purposes, the historic connection between the rise of a "manufacturing civilization" in the Northeast and a "continually advancing frontier line" in the interior was ignored. The centrifugal currents of migration obscured centripetal currents from view. . . . The general approach to the city had been set in 1888 when James Bryce published *The American Commonwealth,* and concluded that cities in America were a very unfortunate development.

Such a negative view, Lampard claimed, particularly as it was contrasted with the positive appraisal of the frontier, profoundly influenced two generations of American historians before 1960. The few who wrote about cities, on the other hand, were unduly impressed by contemporary social scientists. Yet, they too "seem to have accepted the compartmentalization of society into 'urban' and 'rural' types and to have adopted the somewhat superficial distinctions made by economists between 'industry' and 'agriculture.' In studying mainly urban problems, they neglected the study of process of urbanization in the

larger context of social change." He suggested that much sharper conceptual frameworks were needed, perhaps on the basis of models suggested by the well-known urban sociologist Leo Schnore. These involved
the examination of urbanization as a societal process, or the study of
communities within the context of human ecology.[29]

In a survey of urban history in 1963, another young historian,
Charles Glaab, echoed Lampard's complaint. Many of the studies of
the preceding decade, he lamented, were quite adequate as studies of
individual cities, but they led nowhere in terms of explaining urbanization as a process. "A few gleanings from nineteenth-century writing
about cities do not really permit any elaborate conclusions about the
nature of the American urban tradition," he wrote, "in spite of the
tendency of historians of late to generalize about the character of a
movement or an aspect of thought on the basis of one or two literary
products. They do suggest, however, that the concepts of 'city' and
'urban' are sufficiently vague to have lent themselves to a variety of
uses in our past, and certainly these uses ought to be explored more
fully than they have been before one speaks authoritatively of either
the prevalence of urbanism or anti-urbanism in our culture." Glaab
deplored the tendency of historians to dwell on the agrarian roots of
American society. Reflecting the rapid growth of cities in his own
lifetime, he noted that "the United States is now the land of the city
and the super-city and since the historian is as much concerned with
finding a 'usable past' as a real one, we shall undoubtedly see more in
our future general histories about the urban side of the American
experience. One can hope that our national historians in developing
these urban themes will . . . [avoid] arguing . . . a supposed urban–
rural dialogue, which earlier historians artificially imposed on our
past."[30]

At the same time, historians like Glaab were uncovering significant
evidence from contemporaries involved in nineteenth-century urban
development, evidence largely ignored by scholars under the Turnerian
spell between 1890 and 1945. Historians writing in the 1960s increasingly shifted their focus on the cultural influences shaping Western

29. Eric E. Lampard, "The Study of Urbanization," *American Historical Review* 67
(October 1961), 51, 60, 62, 63.
30. Charles N. Glaab, "The Historian and the American Urban Tradition," *Wisconsin Magazine of History* 47 (Autumn 1963), 15, 22, 24.

city growth, and deemphasized geographic or environmental conditions. That tendency reflected a broader trend in Western history. Their emphasis was on individuals and institutions whom they perceived as the prime determinants of Western urban development.

Among the individuals, city boosters were a vital force in promoting Western settlement, and Glaab explored their role in some detail. William Gilpin was one of the most important of these mid-nineteenth-century figures, and one of the few who developed a systematic theory of city location in his day. Not only did he influence Senator Thomas Hart Benton's ideas of empire, but he questioned the perception of the arid West as the Great American Desert. Gilpin postulated the inevitability of a continuing westward stream of population which would make the interior a vital center of world commerce. His doctrine of natural advantages was used by scores of other promoters to boost their own particular communities. Other urban enthusiasts were not as prominent, but produced a large body of pamphlet literature which left its mark. They included Jesup Scott in Toledo, Daniel Drake in Cincinnati, Robert T. Van Horn (and Gilpin) in Kansas City, Logan U. Reavis in St. Louis, among others. "None of these figures can be considered brilliant writers," Glaab declared.

> Their style was unpolished, their ideas were often unoriginal, their
> arguments often inconsistent. Still, their work is important in in-
> dicating that the nineteenth century faith in American progress
> was not always tied to the yeoman in his garden but often instead
> to a West of thriving cities. . . . This is explicitly true in the case
> of Jesup Scott, perhaps the most influential of all the western ur-
> ban promotional writers. Where Drake was a blunt propagandist
> for the economic interests of his section, Gilpin an erudite geo-
> graphical determinist, Van Horn a down-to-earth student of tech-
> nology, and Reavis a rhetorical prophet, Scott might be termed a
> primitive demographer. . . . He predicted accurately . . . the
> highly urbanized upper Middle West of today.[31]

Other historians amplified the role of urban boosters during the nineteenth century. Within a decade, J. Christopher Schnell and Katherine B. Clinton sought to demonstrate that boosters envisioned

31. Charles N. Glaab, "Visions of Metropolism: William Gilpin and Theories of City Growth in the American West," *Wisconsin Magazine of History* 45 (Autumn 1961), 113–21; Glaab, "Jesup W. Scott and a West of Cities," *Ohio History* 73 (Winter 1964), 3–12.

a West tied not to the frontier but to cities. The urban vision was popularized in newspapers, tracts, and pamphlets, the most common form of reading material for most Americans. "The literature proclaimed the bright and prosperous future of the American city and announced the westward march of commerce," Schnell and Clinton noted. "The promoters envisioned towns that would boom on the prairies, would mold the patterns of transcontinental migration, and exploit the wealth of the mountains. Through the grandiose and spectacular proportions of their visions, these men made a significant contribution to American thought about the West," while notable women diarists made their own distinctive contribution toward the same goal.[32]

Although not primarily concerned with the West, the works of Stephan Thernstrom provided an inspiration to scholars working on urban themes. Oriented strongly toward the social sciences, he borrowed especially from sociologists concerned with social mobility. His use of quantitative methods in extracting data from the U.S. Census returns also appealed to his peers. Moreover, they found his ideological perspective appealing. His goal was to write "history from the bottom up," to deal with "the lives of hundreds of obscure men," not with leaders or moneyed individuals. That was the core of the "new social history," and reflected social themes common in the 1960s, in the era of Lyndon B. Johnson's Great Society. The aim of his first book, he declared, was to trace "the initial impact of urbanization and industrialization upon the social life of the community." Thernstrom was cautious, but optimistic about the development of urban history. "It may be premature to claim that a 'new urban history' has emerged as yet," he declared in 1969, "but it is clear that the burgeoning field . . . is now in a state of creative ferment. New questions are being raised, new sources are being exploited, new methods of analysis are being employed."[33]

Thernstrom's positive outlook was conditioned, in part, by the appearance of a growing number of works on Western cities. These

32. J.Christopher Schnell and Katherine B. Clinton, "The New West: Themes in Nineteenth Century Urban Promotion, 1815–1880," *Bulletin of the Missouri Historical Society* 30 (January 1973), 76, 88.

33. Stephan Thernstrom, *Poverty and Progress: Social Mobility in a Nineteenth Century City* (Cambridge, Mass., 1964), 3, 5, 6, 7; Thernstrom (ed.), *Nineteenth Century Cities* (New York, 1969), vii. On his research methodology, see Thernstrom, *The Other Bostonians* (Boston, 1973), 1, 197.

included books on the history of individual cities such as those by A. Theodore Brown and Lyle W. Dorsett on Kansas City, and Kenneth Wheeler and David McComb on cities in Texas. The emphasis of these works was on narrative rather than theoretical analysis such as Lampard and Thernstrom were advocating. Still, they provided significant evidence for the field. Wheeler's main theme was that the founding of the four cities he studied—Austin, San Antonio, Houston, and Galveston—preceded the opening of rural frontiers. By implication, this certainly challenged Turner's frontier thesis. McComb's history of Houston had a similar function. And James B. Allen's history of company towns in the West in 1966 provided still another previously unexplored dimension of Western urban growth. If these studies seemed disparate, they were informative and added to the growing appreciation of urban life in the West.[34]

As the most heavily urbanized part of the trans-Mississippi area, the Pacific Coast was likely to attract attention from historians. Most notably, Earl Pomeroy helped to open up that field. In *The Pacific Slope*, published in 1965, Pomeroy noted that while he did not intend to "disparage romantic history . . . I have not written it." A major focus of the book was on the urban dimension of the Pacific Coast from earliest times to the middle of the twentieth century. Pomeroy explained his views on the urban context of the West a few years later (1971), when he said:

> Historians have been slow to recognize the urban dimension of the
> American West. Their slowness has been especially striking in the
> Far West. . . . Perhaps they could not easily believe in cities that
> not only preceded farms but also employed their populations in
> service trades rather than in either industry or agriculture, and
> whose immorality often was not that of the rough frontiersman
> that Bret Harte described for Eastern readers but rather that of the
> transient who refused to accept social responsibility. The westward
> movement brought forth a continuing Western movement in a
> transurban civilization in which time replaced space.

And Pomeroy wondered aloud with Roy Lubove, who had noted in

34. A. Theodore Brown and Lyle W. Dorsett, *K.C.: A History of Kansas City, Missouri* (Boulder, 1978); Kenneth H. Wheeler, *To Wear a City's Crown: The Beginnings of Urban Growth in Texas, 1836–1865* (Cambridge, 1968), 165; David G. McComb, *Houston, the Bayou City* (Austin, 1969); James B. Allen, *The Company Town in the American West* (Norman, 1966).

1967 that "the city threatens to substitute for the frontier, or settlement of the West, as the key . . . to the evolution of American life."[35]

Although Robert Fogelson had little interest in Western history, his study of the growth of Los Angeles provided useful factual data. His interest lay in tracing the growth of central cities in an industrializing economy, and the growth of suburbs from 1870 to 1920. Los Angeles provided a striking example of these trends and provided a model for the development of other Western cities. While lacking in broad significance, the book was another link in a growing list of histories about individual cities in the West.[36]

Historians like Pomeroy and Fogelson dealt with the large metropolitan centers of the region, but others now began to examine smaller communities as well. One of these was Robert Dykstra, who examined the growth of cattle towns in Kansas during the second half of the twentieth century. Utilizing social science literature on the building of communities, Dykstra attempted to place his treatment in a larger social context. To a considerable extent, he was also inspired by the work of Atherton and Wade in the previous decade. As he noted:

> Richard C. Wade's study of St. Louis and four Ohio Valley cities in their first decades of growth vividly documents the successful urban impulse on the frontier. On the other hand, Lewis Atherton's description of life in the midwestern country towns of the late nineteenth and early twentieth centuries in a sense catalogues its failures. But if we could distribute these communities on a scale according to their success in achieving urban growth—Wade's to the upper end, Atherton's to the lower—it seems apparent that we gain something from this raw discrimination of extremes, [although] much is still to be said about what lies between: the collective experience of numberless villages and towns that may be thought of as aspirants to city status, whose destinies for longer or shorter periods and in greater or lesser degree hung in a precarious balance between urban "success" and small town "failure."[37]

Among the smaller towns in the West, mining communities were

35. Earl Pomeroy, *The Pacific Slope* (New York, 1965), vii; Pomeroy, "The Urban Frontier of the Far West," in John G. Clark (ed.), *The Frontier Challenge: Responses to the Trans-Mississippi West* (Lawrence, Kansas, 1971), 24, 25.

36. Robert M. Fogelson, *The Fragmented Metropolis: Los Angeles, 1850–1930* (Cambridge, Mass., 1967).

37. Robert R. Dykstra, *The Cattle Towns* (New York, 1968), 4.

among the most distinctive, and by the 1960s they were finally re-
ceiving greater attention from historians. In 1967, Duane Smith published *Rocky Mountain Mining Camps: The Urban Frontier*, primarily a
narrative history of individual mining towns in Colorado. But the
volume contributed to a growing awareness among historians that the
West was as much a product of urban life as it was of western pioneering. As Smith put it:

> The mining camp represented something different, and for the
> most part, new in the American frontier experience: urbaniza-
> tion. . . . For centuries the frontier had been . . . the cutting edge
> of civilization. . . . In contrast, on the mining frontier the
> camp—the germ of a city—appeared almost simultaneously with
> the opening of the region. . . . The urban nature of the move-
> ment increased the speed and direction of development. . . . The
> mining frontier also represents another break with traditional pat-
> terns. The miners jumped hundreds of miles of wilderness to reach
> Colorado and Montana. . . . An urban society evolved before the
> rural one. It came to dominate the region. . . . Its taproots have
> gone deep into Western experience.[38]

This same theme was applied to a group of larger cities—San
Francisco, Denver, Minneapolis, and Chicago—by Gunther Barth in
his 1974 volume on *Instant Cities*. Barth argued that these metropolitan
areas were built in advance of frontier settlement. His editor, Richard
Wade, put the issue sharply when he noted that "rapid urbanization
had ended the frontier era in the West," a claim that was open to
discussion. But Barth's volume provided additional data on the impact
of urban communities in the Far West and Rocky Mountain areas.[39]

By 1970 the history of urban development in the West was gathering momentum. The number and variety of studies in the field was
increasing. On the one hand, historians were producing highly specialized works on a wide range of subjects in some way related to urban
development. On the other hand, they were still groping for integrative theories that could provide some direction or structure for practitioners in this emerging specialty. To some extent, changing
contemporary conditions were continuing to shape such directions.

38. Duane A. Smith, *Rocky Mountain Mining Camps: The Urban Frontier* (Bloomington, 1967), 4, 7, 9, 248.
39. Gunther Barth, *Instant Cities: Urbanization and the Rise of San Francisco and
Denver* (New York, 1975), vii.

The concern over poverty by the 1960s generation led to increased interest in social mobility. Increasing consciousness of ethnic, racial, and gender minorities engendered by the civil rights movement opened that dimension in urban history. A growing dominance of the military on Western city development brought the relationship of the military–industrial complex to urban development into sharper focus. Serious environmental problems experienced by Western cities during these years led to an awareness of this previously neglected aspect of Western urban development. And the rapidly growing population of Western metropolitan areas between 1960 and 1990 underscored the increasing importance of Western communities in the context of national life. In terms of age the Western might still be the new kid on the block, but it had become more like a rapidly growing adolescent than a toddler.

A concern for social mobility—or the lack thereof—was reflected in the writings of Howard Chudakoff. In a study of residential and social mobility in Omaha between 1880 and 1920, Chudakoff used many of the same assumptions and methods that Thernstrom had developed a decade earlier. Making imaginative application of computer technology to the U.S. Census returns, he followed the careers of thousands of individuals in Omaha to demonstrate that Western cities did not necessarily provide new economic opportunities and rapid upward mobility. And in a more general book, *The Evolution of American Urban Society*, in 1972 Chudakoff took direct aim at Turner. That venerable scholar was absolutely wrong, he concluded, because cities accompanied or preceded the frontier—whether as commercial outposts or as depots from which settlers radiated.[40]

Social mobility was also one of the concerns of Lawrence Larsen, who published *The Urban West at the End of the Frontier* in 1978. Like Chudakoff, Larsen based much of this work on an analysis of the United States Census returns, particularly for 1880. The volume was one of the first to attempt social analysis of a group of western cities, in this case twenty-four communities. As Larsen wrote: "For decades professional historians produced studies that supported or repudiated Turner. . . . While intensive research . . . contributed in many ways to an understanding of the West, the studies did not tell us much

40. Howard Chudakoff's two volumes include Chudakoff, *The Evolution of American Urban Society* (New York, 1972), 31, 122; and *Mobile Americans: Residential and Social Mobility in Omaha, 1880–1920* (New York, 1972).

about the people themselves. . . . Turner's attempt to formulate a starting point for a chain of reasoning designed to go beyond the surface clutter of history became the end rather than the means." Larsen reasoned that perhaps the urban West lacked the color and romance of the frontier. "The urban frontier was much less colorful than other aspects of the western experience," he noted. "Still, the undramatic processes of organizing towns significantly shaped frontier society."

Larsen also questioned the supposed impact of the frontier on American society. "The urban frontier represented a unique aspect of the Western experience," he declared. "City building was neither a proving ground for democracy nor a battlefield for cowboys and Indians. It was not a response to geographic or climatic conditions. Rather, it was the extension of a process perfected earlier, the promotion and building of sites, no matter how undesirable, into successful localities."[41]

While Larsen dealt with broad issues of social mobility as these became more a matter of public concern in the 1960s, he did not provide the theoretical framework which some historians on the New Left were seeking. That task was undertaken by Ronald Davis in 1979, as he surveyed the literature of Western urban history. "The history of urban places and life in the American West lacks an analytical framework," Davis declared. "The problem is not in the want of literature or scholarship. The nature of the problem seems to have escaped the historians of the American West. What is needed is a conceptual framework enabling us objectively to understand the process resulting in a city." Davis believed that he could offer such an all-embrasive concept in a neo-Marxist framework. It was the exploitative and destructive influence of capitalism which affected every aspect of Western urban growth.

> Urban places in the western United States resulted from and were part of a process of exploitation for private gain. Their eventual success in the concentration of exploitative powers . . . always depended upon their ability to link up to the system . . . of private enterprise functioning under the capitalist mode of production. . . . Class lines are perpetuated, the status quo is institutionalized, redistributive justice is blocked, and planning the common

41. Lawrence H. Larsen, *The Urban West at the End of the Frontier* (Lawrence, 1978), 1, 4, 18.

good is an impossibility because the mode of production requires exploitative justice and competitive social relationships. For the historian interested in understanding the process affecting and including the past development and reality of frontier urban places, such a conceptual framework is a good point of departure.[42]

If few historians followed Davis's advice, more sought conceptualization in ethnic approaches, especially in the urban experiences of Westerners of Hispanic background. In contrast to an earlier generation of writers like Carey McWilliams, who in *North from Mexico* in 1947 had focused attention on Spanish speaking people in agriculture, the historians of the 1970s tended to focus on Chicanos as an urban population. In his study of El Paso, *Desert Immigrants*, Mario García emphasized the importance of such cities to the great ethnic migrations of the twentieth century. "El Paso symbolized to Mexicans what New York had represented to European immigrants," he wrote. It provided "the opening to what they believed would be a better life. Besides being the largest port of entry, this border site between 1880 and 1920 . . . supplied jobs for large numbers of unemployed Mexican workers as it surged from an obscure desert town to an 'instant city.'" And García sought to suggest a new strand in Western urban history— through the study of Mexican-American communities in the cities. "The urban dimension, as reflected by the Mexicans of El Paso," he claimed, "provides a fuller understanding of the part Mexicans played in the economic development of the Southwest and of the United States." A similar theme was developed by Oscar Martínez in his broadly based account of El Paso as the "capital" of the extensive lands strutting the Mexican–American border, one of the largest bicultural border areas in the United States.[43]

Chicano scholars developed similar themes for Los Angeles during these years. In his study of the formation of a Mexican barrio in Los Angeles between 1890 and 1920, Richard Griswold del Castillo noted that "the history of the Mexican community in Los Angeles during the period 1890 to 1920 reflects an urban experience. . . . By examining the social history of the Mexicans within an urban perspective

42. Ronald L. F. Davis, "Western Urban Development: A Critical Analysis," in Jerome O. Steffen (ed.), *The American West* (Norman, 1979), 175, 178, 180, 191.
43. Mario T. García, *Desert Immigrants: The Mexicans of El Paso, 1880–1920* (New Haven, 1981), 2, 3, 234, 235; Oscar J. Martínez, *Border Boom Town: Ciudad Juárez Since 1880* (Austin, 1978).

a fresh and dynamic viewpoint can be introduced. . . . The process of urbanization for Chicanos is a central theme. . . . Only through the study of the Mexican within an urban perspective can we come closer to the historical reality of this group." Ricardo Romo extended such themes in his study of the East Los Angeles barrio in the twentieth century. "Prior to the publication of Stephan Thernstrom's influential study, *Poverty and Progress,* most of the urban studies recorded the activities of political and business elites," Romo noted. He, too, was interested in writing about people "from the bottom up," by emphasizing quantitative analysis of working people, and examining "the impact of the urban process on ethnic communities." That was also the goal of Albert Camarillo's short little monograph on Chicanos in Santa Barbara, while Mauricio Mazón focused on a small aspect of the Chicano experience in Los Angeles with his psychoanalytic interpretation of the Zoot Suit Riots of 1943. While these historians reflected the Chicano activism of their day, their studies contributed to revealing another dimension of Western urban life, one that had been largely untouched by previous scholars.[44]

Yet the ethnic aspect of Western urban history was not sufficiently broad to provide a comprehensive conceptual framework for the field, a search in which other historians engaged in the two decades after 1970. Among the most imaginative was Roger Lotchin who—impressed by the enormous growth of the military–industrial complex in the West after 1940—developed his concept of a metropolitan–military complex. His thesis was that the growth of Western cities was profoundly influenced by military installations and institutions in their environs, from the middle of the nineteenth century to the present. By the 1850s frontier forts maintained by the United States Army to combat Indians were already shaping the development of nearby cities. In the twentieth century such relationships became even more significant as militarization and urbanization became closely intertwined. "Although historians of earlier eras and other countries have noted

44. Pedro G. Castillo, "The Making of a Mexican Barrio: Los Angeles, 1890–1920" (Diss., University of California, Santa Barbara, 1979), vii, 1, 11, 14, 15, 250. Ricardo Romo, *East Los Angeles: History of a Barrio* (Austin, 1983), vii, 3, 4, 7; Albert Camarillo, *Chicanos in a Changing Society: From Mexican Pueblos to American Barrios in Santa Barbara and Southern California,* 1848–1930 (Cambridge, Mass., 1979); Mauricio Mazón, *The Zoot Suit Riots: The Psychology of Symbolic Annihilation* (Austin, 1984).

the frequent convergence of the city and sword," wrote Lotchin, "historians of twentieth century American cities have neglected the topic. Given the enhanced importance of both militarization and urbanization, it would seem appropriate to bring the connection between urban and military history back into focus." Lotchin considered the relationship to be among the most crucial factors explaining Western urban growth. "Western civilian–service ties that have been called the military–industrial complex obviously came before . . . World War II. In . . . the Sunbelt these ties had an urban, rather than an industrial base. They were also significant to both national defense policy and Western economic development. . . . If Western businessmen were not Merchants of Death they surely qualified as Merchants of Defense." And in a detailed examination of the relationships between the United States Navy and San Diego and Los Angeles and San Francisco between 1900 and 1940, Lotchin demonstrated the close contacts between urban politicians, business leaders, voluntary associations, city planners, and city builders and the military establishment in their midst, which shaped many significant decisions affecting urban growth. Lotchin's thesis provided a broad, integrative concept with which to approach the multifaceted development of cities throughout the West.[45]

The search for integrative theories to guide the study of Western urban expansion led Mark Foster to formulate by 1980 his concept of the automobile metropolis. Contrary to the experience of most cities in the United States, Foster declared, those in the West developed only extensively in the age of automobile transportation. Several earlier historians of Western towns—Pomeroy, Dykstra, and Larsen among them—had stressed the imitativeness of Western city boosters and their attempts to replicate their Eastern experiences. But Foster stressed the uniqueness of Western metropolitan centers after 1900, when they developed in a horizontal rather than vertical pattern because of population dispersion made possible by motor cars. In addition, the greater availability of land and open spaces, climatic conditions, and affluent national and regional economies during most of the period of their

45. Roger W. Lotchin, "The Metropolitan–Military Complex in Comparative Perspective: San Francisco, Los Angeles, and San Diego, 1919–1941," in Gerald D. Nash (ed.), *The Urban West* (Manhattan, 1979), 19, 20; Lotchin (ed.), *The Martial City* (New York, 1984); Lotchin, "The Darwinian City: The Politics of Urbanization in San Francisco Between the World Wars," *Pacific Historical Review* 48 (August 1979), 357–58.

rapid growth after 1900 contributed to their particular shapes. As Foster noted:

> The vast majority of cities in the American West were founded in the nineteenth century, or even earlier; yet most developed their essential metropolitan characteristics in the twentieth century. While the post–World War II sprawl of metropolitan regions such as . . . Phoenix and Los Angeles is obvious to the most casual observer, the period between 1900 and the war brought the primary commitment to . . . a unique pattern of development in at least three major cities. Denver, Seattle, and Los Angeles are distinctive, not only in their geographic settings, but in their economic, ethnic, and social variations. . . . During the forty-five years between the turn of the century and V.J. Day, each assumed a largely horizontal pattern of physical development.

This pattern was a distinctive Western innovation.[46]

In their search for themes that could provide keys to an understanding of the urban history of the West, most historians had stressed the importance of cultural influences as distinguished from environmental factors. Whether concerned with social mobility, the impact of capitalism, ethnic considerations, militarism, or technological innovations like the automobile, scholars during the post-1945 era stressed man-made rather than natural phenomena. But a growing environmental consciousness after 1970 left its mark upon a new generation of environmental historians. While eschewing the geographical determinism of their predecessors a century before, they reemphasized the significance of the environment in shaping urban landscapes of the twentieth century. True, their focus was on the cultural determinants of environmental uses, so that, in a sense, their approach was similar to that of other urban historians. Still, their studies were a forcible reminder that even in a highly technologically oriented industrial age, men and women could ignore Mother Nature and the earth's ecology only at their peril. And they forecast an increase of such perils in the future if warnings of the past, and their present, were ignored.

John Opie was one of the ablest of these environmental historians

46. Mark S. Foster, "The Western Response to Urban Transportation: A Tale of Three Cities, 1900–1945," in Nash (ed.), *The Urban West*, 31, 32, 38; Foster, *From Streetcar to Superhighway: American City Planners and Urban Transportation*, 1900–1940 (Philadelphia, 1981).

to deal with the urban West, who also offered this emphasis as one of several theoretical postulates for the field. As Opie noted:

> The history of boomtowns is invariably an environmental history, although it was first examined in terms of the mining frontier. Natural resources . . . create momentum for rapid localized development. This almost invariably means the invasion of a human population far beyond local capacity to support. The results are not only the spoliation of the land, but also community pollution, waste, crowding, violence, and other human hardships. These developments are often justified as an extension of historic American individualism, freedom of opportunity, the entrepreneurial spirit, and acquisition of wealth. . . . In a longer-term perspective, urban centers were conceived . . . as classic American boomtowns.[47]

By 1980 other urban historians turned their attention to the West, and while they did not develop full-blown theoretical approaches, they provided factual evidence for theoreticians. One of these was John Reps, a historian of city planning, who concentrated on the growth of Western cities before 1890. Reps formulated the general theme that towns preceded rural settlement and were the spearheads of the frontier. Thus, he was challenging Turner's hypothesis about the cutting edge of frontier settlement. "The establishment of urban communities," he wrote in 1979, "stimulated rather than followed the opening of the West and agriculture."[48] A similar approach was followed by Bradford Luckingham for the post-1890 period in his historical overview of four major southwestern cities—El Paso, Albuquerque, Phoenix, and Tucson. As Luckingham noted, even in the nineteenth century these communities "served the region as important outposts of civilization. . . . Reflecting the influence of a variety of cultures, Spanish, Mexican, and American, the towns played a dominant role in the military, economic, social and cultural life of the Southwest." That was even truer of the years after 1930 when these cities were "spearheads of the desert frontier. . . . The four cities represented the

47. John S. Opie, "Environmental History in the West," in Gerald D. Nash and Richard W. Etulain (eds.), *The Twentieth Century West: Historical Interpretations* (Albuquerque, 1989), 215.
48. John W. Reps, *The Making of Urban America: A History of City Planning in the United States* (Princeton, 1965); Reps, *Town Planning in Frontier America* (Princeton, 1969); Reps, *Cities of the American West* (Princeton, 1979), ix; Howard Rabinowitz, "Reps on the Range," *Journal of Urban History* 8 (November 1981), 91–97.

focal points around which the Southwest flourished." Such a significance, Luckingham felt, justified an urban approach to Western history. "Scholars have found more meaning in an urban Southwest with
an urban past," Luckingham wrote in 1984. "From their perspective
it is clearly time to redress the balance in southwestern historiography.
As it has for other regions, an urban view should provide a fuller
understanding of the history of the Southwest."[49]

But perhaps the most comprehensive effort to develop a conceptual
framework for understanding the growth of Western cities came with
the formulation of the Sunbelt concept. The term *Sunbelt* was first
used by journalist Kevin Phillips in his 1969 book *The Emerging Republican Majority* to describe a region of conservative voting habits
where the Republican Party might win new voters, mainly in the
South and West. The phrase was popularized a few years later by
Kirkpatrick Sale, who in 1975 published *Power Shift*, a book that
contrasted the burgeoning South and West since 1945 with the declining East. In the following year, the *New York Times* published five
articles on the growth of new metropolitan areas in the West and
South which it designated as the "sunbelt."[50] Soon other journalists
adopted the term, but it was not until 1979 that urban historian Carl
Abbott developed the concept to make it a sophisticated analytical
tool to provide direction for the study of Western urban history. Abbott
noted that "the evolution of a sunbelt region can be traced to the
impact of World War II on southern and western cities, and followed
through the entire post-war era. It is equally important that the Sunbelt is an urban region. By creating similar economic and social environments in historically dissimilar sections of the United States the
explosive metropolitan growth of the last four decades has allowed
Americans to identify a single region stretching around the southern
and western rim of the nation." And Abbott left little doubt about
the approach which the concept required. "The history of the Sunbelt
is urban history," he wrote. "Since World War II . . . it has increasingly

49. Bradford Luckingham, *The Urban Southwest: A Profile History of Albuquerque,
El Paso, Phoenix, and Tucson* (El Paso, 1982), 40, 48; Luckingham, "The City in the
Westward Movement: A Bibliographical Note," *Western Historical Quarterly* 5 (July
1974), 295–306; Luckingham, "The American Southwest: An Urban View," ibid. 15
(July 1984), 280.

50. Carl Abbott, "The American Sunbelt: Idea and Region," in Nash (ed.), *Urban
West*, 6–7; Kirkpatrick Sale, *Power Shift* (New York, 1975); Kevin Phillips, *The Emerging Republican Majority* (New York, 1969); *New York Times*, February 8–12, 1976.

been the cities of the sunbelt which have set the pace for the nation."
Abbott also suggested specific methods which other historians could
utilize in further research. He proposed the use of economic profiles
such as personal income, demographic analysis, state level growth
data, and federal expenditures as indicators of Sunbelt characteristics.
Moreover, the perspective of the Sunbelt provided new insights for
Western urban studies. It altered the locus of national economic power,
reversed the relation between heartland and hinterland, and affected
both politics and ideology.[51] Of the various theories developed by
historians between 1970 and 1990 to promote the analysis of Western
cities, the Sunbelt concept was the most comprehensive.

In the century after 1890, the urban history of the West developed
in fits and starts, primarily because of the overwhelming influence of
the frontier concept. It is true that the urban dimension of the West
was recognized clearly in the 1890s, but that vision was simply swamped
by almost universal acceptance of frontier perspectives. Consequently,
Western historians between 1893 and 1945 paid scant attention to
the urban character of the trans-Mississippi area. But its significance
could not be suppressed forever. Beginning with Turner himself in the
1920s, and mushrooming under the leadership of Arthur M. Schlesinger, Jr., in the 1930s and 1940s, the chorus of those who advocated
greater emphasis on the role of cities in the West slowly swelled by
1945. They were still a small band, but by 1953 there were enough
to form a small association, the Urban History Group.[52] The greatest
impetus to urban studies, however, came from the phenomenal growth
of Western cities between 1945 and 1990, which virtually forced historians to devote greater attention to the subject.

That effort was hardly well organized, and reflected at least four
trends. Between 1945 and 1960 studies of Western cities were scattered
and fragmented, reflecting in part the increasing specialization in the
historical profession. During this period, historians and journalists
wrote histories of individual cities or urban institutions. A second
trend emerged in the 1960s when various writers attempted to provide
broad, general histories of cities in the United States, including those

51. Abbott, "American Sunbelt," in Nash (ed.), *Urban West,* 8, 10, 16. Abbott,
The New Urban America: Growth and Politics in Sunbelt Cities (Chapel Hill, 1981),
118–19.

52. Blake McKelvey, *The Urbanization of America,* 1860–1915 (New York, 1963),
introduction.

of the West. The generation of historians who began to write in the 1960s were increasingly impressed by national problems of the time such as poverty and social mobility; racial, ethnic, and gender inequalities; and environmental destruction. These events profoundly affected their choice of subject matter and interpretation. They led to a third main trend in the writing of Western urban history, namely, an emphasis on social problems, whether social mobility, the role of minorities in the cities, or issues concerning the urban environment. Although the importance of urban development in the West was beginning to receive wider recognition by 1970, the broad range of studies in the field lacked focus. That led to a fourth trend between 1970 and 1990, a search for theories, or for conceptual frameworks that might allow for greater coherence in the subject.

Almost imperceptibly, and at times unconsciously, by 1990 urban historians of the West had wrought a revolution in transforming the image of the West. That transformation perhaps had not yet reached popular perceptions, but was bound to do so in another generation. In 1890 the popular image of the West—as well as that crafted by historians—was that of a sparsely settled region, characterized by mining, livestock, and agriculture. Its symbolic figures were the miner, the cattleman, and the rancher, and—above all—the cowboy. That perception remained deeply rooted in the national psyche for the next one hundred years. But as the studies of urban historians accumulated, they conveyed a very different image. Even in the nineteenth century, they discovered, the area was dominated by towns and cities. Its representatives were businessmen and urban boosters, real estate agents, bankers, railroad builders, and corporate executives. If by 1990 the new image had not displaced the old, that of the cowboy West, in the twenty-first century it was bound to force itself on the consciousness of a majority of Americans.

FIVE

The West as Utopia and Myth, 1890–1990

THROUGHOUT ITS HISTORY the American West has played as large a role in the imagination of men and women as in their daily lives within a geographical or cultural community. At various stages of American development, it has represented different versions of the American Dream. In the seventeenth and eighteenth centuries it was a symbol of a land of unlimited opportunities, of freedom, and as a place of refuge for those escaping from harsh economic or political conditions in the older civilizations of Europe or Asia. During the nineteenth and twentieth centuries it continued to act as a beacon for people around the world, and also for Americans living in older or more settled areas such as New England and the Eastern seaboard. Those who dreamed of a better life often enshrined the West in their imaginations, even if they never made the westward trek. But they were buoyed with hope merely to know what the West represented. For millions of others, however, the dream acted as a spur that fueled successive migrations. These drove the American frontier steadily westward after 1789, until it reached the Pacific Coast and spilled over into the oceans to Hawaii and beyond. Of course, for many in each generation reality was very much unlike the dream, for instead of success they experienced failure. Yet a large enough number of individuals did find sufficient fulfillment of their dreams in the West, enough to keep the notion of the West as a utopia alive through the years, including the latter half of the twentieth century.

In short, the American West has played multiple roles. On the one hand, Americans as well as people around the world have looked to the West of reality—whether frontier, region, or urban civilization. On the other hand, they have also contemplated another West—the West of the imagination, the West of myth. This West was one that was a figment of artful speculation, a fabled land, a utopia which served as a soothing contrast to the harsh realities of the contemporary world. In a way, it served as a mirror for the present. As Earl Pomeroy once noted, the discovery of the West depended on the cultural baggage of the beholder. Few came to discover what there was to see in the real West. Rather, they came with ideas about what they hoped to find. The West was therefore the product of two imaginations—perceiving the unreal and the real—each feeding upon the other. "Every generation seems to define the West anew," Pomeroy wrote.[1] In searching for the West we define ourselves.

In their treatment of the mythical West, historians clearly reflected major issues of their own day which often permeated their perceptions of the subject. The generation that wrote during the years from 1890 to 1920 was overcome with a profound sense of loss, a feeling of nostalgia for the disappearance of a world which they had cherished, a world which had been at the very center of the American Dream, of the national mythology which Americans used to explain themselves not only to each other, but to the rest of the world. That was understandable due to the ecology of this generation. They were men and women usually born in the second half of the nineteenth century, when Western frontier conditions were still very much a reality in many parts of the United States, at least in their youth. By the time of their middle or old age that was no longer true. To them, it seemed that, along with their own aging, the nation had aged as well. In their effort to hold on to their fleeting youth—or at least to its remembrance—they wrote about a mythical West frozen in time, an exhilarating period in the nation's past.

Between 1920 and 1945 a new generation of writers and historians emerged who were born in the late nineteenth or early twentieth

1. Earl Pomeroy, "Rediscovering the West," *American Quarterly* 12 (Spring 1960), 30.

centuries and who had not experienced frontier conditions in their
own life. As they pondered some of the most pressing issues of their
own period with critical acumen—materialism, the questioning of
traditional values, or a spiritual void—they contrasted these negative
trends with the more positive virtues of the mythic West. As the real
frontier receded into time, the mythic West loomed ever larger as a
stark contrast to a dolorous present. But during the 1920s subtle changes
began to surface. Although some writers still held up the mythic West
as a positive alternative to a negative present, a growing group of
critics began to reverse the image. In this undercurrent, the problems
of the present could be traced directly to the negative influences of
the frontier. Not change, but continuity characterized the image of
the mythic West. The Great Depression did much to sharpen this
negative perception, particularly on the political left. Yet in the realm
of popular culture, the positive image of the mythic West of the past
still served a vital role as an antidote to the more dreary present.

World War II ushered in a different era for Americans, spearheaded
by an age of affluence which contributed to the modification of historical perceptions of the West as myth. The war period heightened
an awareness of psychological motivations and stimulated the emi-
gration of an entire generation of German and Austrian psychoanalysts
to the United States who—among their diverse influences—also stimulated psychological analysis of the West as myth. Their coming coincided with another major trend, the expansion of the instruments
of mass culture—radio, musical recordings, museums, and television.
In that realm, the mythic West still played a major positive role in
American life. It assuaged new insecurities, whether stemming from
Cold War tensions, fears of nuclear holocaust, or affluent life-styles.
Historians were quick to read these new concerns into their analyses
of the Western myth.

Sometime in the 1960s the major concerns of a new generation
of Americans coming of age shifted once more, thus affecting interpretations of the Western myth. For the next thirty years they became
preoccupied with racial and ethnic tensions—with problems of minorities, women's rights, and environmental despoliation. In addition,
the war in Vietnam accelerated—even when it did not create—profound feelings of guilt and self-doubts about the nation's values and
policies among a significant number of Americans. It did not take very
long for historians and other commentators on the West as myth to

reflect these changing contemporary trends. In contrast to earlier writers who had perceived the Western experience in positive terms, this
generation viewed it as a profoundly disturbing and negative aspect
of the nation's past. They judged it to be a most destructive heritage
of which Americans should be ashamed. It was, as Patricia Limerick
lamented, a legacy of conquest, surely not a source of pride. This
refrain, in part a result of New Left ideology, reflected a pronounced
negative self-image of the nation's and of the West's history, and
became a dominant theme in the interpretation of the West as myth.[2]
It could be argued that it revealed more about this group of critics
than about the myth itself. But, then, every generation has had its
own distinctive perception of the West as myth.

What is striking is that the West as a mythical land of perfection
was not merely the creation of Europeans and Americans after the
fifteenth century, but had deep roots in the culture of Western civilization stretching back more than two thousand years. The idea of a
Western paradise was already current in classical Greek civilization.
As Loren Baritz has noted: "If men were brave enough, strong enough,
and perhaps good enough, they would be able to climb the mountain
and sail the seas or placate and vanquish the creatures that stood just
east of Thebes. And once there, the condition of men would be
profoundly altered—there nature's bounty was endless, happiness was
certain, and fear banished forever." This composite vision of a mythical
West was not the inspiration of a single individual, but a perspective
shaped by many minds. One of its strands appeared again and again
in the human story—a yearning for a land of laughter, of peace, and
of life. The exact location of this land, whether it was designated as
Elysium, Eden, or the Isle of Women, engaged the attention of sailors
as well as poets, who often placed it in a westerly location. Another
strand of the myth revolved about the concept of the destiny of nations, a notion that the sword must be taken westward. From ancient
Troy, to Greece, to Elizabethan England "westward the course of
empire takes its way." Themes of eternity, happiness, and millennialism
were woven into one fabric in the Western theme. Emphasis on one
or the other of these strands varied as they suited the purposes of those

2. Limerick, *Legacy of Conquest*; Peter Wiley and Robert Gottlieb, *Empires in the
Sun: The Rise of the New American West* (New York, 1982); Mark Reisner, *Cadillac
Desert* (New York, 1986).

who made use of the idea of the West, whether as a concept, a direction, or both.[3]

For thousands of years, therefore, the spokesmen for successive civilizations embraced this dream. In ancient Greece Proteus told Menelaus, a son of Zeus, that the West represented an Elysian plain where life was easiest for men. Plato himself described the glories of Athens in its war against the lost world West of the Pillars of Hercules. This Western land of flowers, the playwright Euripides explained, was reserved for the favorites of the gods. The idea of the imperial West was largely a conception of the Romans. As the poet Virgil proclaimed, Rome must move from Troy to Italy, in a westerly direction. The Islands of the Blest, the Romans believed, were west of Rome. As the poet Horace described this hidden, happy land:

> See, before us the distant glow
> Through the thin dawn-mists of the West
> Rich sunlit plains and hilltops gemmed with snow
> The Islands of the Blest.[4]

The Romans did much to strengthen the concept of a utopia in the West. By the first century B.C. the Elysian plain of Homer had been located. Plutarch described how Sertorius met Spanish sailors who had just returned from an expedition to two distant Atlantic islands. They reported that

> these are called the Islands of the Blest; rain falls there seldom, and in moderate showers, but the most part they have gentle breezes, bringing along with them soft dews, which render the soil not only rich for ploughing and planting, but so abundantly fruitful that it produces spontaneously an abundance of delicate fruits, sufficient to feed the inhabitants, who may here enjoy all things without trouble or labor . . . so that the firm belief prevails, even among the barbarians, that this is the seat of the blessed, and that these are the Elysian fields celebrated by Homer.[5]

Real estate boosters in twentieth-century California could hardly have done better.

3. Loren Baritz, "The Idea of the West," *American Historical Review* 66 (April 1961), 618–19.

4. Quoted in ibid., 621. Howard R. Patch, *The Other World* (Cambridge, Mass., 1950), 26; Max Cary and E. H. Warmington, *The Ancient Explorers* (New York, 1929), 202–3.

5. Quoted in Baritz, "Ideas of the West," *American Historical Review* 66, 621.

By the first century A.D. the westerly direction had been set. The journey to Elysium from the Mediterranean was westward. Utopia—or Elysium—was firmly established in the West in the minds of the founders of Western European civilization.

In succeeding years, the conception of a mythical utopia in the West was further embellished. Almost every European language group throughout Christendom developed some tale of adventure in which a mythical land of plenty beckoned somewhere in the West. One of the most influential was the tale of St. Brendan in seventh- or eighth-century Ireland. This pagan saga about a land of sensual delights located in the West was widely known throughout Europe for many centuries. Hundreds of years earlier, St. Augustine proclaimed that the westward course of empire had divine sanction. By the sixteenth century—the age of the great discoveries—geographers had placed this wondrous utopia somewhere between Ireland and America. Columbus's son believed that one of his father's motives for sailing West was his desire to search for these mysterious islands. Columbus himself believed that he had found a continent on which Eden, an earthly paradise, was located. This essentially Catholic idea was soon anglicized by the British in their own effort to establish their imperial dominance in the world of sixteenth-century Atlantic civilization. Edward Hayes, Sir Humphrey Gilbert's rear admiral, served as a spokesman for this view when he noted that "God's word and religion . . . from the beginning, hath moved from the east towards . . . the West." The creation of English America was the final step in attaining the millennium.[6]

Within a century, the English Puritans in America developed the concept further when they proclaimed that in Massachusetts they had found God's own country, the Western land where His word would be obeyed. As John Winthrop wrote in 1630: "It is true, from the first planting of Religion among men, it has always held a constant way from East to West. . . . Our Saviour's Prophecie Math. 24:27 points out such a progresse of the Gospell." And in 1713 Samuel Sewell wrote that America was best suited for the Government of Christ precisely because it was the Beginning of the East, and the end of the West. Jonathan Edwards was more blunt in proclaiming tersely that God faced West. By the nineteenth century the architects of American

6. Ibid., 623–35.

mythology such as Henry David Thoreau could readily identify the West with freedom. "Eastward I go only by force," he noted. "But westward I go free. . . . That way the nation is moving, and I may say that mankind progresses from east to west." Thoreau combined the West of happiness and eternity—the millennium—with the West of empire and place. "It provided salvation for the nation as well as a sense of identity. From Horace to Horace Greeley the West represented an apocalyptic land where men could live happily ever after."[7]

The major themes of this legend were reinforced by numerous auxiliary tales such as those concerning the naming of California. In a popular novel that appeared about 1500, *Las Sergas de Esplandian*, the Spanish writer Garci Ordóñez de Montalvo referred to a fabled Amazon island named California. Most likely the explorer Hernando Cortés read the book, or at least heard about it. In 1524, he wrote to his king that he expected to find this fabled land. In the novel Montalvo wrote about a certain Esplandian, the son of Amadeus of Gaul, whose character reflected the ideals of the medieval knight. He appeared in a siege of Constantinople, where he confronted Queen Calafia of California. That territory, in the context of contemporary European views of the West, was somewhere in the West, near a terrestrial paradise whose inhabitants used weapons made of gold. Although the novel became obscure during the next three centuries, scholars believe that it was the source for the naming of California.[8]

In addition to the powerful myth of the West as a utopia which Europeans created over the course of more than two millennia, American attitudes toward the West were also profoundly shaped by their Christian heritage. As the famed medievalist Lynn White once declared: "American pioneers took with them, willy-nilly, elements drawn from every epoch of the past." Their attitudes toward the Western wilderness were significantly shaped by the ancient nostalgic Hebrew idealization of the forty years the Israelites spent in the desert between Egypt and Palestine.

7. Ibid., 636–40.
8. Walton E. Bean, *California: An Interpretive History* (New York, 1968), 16–17; Charles E. Chapman, *A History of California: The Spanish Period* (New York, 1923), 56–64; Antonio de Fierro Blanco [Walter Nordhoff], *The Journey of the Flame* (New York, 1933).

Transmitted and refined by the Christian Church Fathers and medieval ascetics, elaborated by mystics and especially by radical An-
abaptists during the Reformation, these doctrines were very
current amongst frontiersmen of the 17th and 18th and 19th centuries. Theirs was the notion that the wilderness was not merely a
dread place of struggle and suffering, but also an arena where spiritual perfection may be won. This idea has played a major role in
American life and emotion. It is doubtful that American westward
expansion would have proceeded as quickly as it did had it not
been for these powerful visions of the wilderness and its redemp-
tive qualities—conditioned by three thousand years of religious tradition—which provided an impetus for the thousands of ambitious
individuals on the frontier.[9]

The millennial vision of the West deserves greater emphasis, perhaps, than it has received from historians, especially those writing in
a secular age. One major theologian, George H. Williams, has lamented the failure of historians, even those as insightful as Henry
Nash Smith and Richard Hofstadter, to give full credence to the
millennial vision of Western American history. As Williams wrote:

> In the retrospect of the nineteenth century the epic gathering of a
> mighty Christian nation beginning in the scattered settlements of
> the eastern seaboard, a nation made up of peoples fleeing in suc-
> cessive generations from the bondage of the Old World across the
> Atlantic Ocean to a land of promise and of liberty, has been seen
> as providential repetition, in majestic, continental proportions, of
> the exodus of God's ancient elect from bondage to Egypt. To be
> an American, has been for successive immigrant generations to
> know a new birth of freedom. . . . This sense of being a new peo-
> ple . . . was perpetuated . . . into the second and even the third
> generation.[10]

Here in the New World the vision of the West as an earthly
manifestation of God's kingdom in heaven was a powerful concept
not only in Christian theology, but in popular secular writings as well.

9. Lynn White, Jr., "The Legacy of the Middle Ages in the American Wild
West," *American West* 3 (Spring 1966), 72–79, 95.
10. George H. Williams, *Wilderness and Paradise in Christian Thought* (Cambridge,
Mass., 1959), 98; for a brief summary, see Williams, "The Wilderness and Paradise
in the History of the Church," *Church History* 28 (March 1959), 3–24.

Cotton Mather in 1693 declared in *The Wonders of the Invisible World,* a discourse based on Revelation 12:12:

> The first Planters of these Colonies were a Chosen Generation of Men . . . and yet withal so peacable that they Embraced a Voluntary Exile in a Squalid, horrid American Desert, rather than to live in Contentions with their Brethren. . . . The New Englanders are a people of God . . . accomplishing the Promise of Old made unto our Blessed Jesus. . . . The Wilderness thro' which we are passing to the Promised Land is all over filled with Fiery flying serpents.

And John Cotton wrote in 1642:

> All the worlde is a wilderness [but] the Church is God's Garden or orchard. As the garden of Paradise was the habitation of Adam in the estate of innocence, so is the Church of all those who are renewed into innocency. As in the garden were all manner of pleasant and wholesome herbs and trees growing, so in the church are all manner of usefull and savoury spirits. As a man walketh in his garden to refresh himselfe, so doth Christ walke in his Churche.[11]

During the eighteenth century, the great Jonathan Edwards expanded on the theme. In a sermon on "The True Christian's Life: A Journey Towards Heaven," he wrote: "The land that we have to travel through is a wilderness; there are many mountains, rocks, and rough places that we must go over in the way. . . . What better end can you propose to your journey than to obtain heaven? . . . Were the children of Israel sorry, after forty years of travel in the Wilderness, when they had almost gone to Canaan?" And in the nineteenth century, this stream of thought was powerfully illustrated by Mormon theology, migration, and settlement. As Williams noted, Joseph Smith's cultural and religious roots were deeply imbedded in preachers like John Cotton. But by 1860 the increasing secularization of the sense of mission in American society led some theologians to be alarmed. As Henry Whitney Bellows, a Unitarian minister, said in 1859:

> I believe wholly and devoutly . . . in the coexistence of the Church with the civilization which is its child, and is now half ready to be its parricide; and I expect confidently, absolutely that

11. Williams, *Wilderness and Paradise,* 108, 109, 111, 117.

memory and hope, history and progress, gratitude and longing, institutions and a free spirit, will all unite again . . . in building up
the waste places of Zion.

From its place as a mythical utopia, from its biblical moorings in a
Christian theological context, the West now became secularized as its
image as utopia was taken out of its theological or religious context
and placed into a secular mold.[12]

In that gradual secularization of the West during the course of the
nineteenth century American writers played a crucial role. The idea
of the West as myth—as distinct from region—was clarified by novelists
like James Fenimore Cooper who enshrined it in the nation's emerging
literary traditions. In their view, they perceived a dualism in American
life, a conflict between wilderness and the civilization established by
Americans. Although the cultural milieu in succeeding years changed,
many writers and artists dealing with the West continued to perceive
this dualism and the conflict it created. The mythical West represented
an escape from the real West. It became an imaginary figment of the
imagination, an antidote to the present, a vision of perfection, not
very different from the visions of men three thousand years before.
Here, heroes enforced the highest and purest standards of manliness
and morality. As John Cawelti once noted: "It represented an ideal
world without the disorder, the ambiguity, the uncertainty, and the
limitations of the world of our experience . . . a type . . . not the
experience of reality."[13]

The transformation of the millennial vision into a secular context
was accelerated by conservationists of the later nineteenth century.
They skillfully combined the romantic with the Christian conceptions
of American prairies and forests, sensing that the wilderness was inextricably bound up with the national character and destiny. After all,
many of these individuals had been born in an agrarian age, but
matured to confront the industrialization of the later nineteenth century. It was no accident that their language resembled that of ancient
prophets as they advocated the saving of nature in order to save society.
Men like John Burroughs or John Muir were the spiritual and secular
descendants of earlier millennial preachers.

12. Ibid., 124, 128.
13. John Cawelti, *Adventure, Mystery, and Romance* (Chicago, 1976), 13; Cawelti,
in Christine Bold, *Selling the Wild West: Popular Western Fiction* (Bloomington, 1987),
74.

Indeed, John Muir's mind resounded with passages from the Bible, three-fourths of which he had committed to memory as a boy. In appealing for a national program of conservation in the 1890s, he hearkened back to earlier traditions when he said that "God began the reservation system in Eden. . . . The forests of America . . . must have been a great delight to God; for they were the best He ever planted. . . . The whole continent was a garden; and from the beginning it seemed to be favored above all the other wild parks and gardens of the globe . . . and happy birds and beasts gave delightful animation." To Muir, the battle conservationists had to fight was "between landscape righteousness and the Devil." In this variation of biblical themes, conservationists like Muir converted the desert, with its variegated flora and fauna, into a kind of paradise, perhaps a national park. The devil prowled outside these wilderness environments, in the person of selfish economic interests and depredators who would despoil the continental garden for the sake of private greed. In Muir's vision, the West in its natural state resembled an erstwhile Eden, that mythical pure land which men had sought for more than three thousand years, and which now had to be protected from devilish onslaughts. In this manner, the conservation movement united not only practical consideration of preservation in a society with an increasing population and diminishing natural resources, but with an age-old spiritual theme of perfection and fulfillment. Wilderness areas nurtured not only man's body, but his soul as well.[14]

In the decade of the 1890s Americans were prone to seek some escape from their rapidly changing society. An increasing number of people now realized that the agrarian civilization that had been characteristic of the United States in the nineteenth century was rapidly declining and was being replaced by a new industrial–urban order. The depression of the 1890s underscored that change, and the anguished cries of the Populists, and their ultimate defeat, reiterated the impression that the day when the United States was a nation of sturdy yeomen-farmers had passed. Within that context, Turner's pronouncement that the frontier was gone only added the finishing touch to the perception that one major era in American life had passed and that another—whose full dimensions were still unknown—was about to start. Since this momentous change took no more than one generation,

14. Williams, *Wilderness and Paradise*, 130.

its shock effect on Americans between 1890 and 1920 can be readily understood.

Between 1890 and 1920, therefore, some historians of the West lost themselves in nostalgia as they invented a lost golden age, an earlier period in Western history which was the very antithesis of the rapidly changing West of their own day. Novelists, artists, and the purveyors of popular culture did much to reinforce their impact. This West of their imaginations was an uncomplicated, sparsely populated area characterized by a majestic, uncluttered landscape rather than by a crowded urban environment. This West was peopled by noble and distinctive individuals, personified by mountain men, trappers, or cowboys, and hardy pioneer farmers. They were a stark contrast to the millions of faceless immigrants from eastern and southern Europe who were just then pouring into the nation's urban centers. And the dominant Anglo settlers of this mythical region displayed great nobility of character and the finest values of the nineteenth-century Protestant Ethic, individualism, self-reliance, courage, and a love for freedom. Their heroic deeds were supported by the equivalent of a Greek chorus in the person of romanticized Native Americans and Hispanics who provided the supporting cast. The clearly defined values of this Western society contrasted markedly with the increasingly ambivalent values of industrial America, seemingly typified, its critics charged, by crass materialism, selfishness, cowardice, deceit, and increasing reliance on government.

Such images of the mythical West found powerful reinforcement at the hands of the architects of popular culture. Novelists such as Owen Wister and a host of other writers embellished the perception during these years. Thousands of others who wrote for popular pulp westerns and magazines filled in the vivid details of the myth. And millions of Americans who never read a book about the West absorbed the myth through the canvases of countless painters and illustrators, of whom Frederic Remington and Charles Russell were only the most famous. Other millions absorbed the legend through the Wild West shows of Buffalo Bill, who artfully presented many of the elements of the mythical West in an entertaining style. After 1905 both young and old could also live, and relive, the supposed glories of a bygone age through the medium of the Western film, once *The Great Train Robbery* provided a model for the genre. At different levels of society, therefore, in the United States and around the world, the perception of the mythical West made a deep impression on the consciousness of people who never actually laid eyes on the region.

Among those reflecting the nostalgic mood, the novelist Frank Norris, writing as a historian, was prominent. Reflecting his generation's sense of loss, a nostalgia for the vanishing frontier, Norris declared that the conquest of the trans-Mississippi West was an achievement of epic proportions that deserved to be celebrated as such. It was comparable, he declared, to some of the greatest epics in the annals of Western civilization. "The Trojan war left to posterity the character of Hector," he proclaimed. "The wars with the Saracens gave us Roland; the folklore of Iceland produced Grettir; the Scotch border poetry brought forth the Douglas; the Spanish epic, the Cid. But the American epic, just as heroic, just as picturesque, will fade into history, leaving behind no finer type, no nobler hero, than Buffalo Bill." Norris also suggested the characteristics of the heroes who personified the epic. Unlike the lawbreakers of the dime novels in the 1870s and 1880s, who had portrayed the adventure of the West, the Western hero was characterized now by Norris as "a lawmaker, a fighter; it is true, as is always the case with epic figures, but a fighter for peace, a calm, grave strong man who hated the lawbreaker as the hound hates the wolf." This hero faced his enemies with tranquil courage, and "fear was not in him even at the end. For such a man as this could die no quiet death, in a land where law went no further than the statute books and life lay in the crook of my neighbor's forefinger. . . . He is of all the world types the one distinctive to us—peculiar, particular, and unique."[15]

Like many of his contemporaries, Norris lamented the end of an era when the frontier had disappeared. "Suddenly we have found that there is no longer any Frontier," he complained.

> Until the day when the first U.S. Marine landed in China we had always imagined that out yonder somewhere in the West was the border land where civilization distintegrated and merged into the untamed. . . . And the Frontier has become so much an integral part of our conception of things that it will be long before we shall all understand that it is gone. We liked the Frontier; it was to-mance, the place of the poetry of the Great March, the firing line where there was action and fighting, and where men held each

15. Frank Norris, "The Frontier Gone At Last," *World's Work* 3, 1729.

other's lives in the crook of the forefinger. Those who had gone
out came back with tremendous tales and those that stayed behind
made up other and even more tremendous tales.

But the fading of the real frontier would only fuel the imagination
about the mythical frontier.

"So, lament it though we may," Norris continued, "the Frontier
is gone, an idiosyncracy that has been with us for thousands of years,
the one peculiar picturesqueness of our life is no more. We may keep
alive for many years yet the idea of a Wild West, but the hired cowboys
and paid rough riders of Mr. William Cody are more like the 'real
thing' than can be found today in Arizona, New Mexico, or Idaho."
And then Norris pointed to the close nexus between the real and the
mythical West. "Today we are the same race, with the same impulse,
the same power, and because there is no longer a Frontier to absorb
our overplus of energy, because there is no longer a wilderness to
conquer . . . we remember the old days when our ancestors before us
found the outlet for their activity."[16]

Among other writers who contributed to the dualism between the
real and the mythical West, Stephen Crane was notable. In 1895, he
embarked on a trip to the West and quickly lost himself in the romantic
aura of the region. He acquired Western clothes and attire, and even
purchased a ranch in Texas, the better to act out his phantasies. In
the West he discovered a capacity for the heroic, and for free will,
which led him to question the determinism and the pessimistic cy-
nicism that he had earlier expressed so strongly in books like *Maggie*
and *The Red Badge of Courage*. In his stories of this later period, he
idolized the courage and stoicism of Western farmers and cattlemen.
"They were strong, fine, sturdy men, not bended . . . but erect and
agile. They are completely American." Westering obviously produced
the quintessential American traits of the nation.[17]

Crane's biographer, Thomas Beer, explained his subject's motivation well. "Like others of his generation," Beer wrote, "Crane sought
to escape the great and elemental facts of American life," the emergence of an industrial order. He lamented the disappearance of the

16. Ibid.; see also Norris, "A Neglected Epic," in ibid. 5 (December 1902) 2904–
6.

17. Robert G. Deamer, "Stephen Crane and the Western Myth," in *Western
American Literature* 7 (Summer 1972), 111.

old under the crushing weight of the new. In criticizing the emergence of a modern city in San Antonio, Texas, Crane wrote in 1895:

> The principal streets and lanes between rows of handsome business blocks and upon them proceeds with important uproar the terrible and almighty trolley car. . . . The serene Anglo-Saxon erects business blocks upon the dreams of transient monks; he strings telegraph wires across the face of their sky of hope and over the energy, the efforts, the accomplishments of these pious fathers of the early church passes the wheel, the hoof, the heel. . . . Here and there . . . one finds in the main part of the town little old buildings yellow with age . . . that have escaped . . . the whirl of modern life. . . . But despite the tenderness which San Antonio feels for these monuments, the unprotected mass of them must get trampled into shapeless dust which lies always behind the march of this terrible century.[18]

Lesser writers wove variations on the theme of the mythical West. In discussing the Western spirit of restlessness, Ray Stannard Baker in 1908 noted that for the people he met in the West, many were "sure that their fortune lay somewhere at the end of the road—a pot of fairy gold. For the West has been a seductive beckoner to the dreamer and the idealist. Hard realities at home, toil for low wages, long hours, no future; over there opportunity lies golden, all the stream bottoms are rich with treasure, all the land is fertile and free, in every town there is a chance of quick wealth. And so they fly to escape realities, and to find only rougher, harder realities." The sociologist E. A. Ross found a similar phenomenon, in stressing the heroic dimension of the West. "The stalwart youth spurned his natal spot as 'too crowded,'" he wrote. "In the last Westernmost decanting of the pioneering breed, courage and love of independence reach their greatest intensity. Today, in the recesses of the Rocky Mountains you come upon steady-eyed eagle faced men . . . whose masterful, unswerving will and fierce impatience of restraint remind you of their spiritual kinsmen, the heroes of the Icelandic sagas."[19]

Western traits were never as unique, wrote William R. Lighton (in discussing "Where is the West"), as in the pages of the border

18. Ibid., 116; Thomas Beer, *Stephen Crane* (New York, 1923), 31.

19. Edward A. Ross, "The Middle West," *Century Magazine* 83 (February 1912), 609–15; Ray S. Baker, "The Western Spirit of Restlessness," *Century Magazine*, 76 (July 1908), 468.

romance. From Bret Harte to the more recent disciples of that school, writers of Western stuff, without exception, exaggerated outward signs. And the foremost advocate of Western irrigation, William F. Smythe, hoped to bridge the gap between reality and dream with his advocacy of irrigation colonies which he designated as the "Real Utopias in the arid West."[20]

An important strand in the new nostalgic mythology of the West came with the enshrouding of the Southwest in the realm of fantasy. Initially, American and European migrants to California, New Mexico, and Arizona between 1850 and 1880 expressed very little appreciation for the Spanish, Mexican, and Indian cultures of that area. Mostly, they were deprecatory. Typical was one newcomer to Los Angeles in 1849, who complained that "an antiquated, dilapidated air pervades all." But the new wave of settlers who came after the 1880s sought to escape from the increasingly crowded industrial East. They manufactured new myths about Hispanic and Indian influences in their search for an instant identity. Helen Hunt Jackson published *Ramona* in 1884. In that work, she romanticized the Spanish era in California as a lost golden age—much as Southern writers at the same time were embellishing the South's plantation myth—hearkening back to a supposedly idyllic, romantic era in the antebellum South. Perhaps the most prominent mythologizer of the Southwest was Charles Lummis, an American aristocrat who, like Brooks Adams, deplored the industrialization of his own day and escaped to his own private dream world in California. In 1892, he walked westward from Ohio to Los Angeles. There, he devoted his life to the development of the romantic myth about the Southwest's golden age in the past. He founded not only the Southwest Museum as a shrine to the lost world of the pre-American era, but through his voluminous writings and a magazine, *The Land of Sunshine*, which he edited, he did much to forge a mythical image for Americans. To the grandeur of Nature and noble savages, he added romantic Hispanic and Indian cultures of the Southwest, emphasizing their quaint and charming customs. Others in his circle who were prominent in polishing this image were Mary Austin and Ambrose

20. William R. Lighton, "Where is the West?" *Outlook* (July 18, 1903), 703; William E. Smythe, "Real Utopias in the Arid West," *Atlantic Monthly* 79 (May 1897), 608–9.

Bierce who were adept in inventing what in effect was a counter-culture which provided them with an escape from their own native land without actually leaving its creature comforts.[21]

The influence of these mythmakers extended beyond the written word, touching both artists and life-styles. The changing mood and the nostalgia also affected Southwestern architecture. The Mission style swept southern California and the Southwest during this period and resulted in a campaign to restore the badly decaying Spanish missions. A generation which absorbed this myth now rebuilt private homes, public buildings, and even the Santa Fe Railroad's stations to conform to the romantic perception of a lost, idyllic world. Educators in the schools revised language curricula to include the Spanish language, and tales of heroic Spanish friars in the seventeenth and eighteenth centuries. In the popular mind, these images were reinforced by annual pageants and fiestas such as the Ramona play in Santa Barbara. And talented painters, such as Charles Nahl, Albert Bierstadt, Thomas Hill, Thomas Ayres, and William Keith were busily at work to broaden—and market—the myth on canvas.[22]

Some historians such as Carey McWilliams and Earl Pomeroy have noted that there was an air of unreality in this sudden admiration of things Hispanic and Indian. By the 1880s most evidences of Spanish and Indian civilizations had disappeared. But by the 1890s Americans suddenly found them to be socially acceptable, and were seeking an instant identity in the West. "It gave the West ancestors," Pomeroy wrote, "which any new family needs, or any new community. Father Serra was an answer to William Bradford, and only a century and a half later."[23] Perhaps the West could have recovered from its inferiority

21. Pomeroy, "Rediscovering the West," *American Quarterly* 12, 26; Charles F. Lummis, *A Tramp across the Continent* (New York, 1892), *The Land of Poco Tiempo* (New York, 1893), *The Spanish Pioneers* (Chicago, 1893); Mary Austin, *The Land of Little Rain* (Boston, 1903), *California, The Land of the Sun* (New York, 1914), *The Trail Book* (Boston, 1918), *The American Rhythm* (Boston, 1930); Ambrose Bierce, *The Shadow of the Dial* (San Francisco, 1909), *Collected Works* (12 vols., New York, 1909–1912).

22. Nash, *American West in the Twentieth Century*, 49–62; Harold Kirker, *California's Architectural Frontier: Style and Tradition in the Nineteenth Century* (San Marino, 1960); Edwin R. Bingham, *Charles F. Lummis, Editor of the Southwest* (San Marino, 1955); Franklin Walker, *San Francisco's Literary Frontier* (New York, 1939), and *A Literary History of Southern California* (Berkeley, 1950).

23. Pomeroy, "Rediscovering the West," *American Quarterly* 12, 27; Carey McWilliams, "Myths of the West," *North American Review* 232 (November 1931), 424, 430.

complex. But the enthusiasm for Hispanic and Indian cultures served a psychological need and provided Southwestern chambers of commerce with a significant theme for commercial boosterism. It was an advertising person's dream because it satisfied the two worlds in which Westerners lived. One was the world of reality—of get-rich-quick real estate schemes. The other was a world of dreams. But by embracing Hispanic and Indian legends they did not have to sacrifice one to embrace the other. Both could flourish in an amiable coexistence. It was good for business, and for the soul.

For the West as a whole, few writers could match the nostalgia articulated by Emerson Hough, prolific in nonfiction and fiction. He mourned the passing of the Old West in what amounted to dirges. "Away with the saddle blanket," he declared.

> The beaver are gone, and the range cattle are all fenced in. Hang up the rifle, for our great game is vanishing. . . . As to the steps in the future development of the West . . . it would seem that every inch of our agricultural lands must come under the plow. . . . The Old West lies in ruins. To pick about among those ruins may, indeed, be to find here and there a bit of local color; but were it not better to reflect that this color may be only the broken bits of a cathedral pane? Restore that cathedral, in recollection, in imagination, at least, if it be within the skill of art and literature to do so. Restore it, and write upon the arch the thought that history may be more than a mere recital of wars and religions. . . . Give the men of the Old West . . . this epitaph—that they had character. Let the heroes have place of honor in their own cathedral.

And he pleaded for the perpetuation of the myth. "Tell us of the West that was, demands humanity. . . . Play for us again the glorious drama of the past, and let us see again the America that was once ours."[24]

By the end of the First World War, therefore, the dimensions of the mythical West within the context of twentieth-century America were well established. At a time when industrialism, urbanization, and immigration were changing the nature of American society, the generation that had known both worlds, agrarian and industrial America, lamented not only the passing of their own youth, but that of

---

24. Emerson Hough, "The Settlement of the Frontier: A Study in Transportatioon," *Century Magazine* (November 1901), 91–107; ibid. (December 1901), 201–16.

the United States as well. This refrain was not restricted to intellectuals, however. It affected Americans at all levels and became part of the national ethos. To millions of people the myth became very real as it left an imprint on their minds through pulps, paintings, illustrations, and western films—not to speak of numerous novels and magazines. In fact, the distinction between the real and the unreal, between myth and reality, became increasingly blurred.

In the years between 1920 and 1945 these patterns established in the early twentieth century were strengthened. Accelerated industrialization, the growth of cities, and a more heterogeneous social order proceeded apace, along with a gnawing sense of dissatisfaction, and at times, disillusionment with the new order that was becoming increasingly typical of most parts of the United States. The desire to escape from this new civilization, even while partaking of its material and other benefits and comforts, became as strong for a new generation as it had been for the old.

By the 1920s historians and writers further sharpened the mythical image of the West. The West became an alternative to the industrial society in America that was emerging during these years. No matter that a return to a simpler age seemed utterly unrealistic for most Americans who now developed a new appreciation and admiration for Native American and Hispanic cultures in the West. By enshrining these in myth they could retain the advantages of a technological age while at the same time giving their allegiance to the mythical anti-industrial civilization they envisaged in their minds, vividly recreated by the mass media and the survivors of the older Indian and Hispanic cultures.

During the 1920s historians of the West came to recognize the potency of the myth even though, like Turner, they professed to be "scientific" and engaged in empirical research. One of the first to pick up the thread was John C. Parish, a historian at the University of California at Los Angeles, who speculated on the subject in a series of essays which he wrote over the course of the decade. In commenting upon the persistence of the westward movement and on Turner, Parish noted in 1926 that "a third of a century has passed . . . since 1890, and it seems pertinent to ask if we have not become so engrossed in the task of writing the obituary of a single frontier—that of settlement—that we have shut our eyes to the fact that the westward movement in its larger sense, with its succession of many kinds of frontiers . . . did not cease in 1890, but has been a persistent factor in our national life, which still tends to distinguish the American people from the people of European nations." And Parish saw the dimension of myth as one major consequence. "Divergent forces will probably always keep us sectional and heterogeneous," he wrote, "but if there ever is discernible an amalgamated American spirit it will be explained only after a clear and comprehensive appreciation of the interrelated phases and elements of the westward movement."[25]

The West as myth was also the major concern of the volume on the West in the *Chronicles of America* series, edited by Allen Johnson of Yale University. Appearing in 1919, the book was written by Emerson Hough, the popular writer. In *The Passing of the Frontier*, Hough wrote in a wistful mood about a past era when men hunted the buffalo and rode the trails. Hough had a deeply felt admiration for what he considered as the advance guard of American civilization. In appraising the volume, Hamlin Garland noted:

> The beauties of the old-time plain, the epic sweep of settlement, and the stern battles of the border inspired Hough with fervor. The book was a threnody, deeply colored by Hough's somber meditation on the days of old. All these old frontiers were now gone, Hough lamented. America had lost its region of mystery, of untracked spaces, of the unknown, and something fine and strong passed from the national scene, something which helped our forefathers to become unconquerable individualists. "We had a frontier once," Hough wrote. "It was our most priceless possession. It has not been possible to eliminate from the blood of the American West . . . all the iron of the old home-bred frontiersman. . . . It was there we showed our fighting edge, our unconquerable resolution, our undying faith. There, for a time at least, we were Americans. We had our frontier. We shall do ill indeed if we forget and abandon its strong lessons, its great hopes, its splendid human dreams."[26]

Henceforth, that frontier had to reside in the minds of Americans, now that its physical vestiges were gone.

The mythical element of the West was also emphasized by Archer

25. John C. Parish, *The Persistence of the Westward Movement, and Other Essays* (Berkeley, 1943), 2, 45.

26. Emerson Hough, *Passing of the Frontier*, 1–3, 172; Hamlin Garland, "The Passing of the Frontier," *Dial* 67 (October 4, 1919), 285–86.

Hulbert, a popular writer and historian. Writing on the subject of *Frontiers* in 1929, Hulbert reflected the nostalgic mood of the decade. "Our United States government has officially declared that the old historic frontier no longer exists," Hulbert wrote. He mourned its passing, for it meant that "robust characters, like Boone, who have defied the unknown, wrought out new tools of agriculture, law and society for the conquest of new soils, new minerals, new rivers— unmindful of sudden death from any quarter," had passed. "But has the passion to explore new worlds departed with that frontier?" Hulbert asked. He thought not. He believed that allegiance to province or section would be "the fountain sources of national stability and freedom. . . . Only by owning our birthplace either in a literal or a figurative sense can we have and keep a 'fatherland.'" The myth of the West thus was the foundation of the nation's spirit of identity. It will "make America a nation, make it American, and make it true to itself."[27]

Textbook writers of the period echoed this theme. When Robert E. Riegel of Dartmouth College published *America Moves West* in 1930, he noted that "it is possible to view the Western movement as a search for mental and spiritual values as much as an endeavor to seek economic opportunity." As Carey McWilliams, a contemporary critic, noted somewhat sarcastically, when the frontier disappeared to the naked eye it seemed to seep inward to survive as myth which tugged fiercely at the heartstrings of Americans.[28]

Students of Western American literature in the 1920s did much to develop further the concept of the West as utopian myth. Inspired by the perception of a lost age which the West represented, T. K. Whipple in 1929 focused directly on "The Myth of the Old West." He noted that in "all the talks about the West—or the frontier—and about how it has formed the character of our nation for better or for worse, one aspect of the subject has been neglected: its value as a national myth or symbol. . . . The sweep across the continent . . . has often been called . . . the American epic, and our own heroic age. The story of the West is our Trojan War. . . . But these parallels are less likely to illuminate than to mislead and confuse." Whipple did not believe that the West was actually heroic.

27. Archer Hulbert, *Frontiers* (New York, 1929), 243, 248, 443.
28. Riegel, *America Moves West*, 564–65; McWilliams, "Myths of the West," *North American Review* 232, 432.

Rather . . . we should take it to mean strong in the primitive virtues—the animal virtues—if you like, physical vigor, physical
courage, fortitude, sagacity, quickness, and the other qualities
which enable a man to thrive in an uncivilized environment, to
take care of himself amid primeval dangers and hardships. These
are the individual, not the social virtues. To those of us who live
in a highly differentiated society, these traits are bound to seem
heroic, because they survive in us as unused but strong potentialities, undeveloped because inappropriate. Although the fact that so
much of the savage is latent in us may make civilization precarious, we ought nevertheless to be thankful, for certainly we cannot
afford to lose the primitive virtues. The frontier myth retains them
in consciousness and provides them with exercise and activity.
. . . The function which the myth of a heroic age has always per-
formed: it has embodied and preserved for a complex culture the
values of a simpler world. . . . Our forefathers had civilization inside themselves, the wild outside. We live in the civilization they
created, but within us the wilderness still lingers. What they
dreamed, we live; and what they lived, we dream. That is why our
western story still holds us, however ineptly it is told.[29]

To intellectuals like Joseph Hergesheimer, who were distraught
over the crass commercialism of the 1920s, the mythical West provided
a soothing antidote. "If the frontier had gone," he declared, "the
frontier that was the parent of democracy . . . was still, a living touch
of memory." Compared to the men of the 1920s, Westerners were a
heroic breed. They were a clear contrast to the "financiers, the present
manipulators of public resources. . . . It was in those older men, who,
when they had gone West . . . I found a trace of what I began to
think [of] as an American spirit. . . . [They had] the shape of a distinctive individuality—that courage, at once practical, and highly
picturesque, romantic." And he concluded that "the conditions of the
West made independence . . . there momentarily the spirit of the
nation was visible . . . a country rose not like other countries. . . .
There was . . . an authentic and heroic part of the earth."[30]

Like many of the disillusioned writers of the decade, Lewis Mumford decried what he considered to be the sterility of contemporary

29. T. K. Whipple, *Study Out the Land* (Berkeley, 1943), 59, 61, 65. Whipple
wrote the essay on myth in 1929.
30. Joseph Hergesheimer, "The Magnetic West," *Saturday Evening Post* 195 (September 2, 1922), 97.

culture, but he questioned the efforts of some regionalists to escape into a mythic West. That West, he declared, was not the product of the American environment but of the European mind. The mythical concept of the West was in the imagination of Europeans long before they ever set foot in the New World. "The pioneer has usually been looked upon as a typical product of the American environment," Mumford wrote in 1926. "But the truth is that he existed in the European mind before he made his appearance here. Pioneering may in part be described as the Romantic movement in action." And he questioned the wisdom of escaping into an artificial past. "The power to escape from this sinister world," he declared, "can come only by the double process of encountering more complete modes of life, and of reformulating of more vital tissue of ideas and symbols to supplant those which have led us into the stereotyped interests and actions [of the present]."[31]

Not all students of the Western myth agreed that its origins lay primarily in Europe. Writing in 1930, Carey McWilliams noted that much of the myth came out of the American environment. Its embellishment in the 1920s, he believed, was an outgrowth of a contemporary perception that the Protestant Ethic was in decline, and that Americans had to search for another identity. "For centuries the Far West was the Dark Continent of America," McWilliams wrote. "Myths arose from this unknown and fabulous region. . . . It was the unknown and unpredictable character of the land that fostered the Myth." In seeking to explain its development, McWilliams noted that

> the South and Middle West were settled and established before the West was thoroughly explored. Not only were these regions settled, but they occupied quite definite niches in the national gallery before the West emerged from its nebulous frontier existence, so that the West, coming into self-consciousness, found that it had a difficult problem to solve. How was it to dispose of the outlandish Myth about its origins, attributes, and identity? It was necessary either to accept the legend or to repudiate it harshly and irrevocably. With childlike genuousness, the West not only accepted the legend but naively built it out to epic proportions. Ethical rather than geographic considerations marked the kingdom of the West. This fiction kept Western bounds flexible. The West was a matter of mood.

31. Mumford, Golden Day, 47, 55, 282.

McWilliams blamed historians for nourishing the myth. "Historical writing on the West since 1900," he noted, "has been given over to the composition of obsequies on the frontier—to funereal laments . . . over the demise of the frontier. This dolorous mood has resulted in an enormous and incredible renaissance of the Western Myth." In this infatuation with the frontier, McWilliams declared, historians and writers lovingly fashioned new versions of the myth, thereby adding other layers. "When the frontier disappeared to the naked eye it seeped inward, and survives today as a subjective force which tugs fiercely at our heart strings."[32]

What McWilliams had in mind were dirges such as those composed by Hamlin Garland which added to Western myth. As Garland contemplated the West during these years, he lamented that

> all these frontiers . . . are now gone, utterly gone. America no
> longer has a region of mystery, of untracked spaces, and something
> fine and strong and free is passing from our national life . . .
> something which helped to make our fathers the unconquerable
> individualists they were. . . . Over against the bitterness which
> springs from the congestion of great cities I like to place the faith
> in which my pioneer sire wrought for over eighty years—a faith in
> the open spaces. In a sense the frontier of American progress will
> never pass. So long as we have faith in the future and in the
> transforming effect of our winds and skies the gate of the sunset is
> open to the intellectual pathfinder."[33]

Lesser writers similarly contributed to the enlargement of the myth, to fasten it into national consciousness. "The settlement of the West," wrote Charles M. Harger, was a "tale of frontier struggle against nature . . . out of such experience come manliness, courage, ability. . . . It would be strange if out of the years of stress there came not a character fitting the freedom, the energy, the enthusiasm of the great West. . . . Is it not fair to anticipate a new kind of American?" Struthers Burt, in his *Diary of a Dude Wrangler*, noted quite bluntly that while the real West was gone, the heritage of the West was a state of mind, and would last much longer than the material circumstances that gave it birth. Katherine Gerould, who recorded her impressions of a trip to

32. McWilliams, "Myths of the West," *North American Review* 232, 424, 425, 427, 429.
33. Garland, "Passing of the Frontier," *Dial* 67, 286.

the West in 1925, contrasted the crassness of her contemporary industrialized environment to the noble grandeur of the West. "Courtesy
is still finer," she wrote, "dignity more implicit, than elsewhere. The
wide spaces give every man room to breathe. . . . That doctrine of
freedom, that conception of personal dignity still mould the Western
mind and manner. . . . In the sheer interest of democracy, it can do
us no harm to ponder on the one period of our history, the one section
of our country, wherein democracy became, for a time . . . a logical,
a desirable, a workable theory, neither glorifying Mammon nor can-
onizing mediocrity."[34] In part, she was reflecting the anguish of her
own age.

It was refrains such as those of Garland, Harger, Burt, Gerould,
and others that led Bernard De Voto, a young literary critic at the
time, to join McWilliams in warning about confusing the myth with
reality. "The frontier has created an extraordinary number of myths,"
he wrote in 1927, "and they have got themselves accepted as realities.
So far as they make the rest of the world think of us in preposterous
symbols, they do no great harm but rather add to our sum of laughter.
But, alas, they have worked into our own thinking, and we see ourselves not as we are but as the myths have made us out to be. The
result is only sometimes amusing, but it is always harmful to us, and
especially to our future." He condemned the myth of the West as the
main source of American individualism, the heroism of American
pioneers, or pretensions to a distinctive Western culture. But in criticizing contemporary Western boosterism, he also reflected some nostalgia of his own. "When I have praised the West . . . ," he declared,
"I have praised its countryside, and when I have rebuked it I have
been talking about its cities."[35]

The rapid industrialization and urbanization of the 1920s, therefore, led to a deepening of the nostalgic mood that had contributed
to the development of the West as myth in the early years of the
century. To this was added the disillusionment with American entry

34. Struthers Burt, *The Diary of a Dude Wrangler* (New York, 1925), 312, 318;
Charles M. Harger, "The New Westerner," *North American Review* 620 (August 2,
1907), 748, 752, 754; and Harger, "Brighter Skies Out West," *Review of Reviews* 70
(October 1924), 423. Katherine Fullerton Gerould, "The Aristocratic West," *Harper's*
151 (September 1925), 472, 476, and more fully in her book, *The Aristocratic West*
(New York, 1925).

35. Bernard De Voto, "Footnote on the West," *Harper's* 155 (November 1927),
717, 721.

into World War I which only strengthened the yearning for a return to a simpler age. Historians and other writers about the West clearly reflected these perceptions and wrote them into their visions of the Western myth. In the process, the real West and the mythical West often became closely intertwined.

Such a combination was strengthened by the crisis of the Great Depression. On the one hand, the Depression did foster further disillusionment with contemporary society and a lack of confidence in existing institutions among historians and intellectuals. But on the other hand, on the level of popular culture, the myth provided millions of Americans with an easy escape into a carefree world. Between 1930 and 1945, however, historians were far more concerned with the West as frontier, region, and urban civilization than they were with the West as myth.

Certainly, the Depression sharpened the criticism of the mythic West by disillusioned intellectuals. Increasingly, they attributed alleged national character traits which they associated with the West as myth— traits such as aggression, greed, and materialism, and swashbuckling— to major causes of the economic crisis. A good example of this trend was James Truslow Adams, one of the most widely read historians of the decade. In his Epic of America, published in 1931, he directly attributed lawlessness and violence to the mythical frontier. In Adams's view, the rise of gangsterism and organized crime in his own times was largely due to the traditions of the mythic West.[36] Similarly, the well-known biographer and literary critic Matthew Josephson, a socialist by political orientation, attacked the mythic West as the main source of acquisitiveness among Americans. And that, he concluded, had greatly contributed to the coming of the Great Depression. The gross materialism of America's business civilization, according to Josephson, was a result of the inheritance of the mythic West. "The primitive environment of the frontier actually created no social philosophy other than the anarchic individualism of the jungle," wrote Josephson in 1931.[37] Along similar lines, the editorial writers of the New Republic in 1934 attacked Herbert Hoover, charging that the

36. James Truslow Adams, The Epic of America (Boston 1931), 270–306; Adams, "Rugged Individualism Analyzed," New York Times Magazine (March 8, 1934), 1–2, 11.

37. Matthew Josephson, "The Frontier and Literature," New Republic 68 (September 2, 1931), 78.

morality that had been spawned by the West needed to be abandoned in the midst of the economic disaster which it had done much to produce.[38]

Yet despite these critics, millions of Americans who endured suffering because of economic want continued to rely on the mythical West as an escape from the terrible problems of their present. The decade witnessed a growing interest in popular literature about the mythic West, as measured by the number of books and articles published in the decade. Percy Boynton, a noted literary scholar, noted in 1931 that the interest in the nostalgic West had a special attraction for writers of his day. Amid the mood of cultural nationalism fostered by the Depression, he proclaimed "The Rediscovery of the Frontier." The popularity of such best-sellers as Edna Ferber's *Cimarron* reflected this trend, but hundreds of lesser authors followed in a similar vein. As Boynton noted in 1935, "many of them were world weary and war weary, turning to the West to celebrate the passage of a heroic age and applauding in that remote setting men and events that could be duplicated in every dramatic detail by the gangsters of the nearest big city." Literary works, however, were only one propagator of the Western myth. Increasingly significant were the instruments of popular culture, Western pulps and magazines, radio network programs during the decade, and hundreds of Western movies churned out by Hollywood. Artists like Thomas Hart Benton and the WPA Arts programs made their own distinctive contributions to the myth. As Boynton noted: "Bill Hart and Tom Mix reached a hundred through the film for every one reached through print; Will Rogers came into his own; in these years the rodeo was brought East . . . thrilling all; frontier songs and ballads proliferated." Gene Autry, Roy Rogers, and the Lone Ranger as well as John Wayne now became more effective mythmakers than the legions of western storytellers of the previous generation.[39]

The negative view of the Western myth was strengthened by the introduction of psychological insights. In that respect, the Second World War had an unexpected impact on the development of the West as a myth. It fostered a very significant migration to the United States of Viennese and German psychologists and psychoanalysts who brought their Freudian and Jungian theories with them. Within a

38. "Exit Frontier Morality," *New Republic* 37 (January 2, 1934), 137–38.
39. Percy H. Boynton, *The Rediscovery of the Frontier* (Chicago, 1931); quote from Boynton, *Literature and American Life* (Boston, 1935), 828, 830, 831–32.

decade, they had succeeded in introducing the use of psychology in the analysis of the West as myth, and provided a new dimension in its perception.

In fact, Franz Alexander, one of the most eminent of these émigrés, began to focus on analysis of the West even in wartime. One of Alexander's main concerns was the behavior of criminals in the United States, which he attributed in large part to the widespread acceptance of the frontier myth. As Alexander noted:

> The study of criminal personalities has revealed that apart from rational motives like the desire for gain, other more powerful emotional factors drive individuals to crime. An excessive desire for prestige, the wish to appear daring and independent—a "tough guy"—has been found frequently as such an emotional factor, especially in the young. The reason for this is probably to be found in the cultural history of the country. The ideal of the successful, resourceful, brave, self-made man who owes everything to himself and nothing to anybody else is the traditional ideal. It is obvious that these virtues were extremely important in the Frontier days and overshadowed any others in the conquest of a vast continent and in the rapid development of a new civilization.

Alexander then went on to explain how such ideals broke down in an urbanized society.

> In a remarkably short period, however, the conditions of the Frontier have changed to those of an organized and standardized industrial structure. We have recognized that spiritual tradition changes more slowly than the social structure, and that this constitutes a major obstacle in the adjustment to the existing social conditions. The great majority of young men are still reared with ideals of individual initiative, endurance, self-reliance and courage like their pioneer forefathers, but when they grow up they are exposed to a world in which opportunities for individual initiative, bravado, and individual accomplishment are extremely limited. . . . The old ideals are alive, but their realization becomes daily more difficult. One escape from this dilemma is criminality.

As a psychiatrist, Alexander believed that contemporary conditions in the 1940s were conducive to such criminal behavior, and that Western films had a role in widening the gap between myth and reality.

> An existence regulated by monotonous routine, so common today,

is diametrically opposed to the Frontier tradition and this explains the appeal of those films in which the life of today is depicted as offering unlimited possibilities. . . . The films adapt the materials of contemporary life to the deceptive revival of past conditions.[40]

Alexander foreshadowed some of the changing conditions between 1945 and 1960 that were to affect so the perceptions of historians of the Western myth. One was obviously the immigration of European psychologists who did much to introduce the psychological analysis of Western myth. In addition, the Cold War created for Americans new insecurities which added to the existing pressures of a techno-logical civilization to prompt them to seek escape from contemporary society, if only in their dreams. Meanwhile, the development of tele-vision during these years produced the most potent of the mass media and greatly extended the scope of the Western myth even more ex-tensively than books, radio, and moving pictures had done in earlier years. Such influences did much to shape public perceptions of the West as that other America—a mythical land which was astride the real America, if only in the imagination of its citizens.

As in earlier years, the myth of the West was pervasive, and reached into many levels of public life. President Franklin D. Roosevelt, it will be remembered, had accepted the myth of the closed frontier in 1932. So, in the 1950s, President Dwight D. Eisenhower reflected other dimensions of the myth, particularly its function as the main depository of American values. In accepting a civil rights award in 1953, Eisenhower reminisced: "I was raised in a little town of which most of you have never heard, but in the West it's a famous place! It's called Abilene, Kansas. We had as marshal for a long time a man named Wild Bill Hickok. If you don't know him read your Westerns more. Now, that town had a code, and I was raised as a boy to prize that code." Eisenhower then went on to detail the qualities he had imbibed. These included facing up to one's enemies in a free society, something, he noted, which Americans as a nation had to do in the dangerous world of the 1950s. Clearly, contemporary conditions left their mark on Eisenhower's perception of the West.[41]

In many ways the stage was set in 1950 for one of the most profound

40. Franz Alexander, *Our Age of Unreason* (New York, 1942), 247–53, 262–71.
41. Rita Parks, *The Western Hero in Film and Television* (Ann Arbor, 1982), 141; quotation in Erik Barnouw, *The Image Empire: A History of Broadcasting in the United States* (3 vols., New York, 1970), vol. 3, 18.

works about the Western myth to appear in the twentieth century—
Henry Nash Smith's *Virgin Land,* which reflected the strong impact of
psychology. What Turner had done for the West as frontier in the
1890s, what Webb had accomplished for the West as region in the
1930s, Smith accomplished for the West as myth in the 1950s. A
student of American Studies, Smith also drew heavily on cultural
anthropology to delve more deeply into the development of the mythical West than anyone else before him. In commenting on the West
as an image of the American past, Smith noted that

> the log cabin and the cowboy are symbols which every member of
> society, regardless of education or social level, recognizes at once.
> Anthropologists call such symbols "cultural images." Many, per-
> haps most cultural images . . . are regarded as versions of actual
> historical events or situations, and they are the principal form in
> which knowledge of the past is really current in the society. The
> cultural images thus define the sense of the past which is common
> to the members of our culture. The experience of sharing these
> images is one of the major forces making for social cohesion, be-
> cause the images express value-judgments that everyone is ex-
> pected to endorse. A symbol of this kind does much more than
> convey a simple declarative statement concerning the past. . . . It
> suggests to the members of the social group a special conception of
> themselves, and tends to impose on them very definite notions of
> what is good and what is desirable in social policy.[42]

The intensified interest in psychology and the social sciences characteristic of this period was also reflected by other scholars of the
Western myth. Among these was Frederick Elkin, who analyzed Western films with the aid of social psychological concepts. Elkin also
attempted to relate changing contemporary values to major variations
in Western motion pictures which depicted the mythical West. As he
noted, between 1920 and 1940 such Westerns stressed a life of constant
action in the great outdoors, providing vicarious adventure for an
audience composed largely of city dwellers. But with the coming of
the affluent society, by 1950 leisure activities came to be prized more
highly. In 1950, Elkin wrote that "in a large percentage of western
features, the action is interspersed with casual leisure, a leisure in
which men ride along, strum their guitars, and sing western songs."

42. Smith, *Virgin Land;* quote from Smith, "The West as an Image of the American
Past," *University of Kansas City Review* 18 (Autumn 1951), 29–30, 31.

Until 1940 western heroes tended to be rugged men. But by 1950 a new trend emerged, emphasizing the role of heroines.

> The western heroine . . . is no longer content with a recessive home-centered role and has proclaimed her equality and identity with man. This newer development in heroine type complements the development in hero type. . . . In this more recent development in a world in which both men and women are prominent, the western hero must not only be brave and rugged; he must also have a certain charm, glamor, popularity, and a willingness to accept the independent woman as his partner. Instead of dominant man and complementary recessive woman, this type of western sets up an ideal of a companiate relationship . . . in which the man and woman particpate in the same activities.

Elkin concluded that in the turmoil of Cold War tensions, the mythical West as portrayed in films had a reassuring value for Americans. "There is little doubt," he wrote, "that a child, as well as many an adult, finds the world to be a complex and confusing place. . . . In the western—as of course, in most hero stories—the child can imagine himself in a world that is simple, clearcut, and well ordered. There are no unnecessary characters, no irrelevant intrusions, no complex personalities, and no problems left unresolved."[43]

Elkin's themes were developed in a more comprehensive manner by Martin Nussbaum, a sociologist who also related changing themes in the genre to contemporary influences. "Every culture has at some precise time in its growth created a folk-type art form in its response to its inner turmoils and strivings to satisfy its need for expression of its character," he wrote.

> What, then, are these recurring ideas or emotions that influence and produce the adult western? . . . First, the western contains the spirit of foreign adventure, of new and exciting places. . . . Coupled with this spirit is the inherent romance of the West. . . . The very landscape breathes heroism between not men but giants. . . . A second feature is the unique Western hero. . . . The format of the Western is shaped further . . . by the protagonist's independence and individualism—and his primitive and uncompli- cated contact with nature. . . . He is a drifter, a vanishing symbol of individualism in an age of togetherness and conformity. For the

43. Frederick Elkin, "Psychological Appeal of the Hollywood Western," *Journal of Educational Sociology* 24 (October 1950), 72, 75, 77.

westerner can do what we can't, when the pressures and monotony of life become depressing and wearisome, he can "saddle-up" and vanish into the setting sun. . . . Our fifth theme is the Aristotelian concept of good and evil in modern dress.

In the 1930s and 1940s, Nussbaum noted, this permeated the B cowboy movies. But that seemed ridiculous to what he considered to be the more sophisticated audiences of the 1950s who had been exposed to theories of psychology. They tended to view the world not in absolute blacks or whites, but in grays. Authors of adult Westerns thus humanized their characters.

"We believe," Nussbaum concluded,

> that the Western has arisen as a revolt against rationalism and reason. Contemporary man is approaching the state where his inventions and machines are speeding ahead of him and getting out of control. . . . he cannot apply reason to the solution of his everyday problems as he can to scientific problems; even science is fast approaching the realization of human finitude. . . . Thus, there is an end to rationalism and reason with our existentialist hero. By accepting this hero we acknowledge that there is a limit to reason.[44]

The presentism that Nussbaum reflected was carried even further by other commentators on the Western myth, such as Harry Schein. Reading the concerns of his own day into an analysis of the Western film, he wrote in 1955 that "the Western moral problem revolves around the Fifth Commandment. One can understand that a country traditionally pacifist but suddenly transformed into the strongest military power in the history of the world must begin to consider, how, with good conscience, it can take life. In somewhat awkward situations it is always good to take shelter behind the lofty example of the mythological gods."

Schein viewed contemporary Western films, such as *High Noon*, as having great contemporary significance. "I see 'High Noon' as having an urgent political message," he declared.

> The little community seems to be crippled with fear before the approaching villains; seems to be timid, neutral, and half hearted, like the United Nations before the Soviet Union, China, and

44. Martin Nussbaum, "Sociological Symbolism of the 'Adult Western,'" *Social Forces* 39 (October 1960), 25, 26, 27, 28.

North Korea; moral courage is apparent only in the very American sheriff. . . . Duty and the sense of justice come first, in spite of the fact that he must suddenly stand completely alone. . . . The point, of course, is that pacifism is certainly a good thing, but that war in certain situations can be both moral and unavoidable.

And with a considerable stretching of his imagination, Schein decided that *High Noon*, artistically, was the most convincing, and likewise certainly the most honest, explanation of American foreign policy. "The mythological gods of the Western, who used to shoot unconcernedly, without any moral complications . . . are now grappling with moral problems and an ethical melancholy which could be called existentialist if they were not shared by Mr. Dulles."[45]

Even those critics who did not accept the present-minded perceptions of the Western myth leaned on psychological theories to support their interpretations. In evaluating the myth of the West in 1961, literary critic John Williams decried the interpretations of his contemporaries. He charged that they were "literary racketeers" who had developed mindless stereotyping. He believed that the Western myth had been greatly misunderstood, and that, in its simplest form, it was an allegory of the conflict between good and evil. "Its persistence demonstrates the evocation of a deep response in the consciousness of the people," he wrote. "It is deeply rooted . . . in . . . the New England Calvinist habit of mind. . . . The early Calvinists saw experience as a neverending contest between Good and Evil. . . . All experience is finally allegorical." Yet, he argued, the "Western landscape . . . [is] not really appropriate to the Calvinist formula." The Western myth is "really a habit of mind emerging from the geography and history of New England. . . . The history of the West is in some respects the record of its exploitation. . . . The western adventure, then, is not really epical." Novelists like Walter van Tilburg Clark, Frederick Manfred, or countless hack writers tried to impose the Calvinist scheme on the West when it was really alien to it. The mythical element of the West had not yet received appropriate treatment, he believed. Thus, "the American frontiersman . . . becomes an archetypal figure, and begins to expand beyond his location in history. He is a nineteenth century man moving into the twentieth century; he

45. Harry Schein, "The Olympian Cowboy," *American Scholar* 24 (Summer 1955), 309, 316.

is a man moving into the unknown, into potentiality, and by that move profoundly changing his own nature. . . . He walks in his time and through his adventure, out of history and into myth. He is an adventurer in chaos, searching for meaning there. He is, in short, ourselves."[46]

The most visible representative of the Western myth to which Williams alluded was the American cowboy, who came in for close analysis in the postwar era. Although some critics had expected the cowboy symbol to fade as the frontier receded into history, they were surprised in the 1950s to witness an enormous embellishment of the myth, not only in books and magazines, but especially in films and television. Historians like Henry Nash Smith sought to explain this phenomenon. "The cultural image of the cowboy . . . suggests to Americans a certain conception of themselves," Smith noted, "and embodies value judgments. Although the cowboy is a relatively recent addition to the roster of American folk heroes, he is heir to an imposing body of emotions associated with the Manifest Destiny of the United States in the Far West. The novelist Frank Norris, for example, was one among many observers who believed that the conquest of the high plains and mountain ranges beyond the Mississippi was an achievement of epic proportions."[47]

Marshall Fishwick, on the other hand, an American Studies scholar, attributed the popularity of the cowboy to his generation's search for freedom. "The hunter and cowboy," he wrote in 1952, "two symbolic figures . . . made identical appeals to the tradition valued above all others in the United States: freedom. . . . There was something nostalgic [when] the cowboy could roam for hundreds of miles with no fences. By 1951 these fences were as distant as speculation over the morals of Grover Cleveland." Although the open range had disappeared, the mass media were reinforcing the tradition.

> Conditions have altered radically, but the stereotype of the open-range cowboy has remained static. We can never surrender the romantic haze that has settled permanently on the Western horizon. Most of us wouldn't want to, even if we could. We like to conjure up untarnished noblemen roaming about in their never-never

46. John Williams, "The Western: Definition of the Myth," *The Nation* 193 (November 18, 1961), 401, 402, 404, 406.

47. Smith, "The West as an Image of the American Past," *University of Kansas City Review* 18, 31.

land, where they make the laws and mete out justice. . . . It is a world in which none of our little problems occur, and where dissatisfaction is unknown. Everyone knows what he is supposed to do and does it. We have never really known the tranquility of the medieval synthesis as long as the tradition of the American West is kept alive.

Fishwick argued that the cowboy represented that other America of dreams.

The American cowboy has come to symbolize freedom, individualism, and a closeness to nature which for most of us has become a mere mirage; hence they serve as a safety valve for our culture. When things get too bad, we slip into a movie house, or into a chair with the latest cowboy magazine or novel and vicariously hit the trail. . . . We become free agents in space and time, and for a while leave our humdrum world behind. . . . The cowboy legend, a tangible safety valve for mechanized and urbanized America is spreading with great rapidity. . . . The cowboy . . . has in abundance those virtues our culture most admires. . . . With him the love of freedom is a passion, and the willingness to accept the accompanying responsibility a dogma. The cowboy symbol quickens young America's belief in personal integrity and ingenuity. . . . Cowboy stories are morality stories; like his predecessor, the knight-errant, the cowboy travels the land, making amends in an unbalanced world; and selling the American landscape and personality to the rest of the world. Even if the Western range disappears forever . . . the memory and legend of the open range American cowboy will follow the imaginary trail.[48]

Some historians, such as David Davis, believed that in the 1950s the symbol of the cowboy took on very distinct traits of contemporary Americans in the Cold War period. The mythical West, Davis declared in 1954, represented an image of a carefree life to most Americans. For adolescents, it represented approaching adulthood; for adults, a mythical reliving of their youth. Cowboys also satisfied the emphasis on leisure which came to characterize the affluent society. In the 1950s, cowboys in films rarely worked. Reflecting the influence of social psychology so typical of students of myth during these years, Davis

48. Marshall W. Fishwick, "The Cowboy: America's Contribution to the World's Mythology," *Western Folklore* 11 (1951–52), 77, 78, 91, 92.

surmised that the emphasis on leisure was a direct reaction to technology which made leisure possible and "a natural reaction against a
civilization which demands increasingly monotonous work." Nor was
the Western environment dull in contrast to the suburban life of most
Americans, for it contained "an element of the unexpected, of surprise
. . . [what with] mirages . . . dust storms, hidden identities, and secret
ranches." The cowboy also represented anti-intellectualism, which
Davis saw all about him in the McCarthy era. But Davis found much
to celebrate in this version of the Western myth. "When we think of
many past ideals and heroes, myths and ethics, when we compare our
placid cowboy with . . . the eager, cold, serious hero of Nazi Germany;
when in an age of violence and questionable public and private morality . . . we think of the many possible heroes we might have had
. . . then we can be thankful for our silly cowboy. We could have
chosen worse."[49]

Soon after the 1950s ended, Kent Steckmesser sought to crystallize
his generation's view of the cowboy as a representative of the Western
myth. He concluded that the various writings on the subject revealed
folklorical and literary patterns rather than historical analysis. The
formulas used by scores of writers about the West since the nineteenth
century had been remarkably uniform.

> The heroes also personify traits which Americans have always ad-
> mired. Courage, self-reliance, and physical prowess have usually
> been rated high on the scale. These traits may seem anachronistic
> in a settled and industrialized society. Indeed, much of the hero's
> appeal seems to be connected with a sentimental nostalgia for the
> freedom of a vanished frontier. The wilderness setting . . . has al-
> ways intrigued and excited Americans . . . [and] represents the
> perennial drama of man facing the unknown. . . . But the basic
> appeal of the legendary heroes is that they served good causes.
> They were servants of justice and truth, defenders of the meek and
> the oppressed. They became actors in the great allegory of Good
> v. Evil, an allegory whose roots lie deep in American History.
> That service in such causes may be unfounded is of little relevance
> in the legend. Because Americans have cast themselves in idealis-
> tic roles, they have been able to identify with the heroic represen-
> tatives of the national character.[50]

49. David B. Davis, "Ten-Gallon Hero," *American Quarterly* 6 (Summer 1954),
111–23, 124–25.

50. Kent L. Steckmesser, *The Western Hero in History and Legend* (Norman, 1965),
241, 245, 250, 255.

In an age of insecurity permeated by three wars—World War II, the Korean War, and the Cold War—Americans between 1945 and 1960 found a special place for the mythic West, and its symbolic representative, the cowboy. By 1950 they were reading at least eighteen million westerns yearly and listening to radio programs featuring the Lone Ranger, Gene Autry, and Roy Rogers. Tens of millions went to see the myth reflected in Western films, while still larger numbers soon joined an even larger television audience to view programs such as "Bonanza" or "Gunsmoke." Perpetuation of the myth fitted the mood of Americans seeking an escape from their own uncertain world into one which was eminently predictable. In this universe, they also found a reaffirmation of basic American values—many of which were being questioned at home while they were challenged in the ideological conflict with the Soviet Union abroad. Such a reaffirmation was soothing and reassuring. And in an era when an increasing number of Americans were enjoying more leisure, the entertainment value of Western myth was obviously prized as well. As time dimmed recollections of the real nineteenth-century West, generations born in the twentieth century intensified the embellishment of its mythic past to meet their own particular needs in a time of turmoil.

Historians and social scientists concerned with the West as myth were deeply influenced by these contemporary trends. That was clearly reflected in their writings about the myth. The most important characteristic of their work between 1945 and 1960 was the use of psychological concepts to examine the various dimensions of the imaginary West. The large-scale migration of European psychoanalysts to the United States during the Hitler years had done much to develop this mode of analysis, for they also trained hundreds of psychologists who became their disciples. However, social science analysis also had deep native roots, and social psychologists, sociologists, and cultural anthropologists were especially concerned with the Western myth. During these years, they found a direct relationship between contemporary problems of the United States in the Cold War and the increasing popularity of the West as myth. These included fears and insecurities due to the Cold War with the Soviet Union, gnawing doubts about life-styles fostered by the affluent society, and increasing leisure and the growth of the entertainment industry, particularly television and the mass media. Such trends encouraged embellishment of the Western myth. As the pace of life in the United States between 1945 and 1960 resulted in new tensions, historians and writers on the mythic West concluded that more Americans than ever found relief in escaping to a land of their imagination—the mythic West.

Sometime in the 1960s the momentous events of the decade began to have an impact on the treatment of the mythic West. Perceptions changed—whether reflected in books or in the many other manifestations of the myth until 1990. The civil rights movement awakened a new consciousness of minorities in the West: Indians, blacks, and Hispanics. By 1963, when Betty Friedan's *The Feminine Mystique* appeared, the scope of the civil rights movement broadened to include women. At the same time, the Vietnam war accelerated a mood of guilt, self-doubt, self-criticism, and negativism among intellectuals and large numbers of the young. Ideology became far more pronounced in historical interpretations, not only among the New Left, but also among many specialists in ethnic, racial, or gender-oriented history who viewed race, class, or sex as the major determinants of historical events. Such an orientation encouraged an increasing present-mindedness and narrowness which brought benefits as well as new problems.

The years between 1960 and 1990 also witnessed an enormous expansion in the scope and influence of the mass media on politics, society, and culture. Indeed, some critics argued that television had usurped the functions of family and church as one of the major purveyors of values for large numbers of the American people. And while the emphasis of global perceptions on the West was not as pronounced as it had been in the decade after 1945, students of the mythic West during these years clearly reflected an international perspective in their approach to the subject.

In short, three major trends permeated writings about the mythic West between 1960 and 1990. Most pronounced was the negativism, and also pessimism, of a generation on whom the 1960s had left a deep impact. Another trend was the central role of the mass media in propagation of the myth which now concerned an increasing number of scholars. Less explicit, but in the mainstream, was the international perspective on the West.

Such trends were aptly reflected in changing perceptions of the mythic West. The strong doubts which scholars of this generation had about traditional values were clearly reflected in their rather negative appraisals of the imaginary West. Others merely expressed a pessimistic mood, or continued to view the West of romance as an escape hatch for contemporary pressures. But the study of myth during this period was more extensive than in any other comparable span of years before. Scholars explored the impact of myth much more fully, and in greater depth. In addition, they provided new dimensions, and delved in the reflection of myth not only in literature and art, but in the mass media, including radio, films, and television. That interest reflected a growing awareness of the importance of the mass media in shaping popular perceptions (and misconceptions) as well as myths. Certainly, books and magazines had given form to the mythic West since the nineteenth century, but the electronic media of the twentieth century did much to expand their role. And the global role of the United States during this period no longer made it possible for scholars to view the West as a unique phenomenon.

That the awareness of the West as myth was profoundly influenced by contemporary conditions was well recognized by historians of this era, of whom Paul Hutton was among the most articulate. Writing in 1976, he noted:

> Heroes are not born, they are created. Their lives so catch the imagination of their generation, and often the generations that follow, that they are repeatedly discussed and written about. The lives of heroes are a testament to the values and aspirations of those who admire them. If their images change as time passes they may act as a barometer of the fluctuating attitudes of a society. Eventually, if certain attitudes change enough, one hero may re-place another. Such is the case with George Armstrong Custer. Once a symbolic leader of civilization's advance into the wilder-ness, within one hundred years he came to represent the supposed moral bankruptcy of Manifest Destiny.

And then Hutton concluded:

> As the values of society change so does its vision of history, and one Custer myth is replaced with another. The collective pop-ular mind is unable or unwilling to deal with the complexities of character; its heroes are pure and its villains are evil with no shad-ing in between. As the American view of militarism and Indians changed, so the view of Custer changed. As society's image of the frontier altered from that of a desert stubbornly resisting the prog-ress of civilization to that of a garden of innocence offering refuge from the decadence of civilization, so the expectations for the western hero changed. The conquering military hero was replaced

by the frontiersman or Indian who could live in harmony with nature. Thus, from a symbol of courage and sacrifice in the winning of the West, Custer's image was gradually altered into a symbol of the arrogance and brutality displayed in the white exploitation of the West. The only constant factor in this reversed legend is a remarkable disregard for historical fact.[51]

Historians continued to treat the mythic West as an escape for Americans from an urban, industrial society, a function which it continued to have during this period. Writing in 1967 about *Wilderness and the American Mind,* Roderick Nash noted that

> America was ripe for the widespread appeal of the uncivilized. The cult had several facets. In the first place, there was a growing tendency to associate wilderness with America's frontier and pioneer past that was believed responsible for many unique and desirable national characteristics. Wilderness also acquired importance as a source of virility, toughness, and savagery, qualities that defined fitness in Darwinian terms. Finally, an increasing number of Americans invested wild places with aesthetic and ethical values, emphasizing the opportunity they afford for contemplation and worship.[52]

Almost a decade later, Richard Etulain enlarged on this function of the Western myth. "Some Americans of the Progressive Era feared that an industrial society was creeping upon them," Etulain wrote,

> and devouring their lives. To recapture a past that was less coercive and less dominated by the city, the immigrant, and worker, they turned to the West as a palliative. The West as frontier symbolized a simpler and more primitive and pristine past that many Progressives wished to retain. Confronted with a present and a future that conjured a diminished individualism, they embraced, instead, a region in popular literature that was the last opportunity for democracy, individualism, and decency. The West, to these Americans, was more than a satisfactory symbol; it was an attractive emotional experience. The Western was in large part the literary byproduct of this haunting and fractured emotional experience.

51. Paul A. Hutton, "From Little Big Horn to Little Big Man: The Changing Image of a Western Hero in Popular Culture," *Western Historical Quarterly* 7 (January 1976), 19, 45.
52. Roderick Nash, *Wilderness and the American Mind* (New Haven, 1967), 145.

Etulain then related the myth to his own times. "Perhaps Americans in our time can comprehend this tendency of the Progressive Era to evade the most pressing issues of the time and to revert to a nostalgic and sentimental view of the West," he declared.

> Some contemporary Americans avoid the nagging problems of poverty, racism, and pollution by allowing themselves to escape to the mountains or countryside and lose their worries in a symbolic wilderness. In several ways the popularity of Charles Reich's *The Greening of America* and the writings of Theodore Roszak illustrate this tendency of avoiding harsh realities and of dreaming of what might be. Instead of realizing that the best answer is some kind of difficult but necessary compromise between extremes, many Americans choose to think that back-to-the-land movements or the championing of what they consider the mystical and land-oriented philosophies of Native Americans will solve our complex and traumatic social problems. This desire to avoid a depressing present and the increasing tendency to escape into the past is much with us today; if we comprehend this impulse, it is less difficult to understand the climate of opinion that helped spawn the Western.[53]

A significant number of scholars who examined the myth of the West during these years wrote from New Left perspectives. Their view of the American—and Western past—was profoundly influenced by their contemporary self-deprecatory mood. Essentially, they applied their political outlook to the study of the mythic West. Representative were literary critics such as Leslie Fiedler and Richard Slotkin, and historians such as Brian Dippie and Richard Drinnon. Their works were present-minded, and sometimes provided new perspectives on familiar topics.

Leslie Fiedler, one of the most widely read literary critics of this period, well reflected the negativism of this generation. In *The Return of the Vanishing American,* Fiedler sought to interpret contemporary trends in American culture within the context of the Western myth. In his analysis of the literature of the West, Fiedler now perceived the theme of racial and ethnic conflict as a major determinant. As whites had corrupted Indians with whiskey centuries ago, so now Indians were reaping their revenge on whites who were seeking new frontiers through the use of drugs—the Indians' hallucinogens.

53. Richard W. Etulain, "The Historical Development of the Western," *Journal of Popular Culture* 7 (Winter 1973), 718, 719.

An astonishing number of novelists have begun to write fiction in which the Indian character—whom only yesterday we were comfortably bidding farewell . . . has disconcertingly reappeared. . . . But in the last several years, beginning somewhere around 1960, John Barth and Thomas Berger and Ken Kesey and David Markson and Peter Mathiessen . . . and I . . . have, perhaps without being even aware, been involved in a common venture: the creation of a New Western, a form which not so much redeems the Pop Western as exploits it with irreverence and pleasure, in contempt of the "serious reader" and his expectations.

Fiedler argued that Indians were central to the Western myth. "What is the Western in its classic or traditional form, and second, what precisely is new about the New Western?" he asked.

To begin answering the first of these questions, we need only notice the fact . . . that geography in the United States is mythological. . . . The heart of the Western is not the confrontation with the alien landscape . . . but the encounter with the Indian. . . . No grandchild of Noah, he escapes completely the mythologies we brought with us from Europe, demands a new one of his own. . . . everything else which belongs to the Western theme has long since been assimilated; the prairies subdivided and landscaped; the mountains staked off as hunting preserves and national parks; fabulous beasts, like the grizzlies and the buffalo, killed or fenced in as tourist attractions. . . . Only the Indian survives . . . to remind us with his alien stare of the new kind of space in which the baffled refugees from Europe first found him. . . . It is for this reason that tales set in the West seem to us not quite Westerns . . . when no Indian . . . appears in them.

Given his emphasis on Indians, Fiedler interpreted the mythic West as one major theater of racial conflict in the United States. "The Western story in archtypal form is, then, a fiction dealing with the confrontation in the wilderness of a transplanted WASP and a radically alien other, an Indian, leading either to a metamorphosis of the WASP into something neither White nor Red . . . or else to the annihilation of the Indian. In either case, the tensions of the encounter are resolved by eliminating one of the mythological partners, by ritual or symbolic means [or] by physical force."

Reflecting the drug culture of the 1960s, Fiedler had advice for those who might join his search for a new mythic West. "Obviously,

not everyone is now prepared . . . to make a final and total commitment to the Newest West via psychosis," he wrote. "But a kind of
tourism into insanity is already possible for those . . . ready . . . to
migrate from the world of reason. We can take, as the New Westerns
suggest what is already popularly called . . . a 'trip,' an excursion into
the unknown with the aid of drugs." That seemed logical to him
because "the West has seemed to us for a long time a place of recreation
as well as of risk."[54]

Another searing critique of American society through the medium
of the Western myth came from the pen of Richard Slotkin in his
Regeneration Through Violence, published in 1973. Slotkin was particularly critical of most traditional American values, including an alleged
violent strain. He reflected his own era by extensive integration of
Jungian psychology into his work. His major theme was that "an entire
set of national attitudes and traditions informing our literature and
defining our social responses has evolved from the myth of the hunter–
hero struggling in a savage new world to claim the land, to displace
the Indian." In his study, Slotkin reflected the guilt feelings of many
Americans in the 1960s about alleged injustices they inflicted on
minorities such as the Indians. Like many ideologically oriented studies
of this period, Slotkin analyzed not individuals, but faceless types so
that he created new stereotypes of both Indians and non-Indians. The
former could do no wrong, and the latter could do no right.

With such a perspective, Slotkin attempted to provide a complex
analysis of the mythic West. In an effort to integrate Indian myths
with those of American heroes, he subjected them to Jungian analysis.
Thus, he was not interested in socioeconomic details since he set up
his ideological framework before arrangement of his data. Whereas
Western myth before 1945 had largely ignored or denied the extraordinary complexity of the Indian's culture, Slotkin now gave it primary
emphasis. In Slotkin's world, Indian myths were always "genuine"
while the myths of Western heroes were invariably "spurious." In this
form of reverse racism, moral and ethical judgments tended to become
doctrinaire. His exhaustive analyses of frontier narratives were filtered
through such an ideological prism. Despite the sophistication of the
work, Roy Harvey Pearce (a well-known literary historian) noted,

54. Leslie A. Fiedler, *The Return of the Vanishing American* (New York, 1968), 13,
15, 24, 27, 186.

Slotkin really was typical of a rather uncritical and admiring neo-primitivist. In developing a typology of archetypes, he made ideological commitments which deliberately ignored and devalued the unique, distinctive aspects of individuals and their particular historical experience. It was New Left history in the tradition of Herbert Marcuse's *One-Dimensional Man*.[55]

The directions taken by Fiedler and Slotkin were amplified in 1982 by Brian Dippie in *The Vanishing American*. "The myth of the Vanishing American lives on," he declared,

> sustained by literary and artistic tradition older than the Republic. . . . The psychological imperative of cultural guilt periodically infuses it with new vigor. . . . Today the modish word "genocide" carries the burden of the Vanishing American. It implies a deliberate program of extermination and a devastating moral judgment. . . . The presence of those who were wronged seems unbearable. Avoidance and denial become the most reassuring responses. . . . The myth of the Vanishing American accounted for the Indians' future by denying them one, and stained the tissue of policy debate with fatalism.[56]

Perhaps the shrillest voice on the New Left with regard to Western myth was that of Richard Drinnon. In his discussion of "the problem of the West" in 1980, he reflected the intrusion of contemporary concerns.

> Four centuries after Columbus, Frederick Jackson Turner had pronounced the continental frontier . . . gone; three-quarters of a century later the second period closed, with the westward course of empire rolling back from the Pacific rim. . . . [With] Viet Nam America's historic westward-driving wave has crested. That wave has carried us along. . . . But before turning about and facing home again, we had better cast an apprehensive glance over our shoulder. . . . Despite his geographical determinism . . . Turner saw clearly the direction the empire was headed in and even foresaw the inner identities of the New Frontier and the old long before John F. Kennedy so christened the former. Turner added his

---

55. Richard Slotkin, *Regeneration through Violence: The Mythology of the American Frontier, 1600–1860* (Middletown, Conn., 1973), and the review by Roy Harvey Pearce, in *Pacific Historical Review* 43 (February 1974), 111–12.

56. Brian W. Dippie, *The Vanishing American: White Attitudes and U.S. Indian Policy* (Middletown, Conn., 1982), xii, 351.

monumental chapter to the national metaphysics of Indian-hating. At bottom, that doctrinal hate rested on the collective refusal to conceive of Native Americans as persons, a refusal Turner shared in full measure. No less than [others] did he glorify Indian-killers as pathfinders of "civilization," glorify their mastery over every dusky tribe, and throw sheaves of patriotic rhetoric over the real human bodies left behind.

Drinnon's strong ideological bias profoundly affected his analysis of the mythic West. "To my mind," he wrote,

> the intricate inter-relationships among a society's subterranean emotions, its channeling of these into myths that seemingly give coherence to the past and bearing for the future, and its institutional means of making that destiny manifest—all these complex and reciprocal relationships foredoom any such attempt [to offer a theory]. I do suggest these metaphysics helped shape [and were shaped by] political, social, and economic structures; provided substance for fundamental declarations of doctrine, laws, and policy; established core themes in literature, sculpture, painting, and film; and determined how individuals perceived their world and acted in it. It gave them their astonishing assurance . . . that they had a right to be in every West they could "win" . . . down to Lodge and Calley in Indochina. . . . He would indeed be a rash prophet who should assert that the metaphysics of Indian-hating will be lightly cast aside. The Vietnam veterans came home from the war to the Pentagon Papers, Watergate, the CIA scandals, and all the rest—all of which provide compelling evidence that the methods and instrumentalities designed originally for dealing with natives had beat them home. . . .[57]

If not all of the critics of the mythic West were as ideological as Fiedler, Slotkin, and Drinnon, they still shared to some extent their pessimistic mood. In a notable regional study of *The California Dream*, published in 1972, Kevin Starr announced that "this book attempts to deal with the imaginative aspects of California's journey to identity. While barely on the map, it entered American awareness as a symbol of the renewal. It was a final frontier: of geography and of expectation." In explaining his method, Starr noted that he hoped to integrate fact and imagination in the belief that the record of their interchange

57. Richard Drinnon, *Facing West: The Metaphysics of Indian-Hating and Empire-Building* (Minneapolis, 1980), 460, 462–63, 464, 465.

through symbolic statement was the most precious legacy from the past. "Obscurely . . . at a distance . . . Americans glimpsed a California of beauty and justice, where on the land or in well ordered cities they might enter into prosperity and peace. Of course, the dream outran the reality, as it always does. California experienced more than its share of social problems because its development was so greedy and so unregulated. No evocation of imaginative aspiration can atone for the burdens of the California past," he wrote in the self-deprecatory tone common of his generation. Almost as if he were involved in an act of catharsis—of public atonement for the sins of the past—he added: "Acknowledging the tragedy, however, Californians must also attune themselves to the hope." Such hope was necessary, he believed, because he shared the pessimistic outlook of the decade. "In this more complicated time, when hope is not so certain and the promise is unclear, the faith of those years must come to our aid."[58]

Such a pessimistic note was also struck by Don Walker, a literary historian, in his 1981 discussion of the cowboy myth. "It should be clear," he wrote,

> that when we speak of this cowboy past we do not mean an objective history. . . . It may well be that the deep structures of all histories are finally mythic. Yet short of enclosing ourselves in this final circle we can continue to make practical distinctions between history as a critical reconstruction of "things as they actually were," and the past as a "psychological reality" used to give ideological sanction. . . . All of the versions of the cowboy past . . . are perceptions of the past in this sense. . . . They are ideological creations, not critical reconstructions. Indeed, they are fictions. . . . The past as psychological reality may prove to be more important than the past as history.

Walker reflected his generation's lack of confidence as he noted that

> all of this should be humbling; all of this should remind us that tentative answers are all we are ever likely to find. All of this, in our time, should indeed test our intellectual nerve. For however complicated historiography may have seemed in the past, whatever the problems of separating fact from opinion, history from myth . . . in our time we have seemed to flounder in an epistemological

58. Kevin Starr, *Americans and the California Dream, 1850–1915* (New York, 1973), vii–viii.

sinkhole. Old structures have failed us. The time-honored chain of time no longer binds our meanings together. Configuration may be as much spatial as chronological.[59]

Clearly, contemporary events between 1960 and 1990 left a deep imprint on those who were writing about the mythic West. Most striking was a pronounced mood of self-doubt, guilt, pessimism, and negativism—all reflecting pervasive fears that were beginning to appear in the outlook of many Americans during these years. In a sense, the scholars served as the weather vanes of society.

Also prominent during this period was an enormous expansion of writings about the mythic West as it was reflected in the mass media. Scholars continued to give attention to the role of literature in the propagation of the myth. But now they also expanded their research to include the mass media, which previously had not been seriously considered by academics. These media included various instruments of popular culture such as pulp Westerns, radio programs, Western films, and television. Moreover, these years saw the first serious efforts by scholars to deal with the social history of Western art, to view it not only from the perspective of artistic excellence, but as social documents reflecting the mythic West. Between 1960 and 1990 scholars did more to extend the scope and breadth of the mythic West than they had in the entire seventy-year era before.

Among those who called attention to the importance of the mass media in developing myths about the West, Richard Etulain was prominent. Writing in 1974, he bemoaned the lack of serious study of the mythic West, particularly as portrayed in Westerns. "Like other forms of popular literature, the Western has not received much scholarly attention," Etulain wrote. "More serious scholarship has been published in fact, on science fiction and the detective novel than on the Western. There are, however, signs of change . . . in the last decade." Alluding directly to the West as myth, Etulain declared that "we need to know more about . . . movies, television, popular music, rodeos, festivals, county fairs, museums, and historical exhibits. We have utilized too sparingly the techniques that social scientists employ in analyzing audiences and their reactions to what they read or see."[60]

59. Don Walker, *Clio's Cowboys: Studies in the Historiography of the Cattle Trade* (Lincoln, 1981), 162, 164.
60. Richard W. Etulain, "Riding Point: The Western and Its Interpreters," *Journal of Popular Culture* 7 (Winter 1973), 647–51.

Etulain also sought to explore the origins of this myth. "The West as a physical and spiritual frontier was an important symbol for America," he wrote.

> To lose it or the idyllic existence that it represented was to lose part of their past and to bargain away their future. It is not difficult to perceive how this psychological necessity encouraged authors to devote most attention to the West in their writings. The need and mood were apparent, and writers who were a part of this identity crisis could assure themselves of a larger audience if they portrayed the West romantically. So the conflict between industrial and agricultural America and the resultant nostalgia for the past were large encouragements for the rise of the Western.

And in a series of suggestive articles, Etulain provided detailed analyses of the literary development of the Western myth, particularly in the realm of popular culture.[61]

Other historians also emphasized that the popular Western met basic psychic needs of Americans. As M. T. Marsden emphasized in 1978, the genre was one of the nation's cultural artifacts, "providing both literary critic and historian invaluable insight into popular attitudes and values, not only about the historical West, but also about 'the West' of our contemporary imagination. Popular western literature is also an ever-changing, yet constant window into the cultural needs and values of a people who enjoy the ritualistic retelling of the winning of the West, not as it was won, but as it should have been won." The psychological functions of the Western were not a passing fancy, Mardsden concluded. "The Western helps us to define who we are by carefully examining where we should have been, and by implication, where we should be headed. The West is national self-awareness. In the West the American people are unified imaginatively through time, and by traditions."[62]

Perhaps the most comprehensive and most incisive analysis of the West as myth revealed in popular culture was made by John Cawelti, an American Studies scholar, in 1974. Synthesizing many of the major

61. Etulain, "Historical Development of the Western," *Journal of Popular Culture* 7, 717–26; Etulain, "Origins of the Western," *Journal of Popular Culture* 5 (Spring 1972), 802.

62. Michael T. Marsden, "The Popular Western Novel as a Cultural Artifact," *Arizona and the West* 20 (Autumn 1978), 203, 206, 208.

strands developed by others in the preceding two decades, he crystallized his generation's view of the Western myth. "The West has not
only been an important historical reality," he wrote,

> but a landscape of the imagination, a setting for symbolic dramas
> which continue to preoccupy many of our most creative as well as
> our most popular novelists, dramatists, and filmmakers. And the
> imaginative role of the West . . . has also generated a vital set of
> symbols which fascinate Easterners as well. . . . The American
> West has always had fascination for Europeans . . . has cast its
> spell in Asia and Africa as well, becoming the basis of what may
> be one of the first truly international popular mythologies.

Cawelti acknowledged the negative outlook of some of his contemporaries about the mythic West. "The myth of the West is the
myth of America in this very special sense," he declared,

> that men can leave their history behind and father a higher hu-
> man possibility on a virgin continent. The power of this imagina-
> tive vision . . . the American dream . . . has, until recently,
> survived our growing realization that there is no escape from his-
> tory, and our increasing awareness that our approach to the New
> World was less analogous to marriage with a virgin than to the
> rape and murder of a neighbor's wife. We are still struggling to
> come to terms with this new awareness of our tragic betrayal of
> the American dream, and this struggle is reflected in the guilt-
> ridden and ironic undertones of many contemporary treatments of
> the Western myth, such as Thomas Berger and Arthur Penn's *Little
> Big Man*.[63]

In brilliant fashion, Cawelti chronicled the transformation of the
optimistic views of the Western myth before 1945 to the increasingly
pessimistic and negative outlook in the half-century thereafter.

> In harmonizing our conflicting Western myths . . . the Western
> novel and film of the early twentieth century was . . . in tune
> with the upsurge of moral optimism which seemed to be shared by
> much of the American public during this period of confident pro-
> gressivism. It seems appropriate that Wister dedicated his *Virginian*
> to Theodore Roosevelt. . . . the novel can be interpreted as a pro-
> gressive parable in which courageous individual leadership drives

63. John Cawelti, "God's Country . . . Differing Visions of the West," *Western
American Literature* 9 (Winter 1975), 273–74.

the rascals out and regenerates the community. . . . But this vibrantly optimistic feeling about the moral future and rich human possibility of American life was deeply shaken by many factors in the late twenties, thirties, and forties. If it was to survive, the Western had to develop a new kind of imaginative orientation. That it did, by the late 1930s especially. In the 1940s and 1950s the western hero's relation to the pioneer community became the dominant subject of serious westerns. He became an individual isolated from the community—reflecting the feelings of Americans in the 1950s. . . . But the accumulating crises of the twentieth century made Americans increasingly uncertain of the meaning of the American dream. The central symbols of the Western became darker and more complex. Negativism set in. . . . The Western today is clearly a mythical form in search of a new set of cultural meanings. The dialectic of social redemption and individual freedom on which the popular Western has been essentially grounded has given way to a more enigmatic and pessimistic view of the meaning of America. . . . If the myth is to remain a vital one . . . the Western must confront our new understanding of ourselves and to begin to articulate and explore the conflicts of value and meaning which now dominate our lives. If not, it will become at long last a truly dead myth.[64]

But other literary critics argued that the vitality of the myth was essential to the American experience. In his analysis of *American Myth, American Reality,* in 1980, James Oliver Robertson declared that

the sense of the existence of wilderness, the powerful imagery of contrast between civilization and wilderness, must be maintained if the logic of New World mythology is to be maintained. American myths tell us still that there is no New World without wilderness. If we are to be true Americans . . . there *must* be wilderness. The symbol is an imperative for our real world. . . . Since its birth, the American nation has tied itself to a dream of expansion into the wilderness. The destiny of the New World and the mission of America have been the interchangeable focuses of powerful, still-living American myth. The actual demise of a New World to conquer—the American West, the American wilderness—has not destroyed the power of the myth to generate energy in Americans, to provide a dynamic for American society, to make a logical explanation of the American universe. The imperative of the mission

64. Ibid., 281–83.

myth requires new worlds . . . to conquer. Americans—pathfinders, discoverers, pioneers, explorers, crusaders, reformers—have
not ceased to seek the liberty, democracy, equality, independence,
and happiness those new worlds offer, *in new worlds.*[65]

This period saw the first efforts by serious scholars to assess the
mythic West as it was portrayed in films and television. Writing in
1982, Rita Parks reflected on the contemporary influences which led
to her study. "Less than four hundred years after the beginnings of
European colonization," she wrote,

> barely two hundred years after the first trembling steps taken to-
> wards sovereignty as a nation, the United States of America has
> climbed to the summit of world power and is struggling for equal
> footing with nations whose history extends back into the unchron-
> icled darkness of ancient times. . . . Europe is unable to under-
> stand this United States. This apparent paradox between history
> and myth . . . may very likely have produced . . . mass media en-
> tertainment. The Western hero is a subject whose roots are in his-
> tory, whose image has been transformed into myth, and whose
> chief function for the contemporary audience is to provide enter-
> tainment . . . [and] the vitality and stability of recurrent themes of
> ancient myth.

Parks chronicled the mood of negativism and despair that reflected
itself in depictions of the mythic West.

> The Western, of course, represents a way of life that was eclipsed
> at the time of the closing of the frontier. Once the new Adam and
> Eve of symbol and story, today's Americans are less sure of their
> strength, less confident of success through their own efforts. At
> one time reborn of American idealism and hope for the future, we
> no longer feel that we are in control of our environment, ultimate
> victors in the battle against evil. Both the land itself and the mas-
> tery of the land have become a memory and an impossible dream
> for technological society. We often feel now that we have little
> choice but to place our confidence and existential hope . . . in the
> power of the machine. . . . More seriously, perhaps, the contem-
> porary American's inner landscape has been befogged by shades of
> gray. No longer is the cause clearly and unmistakably good or evil;
> no longer can the good guys be recognized by their color, gentle

65. James Oliver Robertson, *American Myth, American Reality* (New York, 1980),
124.

birth, cleanliness of speech and dress. . . . No longer do the good
guys receive their just deserts [sic]; on the contrary, more frequently they become the possessors of the earth while the heroes
are outsiders—symbolic of anti- or non-heroism. Contemporary
Americans, moreover, are less able to account for their own conflicting desires, motivations, and impulses. We have few and immediate goals, we often find striving for them futile, and it is
increasingly difficult to see purpose in what we do or are. . . .
[But] for Americans the Western genre has played a cyclic but consistent role sustaining and enriching . . . cultural images. . . . The
story in whatever form still responds to our needs and represents
our dreams.[66]

While Parks focused on the mythic West in television, John Lenihan concentrated his energies on the Western film. Writing in 1980,
he noted that Western films were

especially revealing of how a particular form is modified in accor-
dance with the constantly changing concerns and attitudes of a society . . . with fundamental American beliefs about individual and
social progress. The post–World War II years were a period of
acute national self-examination of America's direction in foreign
affairs, the social assimilation of ethnic minorities, and the ability
of the corporate welfare state to serve the collective needs of a
mass society while respecting individual rights and interests.

Then, in the 1950s the "organization man, lonely crowd, alienated
individuals, conformity, consensus, anxiety, and complacency" became
major themes in Western films. That changed again in the 1960s,
when Vietnam, the New Left, riots, and the counter-culture directly
affected the themes of most Westerns. Lenihan believed that "the
Western movie is one of the mechanisms a democratic society used
to give form and meaning to its worries about its own destinies at a
time its position seemed more central and its values less secure than
ever before." In view of such sensivitity, Lenihan concluded that "from
World War II through the troubled Cold War years, the Western
accommodated a variety of issues and ideas that echoed feelings of
confidence and commitment, as well as alienation and disillusionment.

66. Parks, *Western Hero in Film and Television*, 1, 6, 156–57.

Its proved capacity for redefining America's mythic heritage in contemporary terms would suggest . . . that the Western is an unlikely
candidate for cultural oblivion."[67]

It was only in the 1980s that historians began the serious inquiry
into the important role of art in disseminating images of the mythic
West. Charles Eldredge was one of the earliest art historians to discern
that significance. As he noted in 1984,

> To those raised on the films of William Boyd, the tales of Zane
> Grey, the illustrations of Frederic Remington or William R. Leigh,
> the West may forever be a land of brave men, heroic exploits, and
> derring do. Their portrayals of the region and its legendary charac-
> ters, all larger than life, inspired awe, even reverence among the
> young. But the world of Hopalong Cassidy was only one part of
> the West. It was part of a legend whose genesis lay in the nine-
> teenth century. It was an apparently simpler era when cowboys
> and Indians, cavalry and prospectors, Wyatt Earp and dance-hall
> girls populated rude streets and unspoiled landscape. These historic
> roles of the characters have been replayed in the movies, in books,
> and in art—and in our modern imagination—until the West has
> assumed a mythic and psychological importance quite independent
> of geography or history. The region's rich legends and landscapes
> of Catlin, Remington, Bierstadt continue to provide imaginative
> escape from the realities of modern life. But the West today also
> boasts boom towns matured into major metropolises. . . . It is a
> complex region and can no longer be understood as an idyllic
> grand garden, or an American Eden.[68]

In fact, it was the belief of Patricia Janis Broder, a leading art
historian, that the artistic portrayal of the twentieth-century West
would provide an as yet unrecognized dimension of the mythic West.
"It has been a long-standing tradition to idealize and romanticize the
American West," she wrote in 1984.

> In the twentieth century, however, the American West is neither a
> paradical Eden nor a wilderness to be conquered and given the gift
> of civilization. The cowboy who rode the open range vanished al-
> most a century ago, and the Indian is not the last of his race.

67. John H. Lenihan, *Showdown: Confronting Modern America in the Western Film*
(Urbana, 1980), 3, 5, 9–10, 176.
68. Charles Eldridge, in Patricia Janis Broder, *The American West: The Modern
Vision* (Boston, 1984), foreword.

Nevertheless, there is a strong temptation to retain these and other fantasies rather than face the reality of the twentieth century West: towns and cities with large, ethnic populations, highways, railroads, jetports, industrial complexes and tourist attractions. The West is part of contemporary America. Fortunately, many American artists have accepted the challenge to paint a land and culture in transition.[69]

The importance of these visual-image makers was the primary subject of an important book by William Goetzmann in 1986, which also became the basis of a television series. This was *The West of the Imagination,*

> a country and a saga peopled by characters who, because they have a special place in our collective national consciousness, are as alive today as they were a hundred years ago. Tracing the stories and analyzing the works of the artists and photographers and other image-makers who portrayed the West, we hope to point up the elemental power of their visions, their magic, and the ways in which they contributed to what might be called "the tale of the American tribe." For the visual image-makers have contributed as much as the writers to the fundamental myth of the American experience—the story of the peopling of a vast new continent by emigrants from the old European world who were forever moving West. To a surprising degree, the men and women who were engaged in this movement West . . . were conscious of their place in history. . . . The artist, and a bit later, the photographers, were also part of this process of history-making and as they nostalgically looked backward upon the whole experience they, too, like the writers and the storytellers, became America's premier mythmakers. And the more we look at the way in which these artists pictured the Western experience and brought it to life . . . the more . . . we realize that history, or myth, is in the eye of the beholder.[70]

Goetzmann emphasized that the visual image makers—whom historians had largely ignored—were among the most important shapers of the West as myth.

They should serve to illustrate just how myth or the story of a

69. Broder, *American West*, 1, 2, 4, 5, 8.
70. William H. Goetzmann and William N. Goetzmann, *The West of the Imagination* (New York, 1986), ix.

people—the tale of the tribe—weaves together the many strands and layers of complex human experience into one understandable story that inspires the people or the tribe to go on as one into succeeding epochs, sustained by an increasingly timeless tradition. It should also be clear that this myth or story that we tell ourselves about the historic Western experience has become part of that experience. Hence, in describing the myth, we are also describing a perceived reality that has profoundly affected both Western and American behavior patterns and values. . . . Thus the West lives on, even today, in the hearts of most Americans.[71]

In examining artistic representations of the Western myth, historians now explored its various components. One of these Kirsten Powell, a literary scholar, found to stem directly from the medieval European heritage. In an incisive essay, Powell analyzed this aspect of medieval European influence on the mythic West. "At the turn of the century," she wrote,

American artists were introduced to a Yankee variant of Pre-Raphaelitism through the writings and illustrations of Howard Pyle . . . [who] had fallen under the spell of the English artists. . . . Why was this imagery of England's remote past applied to the American experience with such enthusiasm? One explanation may stem from the problem of defining heroes in a democratic society based on equality. To differentiate special individuals from the general population, artists and writers borrowed hierarchical structures from the English monarchy, so that Buck Taylor was "king" of the cowboys; the "Virginian" was a "noble" young cowboy; Deadwood Dick was the "Black Prince" of the Black Hills; and more recently, John Wayne was the "Duke." The direct line of figurative descent from the heroes of Anglo-Saxon history to the cowboys of the plains had been firmly traced to Owen Wister. . . . Frederic Remington's illustrations for Wister's essay also made this point . . . that "in personal daring and in skill as to the horse, the knight and the cowboy are nothing but the same Saxon of different environments."

Powell thus emphasized the importance of medieval European imagery in shaping components of the Western myth—a rather unusual combination. "When we examine our frontier heritage with attention

71. Ibid., 434.

to the emphasis that has been placed on idealization, the importance of Pre-Raphaelite precedents is clear," she declared.

> Not only has our vocabulary of hero definition been dependent upon what Theodore Roosevelt called "the reproduction here on this continent of essentially the conditions of ballad growth which obtained in medieval England," but more precisely it has been dependent upon the pre-Raphaelite restatement of these conditions. Looking back on the popular art and literature that dealt with the plains, it is not surprising that it was dependent upon European antecedents. . . . Wister's and Remington's impressions of the West set the stage for other eastern artists and writers to apply their assumptions about medieval adventure and chivalry to the Western experience. . . . Their paintings and drawings codified the image of the American western hero and heroine as the heirs and heiresses to a rich imaginative tradition formed in nineteenth century Britain by the artists of the Pre-Raphaelite Brotherhood.[72]

The years from 1960 to 1990 thus witnessed an extraordinary broadening of the Western myth by historians and scholars from other disciplines. Until 1960 the West as myth had been considered largely as a product of the written word, reflected in pulps, magazines, Westerns, and serious works of fiction and non-fiction. But during this period scholars greatly expanded the range of influences which contributed to the myth by analyzing films, radio, television, art, photography, illustrations, and were sensitive to the significance of music in the formulation of widely accepted images. In so doing they revealed much about the complexity of the myth, a complexity which added a new dimension to its understanding.

Most of the historians who wrote about the West in the three decades after 1960 did so not from a narrow nationalistic perspective, but from a broader global view. Unlike scholars before 1945, they did not consider the American experience to be entirely unique. This worldwide context was also reflected in various new studies of the Western myth which emphasized worldwide acceptance of the image of the West. Although this international dimension had been recognized for many years, historians did not begin to write about it until the 1970s. One of these studies was by a Germanist, D. S. Ashliman,

72. Kirsten Powell, "Cowboy Knights and Prairie Madonnas: American Illustrations of the Plains and Pre-Raphaelite Art," *Great Plains Quarterly* 5 (Winter 1985), 41, 42–43, 50–52.

who focused on the German reaction to the myth of the West. That reaction was shaped by the nineteenth-century novelist Karl May, who was one of Germany's most popular novelists for more than one hundred years after 1890. May's pulp novels fabricated a West that never was, but millions of Germans each year absorbed the images he designed. By 1953 May had sold more than twenty-five million copies of his books, even though he himself died in 1912. Moreover, in the 1960s at least five hundred new novels about the supposedly wild nineteenth-century West appeared yearly while Western films also enjoyed great popularity.

As Ashliman explained, the cult of the imaginary West suited German culture. It provided an escape from contemporary problems, reinforced basic values such as courage and heroism, and provided entertainment. The myth developed in books, films, and television depicted an imaginary land peopled by cowboys and Indians. The books usually had plots encompassing simple morality tales which pitted good against evil. They also placed great emphasis on physical prowess. The mythic West, in addition, provided an exotic setting for discussions of the conflict between man and nature. As German scholar Herbert Frenzel noted in 1969, the American pioneer epoch was complementary to the medieval age of knighthood, and represented one of the two major fantasies of the literary world, "a heroic saga of our time."[73] In short, the West as myth had attained an international dimension.

But the mythic West had a strong attraction not only in Germany, but in Italy and France as well as Japan, as Ray Allen Billington pointed out in his last book, a distinguished analysis of the mythic West as viewed from around the world. "For half a century after Christopher Columbus's landfall the New World remained a *terra incognita*," Billington wrote.

> Yet an image of that distant frontier was already shaping in the minds of Europeans, based not on what they knew but on what they hoped would be there. They saw America as a slightly improved version of the Garden of Eden, overflowing with Nature's bounties, and peopled by a race of superior beings who lived in a perfect state of equality, without want and without masters—a model that would lead decadent Europe into a better future of

73. D. S. Ashliman, "The American West in 20th Century Germany," *Journal of Popular Culture* 2 (Summer 1968), 81–92.

which philosphers dreamed. Then, as colonists brought back word
of the realities of pioneer life, that image changed . . . and . . .
changed with the changing environment.

Billington argued that the mythic West had become more important than the West of reality. "The image-makers had played their
role in a drama that had been acted on both sides of the Atlantic,"
he declared. The

> frontier refused to die. It lived on through the twentieth century,
> not as a haven for the dispossessed, but as a legend to stir the
> blood of armchair voyagers and thrill seekers after vicarious adven-
> ture in Europe as well as in America. In this new garb the West as
> a land of opportunity was forgotten, and the West as a land of sav-
> agery perpetuated. . . . The frontier . . . was destined to live on
> . . . as a land of legend, perpetuted by image-makers on both sides
> of the Atlantic . . . a wonderland of their creation.[74]

Like most Western historians of his time, Billington reflected a
profoundly pessimistic view concerning interpretations of the West as
myth, perhaps in reaction against New Left historians and their disciples. "That the image of America as a land of equality and a champion
of democracy has eroded alarmingly since World War II cannot be
questioned," he despaired.

> The reasons for this erosion are less obvious. Peoples . . . insist
> that their faith in the United States crumbled when its interven-
> tion in Viet Nam and its meddling in Southeast Asia revealed its
> imperialistic ambitions. They maintain, too, that the nation's will-
> ingness to support any dictatorial government that promised to re-
> tain the status quo revealed that it was out of step with the spirit
> of progress on which its greatness was built. . . . An alarming
> number of people see the nation as a ruthless predator, a foe of
> minorities, an enemy of progress. . . . Tragically, those views are
> rooted in the long-held belief that frontier America . . . was a
> land where might ruled over right, where brutality was the way of
> life, and where an Indian minority was heartlessly wiped out by
> white aggressors.

Such perceptions, Billington emphasized, were shaped primarily by
image makers, and underscored the importance of the West as myth.

74. Ray Allen Billington, *Land of Savagery, Land of Promise: The European Image
of the American Frontier in the Nineteenth Century* (Norman, 1981), 1, 310.

If such views shaped the attitude of many of his contemporaries, Billington concluded, then "the image-makers played a larger role in history than they anticipated, and must be recognized if we are to understand the world we live in."[75]

Perhaps the most comprehensive broad assessment of the Western myth came from the prolific pen of the well-known Western historian, Robert Athearn. In *The Mythic West*, published posthumously in 1986, Athearn effectively synthesized many of the voluminous writings on the Western myth which appeared since 1960. "The mythic West, then, is more than an emotion or a state of mind," Athearn noted.

> It is real. It is not only the westerner, but also the American at large, who, knowingly or not, lives in two worlds: the day-to-day scene and the make-believe or fantasized world that has, for a great many people, actual substance. And there is no real conflict between the two. We live with both quite comfortably—one world filled with the immediate problems at hand, the other serving as a spare tire, a numbered emotional bank account, a fall-back position that is reassuring, comforting. Agreed, the factual frontier is gone, but the possibilities, the promise that it held are very much alive in the national mind. This quality may be fugitive, buried deep in one's conscience, but it is there, and this is the place where dreams are manufactured.

Unlike Billington, Athearn chose not to reflect on the negativism of his times. The West, he wrote, "is home to the loveliest and most enduring of our myths, the only one to be universally accepted." As Bernard De Voto once wrote, the Western myth wore many faces. It meant escape, relief, freedom, and sanctuary. It has meant opportunity, a new start, the saving chances. "We created this dream as we were growing up as a people," Athearn declared, "though we realized it only dimly as it was happening, and in turn the dream has continued to give us back a sense of who we are. It has been a case of mutual midwifery, with Americans and the myth helping each other into the world. For a dozen generations Americans fought their way into the wilderness. . . . The western mystique will be with us for a while longer. With so much to keep it alive, within us and all around, how could we ever forget?"[76]

75. Ibid., 332.
76. Robert G. Athearn, *The Mythic West in Twentieth-Century America* (Lawrence, 1986), 274.

Between 1945 and 1990 the West as myth underwent another metamorphosis in its development. The negativism of many scholars during these years resulted in a reversal of roles. From 1890 to 1945 most historians had hailed the westward movement as one of America's crowning achievements, and glowingly described its encapsulation in a growing myth. But in the four and a half decades after 1945 many academicians pictured Western development as a shameful record of exploitation and oppression which needed to be reflected in perceptions of the mythic West. Instead of offering unlimited opportunities to millions, historians charged that the West was the scene which witnessed the suppression and even extermination of native peoples and other minorities, and wanton destruction of the environment. Instead of revealing the sterling qualities of the American character— individualism, courage, self-reliance—their version of the myth reflected only selfishness and greed, cruelty and violence. This was the bleak outlook of the Vietnam generation, which was reading its own prejudices into the study of the Western myth and forming new myths to replace the old. Not all historians were quite as pessimistic or condemnatory, of course. Others focused on the increasingly powerful role of the mass media in shaping the perceptions of millions of people concerning the supposed contours of the mythic West. And, whatever their persuasion, historians of this era were far more conscious of the global context of the Western myth than their predecessors had been during the first half of the twentieth century.

In the century after 1890 the American image of the mythical West underwent many changes, but also reflected continuities. Between 1890 and 1920 it mirrored the nostalgia of Americans for a recent bygone age, and the end of an agrarian epoch; from 1920 to 1945 it reflected major strains of the American character as that generation perceived it; between 1945 and 1960 the myth provided needed assurance for Americans in a time of domestic anxiety and international insecurity as American ideals came under attack during the Cold War, both at home and abroad. From 1960 to 1990 historians subjected the myth to increasing criticism and charged it with reflecting many of the alleged wrongs of their own era, whether racism, sexism, class conflict, or environmental despoliation. And instead of dealing with individuals as carriers of the myth, these scholars—reflecting the organizational society in which they lived—dealt primarily with abstract types or faceless masses.

Throughout the course of the century, however, one major function of the myth remained stable. The mythic West continued to represent the other America—a mirror to contemporary society that served to explain Americans to themselves. For many, it represented that ideal, perfect society which served as a marked contrast to the imperfect civilization of the present. To them, it was a mirror which provided a reflection of how they would like to see themselves, whether in their dreams, fantasies, or imagination. The mythic West still provided the Great American Escape.

Conclusion

IN WRITING about the West, historians have also been writing about themselves, about their own social, economic, and cultural backgrounds, their geographical location and their environment. In this book, we have designated these factors as their ecological context. Such influences were related to their generational background, the juncture in their lives when men and women entered the world and their chosen profession and developed a vantage point from which to view the history of the West from a particular perspective. The visions of the West which successive generations had in mind were as determining in shaping their particular interpretations as the historical record. Although some in each generation believed that they had found the key to an understanding of the true dimensions of the subject, that eventually came to constitute a self-deception. Essentially, they were engaged in replacing one set of myths with another—with those that seemed more satisfying to their own generation. Given the rhythms of biological existence, these myths usually enjoyed some currency for about one generation before they were replaced. Whether they were embodied in the concepts of the West as frontier, region, urban civilization, or utopian mythical visions, or in cultural determinants such as gender, race, class, or ethnic components, these myths were but passing phases, temporary keys that served to explore different dimensions of the complex fabric of Western life.

The generation between 1890 and 1920 well illustrated this process. It was a generation largely composed of men whose social and cultural milieu was very similar. Overwhelmingly WASPs, they came from rural or small-town New England or Middle Western backgrounds, or upbringing.[1] Their common experience encompassed the maturing of frontier settlements in the Middle West, the farm protest movements of the 1880s and 1890s, the rapid emergence of the United States as the world's leading industrial nation, and its dramatic overseas expansion. The historians who shared this common heritage were a small, close-knit group of no more than a few hundred men. No wonder that they readily reached a consensus on the significance of the West within the American experience, and that someone like Turner quickly became the spokesman for his generation.

But by the time of the First World War the world which they had known changed significantly, and the ecology of the historical profession was altered accordingly. Between 1920 and 1945 those who wrote about the West tended to come from more urban backgrounds than the preceding generation, although precise generalizations on the sociology of the profession still await detailed statistical studies. The profession also grew in numbers, and reflected greater ethnic, class, and cultural diversity. When John Higham took a sample of ninety-seven leading native-born historians during the 1882–1946 period, he found that almost all came from New England or the Middle West. Only two were born in states west of Kansas. At least one-half of those who took degrees in the 1882–1929 period grew up in communities of less than ten thousand population. By the 1920s, however, the profession began to include a larger number of individuals with immigrant backgrounds, first or second generation, still somewhat outside the mainstream of the earlier dominant WASP establishment. Throughout the years 1882–1929, the percentage of those with upper-class status or with considerable wealth declined.[2]

Certainly many of the newcomers lacked the sense of self-assurance and security of status displayed by the patricians. Moreover, the post–World War I disillusionment of the 1920s, the ensuing Great Depression in the 1930s, and American involvement in World War II made theirs a far more unstable world than that of the gentleman-scholars

1. John Higham, *History: Professional Scholarship in America* (rev. ed., Baltimore, 1983), 62–63, 150–70; Novick, *Noble Dream*, 47–60, 68–69, 169–72.
2. Higham, *History*, 183–97; Novick, *Noble Dream*, 111–225.

of the earlier age. And their consciousness of European backgrounds tended to make them more sensitive to the impact of European cultural influences on American civilization. No wonder, therefore, that compared to historians in the era from 1890 to 1920, this generation had a waning sense of optimism and less self-assurance. The West which they discovered was more varied and more complex, contained not only an Anglo culture but Hispanic and Native American civilizations, and suffered from some of the tribulations of colonialism. To write the history of the West was no longer an unbroken story of heroic deeds—as in Theodore Roosevelt's vision—but a far more complex tapestry that reflected not only successes, but as Ole Rölvaag emphasized, failures as well.

World War II had a considerable effect on the ecology of historians, including, by 1945, the two to three hundred specialists on the West. The war ushered in the G.I. Revolution, which resulted in a quintupling of the historical profession within a decade as college and university enrollments soared. Not only did the numbers of Western historians grow, but their social and cultural backgrounds became even more varied than in the preceding period. Increasingly, they were more likely to have urban rather than rural backgrounds, and their ethnic and religious origins were more diverse. If Catholics and Jews had been represented only sparsely in the historical profession before 1945, their numbers began to increase significantly during the second half of the twentieth century.[3] Most of this generation had grown up knowing depression and war, and they were far less self-confident and much more cynical than the founding fathers of the discipline. Their views on Western history began to change accordingly. More skeptical of seemingly simple explanations like the Turner Thesis, they probed hitherto unexplored complexities of the Western experience. They focused more sharply on the urban, intellectual, and cultural dimensions of the West, emphases to which their background attuned them much more fully than those who had grown up in rural or frontier conditions. If the Turnerian approach to Western history still enjoyed considerable acceptance between 1945 and 1960, yet it had to share its primacy with an ever broadening range of alternate approaches.

And during the 1960s the tumultuous events of that decade were to leave other imprints on the interpretation of Western history. These

3. Novick, Noble Dream, 69, 172–74, 203, 339–41, 364–66.

years ushered in a greater awareness of fissures in American society. It was a period of social turmoil, the questioning of traditional values, the trauma of Vietnam, and a familiar litany including racism, women's rights, poverty, and destruction of the environment. Whatever consensus might have existed among historians of the previous generation was rudely disrupted by the new generation. Their own primary orientation now shifted largely to issues of their own lifetime—to civil rights, women's rights, ethnic problems, class conflict, the underclass in the United States, and the ravaging of the environment. Their historical universe centered mostly on these controversies—and relegated other subjects, if not to oblivion, to greater obscurity. One historian has even charged that this generation had a higher degree of present-mindedness than any of its predecessors, although this is debatable.[4] In their writings over the next thirty years they produced some welcome correctives to omissions and distortions made by previous historians. Yet they also ignored a wide range of other significant subjects, whether in the realm of technological, cultural, intellectual, and economic influences. On the other hand, consensus could hardly be expected from the more than two thousand Western historians in 1990—compared to fewer than two hundred in 1890—with diverse ethnic, racial, gender, social, and cultural origins. Like the nation at large, the profession had come to be a conglomeration of special interests, each with its own agenda, but without a common core. Although knowing more about the West than any previous generation, paradoxically they also found it more difficult to explain its broad significance in the nation's experience to Americans at large.

By 1990, therefore, Western historians had traveled far from their beginnings as professionals in 1890 in their search for a fuller understanding of the West as they reflected trends that grew out of their changing contemporary environments. Striking was a growing pessimism, or negativism, about the past and present of the West. With this feeling came a second trend, increasing specialization and fragmentation of the field. If consensus on the significance of the Western experience broke down, yet the overwhelming number of historians shared a common orientation, namely, an emphasis on cultural rather than environmental determinants in the shaping of the West. This

4. Higham, *History*, 52. John Higham, "Paleface and Redskin in American Historiography: A Comment," *Journal of Interdisciplinary History* 16 (Summer 1985), 1111–16.

was in part related to a fourth tendency, an increasing resort to social science theories and methods, particularly after 1945. While this was true of a wide range of disciplines, many historians reflected a partiality to psychology as an aid to historical analysis, especially in the sphere of Western myths, perceptions of regional identities, or symbols of popular culture. Broadening vistas also led to a sixth trend, a greater awareness of the global context of Western history, and a questioning of American exceptionalism. By the 1980s another direction became evident, a gnawing dissatisfaction with the fragmentation of the subject and a search for more general interpretive or synthetic concepts. Certainly, these were not the only trends that could be discerned in Western history, but they were among those that were closely rooted in the ecology of historians in the field.

In the course of the twentieth century, historians developed an increasingly negative attitude toward the West, sometimes unconsciously, and sometimes deliberately so. Scholars of Turner's generation took great pride in pointing to the positive impact of the West. In an era of nationalism (1890–1920), the conquest of a virgin wilderness represented a unique achievement of heroic proportions, a triumph of the will reflecting on the strong character of the American people. If not all of the writers were as ebullient as Theodore Roosevelt or Emerson Hough, most pointed with pride not only to the material accomplishments of the great march across the continent, but to its profound spiritual consequences. It was Turner who detailed the assumed impact of the frontier most succinctly, whether it was to produce political democracy, or the fostering of distinctive American traits such as individualism, self-reliance, or the cooperative spirit. But his generation was also aware that the conditions which had bred this idealized society were on the verge of disappearance. Their writings reflected not only a deep sense of nostalgia, but some apprehension as well about the future.

That apprehension was more fully developed by the succeeding generation (1920–1945). Less sanguine about the pervasive impact of the West on American society, and more global in their orientation, they began to question the uniqueness of the American experience. As they lived through the post–World War I disillusionment of the 1920s, the world Depression, and the Second World War, they could not help but realize that the American experience was perhaps not quite as unique as their predecessors had proclaimed. And increasingly, they began to question the positive impact of the West, and instead focused on its assumed negative influences. Writers as diverse as John Dewey, Lewis Mumford, and Ole Rölvaag now stressed the negative or destructive impact of the West—whether it was anti-intellectualism, or crass materialism. Historians during the Great Depression lengthened that list, adding extreme selfishness, hypocrisy, the myth of rugged individualism, and destructive competition.

If the pessimism became more muted during the affluent years from 1945 to 1960, it burst out as the dominant mood of the generation that wrote about the West in the thirty years after 1960. Their disaffection with American society and the disillusionment with the Vietnam war became major themes of historians and social scientists writing about the West—sometimes to the point of obsession. They focused on the alleged mistreatment of Indians, blacks, Hispanics, Orientals, women, and other minorities, and on the desecration of the natural environment. Many of them viewed the history of the West as a shameful chapter in the American experience, finding little to praise but much to condemn. The laments covered a wide range of alleged injustices and oppressions ingrained in the Western movement. If the twentieth century had opened with an era of muckraking journalists who had highlighted the shortcomings of American life, so the century entered upon its last decade with a chorus of academicians echoing a similar refrain. The emphasis was on what was wrong, not much on what might have been right.

Perhaps this mood contributed to the increasing specialization and fragmentation of the field. That, of course, was part of a similar trend throughout writings in American history. At the beginning of the century, historians like Turner still felt confident that they could embrace the totality of the Western experience. They did not shrink from formulating generalizations and hypotheses that embraced long periods of time. But the succeeding generation became more dubious about all-encompassing themes, developing alternatives to the Turner Thesis. By the 1920s Charles A. Beard's economic determinism, A. W. Schlesinger, Sr.'s urbanism, and Marcus Hansen's emphasis on the role of immigrants and ethnic groups competed with the Turner Thesis in illuminating the American experience. Although the frontier hypothesis still enjoyed popularity in the teaching of American history, it no longer had the near monopoly it had held in the previous generation.

The breakup of the Turnerian synthesis between 1945 and 1960 contributed to the fragmentation of Western history. The enormous increase of historians in the profession, and their diverse backgrounds and interests, was one factor in the specialization. Another was the increasing prestige of the social sciences during the era of the Behavioral Revolution (1945–1960), which induced some historians to follow paths charted by social scientists, not by historians. Economists like Douglass North; anthropologists like Alfred Kroeber, Clyde Kluckhohn, or Clifford Geertz; social psychologists like B. F. Skinner or David Riesman; sociologists like Seymour Lipset; political scientists such as Daniel Elazar; all played a role as pied pipers who led some historians down divergent paths to explore subjects that initially had not been developed in a historical context. As various Western historians thus wandered down different avenues, they found that some were fruitful and enriched the field, while others were dead ends that did little in a constructive way for the subject, but only contributed to fragmentation.

Other influences hastened the splintering between 1945 and 1960. The rapid growth of the profession also resulted in an explosion in the number of books and articles produced each year. Certainly, new technology and new methods such as quantification lent themselves especially well to intensive specialization, and in-depth analysis of narrow subjects. Moreover, the increasing pluralism in American society and the breakup of whatever consensus might have existed in earlier years further promoted increasing specialization. This pluralism also contributed to the growing politicization of academic professions, including history, that led historians, more so than in earlier years, into a presentism and a preoccupation with contemporary issues— whether civil rights, or gender, ethnic, or class conflict. The task of historians, New Left advocates argued, was to write in support of social action, and reform as they conceived it. Historians of previous generations who had been trained in a neo-Rankean tradition and who assumed that their task was to be more than social critics, but to carry on the historical record from one generation to the next, were viewed by some New Left historians and their followers as pedants who had become irrelevant. Pluralism also led to the development of special interest groups—in academe as in politics—who were primarily concerned with the specialized studies in their own particular sphere.[5]

5. I do not wish to imply that all New Left historians shared the same views on

The periphery of historical studies in the West therefore rapidly expanded without reference to much of a center of the subject. In fact, by 1990 the center had become engulfed by thousands of specialized studies within a multitude of narrow fields. Certainly, many of these provided much needed depth, and contributed a great deal to a fuller understanding of the complexities of Western history. By 1990 historians knew much more about the Western experience than previous generations. Paradoxically, they were far less sure about the significance of their findings in the broader context of the American experience, if indeed a broader context was discernible. The situation brought to mind a question once posed a generation earlier by a leading sociologist, Robert S. Lynd in the title of his book, *Knowledge for What?* (1939).

If Western historians revealed increasing fragmentation, on the other hand they shared a common *Weltanschauung* in their pronounced emphasis on cultural rather than environmental influences as the major determinants of Western history. The men and women of Turner's generation had tended to emphasize the significant impact of geographical factors such as topography and climate on the West. It was a generation very much under the Darwinian spell, a time when major advances were being made in geological and geographic studies in Europe and the United States. But the succeeding generation was far more impressed by the marvels of technology than by nature, and the awesome influence of a virgin wilderness. In their lifetime, electricity, railroads, automobiles and airplanes, heavy farm machinery, dams and reclamation projects seemed to be modifying the Western environment in significant ways, and no less importantly, altering the perceptions of the environment by Americans. Technology made deserts bloom— as in California's Imperial Valley. Distances shrank and isolation was diminished as new means of communication—whether telephones, moving pictures, rural free delivery, newspapers and magazines, and the products of mail-order houses like Sears and Roebuck Company reached parts of the West which only a few decades before had been considered too isolated to be inhabitable. The generation of historians between 1920 and 1945 thus reflected a very different perception of

---

historical objectivity since significant differences existed among them. See Irwin Unger, "The 'New Left' and American History: Some Recent Trends in United States Historiography," *American Historical Review* 72 (July 1967), 1237.

the West than their predecessors. In their view, the natural environment of the West played only a minor role in explaining patterns of settlement. Far more important were cultural influences such as ideals and values, religion, languages, and traditions brought by new settlers to a particular community. Geographers like Carl O. Sauer and Isaiah Bowman were in the forefront of this shift in interpretation, which gathered momentum after 1920 and received support from an increasing number of historians. Even those who like Walter P. Webb stressed the importance of environment nevertheless placed even greater emphasis on the significance of technology in modifying that environment. In these years, historians also began to emphasize the importance of economic, political, and legal institutions and ideas, religion, language, ethnic and racial backgrounds, cultural inheritances such as literature, or educational systems in the shaping of Western history.

After 1945 this preoccupation with the importance of cultural variables as major determinants of Western history became much more pronounced. Jet travel and climate control (such as air conditioning) seemed further to lessen the impact of the natural environment. The sense of confidence in the immediate postwar era (1945–1960) only strengthened the belief of this generation that they had mastered control over Nature. As Roderick Nash noted, Americans had come to view Nature as an impediment to be subdued.[6] This was the great age of major irrigation and reclamation projects in the West, during which engineers changed the courses of mighty rivers such as the Colorado, and diverted streams such as the Salt River to make deserts green. Road builders leveled valleys and moved mountains to "correct" what they considered to be the imperfections of nature in their rush to build the interstate highway system. No wonder that by the 1960s many Western historians paid scant heed to the influence of the environment in Western history, but emphasized instead the dominant role of cultural forces. So great was this emphasis that in 1975 a professional geographer like Raymond Gastil could openly declare that environmental factors were of no consequence in explaining the distinctiveness of regions like the West, but that cultural influences were all-encompassing. Such a preoccupation with self led the contemporary social critic Tom Wolfe to characterize his peers as the "Me-Generation."[7] Gastil's cultural determinism had become as extreme,

6. Roderick Nash, *Wilderness*.

7. Tom Wolfe, "The Me Decade and the Third Great Awakening," in *Mauve Gloves and Madmen, Clutter and Vine* (New York, 1976), 126–67.

perhaps, as Ellen Semple's geographical determinism had been sixty
years before. And historians of the 1970s and 1980s who became
preoccupied with the dominant impact of race, gender, or ethnic and
class background further accentuated the importance of man-made or
woman-made influences over environmental forces.

But this faith in the dominance of Kultur over environment came
to be rudely shattered by the 1980s. The emergence of major new
environmental problems, whether air and water pollution, the storage
of nuclear wastes, lands ravaged by strip-mining and wasteful exploitation, destructive lumbering, depletion of fish and wildlife, natural
disasters such as earthquakes and hurricanes, and the salting of irrigated
lands altered the perception that the environment could be largely
ignored by historians. To call attention to these alarming trends was
one of the primary contributions of environmental historians like
Donald Worster, who emerged in the 1980s to warn that his colleagues
could ignore the natural environment in the shaping of the West only
at their peril. As James C. Malin had warned a generation earlier, in
the ecological balance which was being altered by technology, human
beings were not disinterested or amoral observers, but direct participants. Their interest in maintaining some equilibrium established by
Nature was as great as that of animals, plants, and minerals.

In part, the growing emphasis on the role of Kultur in the West
had been reinforced by another trend, the increasing prominence of
the social sciences in American scholarship. Of course, historians of
the West had drawn freely from the social sciences throughout the
century, whether in the realm of theory or method, but that influence
became steadily more important. Turner himself dabbled in geography,
sociology, demography, political science, economics, statistics, and
geology. If historians between 1920 and 1945 were not as broadly
versed as he because of increasing specialization, they continued the
tradition. A. M. Schlesinger, Sr., and Marcus Hansen drew on sociology for their studies of immigration. New urban historians like
Schlesinger, Sr., William Diamond, or Bayrd Still were well ac-
quainted with the work of urban sociologists such as Louis Wirth.

But the generation between 1945 and 1960 was much more heavily
drawn into the world of the social scientists. Historians of the Indian
experience in the West borrowed significantly from cultural anthropologists like Kluckhohn, Kroeber, and Vogt. Students of community
settlement on the frontier and of ethnic adaptation—the names of

Berkhofer, Bogue, Curti, Elkins and McKittrick, and Luebke come to mind—borrowed not only from the anthropologists, but from sociologists and social psychologists. And scholars concerned with Western myth derived much of their theory and method from the psychologists.

After 1960 the social sciences continued to exert a profound influence. Historians like Carl Abbott read deeply in urban demography, economics, sociology, and statistics. Newcomers to the field like Walter Nugent hoped to bring insights from demography. At the same time, a growing number of social scientists began to draw on the work of historians to facilitate their own particular studies of the West, especially to extend their models or theoretical analyses in a temporal dimension. Sharkansky and Elazar in political science, Lipset and Lee in sociology, Sauer and Block in geography, and North in economics were only a few of the legion of social scientists concerned with the West. For one hundred years, therefore, Western historians and social scientists interacted, although the relationships became much closer after 1945.

Of the various social sciences, psychology came to have a particularly important impact on Western history. That the West occupied a significant place in American mythology had of course been recognized long before 1890, as Henry Nash Smith demonstrated so well. But historians began to write about this aspect only gradually. Certainly Turner himself was aware of the psychological dimension in Western history, alluding to it in his presidential address to the American Historical Association in 1910. But neither he nor the men and women of his generation did much to explore it further. It was not until the vogue of Freudianism in the United States during the 1920s and 1930s that students of the West began to explore this aspect of the Western experience more seriously. Psychologists like William McDougall made the first exploratory studies. More significant were literary scholars and critics such as T. K. Whipple, Carey McWilliams, Lucy Hazard, Lewis Mumford, and Howard Mumford Jones who examined the significance of the West through literary forms. This trend was greatly strengthened by the migration of European psychologists and psychiatrists during the Nazi era, who did much to augment students of the West of the imagination. Franz Alexander was one of the first to analyze the West in psychoanalytic terms during the Second World War. But his influence, and that of fellow émigrés such as Erik Erikson, Karen Horney, Bruno Bettelheim, and Paul Lazarsfeld was to have much greater impact in succeeding decades. After 1945 their works did much to raise historians' levels of awareness concerning the relevance of social and psychological influences and myth to the Western experience. Historians of the West as diverse as Bogue and Berkhofer, Richard Hofstadter, David B. Davis, John Cawelti, Marshall Fishwick, and Henry Nash Smith utilized the insights provided by these psychologists to examine hitherto unexplored dimensions of the Western myth— and the Western experience.

Between 1960 and 1990, especially, Western historians intensified the range and depth of their studies of the West as myth and utopia. The number of such works was greater in these thirty years than in the entire seventy-year period before. The enormous expansion of television and the mass media, and of cultural institutions such as art museums, historical societies, and concert halls in the West after 1960 undoubtedly heightened the consciousness of scholars concerning the importance of popular culture in projecting the West of the imagination. Historians like Richard Etulain or Kevin Starr now wrote of the function of literature, whether classic or popular, in the shaping of the West. Others, like John Lenihan and Jon Tuska, analyzed the contributions of the Western film to the formulation of images about the West. By the 1980s scholars extended the range of such work by examining the role of television in the propagation of the myth. And a few historians began to assess the role of Western art in the formation of mental images which Americans had of the West. Just as the geographers Joel Garreau and Ti Fi Yuan who, under the influence of psychologists, were proclaiming that the perceptions of people were a major element in defining regions, so historians were now stressing the importance of psychological perceptions in explanations of the mythic West. That led to more intensive exploration of the instruments of popular culture that contributed to such perceptions, whether movies, television, mass media, art, or music. Clearly, by 1990 the development of psychology had made a deep impression on historical writing about the West.

Another trend was increasing global awareness. In fact, a direct relationship seemed discernible between a gradual waning of isolationist sentiment in American diplomacy and the more conscious global outlook of Western historians. The generation of Turner was caught up in the intense nationalism of their era, prompted in part by the emergence of the United States as a world power at the opening of the century. Historians like Turner, Roosevelt, and Wilson emphasized the uniqueness of the American experience, and much of that uniqueness they attributed to the westward movement. By the time of World War I they broadened their vision, and extended the erstwhile Puritan concept of a "city on a hill" to the entire world. They held up the American experience as a federation of geographical sections as a model for the League of Nations on a worldwide basis. But in the 1920s historians began to question the uniqueness of the United States as improvements in transportation and communications literally shrank the world. Economic determinists like Beard and Hacker stressed the similarities of class conflict in the West and in other nations. Social and intellectual historians like Lewis Mumford and Dixon Ryan Fox focused on the interchange of cultures and the transit of civilization. Not unlike the historians of the 1880s, they stressed the importance of European influences on American civilization. Immigration historians such as Schlesinger, Sr., and Marcus Hansen concentrated on the significance of ethnic and urban factors imported from other nations that mingled with American conditions such as the frontier. This global perception was greatly expanded by the post–World War II generation between 1945 and 1960. Impressed by the new role of the United States as a superpower, historians like Carlton Hayes, Arnold Toynbee, Walter P. Webb, Leonard Arrington, and C. Vann Woodward now placed the frontier experience in a worldwide context. At the same time, Western historians began to enter upon a wide range of comparative studies, comparing the American frontier with frontiers around the globe.

By 1960 this emphasis on globalism waned. Although it did not fade completely between 1960 and 1990, historians became preoccupied with race, class, gender, and environment. Correspondingly, the international context of the West received less emphasis. The Vietnam war seemed to have contributed an orientation that placed greater emphasis on domestic issues. Such an orientation also reflected contemporary trends in American foreign and domestic affairs. Writers like Leslie Fiedler, Richard Drinnon, or Richard Slotkin found themes in the Vietnam experience which they read into the mainstream of Western history—themes such as racism, oppression of minority peoples, violence, imperialism, and rape of the environment. It was at times difficult to discern whether they were writing about the West, or engaging in contemporary social criticism. Yet by 1990 far fewer historians clung to the view that the Western experience had been unique than a century before. The changing role of the United States in world affairs had certainly affected the ecology of historians writing about the West.

By the 1980s another clear trend emerged, a renewed search for broader studies and creative synthesis. For the first time in several generations, historians were reacting against the fragmentation of American and Western history, and began to call for more integrative studies rather than for more extreme specialization. Bernard Bailyn issued such a general appeal in his presidential address to the American Historical Association in 1981, and five years later Thomas Bender spelled out a more detailed prognosis with specific reference to the history of the United States.[8]

A similar trend manifested itself in the field of Western history. The prescriptions varied, but were highly suggestive. "The task of coordination and synthesis is particularly essential in the field of western American history," Spencer Olin declared, "which to a great extent has abandoned an older tradition . . . represented by Frederick Jackson Turner. . . . Historians of the American West, therefore, would do well to accept the challenge of combining diverse approaches to historical inquiry."[9] Not everyone was as ready to abandon Turner, however. Martin Ridge argued that historians should continue to utilize the frontier theories of Turner and Billington, but to provide new answers to the questions which they posed. "The history of frontier theory is too valuable to abandon," he declared. "We should be interested in many of the questions that Turner and Billington asked, partly because we have new answers based on newer methods as well as research, and partly because our professional and perhaps even our personal lives have been so influenced by them."[10] Similarly, William Cronon urged his colleagues not to abandon the Turnerian synthesis. He urged a broadening of the concept to encompass the adaptation of human communities to landscapes in the West. The central problem

8. Bernard Bailyn, "The Challenge of Modern Historiography," *American Historical Review* 87 (February 1982), 6–8; Thomas Bender, "Wholes and Parts: The Need for Synthesis in American History," *Journal of American History* 73 (June 1986), 123–30.

9. Spencer Olin, Jr., "Toward a Synthesis of the Political and Social History of the American West," *Pacific Historical Review* 55 (November 1986), 600.

10. Martin Ridge, "Frederick Jackson Turner, Ray Allen Billington, and American Frontier History," *Western Historical Quarterly* 19 (January 1988), 20.

of Western history, he noted, concerned "American uses of, and attitudes toward, regional landscapes," and how they "shifted with the dialectical interaction of scarcity and abundance." In seeking to revitalize Turner, Cronon concluded that he "gave American history its central and most persistent story. However much we may modify the details and outline of that story, we are unlikely ever to break entirely free of it."[11]

But not all the searchers for synthesis were as wedded to Turnerianism as these historians. William G. Robbins offered a gentle neo-Marxian approach, largely derived from the framework developed by William Appleman Williams for the general field of American history. "In the quest for a more convincing interpretive model," Robbins wrote, "it is important to begin with the work of Karl Marx, whose historic achievement was to show the tremendous productive powers generated by capitalism." He found that "the West is a prototype for modern capitalism with its uneven development, its far-flung extractive economies, its turbulent community histories, and its highly mobile populations."[12] Walter Nugent offered an alternative approach by suggesting that "the key to . . . typology . . . is demography. Demographic stability, or the lack of it, provided firmness or transiency for frontiers and empires. In general, empires proved transient, and frontiers evolved into permanent societies."[13]

Nor were environmental historians enamored of Turnerian approaches. Donald Worster suggested that Western historians take another look at the concept of regionalism as an integrative concept. "For those with imagination to find it," he declared, "there is plenty of thick history to be written about this region [the West]. Within its spacious boundaries . . . this region offers for study all the greed, violence, beauty, ambition, and variety anyone could use. Given enough time and effort, it may someday also offer a story of careful, lasting adaptation of people to the land."[14]

Gene Gressley suggested, on the other hand, that a unique Western

11. William J. Cronon, "Revisiting the Vanishing Frontier," *Western Historical Quarterly* 18 (April 1987), 175, 176.

12. William G. Robbins, "Western History: A Dialectic on the Modern Condition," *Western Historical Quarterly* 20 (November 1989), 434, 439.

13. Walter Nugent, "Frontiers and Empires in the Late Nineteenth Century," ibid. 20 (November 1989), 394.

14. Donald Worster, "New West, True West: Interpreting the Region's History," ibid. 18 (April 1987), 156.

spirit could provide a unifying theme for Western studies. "A western distinctiveness remains," he concluded, "between the way westerners personally and privately behave and the way they maneuver as public personae. Self-awareness survives primarily because transcendentalism has been thwarted. . . . Whether the westerner realizes the fact or, even more important, comprehends that spirit is another matter."[15]

By the end of the 1980s the efforts to combat fragmentation became increasingly ambitious, as Michael Malone's plea for a new approach to Western American history indicated. "Most of us who labor in western studies still bear the onus . . . of working in a field that is deemed by many to be intellectually barren and cluttered with trivia," he lamented. "It is my contention . . . that western regional history is stigmatized because western historians rely on the frontier thesis advanced by Frederick Jackson Turner." To free themselves from Turner's timeworn paradigm, Malone suggested that "Western historians . . . must learn from the best work in national and international scholarship. . . . It is the greatest of all challenges to western historians . . . to work out the contours of the new synthesis that must surely replace the older interpretations. While earlier interpretations continue to bear considerable truth and relevance, they cannot begin to explain the complexities of this diverse and changing region."[16]

At the same time, various book-length studies also called attention to the need for creative synthesis. Patricia Limerick's survey attempted to provide an interpretive stance for the whole sweep of Western history. Michael Malone and Richard Etulain wrote a comprehensive integrative synthesis of Western history in the twentieth century to demonstrate that they practiced what they preached; and Gerald Nash and Richard Etulain edited a collection of essays by distinguished scholars then writing about the West in the twentieth century, which reflected the range and depth of the best research and writing in the field.[17]

By 1990 this ferment promised much for the ensuing decade. It appeared that the specialization during the years between 1960 and

15. Gene Gressley, "The West: Past, Present, and Future," ibid. 17 (January 1986), 23.

16. Michael P. Malone, "Beyond the Last Frontier: Toward a New Approach to Western American History," ibid. 20 (November 1989), 409, 410, 427.

17. Limerick, Legacy; Malone and Etulain, The American West; Gerald D. Nash and Richard W. Etulain (eds.), The Twentieth Century West: Historical Interpretations (Albuquerque, 1989).

1990 had succeeded in opening many new vistas which enabled scholars in the field finally to emancipate themselves from constricting ideas and concepts that had inhibited fresh approaches for many decades. This flurry of activity promised to restore that sense of excitement about Western history that had been experienced by the founding fathers in 1890—but had not been felt again for many decades in the intervening period.

Throughout the course of the twentieth century historians reflected a present-mindedness. At no time during this period were they able or desirous of dissociating themselves from their contemporary environments. The generation between 1890 and 1920 was profoundly influenced by the depression of the 1890s and the rise of industrial America. Still, they had enormous confidence in their ability to arrive at scientific truth. "The first generation or two of professional historians," Theodore Hamerow noted, "was sustained by a belief that the growing mass of primary materials and monographic studies would ultimately help scholarship arrive at . . . broader insight into the past."[18] Their successors between 1920 and 1945 were not as sure, having their faith shaken by depression, totalitarianism, and war, and that was even truer of the group between 1945 and 1960. One member of this generation, Raymond Sontag, phrased it well when he noted that he sensed a clear break between "those whose minds were formed before 1914, and those, whatever their age, who began to think only in the years after 1918." He looked with admiration, but across a great chasm, at his elders, who were "confident that they understood the forces which shaped the past and that they could describe the past objectively and correctly." It was a confidence not shared by his generation, "formed by a time of troubles."[19]

Such troubles led to a further decline of faith in the years from 1960 to 1990. "The historians of today," Hamerow declared in 1986, "have largely abandoned this faith. The course of scholarship made it appear visionary. They are intimidated by the complexity of the past, by the bewildering array of what mankind has experienced on earth. They despair of being able to bring order out of chaos." That presentism

18. Theodore Hamerow, "The Professionalization of Historical Learning," *Reviews in American History* 14 (September 1986), 327; Novick, *Noble Dream*, 578–85; see also Higham, "Paleface and Redskin in American Historiography: A Comment," *Journal of Interdisciplinary History* 16, 1111–12.

19. Sontag, in *American Historical Review* 67 (February 1961), 90–91.

and loss of confidence was widely shared by working historians in this period, experiencing social disruptions, political turmoil, and inter-national strife. Many in this generation openly abandoned any effort to retain a measure of historical objectivity. They became relativists with a vengeance, although they did not always regard themselves as such. In their view, the main role of historians was to be social critics whose task it was to espouse social causes. Ignoring the experiences of Fascist, Nazi, or Stalinist eras earlier in the century—before they had been born—they became devotees of moral missions. This was the position not only of those on the New Left, but also of those who followed in their path without an explicit ideological commitment.[20] That the historian perhaps also had a responsibility to transmit the experiences of one generation to the next was a function which seemed less important on their scale of priorities than social commentaries.

By 1990 it was clear that historians of the West had discovered much that was right, and much that was wrong with the story of the West. If the founding fathers had erred in overemphasizing what was right, the generation of the 1960s concentrated on discovering what was wrong, leading to a lack of balance in the field. Perhaps the task of the generation entering the 1990s is to restore greater balance to the subject. A one-sided emphasis created an increasing gap between popular writers about the West and the professional historians. The former, utilizing positive approaches, were clearly reaching large pop-ular audiences who were disinclined to immerse themselves in the jeremiads of Cassandras. If historians are also keepers of a nation's soul, the custodians of its sense of identity, one-sided indictments can serve the function of destroying the very fabric of national identity. To teach America's youth exclusively about the alleged depravity of the Western experience is to do a disservice to the profession.

If the theory of generational change has any validity, the negative views of the past thirty years will soon run their course. They will be replaced by other perceptions of the West whose dimensions are not yet readily visible. But of one element we can be sure. Interpretations of the West in the next decade are bound to reflect changes in con-temporary conditions, to be influenced by events that have not yet occurred. As this study has indicated, historians cannot free themselves

20. Hamerow, "The Professionalization," in *Reviews in American History* 14, 327; Novick, *Noble Dream*, 578–85.

from contemporary influences. Yet it is their responsibility as historians—as distinct from journalists or politicians—to use a measure of self-restraint to prevent their political and moral views from engulfing their historical interpretations, even if such views can never be totally excluded. Toward that end, a clearer understanding of the ecology of Western historians can make a contribution to the constant effort of historians to provide a useful past for society at large.

Bibliography

BOOKS

Abbott, Carl. *The New Urban America: Growth and Politics in Sunbelt Cities.* Chapel Hill, 1981.
Abernethy, Thomas P. *From Frontier to Plantation in Tennessee.* Chapel Hill, 1932.
Acuña, Rodolfo. *Occupied America: A History of Chicanos.* 3d ed., New York, 1987.
Adams, Brooks. *The Law of Civilization and Decay.* New York, 1896.
Adams, Henry. *The Education of Henry Adams.* Boston, 1918.
Adams, James Truslow. *The Epic of America.* Boston, 1931.
Alexander, Franz. *Our Age of Unreason.* New York, 1942.
Allen, James B. *The Company Town in the American West.* Norman, 1966.
Alvord, Clarence A. *The Mississippi Valley in British Politics.* 2 vols., Urbana, 1917.
Armitage, Susan, and Elizabeth Jameson (eds.). *The Women's West.* Norman, 1987.
Arrington, Leonard J. *Great Basin Kingdom: An Economic History of the Latter-day Saints, 1830–1900.* Cambridge, Mass., 1958.
Atherton, Lewis. *Main Street on the Middle Border.* Bloomington, 1954.
Athearn, Robert G. *In Search of Canaan: Black Migration to Kansas, 1879–1880.* Lawrence, 1978.
——. *The Mythic West in Twentieth-Century America.* Lawrence, 1986.
Austin, Mary. *The Land of Little Rain.* Boston, 1903.
——. *California: The Land of the Sun.* New York, 1914.
Barnouw, Erik. *The Image Empire: A History of Broadcasting in the United States.* 3 vols., New York, 1970.
Barth, Gunther. *Instant Cities: Urbanization and the Rise of San Francisco and Denver.* New York, 1975.

Bataille, Gretchen, and Kathleen M. Sands. *American Indian Women: Telling Their Lives*. Lincoln, 1984.

Bean, Walton E. *California: An Interpretive History*. New York, 1968.

Becker, Carl. *Everyman His Own Historian*. New York, 1935.

Beer, Thomas. *Stephen Crane*. New York, 1923.

Bemis, Samuel Flagg. *Jay's Treaty*. New York, 1923.

———. *Pinckney's Treaty*. Baltimore, 1926.

Benson, Lee. *Turner and Beard: American Historical Writing Reconsidered*. New York, 1960.

Berge, Wendell. *Economic Freedom for the West*. Lincoln, 1946.

Berkhofer, Robert F., Jr. *Salvation and the Savage: An Analysis of Protestant Missions and American Indian Response, 1787–1862*. Lexington, 1965.

Berwanger, Eugene H. *The Frontier against Slavery: Western Anti-Negro Prejudice and the Slavery Extension Controversy*. Urbana, 1967.

Bierce, Ambrose. *The Shadow of the Dial*. San Francisco, 1909.

———. *Collected Works*. 12 vols., New York, 1909–1912.

Billington, Ray Allen. *Frederick Jackson Turner, Historian, Scholar, Teacher*. New York, 1973.

———. *The Genesis of the Frontier Thesis: A Study in Historical Creativity*. San Marino, 1971.

———. *Land of Savagery, Land of Promise: The European Image of the American Frontier in the Nineteenth Century*. New York, 1981.

Bingham, Edwin R. *Charles F. Lummis: Editor of the Southwest*. San Marino, 1955.

Blakey, George T. *Historians on the Homefront: American Propagandists for the Great War*. Lexington, 1970.

Bold, Christine. *Selling the Wild West: Popular Western Fiction*. Bloomington, 1987.

Bolton, Herbert E. (ed.). *Spanish Exploration in the Southwest, 1542–1706*. New York, 1925.

Bowman, Isaiah. *The Pioneer Fringe*. New York, 1931.

Boynton, Percy H. *The Rediscovery of the Frontier*. Chicago, 1931.

———. *Literature and American Life*. Boston, 1935.

Branch, E. Douglas. *Westward: The Romance of the American Frontier*. New York, 1930.

Bridenbaugh, Carl. *Cities in the Wilderness*. New York, 1938.

Brigham, Alfred P. *Geographic Influences in American History*. Boston, 1903.

Broder, Patricia Janis. *The American West: The Modern Vision*. Boston, 1984.

Brown, A. Theodore, and Lyle W. Dorsett. *K.C.: A History of Kansas City, Missouri*. Boulder, 1978.

Brown, Dee. *The Gentle Tamers: Women of the Old West*. New York, 1958.

Burt, Struthers. *The Diary of a Dude Wrangler*. New York, 1925.

Camarillo, Albert. *Chicanos in a Changing Society: From Mexican Pueblos to American Barrios in Santa Barbara and Southern California, 1848–1930*. Cambridge, Mass., 1979.

Camden, Carroll (ed.). *Literary Views: Critical and Historical Essays*. Chicago, 1964.

Cary, Max, and E. H. Warmington. *The Ancient Explorers*. New York, 1929.

Castillo, Pedro G. "The Making of a Mexican Barrio: Los Angeles, 1890–1920." Diss., University of California, Santa Barbara, 1979.

Cawelti, John. *Adventure, Mystery, and Romance.* Chicago, 1976.

Chapman, Charles E. *A History of California: The Spanish Period.* New York, 1923.

Chudakoff, Howard. *Mobile Americans: Residential and Social Mobility in Omaha, 1880–1920.* New York, 1972.

――――. *The Evolution of American Urban Society.* New York, 1972.

Clark, Andrew Hill. *Acadia: The Geography of Early Nova Scotia to 1760.* Madison, 1968.

Coman, Katherine. *Economic Beginnings of the Far West.* New York, 1911.

Cowley, Malcolm (ed.). *Books that Changed Our Minds.* New York, 1939.

Croly, Herbert. *The Promise of American Life.* New York, 1909.

Cronon, William. *Changes in the Land: Indians, Colonists, and the Ecology of New England.* New York, 1983.

Curti, Merle, et al. *The Making of an American Frontier Community.* Stanford, 1959.

Daniels, Roger. *Concentration Camps, U.S.A.* New York, 1971.

Deutsch, Sarah. *No Separate Refuge: Culture, Class, and Gender on an Anglo-Hispanic Frontier in the American Southwest, 1880–1940.* New York, 1987.

Dippie, Brian W. *The Vanishing American: White Attitudes and U.S. Indian Policy.* Middletown, Conn., 1982.

Drinnon, Richard. *Facing West: The Metaphysics of Indian-Hating and Empire-Building.* Minneapolis, 1980.

Driver, Harold E. *Comparative Studies of North American Indians.* Philadelphia, 1957.

――――. *Ethnology and Acculturation of the Chichimeca-Jonaz of Northeast Mexico.* Bloomington, 1963.

――――. *Hoof Rattles and Girls' Puberty Rites in North and South America.* Baltimore, 1950.

――――. *Indians of North America.* Chicago, 1961.

――――. *The Contributions of A. L. Kroeber to Culture Areas—Theory and Practice.* Baltimore, 1962.

Driver, Harold E., and James L. Coffin. *Classification of North American Indian Cultures.* Philadelphia, 1975.

Durham, Philip, and Everett L. Jones. *The Negro Cowboys.* New York, 1965.

Dykstra, Robert R. *The Cattle Towns.* New York, 1968.

Elazar, Daniel. *American Federalism: A View from the States.* New York, 1966.

――――. *Cities of the Prairie.* New York, 1970.

Ewers, John C. *The Horse in Blackfoot Indian Culture.* Washington, 1955.

――――. *The Blackfeet: Raiders on the Northwest Plains.* Norman, 1958.

――――. *Crow Indian Beadwork.* New York, 1959.

――――. *Artists of the Old West.* New York, 1965.

Fiedler, Leslie A. *The Return of the Vanishing American.* New York, 1968.

Fierro Blanco, Antonio de [Walter Nordhoff]. *The Journey of the Flame.* New York, 1933.

Fixico, Donald L. *Termination and Relocation: Federal Indian Policy, 1945–1960.* Albuquerque, 1986.

Fogelson, Robert M. *The Fragmented Metropolis: Los Angeles, 1850–1930.* Cambridge, Mass., 1967.

Foster, Mark S. *From Streetcar to Superhighway: American City Planners and Urban Transportation, 1900–1940.* Philadelphia, 1981.

Fowler, Arlen F. *The Black Infantry in the West.* Westport, Conn., 1971.

Fox, Dixon Ryan (ed.). *Sources of Culture in the Middle West: Backgrounds versus Frontiers.* New York, 1934.

Gabriel, Ralph H. *The Course of American Democratic Thought.* New York, 1940.

Galarza, Ernesto. *Merchants of Labor: The Mexican Bracero Story.* Santa Barbara, 1964.

García, Mario T. *Desert Immigrants: The Mexicans of El Paso, 1880–1920.* New Haven, 1981.

Garreau, Joel. *The Nine Nations of North America.* Boston, 1981.

Gastil, Raymond. *Cultural Regions of the United States.* Seattle, 1975.

Gates, Paul W. *The Farmer's Age: Agriculture, 1815–1860.* New York, 1960.

Geertz, Clifford. *Interpretation of Cultures.* New York, 1973.

Gerould, Katharine Fullerton. *The Aristocratic West.* New York, 1925.

Goetzmann, William H., and William N. Goetzmann. *The West of the Imagination.* New York and London, 1986.

Green, Constance M. *American Cities.* London, 1957.

Green, Fletcher M. *Constitutional Development in the South Atlantic States, 1776–1860.* Chapel Hill, 1930.

Griswold del Castillo, Richard. *The Los Angeles Barrio, 1850–1890: A Social History.* Berkeley, 1979.

Hagan, William T. *American Indians.* Chicago, 1961.

Hague, John A. (ed.). *American Character and Culture: Some Twentieth Century Perspectives.* DeLand, Fla., 1964.

Hamilton, William B. (ed.). *The Transfer of Institutions.* Durham, N.C., 1964.

Hansen, Alvin. *Fiscal Policy and Business Cycles.* New York, 1941.

Hansen, Marcus L. *The Immigrant in American History.* Cambridge, Mass., 1940.

Hicks, John D. *The Constitutions of the Northwest States.* University of Nebraska Studies Series, vol. 23. Lincoln, 1924.

Higham, John. *History: Professional Scholarship in America.* Rev. ed., Baltimore, 1983.

Hofstadter, Richard. *The Progressive Historians: Turner, Beard, Parrington.* New York, 1968.

Hough, Emerson. *The Passing of the Frontier.* New Haven, 1919.

Howard, Joseph K. *Montana, High, Wide, and Handsome.* New Haven, 1943.

Hulbert, Archer. *Frontiers.* New York, 1929.

Huntington, Ellsworth. *The Climatic Factor.* New York, 1914.

———. *Civilization and Climate.* New York, 1924.

Hutchinson, William T. (ed.). *The Marcus W. Jernegan Essays in American Historiography.* Chicago, 1937.

Isaacs, Harold R. *Idols of the Tribe: Group Identity and Political Change.* New York, 1975.

Iverson, Peter (ed.). *The Plains Indians of the Twentieth Century.* Norman, 1985.

Jacobs, Wilbur R. *The Historical World of Frederick Jackson Turner.* New Haven, 1968.

James, Preston E. *A History of Geographical Ideas.* New York, 1972.

Jeffrey, Julie Roy. *Frontier Women: The Trans-Mississippi West, 1840–1880.* New York, 1979.

Jensen, Joan, and Gloria Ricci Lothrop. *California Women: A History*. San Francisco, 1987.

Jensen, Merrill (ed.). *Regionalism in America*. Madison, 1951.

Jones, Howard Mumford. *America and French Culture, 1750–1848*. Chapel Hill, 1927.

Josephy, Alvin. *The Indian Heritage of America*. New York, 1968.

Katz, William Loren. *The Black West*. Garden City, N.Y., 1971.

Kelly, Lawrence C. *The Assault on Assimilation: John Collier and the Origins of Indian Policy Reform*. Albuquerque, 1983.

Kirker, Harold. *California's Architectural Frontier: Style and Tradition in the Nineteenth Century*. San Marino, 1960.

Kitano, Harry L. *The Japanese-Americans: The Evolution of a Sub-culture*. Englewood Cliffs, 1969.

Krout, John A., and Dixon Ryan Fox. *The Completion of Independence*. New York, 1944.

Lamar, Howard R. *Dakota Territory, 1861–1889: A Study of Frontier Politics*. New Haven, 1956.

———. *The Far Southwest, 1846–1912: A Territorial History*. New Haven, 1966.

———, and Leonard Thompson (eds.). *The Frontier in History*. New Haven, 1981.

Larsen, Lawrence H. *The Urban West at the End of the Frontier*. Lawrence, 1978.

Leach, Douglas E. *The Northern Colonial Frontier, 1607–1763*. New York, 1966.

Leckie, William H. *The Buffalo Soldiers: A Narrative of the Negro Cavalry in the West*. Norman, 1967.

Lenihan, John H. *Showdown: Confronting Modern America in the Western Film*. Urbana, 1980.

Limerick, Patricia Nelson. *The Legacy of Conquest: The Unbroken Past of the American West*. New York, 1987.

Lipset, Seymour M. *Agrarian Socialism: The Cooperative Commonwealth Federation in Saskatchewan*. Berkeley, 1950.

———. *The First New Nation*. New York, 1963.

———. *Revolution and Counter-Revolution: The United States and Canada*. New York, 1968.

———, and Richard Hofstadter (eds.). *Sociology and History*. New York, 1968.

——— (eds.). *Turner and the Sociology of the Frontier*. New York, 1968.

Lotchin, Roger W. (ed.). *The Martial City*. New York, 1984.

Lowitt, Richard. *The New Deal and the West*. Bloomington, 1984.

Luckingham, Bradford. *The Urban Southwest: A Profile History of Albuquerque, El Paso, Phoenix, and Tucson*. El Paso, 1982.

Luebke, Frederick C. *Immigrants and Politics: The Germans of Nebraska, 1800–1900*. Lincoln, 1969.

Lummis, Charles F. *The Land of Poco Tiempo*. New York, 1893.

———. *The Spanish Pioneers*. Chicago, 1893.

Malin, James C. *The Contriving Brain and the Skillful Hand*. Lawrence, 1955.

———. *Essays in Historiography*. Lawrence, 1946.

———. *The Grassland of North America: Prologomena to Its History*. Lawrence, 1961.

Malone, Michael P. (ed.). *Historians and the American West*. Lincoln, 1983.

Malone, Michael P., and Richard W. Etulain. *The American West: A Twentieth-Century History*. Lincoln, 1989.

Martin, Geoffrey J. *The Life and Thought of Isaiah Bowman*. Hamden, Conn., 1980.

Martínez, Oscar J. *Border Boom Town: Ciudad Juárez Since 1880*. Austin, 1978.

Mattson, Vernon E., and William E. Marion (comps.). *Frederick Jackson Turner: A Reference Guide*. Boston, 1985.

Mazón, Mauricio. *The Zoot-Suit Riots: The Psychology of Symbolic Annihilation*. Austin, 1984.

McComb, David G. *Houston, the Bayou City*. Austin, 1969.

McDougall, William. *The Indestructible Union: Rudiments of Political Science for the American Citizen*. Boston, 1925.

McKelvey, Blake. *The Urbanization of America, 1860–1915*. New York, 1963.

McWilliams, Carey. *The New Regionalism in American Literature*. Seattle, 1930.

———. *North from Mexico: The Spanish-Speaking People of the United States*. Philadelphia, 1949.

Meier, Matt S., and Feliciano Rivera. *The Chicanos: A History of Mexican Americans*. New York, 1972.

Meinig, Donald W. *The Great Columbia Plain: A Historical Geography, 1805–1910*. Seattle, 1968.

———. *Southwest: Three Peoples in Geographical Change, 1600–1970*. New York, 1971.

Melendy, H. Brett. *The Oriental Americans*. New York, 1972.

———. *Asians in America: Filipinos, Koreans, and East Indians*. Boston, 1977.

Melosi, Martin. *Coping with Abundance: Energy and Environment in Industrial America*. Philadelphia, 1985.

Mezerik, A. G. *The Revolt of the South and West*. New York, 1946.

Miller, Perry. *Errand into the Wilderness*. Cambridge, Mass., 1956.

Miyakawa, T. Scott. *Protestants and Pioneers: Individualism and Conformity on the American Frontier*. Chicago, 1964.

Mock, James R., and Cedric Larson. *Words that Won the War: The Story of the Committee on Public Information, 1917–1919*. Princeton, 1939.

Modell, John. *The Economics and Politics of Racial Accommodation*. Urbana, 1977.

Moog, Vianna. *Bandeirantes and Pioneers*. New York, 1964.

Moore, Arthur K. *The Frontier Mind*. Lexington, 1957.

Morison, Elting E. (ed.). *Letters of Theodore Roosevelt*. 8 vols., Cambridge, Mass., 1951–1954.

Mumford, Lewis. *The Golden Day*. New York, 1926.

———. *The City in History*. New York, 1938.

Myres, Sandra. *Westering Women and the Frontier Experience, 1800–1915*. Albuquerque, 1982.

Nash, Gerald D. *The American West in the Twentieth Century*. Albuquerque, 1977.

———. *The American West Transformed: The Impact of the Second World War*. Bloomington, 1985.

Nash, Gerald D., and Richard W. Etulain (eds.). *The Twentieth-Century West: Historical Interpretations*. Albuquerque, 1989.

Nash, Roderick. *Wilderness and the American Mind*. New Haven, 1967.

North, Douglass C. *The Economic Growth of the United States, 1790–1860.* Englewood Cliffs, 1961.

Novick, Peter. *That Noble Dream.* Cambridge, England or New York, 1988.

Odum, Howard W. (ed.). *American Masters of Social Science.* New York, 1927.

O'Neill, William. *Coming Apart: The United States in the 1960s.* Chicago, 1971.

Oswalt, Robert L. *Kashaya Texts.* Berkeley, 1964.

Oswalt, Wendell H. *This Land Was Theirs: A Study of the North American Indians.* New York, 1966.

——. *Alaskan Eskimos.* San Francisco, 1967.

——. *Habitat and Technology.* New York, 1973.

——. *Eskimos and Explorers.* Novato, Cal., 1979.

——. *Napaskiak: An Alaskan Eskimo Community.* Tucson, 1963.

Paredes, Raymund. *The Evolution of Chicano Literature.* New York, 1989.

Parish, John C. *The Persistence of the Westward Movement, and Other Essays.* Berkeley, 1943.

Parks, Rita. *The Western Hero in Film and Television.* Ann Arbor, 1982.

Parman, Donald L. *The Navajos and the New Deal.* New Haven, 1976.

Patch, Howard R. *The Other World.* Cambridge, Mass., 1950.

Paul, Rodman W., and Richard W. Etulain (comps.). *The Frontier and the American West.* Arlington Heights, 1977.

Paxson, Frederic L. *When the West Is Gone.* New York, 1930.

Perloff, Harvey, et al. *Regions, Resources, and Economic Growth.* Baltimore, 1960.

——. *How a Region Grows.* New York, 1963.

Phillips, Kevin. *The Emerging Republican Majority.* New York, 1969.

Philp, Kenneth R. *John Collier's Crusade for Indian Reform, 1920–1954.* Tucson, 1977.

Pitt, Leonard. *The Decline of the Californios: A Social History of Spanish-Speaking Californians, 1846–1890.* Berkeley, 1966.

Pomeroy, Earl S. *The Territories and the United States, 1861–1900: Studies in Colonial Administration.* Philadelphia, 1947.

——. *The Pacific Slope.* New York, 1965.

Porter, Kenneth Wiggins. *The Negro on the American Frontier.* New York, 1971.

Potter, David. *People of Plenty.* Chicago, 1954.

Prucha, Francis Paul. *The Great Father: The United States Government and the American Indians.* 2 vols., Lincoln, 1984.

Pyne, Stephen J. *Fire in America: A Cultural History of Wildland and Rural Fire.* Princeton, 1982.

Reisner, Marc. *Cadillac Desert.* New York, 1986.

Reps, John W. *The Making of Urban America: History of City Planning in the United States.* Princeton, 1965.

——. *Town Planning in Frontier America.* Princeton, 1969.

——. *Cities of the American West.* Princeton, 1979.

Riegel, Robert E. *America Moves West.* New York, 1930.

Riesman, David. *The Lonely Crowd.* New York, 1950.

Rikoon, J. Sanford, and Judith Austin (eds.). *Interpreting Local Culture and History.* Boise, 1987.

Riley, Glenda. *Women and Indians on the Frontier, 1825–1915.* Albuquerque, 1984.

————. *The Female Frontier: A Comparative View of Women on the Prairie and the Plains*. Lawrence, 1988.

Robbins, William G., Robert Frank, and Richard E. Ross (eds.). *Regionalism and the Pacific Northwest*. Corvallis, 1983.

Robertson, James Oliver. *American Myth, American Reality*. New York, 1980.

Rölvaag, Ole. *Giants in the Earth*. New York, 1928.

Rolle, Andrew F. *The Immigrant Upraised: Italian Adventurers and Colonists in an Expanding America*. Norman, 1968.

Romo, Ricardo. *East Los Angeles: History of a Barrio*. Austin, 1983.

Roosevelt, Franklin D. *Public Papers and Addresses*. 13 vols., New York, 1938–1950.

Roosevelt, Theodore. *Works of Theodore Roosevelt*, edited by Herman Hagedorn. 24 vols., New York, 1923–1926.

Royce, Josiah. *Basic Writings*, edited by John J. McDermott. 2 vols., Chicago, 1969.

Sale, Kirkpatrick. *Power Shift*. New York, 1975.

Sánchez, George I. *Forgotten People: A Study of New Mexicans*. Albuquerque, 1940.

Sauer, Carl O. *The Morphology of Landscape*. Berkeley, 1925.

Saveth, Edward N. *American Historians and European Immigrants, 1875–1925*. New York, 1948.

Schlesinger, Arthur M., Sr. *New Viewpoints in American History*. New York, 1922.

————. *The Rise of the City, 1878–1898*. New York, 1933.

————. *Paths to the Present*. New York, 1949.

Semple, Ellen Churchill. *American History and Its Geographic Conditions*. Boston, 1903.

————. *Influences of Geographic Environment*. New York, 1911.

Sharkansky, Ira. *Regionalism in American Politics*. New York, 1970.

Simons, Algie M. *Social Forces in American History*. New York, 1911.

Slotkin, Richard. *Regeneration through Violence: The Mythology of the American Frontier, 1600–1860*. Middletown, 1973.

Smith, Duane A. *Rocky Mountain Mining Camps: The Urban Frontier*. Bloomington, 1967.

Smith, Henry Nash. *Virgin Land: The American West as Symbol and Myth*. Cambridge, Mass., 1950.

Spicer, Edward A. *Pascua: A Yaqui Village in Arizona*. Chicago, 1940.

————. *Cycles of Conquest: Impact of Spain, Mexico, and the United States on the Indians of the Southwest, 1533–1960*. Tucson, 1962.

————. *The American Indians*. Cambridge, Mass., 1980.

———— (ed.). *Perspectives in American Indian Cultural Change*. Chicago, 1956.

Starr, Kevin. *Americans and the California Dream, 1850–1915*. New York, 1973.

Steckmesser, Kent L. *The Western Hero in History and Legend*. Norman, 1965.

Stegner, Wallace. *Beyond the Hundredth Meridian: John Wesley Powell and the Second Opening of the West*. Boston, 1954.

Swierenga, Robert P. (ed.). *James Malin: History and Ecology*. Lincoln, 1984.

Taylor, Griffith (ed.). *Geography in the Twentieth Century*. London, 1951.

Terborgh, George W. *The Bogey of Economic Maturity*. New York, 1945.

Thernstrom, Stephan J. *Poverty and Progress: Social Mobility in a Nineteenth Century City*. Cambridge, Mass., 1964.

———. *The Other Bostonians*. Boston, 1973.

——— (ed.). *Nineteenth Century Cities*. New York, 1969.

Tobin, Gregory M. *The Making of a History: Walter Prescott Webb and "The Great Plains."* Austin, 1976.

Tuma, Elias H. *Economic History and the Social Sciences*. Berkeley, 1971.

U.S. Country Life Commission. *Report of the Commission on Country Life—with an introduction by Theodore Roosevelt*. New York, 1911.

Vogt, Evon Z. *Navajo Veterans: A Study of Changing Values*. Cambridge, Mass., 1951.

———. *Modern Homesteaders: The Life of a Twentieth Century Frontier Community*. Cambridge, Mass., 1955.

———. *Navajo Means People*. Cambridge, Mass., 1951.

——— (ed.). *People of Rimrock: A Study of Values in Five Cultures*. Cambridge, Mass., 1966.

——— (ed.). *Culture and Life: Essays in Memory of Clyde Kluckhohn*. Carbondale, 1973.

Wade, Richard C. *The Urban Frontier: The Rise of Western Cities, 1790–1830*. Cambridge, Mass., 1959.

Wagley, Charles. *An Introduction to Brazil*. New York, 1963.

Walker, Don. *Clio's Cowboys: Studies in the Historiography of the Cattle Trade*. Lincoln, 1981.

Walker, Franklin. *San Francisco's Literary Frontier*. New York, 1939.

———. *A Literary History of Southern California*. Berkeley, 1950.

Wallace, Anthony F. C. *Culture and Personality*. New York, 1970.

———. *The Death and Rebirth of the Seneca*. New York, 1970.

———. *The Modal Personality Structure of the Tuscarora Indians*. Washington, 1952.

——— (ed.). *Men and Cultures*. Philadelphia, 1960.

Wallace, Henry A. *New Frontiers*. New York, 1934.

Washburn, Wilcomb E. (ed.). *The American Indian and the United States: A Documentary History*. 4 vols., New York, 1973.

Webb, Walter P. *Divided We Stand: The Crisis of a Frontierless Democracy*. New York, 1937.

———. *The Great Frontier*. Austin, 1964.

———. *The Great Plains*. Boston, 1931.

Weber, Adna F. *The Growth of Cities in the Nineteenth Century*. Studies in History, Economics, and Public Law. Columbia University. Vol. 2, New York, 1899.

West, Elliott. *Growing Up with the Country: Childhood on the Far Western Frontier*. Albuquerque, 1989.

West, Ray B. (ed.). *Rocky Mountain Cities*. New York, 1949.

Weyl, Walter E. *The New Democracy: An Essay on Certain Political and Economic Tendencies in the United States*. New York, 1913.

Wheeler, Kenneth H. *To Wear a City's Crown: The Beginnings of Urban Growth in Texas, 1836–1865*. Cambridge, Mass., 1968.

Whipple, T. K. *Study out the Land*. Berkeley, 1943.

White, G. Edward. *The Eastern Establishment and the Western Experience: The West of Frederic Remington, Theodore Roosevelt, and Owen Wister*. New Haven, 1968.

White, Morton. *Foundations of Historical Knowledge*. New York, 1965.

Wildavsky, Aaron, and Mary Douglas. *Risk and Culture: An Essay on the Selection of Technical and Environmental Dangers.* Berkeley, 1982.

Wiley, Peter, and Robert Gottlieb. *Empires in the Sun: The Rise of the New American West.* New York, 1982.

Willard, James F., and Colin B. Goodykoontz (eds.). *The Trans-Mississippi West.* Boulder, 1930.

Williams, George H. *Wilderness and Paradise in Christian Thought.* Cambridge, Mass., 1959.

Williams, William Appleman. *The Contours of American History.* Cleveland, 1961.

Wittke, Carl. *We Who Built America.* New York, 1939.

Wohl, Robert. *The Generation of 1914.* Cambridge, Mass., 1979.

Wolfe, Tom. *Mauve Gloves and Madmen, Clutter and Vine.* New York, 1976.

Worster, Donald. *Dust Bowl: The Southern Plains in the 1930s.* New York, 1979.

———. *Rivers of Empire: Water, Aridity, and the Growth of the American West.* New York, 1986.

Wright, Louis B. *Culture on the Moving Frontier.* Bloomington, 1955.

Wyman, Walker D., and Clifton B. Kroeber (eds.). *The Frontier in Perspective.* Madison, 1957.

Zelinsky, Wilbur. *The Cultural Geography of the United States.* Englewood Cliffs, 1973.

ARTICLES

Abbott, Carl. "The American Sunbelt: Idea and Region." In Gerald D. Nash (ed.), *The Urban West.* Manhattan, Kansas, 1979, 9–16.

Abernethy, Thomas P. "Democracy and the Southern Frontier." *Journal of Southern History* 4 (February 1938), 3–13.

Adams, James Truslow. "Rugged Individualism Analyzed." *New York Times*, March 8, 1934, pp. 1–2, 11.

Almack, John C. "The Shibboleth of the Frontier." *Historical Outlook* 16 (May 1925), 197–202.

Arensberg, Conrad. "American Communities." *American Anthropologist* 57 (December 1955), 1143–62.

Armitage, Susan. "Women and Men in Western History: A Stereoptical Vision." *Western Historical Quarterly* 16 (October 1985), 381–95.

Ashliman, D. S. "The American West in 20th Century Germany." *Journal of Popular Culture* 2 (Summer 1968), 81–92.

Bailyn, Bernard. "The Challenge of Modern Historiography." *American Historical Review* 87 (February 1982), 1–24.

Baker, Ray Stannard. "The Western Spirit of Restlessness." *Century Magazine* 76 (July 1908), 468–69.

Baritz, Loren. "The Idea of the West." *American Historical Review* 66 (April 1961), 618–40.

Barker, Eugene C. "Three Types of Historical Interpretation." *Southwestern Historical Quarterly* 45 (April 1942), 323–34.

Bartlett, Richard A. "Freedom and the Frontier: A Pertinent Re-examination." *Mid-America* 40 (July 1958), 131–38.

Beard, Charles A. "The Frontier in American History." *New Republic* 25 (February 16, 1921), 349–50.

———. "Culture and Agriculture." *Saturday Review of Literature* 5 (October 20, 1928), 272–73.

———. "The Myth of Rugged American Individualism." *Harper's* 164 (December 1931), 13–22.

———. "The Frontier in American History." *New Republic* 97 (February 1, 1939), 359–62.

Becker, Carl. "Frederick Jackson Turner." In *American Masters of Social Science,* ed. by Howard W. Odum (New York, 1927), 273–318.

———. "Some Aspects of the Influence of Social Problems and Ideas upon the Study and Writing of History." *American Journal of Sociology* 18 (March 1913), 641–75.

Beckman, Allen. "Hidden Themes in the Frontier Thesis: An Application of Psychoanalysis to Historiography." *Comparative Studies in Society and History* 8 (April 1966), 361–82.

Bender, Thomas. "Wholes and Parts: The Need for Synthesis in American History." *Journal of American History* 73 (June 1986), 123–30.

Benson, Lee. "Achille Loria's Influence on American Economic Thought: Including His Contributions to the Frontier Hypothesis." *Agricultural History* 24 (October 1950), 182–99.

Berkhofer, Robert, Jr. "Space, Time, Culture, and the New Frontier." *Agricultural History* 38 (January 1964), 21–30.

———. "The Political Context of a New Indian History." *Pacific Historical Review* 40 (August 1971), 357–82.

Berthoff, Roland W. "The American Social Order: A Conservative Hypothesis." *American Historical Review* 65 (April 1961), 495–526.

Bestor, Arthur. "Patent Office Models of the Good Society: Some Relationships Between Social Reform and Westward Expansion." *American Historical Review* 58 (April 1953), 505–26.

Bezanson, Anne. "Some Historical Aspects of Labor Turnover." In *Facts and Factors in Economic History,* ed. by Arthur H. Cole, et al. Cambridge, 1932.

Billington, Ray Allen. "Why Some Historians Rarely Write History: A Case Study of Frederick Jackson Turner." *Mississippi Valley Historical Review* 50 (June 1963), 3–27.

———. "The Frontier and I." *Western Historical Quarterly* 1 (January 1970), 4–20.

Bledstein, Burton J. "Frederick Jackson Turner: A Note on the Intellectual and the Professional." *Wisconsin Magazine of History* 54 (Autumn 1970), 50–55.

Block, Robert B. "Frederick Jackson Turner and American Geography." *Annals of the Association of American Geographers* 70 (March 1980), 31–42.

Bogue, Allen G. "Pioneer Farming and Innovation." *Iowa Journal of History* 56 (January 1958), 1–36.

———. "Social Theory and the Pioneer." *Agricultural History* 34 (January 1960), 21–34.

———. "The Iowa Claim Clubs: Symbol and Substance." *Mississippi Valley Historical Review* 45 (September 1958), 231–53.

Bold, Christine. "Return of the Native: Some Reflections on the History of American Indians." *Journal of American Studies* 8 (August 1974), 247–59.

Bolton, Herbert E. "The Mission as a Frontier Institution in the Spanish-American Colonies." *American Historical Review* 23 (October 1917), 42–61.

———. "Epic of Greater America." *American Historical Review* 38 (April 1933), 448–74.

Boyd, Carl. "Growth of the Cities in the United States During the Decade, 1880–1890." *Publications of the American Statistical Association* 3 (September 1893), 416–25.

Brown, George W. "Some Recent Books on the History of the United States." *Canadian Historical Review* 19 (December 1938), 411–14.

Burr, George Lincoln. "The Place of Geography in the Teaching of History." *New England History Teachers Association, Annual Report for* 1907 (Boston, 1908), 1–13.

Burton, David H. "The Influence of the American West on the Imperialist Philosophy of Theodore Roosevelt." *Arizona and the West* 4 (Spring 1962), 5–26.

Careless, J. M. S. "Frontierism, Metropolitanism, and Canadian History." *Canadian Historical Review* 35 (March 1954), 1–21.

Carpenter, Ronald H. "The Rhetorical Genius of Style in the 'Frontier Hypothesis' of Frederick Jackson Turner." *Southern Speech Communication Journal* 37 (Spring 1972), 233–48.

———. "The Stylistic Identification of Frederick Jackson Turner with Robert M. LaFollette: A Psychologically Oriented Analysis of Language Behavior." *Wisconsin Academy of Sciences, Arts, and Letters—Transactions*, 63 (Madison, 1975), 102–15.

Carter, Clarence E. "The Transit of Law to the Frontier: A Review Article." *Journal of Mississippi History* 16 (July 1954), 183–94.

Caughey, John W. "The Mosaic of Western History." *Mississippi Valley Historical Review* 33 (March 1947), 595–606.

———. "Historians' Choice: Results of a Poll on Recently Published American History and Biography." *Mississippi Valley Historical Review* 39 (September 1952), 289–302.

———. "The Insignificance of the Frontier in American History or 'Once Upon a Time There Was an American West.'" *Western Historical Quarterly* 5 (January 1974), 5–16.

Cawelti, John. "God's Country . . . Differing Visions of the West." *Western American Literature* 9 (Winter 1975), 273–83.

Clark, Thomas D. "The Heritage of the Frontier." *West Virginia History* 34 (October 1972), 1–17.

Coleman, Peter J. "Beard, McDonald, and Economic Determinism in American Historiography." *Business History Review* 34 (Spring 1960), 113–21.

Commager, Henry Steele. "The Literature of the Pioneer West." *Minnesota History* 8 (December 1927), 319–28.

———. "Farewell to Laissez-Faire." *Current History* 38 (August 1933), 513–20.

Craven, Avery. "Frederick Jackson Turner." In *The Marcus W. Jernegan Essays in American Historiography*, ed. by William T. Hutchinson (Chicago 1937), 252–70.

Cronon, William J. "Revisiting the Vanishing Frontier." *Western Historical Quarterly* 18 (April 1987), 157–76.

Crowe, Charles. "The Emergence of Progressive History." *Journal of the History of Ideas* 27 (January–March 1966), 109–24.

Davis, David B. "Ten-Gallon Hero." *American Quarterly* 6 (Summer 1954), 111–25.

Davis, Ronald L. F. "Western Urban Development: A Critical Analysis." In Jerome O. Steffen (ed.) *The American West* (Norman, 1979), 175–96.

Davis, William N. "Will the West Survive as a Field in American History? A Survey Report." *Mississippi Valley Historical Review* 50 (March 1964), 672–85.

Deamer, Robert G. "Stephen Crane and the Western Myth." *Western American Literature* 7 (Summer 1972), 111–23.

Degler, Carl. "Why Historians Change their Minds." *Pacific Historical Review* 45 (May 1976), 167–84.

———. "Remaking American History." *Journal of American History* 67 (June 1980), 7–25.

DeGraaf, Lawrence B. "Recognition, Racism, and Reflections on the Writing of Western Black History." *Pacific Historical Review* 44 (February 1975), 22–51.

De Voto, Bernard. "Footnote on the West." *Harper's* 155 (November 1927), 714–22.

———. "The West: A Plundered Province." *Harper's* 169 (August 1934), 355–64.

———. "The Anxious West." *Harper's* 193 (December 1946), 489–95.

Dewey, John. "The American Intellectual Frontier." *New Republic* 30 (May 10, 1922), 303–5.

Diamond, William. "On the Dangers of an Urban Interpretation." In Eric F. Goldman (ed.), *Historiography and Urbanization: Essays in Honor of W. Stull Holt* (Baltimore, 1941), 98–112.

———. "American Sectionalism and World Organization, by Frederick Jackson Turner." *American Historical Review* 47 (April 1942), 545–51.

Dowd, Douglas F. "A Comparative Analysis of Economic Development in the American West and South." *Journal of Economic History* 16 (December 1956), 558–74.

Elkin, Frederick. "Psychological Appeal of the Hollywood Western." *Journal of Educational Sociology* 24 (October 1950), 72–87.

Elkins, Stanley M., and Eric L. McKittrick. "A Meaning for Turner's Frontier, Part I: Democracy in the Old Northwest." *Political Science Quarterly* 69 (September 1954), 321–53.

———. "A Meaning for Turner's Frontier, Part II: The Southwest Frontier and New England." *Political Science Quarterly* 69 (December 1954), 565–602.

———. "Institutions in Motion." *American Quarterly* 12 (Summer 1960), 188–97.

Entriken, J. Nicholas. "Carl O. Sauer, Philosopher in Spite of Himself." *Geographical Review* 74 (October 1984), 387–408.

Etulain, Richard W. "Origins of the Western." *Journal of Popular Culture* 5 (Spring 1972), 799–805.

———. "Riding Point: The Western and Its Interpreters." *Journal of Popular Culture* 7 (Winter 1973), 647–51.

———. "The Historical Development of the Western." *Journal of Popular Culture* 7 (Winter 1973), 717–26.

———. "Frontier, Region, and Myth: Changing Interpretations of Western American Culture." *Journal of American Culture* 3 (Summer 1980), 268–84.

"Exit Frontier Morality." *New Republic* 37 (January 2, 1934), 137–38.

Fish, Carl Russell. "The Frontier, a World Problem." *Wisconsin Magazine of History* 1 (December 1917), 121–41.

Fisher, James A. "The Political Development of the Black Community in California, 1850–1950." *California Historical Quarterly* 50 (September 1971), 256–66.

Fishwick, Marshall W. "The Cowboy: America's Contribution to the World's Mythology." *Western Folklore* 11 (1951–52), 77–92.

Fite, Gilbert C. "Daydreams and Nightmares: The Late Nineteenth-Century Agricultural Frontiers." *Agricultural History* 40 (October 1966), 285–93.

Forbes, Jack D. "The Indian in the West: A Challenge for Historians." *Arizona and the West* 1 (Autumn 1959), 206–15.

———. "Frontiers in American History." *Journal of the West* 1 (July 1962), 63–73.

Foster, Mark S. "The Western Response to Urban Transportation: A Tale of Three Cities, 1900–1945." In Gerald D. Nash (ed.), *The Urban West* (Manhattan, Kansas, 1979), 31–39.

Fowke, Vernon C. "National Policy and Westward Development in North America." *Journal of Economic History* 16 (December 1956), 461–79.

Fox, Dixon Ryan. "The Transit of Civilization." *American Historical Review* 32 (July 1927), 753–68.

Frost, James. "The Frontier Influence—A Perspective." *Social Education* 11 (December 1947), 361–63.

Garland, Hamlin. "The Passing of the Frontier." *Dial* 67 (October 4, 1919), 285–86.

Gates, Paul W. "The Homestead Law in an Incongruous Land System." *American Historical Review* 41 (July 1936), 652–81.

Gerhard, Dietrich. "The Frontier in Comparative View." *Comparative Studies in Society and History* 1 (March 1959), 205–29.

Gerould, Katherine. "The Aristocratic West." *Harper's* 151 (September 1925), 466–77.

Glaab, Charles N. "Visions of Metropolism: William Gilpin and Theories of City Growth in the American West." *Wisconsin Magazine of History* 45 (Autumn 1961), 113–21.

———. "The Historian and the American Urban Tradition." *Wisconsin Magazine of History* 47 (Autumn 1963), 13–25.

———. "Jesup W. Scott and a West of Cities." *Ohio History* 73 (Winter 1964), 3–12.

Goetzmann, William H. "The West and the American Age of Exploration." *Arizona and the West* 2 (Autumn 1960), 265–78.

———. "The Mountain Man as Jacksonian Man." *American Quarterly* 15 (Spring 1963), 402–15.

Gómez-Quiñones, Juan, and Luis Leobardo Arroyo, "On the State of Chicano History: Observations on Its Development, Interpretations, and Theory, 1970–1974." *Western Historical Quarterly* 7 (April 1976), 155–85.

Goodrich, Carter C., and Sol Davidson, "The Wage-Earner in the Westward Movement." *Political Science Quarterly* 50 (June 1935), 161–85.

Gressley, Gene. "The West: Past, Present, and Future." *Western Historical Quarterly* 17 (January 1986), 5–23.

Hacker, Louis M. "Sections—or Classes." *Nation* 137 (July 26, 1933), 108–10.

Hague, Harlan. "Eden Ravished: Land, Pioneer Attitudes, and Conservation." *American West* 14 (May–June 1977), 30–33, 65–69.

Hamerow, Theodore. "The Professionalization of Historical Learning." *Reviews in American History* 14 (September 1986), 319–33.

Hamilton, William B. "The Transmission of English Law to the Frontier of America." *South Atlantic Quarterly* 67 (Spring 1968), 243–64.

Harger, Charles M. "The New Westerner." *North American Review* 620 (August 2, 1907), 748–58.

———. "Brighter Skies Out West." *Review of Reviews* 70 (October 1924), 420–23.

Harper, Norman D. "Turner, the Historian: 'Hypothesis' or 'Process'? With Special Reference to Frontier Society in Australia." *University of Kansas City Review* 18 (Autumn 1951), 76–86.

Hartz, Louis. "American Historiography and Comparative Analysis: Further Reflections." *Comparative Studies in Society and History* 5 (July 1963), 365–77.

Hauptman, Lawrence M. "Mythologizing Westward Expansion: Schoolbooks and the Image of the American Frontier before Turner." *Western Historical Quarterly* 8 (July 1977), 269–82.

Hayes, Carlton J. H. "The American Frontier—Frontier of What?" *American Historical Review* 51 (January 1946), 199–216.

Heaton, Herbert. "Other Wests than Ours." *Journal of Economic History* 6, Supplement (1946), 50–62.

Heimert, Alan. "Puritanism, the Wilderness, and the Frontier." *New England Quarterly* 26 (September 1953), 361–82.

Hergesheimer, Joseph. "The Magnetic West." *Saturday Evening Post* 195 (September 2, 1922), 97.

Herring, Pendleton. "A Political Scientist Considers the Question." *Pennsylvania Magazine of History and Biography* 72 (April 1948), 118–36.

Hicks, John D. "The 'Ecology' of the Middle-Western Historians." *Wisconsin Magazine of History* 24 (June 1941), 377–84.

———. "American History." *Saturday Review of Literature* 36 (March 14, 1953), 14–15.

———. "Changing Concepts of History." *Western Historical Quarterly* 2 (January 1971), 21–35.

Higham, John. "Paleface and Redskin in American Historiography: A Comment." *Journal of Interdisciplinary History* 16 (Summer 1985), 1111–16.

Hofstadter, Richard. "Turner and the Frontier Myth." *American Scholar* 18 (Autumn 1949), 433–43.

Hough, Emerson. "The Settlement of the Frontier: A Study in Transportation." *Century Magazine* 63 (November 1901), 91–107 and 63 (December 1901), 201–16.

Hutton, Paul A. "From Little Big Horn to Little Big Man: The Changing Image of a Western Hero in Popular Culture." *Western Historical Quarterly* 7 (January 1976), 19–45.

Jacobs, Wilbur R. "British Colonial Attitudes and Policies towards the Indian in the American Colonies." In Howard Peckham and Charles Gibson (eds.), *Attitudes of Colonial Powers toward the American Indian* (Salt Lake City, 1969), 81–106.

———. "The Fatal Confrontation: Early Native–White Relations on the Frontiers of Australia, New Guinea, and America: A Comparative Study." *Pacific Historical Review* 40 (August 1971), 283–309.

———. "The Indian and the Frontier in American History—A Need for Revision." *Western Historical Quarterly* 4 (January 1973), 43–56.

———. "The Great Despoliation: Environmental Themes in American Frontier History." *Pacific Historical Review* 47 (February 1978), 1–26.

James, Edmund J. "The Growth of Great Cities." *Annals of the American Academy of Political and Social Science* 13 (January 1899), 1–30.

Jensen, Joan, and Darlis A. Miller. "The Gentle Tamers Revisited: New Approaches to the History of Women in the American West." *Pacific Historical Review* 49 (May 1980), 173–213.

Jensen, Richard. "On Modernizing Frederick Jackson Turner: The Historiography of Regionalism." *Western Historical Quarterly* 11 (July 1980), 307–22.

Josephson, Matthew. "The Frontier and Literature." *New Republic* 68 (September 2, 1931), 78–79.

Kaplan, Lawrence S. "Frederick Jackson Turner and Imperialism." *Social Science* 27 (January 1952), 12–16.

Krey, August C. "My Reminiscences of Frederick Jackson Turner." *Arizona and the West* 3 (Winter 1961), 377–81.

Lamar, Howard R. "Persistent Frontier: The West in the Twentieth Century." *Western Historical Quarterly* 4 (January 1973), 5–25.

Lampard, Eric E. "The Study of Urbanization." *American Historical Review* 67 (October 1961), 51–63.

Larson, T. A. "Women's Role in the American West." *Montana: The Magazine of Western History* 24 (Summer 1974), 2–11.

Laut, Agnes C. "The Last Trek to the Last Frontier: The American Settler in the Canadian Northwest." *Century Magazine* 56 (May 1909), 99–110.

Lawson, Merlin P., and Charles W. Stockton. "Desert Myth and Climatic Reality." *Annals of the Association of American Geographers* 71 (December 1981), 527–35.

Lee, Everett S. "The Turner Thesis Reexamined." *American Quarterly* 13 (Spring 1961), 77–83.

Lerner, Max. "America—A Young Civilization?" *Antioch Review* 6 (Fall 1946), 368–75.

———. "History and American Greatness." *American Quarterly* 1 (Fall 1949), 209–17.

Lewis, Merrill E. "The Art of Frederick Jackson Turner." *Huntington Library Quarterly* 35 (May 1972), 241–55.

Lighton, William R. "Where Is the West?" *Outlook* (July 18, 1903), 703.

Lotchin, Roger W. "The Metropolitan–Military Complex in Comparative Perspective:

San Francisco, Los Angeles, and San Diego, 1919–1941." In Gerald D. Nash (ed.), *The Urban West* (Manhattan, Kansas, 1979), 19–29.

———. "The Darwinian City: The Politics of Urbanization in San Francisco Between the World Wars." *Pacific Historical Review* 48 (August 1979), 357–81.

Luckingham, Bradford. "The City in the Westward Movement: A Bibliographical Note." *Western Historical Quarterly* 5 (July 1974), 295–306.

———. "The American Southwest: An Urban View." *Western Historical Quarterly* 15 (July 1984), 261–80.

Luebke, Frederick C. "Ethnic Group Settlement on the Great Plains." *Western Historical Quarterly* 8 (October 1977), 405–30.

———. "Ethnic Minority Groups in the American West." In Michael P. Malone (ed.), *Historians and the American West* (Lincoln, 1983), 387–413.

———. "Regionalism and the Great Plains: Problems of Concept and Method." *Western Historical Quarterly* 15 (January 1984), 19–38.

Lynd, Staughton. "On Turner, Beard, and Slavery." *Journal of Negro History* 48 (October 1963), 235–50.

Malin, James C. "The Turnover of Farm Population in Kansas." *Kansas Historical Quarterly* 4 (November 1935), 339–72.

———. "Space and History: Reflections on the Closed-Space Doctrines of Turner and Mackinder and the Challenge of Those Ideas by the Air Age, Part II." *Agricultural History* 18 (July 1944), 107–26.

Malone, Michael P. "Beyond the Last Frontier: Toward a New Approach to Western American History." *Western Historical Quarterly* 20 (November 1989), 409–27.

Marsden, Michael T. "The Popular Western Novel as a Cultural Artifact." *Arizona and the West* 20 (Autumn 1978), 203–10.

Martin, Curtis. "Impact of the West on American Government and Politics." *Colorado Quarterly* 13 (Summer 1964), 51–69.

Marty, Martin. "Religion in America Since Mid-Century." *Daedalus* 111 (Winter 1982), 149–63.

McKelvey, Blake. "American Urban History Today." *American Historical Review* 57 (July 1952), 919–29.

McWilliams, Carey. "Myths of the West." *North American Review* 232 (November 1931), 424–32.

Mead, W. R. "Frontier Themes in Finland." *Geography* 44 (July 1959), 145–56.

Meany, Edward S. "The Towns of the Pacific Northwest Were Not Founded on the Fur Trade." American Historical Association, *Annual Report*, 1910. Washington, 1911.

Meinig, Donald W. "American Wests: Preface to a Geographical Interpretation." *Annals of the Association of American Geographers* 62 (June 1972), 159–84.

Mikesell, Marvin W. "Comparative Studies in Frontier History." *Annals of the Association of American Geographers* 50 (March 1960), 62–74.

Nichols, David. "Civilization over Savage: Frederick Jackson Turner and the Indian." *South Dakota History* 2 (Fall 1972), 383–405.

Nettels, Curtis P. "Frederick Jackson Turner and the New Deal." *Wisconsin Magazine of History* 17 (March 1934), 257–65.

Norris, Frank. "The Frontier Gone at Last." *World's Work* 3 (February 1902), 1728–31.

———. "A Neglected Epic." *World's Work* 5 (December 1902), 2904–6.

North, Douglass C. "Location Theory and Regional Economic Growth." *Journal of Political Economy* 63 (June 1955), 243–58.

———. "International Capital Flows and the Development of the American West." *Journal of Economic History* 16 (December 1956), 493–505.

Nugent, Walter. "Frontiers and Empires in the Late Nineteenth Century." *Western Historical Quarterly* 20 (November 1989), 393–408.

Nussbaum, Martin. "Sociological Symbolism of the 'Adult Western.'" *Social Forces* 39 (October 1960), 25–28.

Olin, Spencer, Jr. "Toward a Synthesis of the Political and Social History of the American West." *Pacific Historical Review* 55 (November 1986), 599–611.

Opie, John S. "Environmental History in the West." In Gerald D. Nash and Richard W. Etulain (eds.), *The Twentieth Century West: Historical Interpretations* (Albuquerque, 1989), 210–30.

Ostrander, Gilman. "Turner and the Germ Theory." *Agricultural History* 32 (October 1958), 258–61.

Parsons, James J. "Carl Ortwin Sauer." *Geographical Review* 66 (January 1976), 83–89.

Paxson, Frederic L. "The Pacific Railroads and the Disappearance of the Frontier in America." American Historical Association, *Annual Report, 1907* (Washington, 1908), vol. 1, 107–18.

———. "A Generation of the Frontier Hypothesis: 1893–1932." *Pacific Historical Review* 2, no. 2 (1933), 34–51.

———. "The New Frontier and the Old American Habit." *Pacific Historical Review* 4, no. 4 (1935), 309–27.

Petersen, William J. "Population Advance to the Upper Mississippi Valley, 1830–1860." *Iowa Journal of History and Politics* 32 (October 1934), 312–53.

Pierson, George W. "American Historians and the Frontier Hypothesis in 1941." *Wisconsin Magazine of History* 26 (September 1942), 36–60.

———. "American Historians and the Frontier Hypothesis in 1941." *Wisconsin Magazine of History* 26 (December 1942), 170–85.

Pomeroy, Earl. "Toward a Reorientation of Western History: Continuity and Environment." *Mississippi Valley Historical Review* 41 (March 1955), 579–600.

———. "Rediscovering the West." *American Quarterly* 12 (Spring 1960), 20–30.

———. "Old Lamps for New: The Cultural Lag in Pacific Coast Historiography." *Arizona and the West* 2 (Summer 1960), 107–26.

———. "Josiah Royce: Historian in Quest of Community." *Pacific Historical Review* 40 (February 1971), 1–20.

———. "The Urban Frontier of the Far West." In John G. Clark (ed.), *The Frontier Challenge: Responses to the Trans-Mississippi West* (Lawrence, Kansas, 1971), 7–29.

Potter, David. "American Women and the American Character." In John A. Hague (ed.), *American Character and Culture: Some Twentieth Century Perspectives* (Deland, Fla., 1964), 65–84.

Powell, Kirsten H. "Cowboy Knights and Prairie Madonnas: American Illustrations of the Plains and Pre-Raphaelite Art." *Great Plains Quarterly* 5 (Winter 1985), 39–52.

Rabinowitz, Howard. "Reps on the Range." *Journal of Urban History* 8 (November 1981), 91–97.

Ridge, Martin L. "Ray Allen Billington (1903–1980)." *Western Historical Quarterly* 12 (July 1981), 245–50.

———. "Ray Allen Billington, Western History, and American Exceptionalism." *Pacific Historical Review* 56 (November 1987), 495–511.

———. "Frederick Jackson Turner, Ray Allen Billington, and American Frontier History." *Western Historical Quarterly* 19 (January 1988), 5–20.

Riegel, Robert E. "Current Ideas of the Significance of the United States Frontier." *Revista de Historia de America* 33 (June 1952), 25–43.

Riley, Glenda. "Images of the Frontierswoman: Iowa as a Case Study." *Western Historical Quarterly* 8 (April 1977), 189–202.

———. "Women on the Great Plains: Recent Developments in Research." *Great Plains Quarterly* 5 (Spring 1985), 81–92.

Robbins, William G. "The Conquest of the American West: History as Eulogy." *Indian Historian* 10 (Winter 1977), 7–13.

———. "Western History: A Dialectic on the Modern Condition." *Western Historical Quarterly* 20 (November 1989), 429–49.

Ross, Earle D. "A Generation of Prairie Historiography." *Mississippi Valley Historical Review* 33 (December 1946), 391–410.

Ross, Edward A. "The Study of the Present as an Aid to the Interpretation of the Past." *Mississippi Valley Historical Association, Proceedings* 11 (1908–1909), 128–36.

———. "The Middle West." *Century Magazine* 83 (February 1912), 609–15.

Rundell, Walter, Jr. "Walter Prescott Webb: Product of Environment." *Arizona and the West* 5 (Spring 1963), 4–28.

Saloutos, Theodore C. "Cultural Persistence and Change: Greeks in the Great Plains and Rocky Mountain West, 1890–1970." *Pacific Historical Review* 49 (February 1980), 77–103.

Sauer, Carl O. "The Morphology of Landscape." *University of California Publications in Geography* 2 (October 12, 1925), 19–53.

Schafer, Joseph. "The Yankee and the Teuton in Wisconsin." *Wisconsin Magazine of History* 6 (December 1922), 125–45; 6 (March 1923), 261–79; 6 (June 1923), 286–302; 7 (September 1923), 3–19; 7 (December 1923), 148–71.

———. "Editorial Comment." *Wisconsin Magazine of History* 17 (June 1934), 447–65.

———. "Turner's Frontier Philosophy." *Wisconsin Magazine of History* 16 (June 1933), 451–69.

Scheiber, Harry N. "Turner's Legacy and the Search for a Reorientation of Western History: A Review Essay." *New Mexico Historical Review* 44 (July 1969), 231–48.

Schein, Harry. "The Olympian Cowboy." *American Scholar* 24 (Summer 1955), 309–17.

Schlesinger, Arthur M., Sr. "The Influence of Immigration on American History." *American Journal of Sociology* 27 (July 1921), 71–85.

————. "The City in American History." *Mississippi Valley Historical Review* 27 (June 1940), 43–66.

————. "What Then Is the American, This New Man?" *American Historical Review* 48 (January 1943), 225–44.

Schnell, J. Christopher, and Katherine B. Clinton. "The New West: Themes in Nineteenth Century Urban Promotion, 1815–1880." *Bulletin of the Missouri Historical Society* 30 (January 1973), 75–88.

Schroeder, Fred E. H. "The Development of the Super-Ego on the American Frontier." *Soundings* 57 (Summer 1974), 189–205.

Semple, Ellen Churchill. "Geographical Location as a Factor in History." *Bulletin of the American Geographical Society* 40 (1908), 65–81.

Shannon, Fred A. "The Homestead Act and Labor Surplus." *American Historical Review* 41 (July 1936), 637–51.

Sharp, Paul F. "The American Farmer and the 'Last Best West.'" *Agricultural History* 21 (April 1947), 65–75.

Simonson, Harold P. "The Closed Frontier and American Tragedy." *Texas Quarterly* 11 (Spring 1968), 56–69.

Smith, Henry Nash. "The West as an Image of the American Past." *University of Kansas City Review* 18 (Autumn 1951), 29–40.

Smythe, William E. "Real Utopias in the Arid West." *Atlantic Monthly* 79 (May 1897), 599–609.

Steiner, Michael C. "The Significance of Turner's Sectional Thesis." *Western Historical Quarterly* 10 (October 1979), 437–66.

————. "Regionalism in the Great Depression." *Geographical Review* 73 (October 1983), 430–46.

Still, Bayrd. "Evidences of the Higher Life on the Frontier." *Journal of the Illinois Historical Society* 28 (July 1935), 81–99.

————. "Patterns of Mid-Nineteenth Century Urbanization in the Middle West." *Mississippi Valley Historical Review* 28 (September 1941), 187–206.

Sussman, Warren I. "The Useless Past: American Intellectuals and the Frontier Thesis, 1910–1930." *Bucknell Review* 11 (March 1963), 1–24.

————. "History and the American Intellectual: Uses of a Usable Past." *American Quarterly* 16, part 2, Supplement (Summer 1964), 242–55.

Tattersall, James N. "The Turner Thesis in the Light of Recent Research in Economic History." Western Economic History Association, *Proceedings, 1958* (Pullman, Wash., 1959), 46–51.

Toynbee, Arnold S. "Encounters between Civilizations." *Harper's* 194 (April 1948), 289–94.

Turner, Frederick Jackson. "The Winning of the West." *The Dial* (August 1889), 7.

————. "The Significance of History." *Wisconsin Journal of Education* 21 (October–November 1891), 230–34, 253–56.

————. "The Significance of the Frontier in American History." In *The Frontier in American History* (New York, 1920), 3–43.

————. "Report on Conference on the Relation of Geography and History." *Annual Report of the American Historical Association for 1907* (Washington, 1908), vol. 1, 45–48.

——. "Social Forces in American History." *American Historical Review* 16 (January 1911), 217–33.

——. "Sections and Nation." *Yale Review* 12 (October 1922), 1–21.

——. "The Significance of the Section in American History." *Wisconsin Magazine of History* 8 (March 1925), 255–80.

——. "Geographical Sectionalism in American History." *Annals of the Association of American Geographers* 16 (June 1926), 85–93.

Unger, Irwin. "The 'New Left' and American History: Some Recent Trends in United States Historiography." *American Historical Review* 72 (July 1967), 1237–63.

Vogt, Evon Z. "American Subcultural Continua. . . ." *American Anthropologist* 57 (December 1955), 1163–72.

Vorpahl, Ben M. "Presbyterianism and the Frontier Hypothesis: Tradition and Modification in the American Garden." *Presbyterian Historical Society Journal* 45 (September 1967), 180–92.

Ward, John W. "Cleric or Critic? The Intellectual in the University." *American Scholar* 35 (Winter 1965), 101–13.

Washburn, Wilcomb E. "The Writing of American Indian History." *Pacific Historical Review* 40 (August 1971), 261–81.

Webb, Walter P. "Ended: Four Hundred Year Boom: Reflections on the Age of the Frontier." *Harper's* 203 (October 1951), 25–33.

——. "Geographical–Historical Concepts in American History." *Annals of the Association of American Geographers* 50 (June 1960), 85–93.

Wecter, Dixon. "Instruments of Culture on the Frontier." *Yale Review* 36 (Winter 1947), 242–56.

Wertenbaker, Thomas J. "The Molding of the Middle West." *American Historical Review* 53 (January 1948), 223–34.

White, Lynn, Jr. "The Legacy of the Middle Ages in the American Wild West." *American West* 3 (Spring 1966), 72–79, 95.

White, Richard. "American Environmental History: The Development of a New Historical Field." *Pacific Historical Review* 54 (August 1985), 297–335.

Williams, Burton J. "The Twentieth Century American West, the Old versus the New." *Rocky Mountain Social Science Journal* 6 (October 1969), 163–67.

Williams, George H. "The Wilderness and Paradise in the History of the Church." *Church History* 28 (March 1959), 3–24.

Williams, John. "The Western: Definition of the Myth." *Nation* 193 (November 18, 1961), 401–6.

Williams, William Appleman. "The Frontier Thesis: An American Foreign Policy." *Pacific Historical Review* 24 (November 1956), 379–95.

Wilson, Joan Hoff. "The Plight of a Mom and Pop Operation." *OAH Newsletter* 13 (May 1985), 2.

Wilson, Woodrow. "The Proper Perspective of American History." *Forum* 19 (July 1895), 544–59.

——. "The Making of the Nation." *Atlantic Monthly* 80 (July 1897), 1–14.

Woodward, C. Vann. "The Age of Reinterpretation." *American Historical Review* 66 (October 1960), 1–19.

Worster, Donald. "New West, True West: Interpreting the Region's History." *Western Historical Quarterly* 18 (April 1987), 141–56.

Wright, Benjamin F. "American Democracy and the Frontier." *Yale Review* 22 (December 1930), 349–65.

Wright, Louis B. "The Westward Advance of the Atlantic Frontier." *Huntington Library Quarterly* 11 (May 1948), 261–75.

———. "Culture and Anarchy on the Frontier." In Carroll Camden (ed.), *Literary Views: Critical and Historical Essays* (Chicago, 1964), 131–43.

Zaslow, Morris. "The Frontier Hypothesis in Recent Historiography." *Canadian Historical Review* 29 (June 1948), 153–67.

Zelinsky, Wilbur. "Personality and Self-Discovery: The Future of Social Geography of the United States." In Ronald Abler et al. (eds.), *Human Geography in a Shrinking World* (North Scituate, Mass., 1975), 108–21.

———. "North America's Vernacular Regions." *Annals of the Association of American Geographers* 70 (March 1980), 1–16.

Index